CW00369204

E·A·S·Y
HOME
IMPROVEMENTS

A J.B. Fairfax Press Publication

EDITORIAL
Managing Editor: Sheridan
Carter
Consultant Editors: Dieter
Mylius; Susan Tomnay; How-To
Publications (UK)
Editorial Coordination: Rachel
Blackmore; Margaret Kelly
Editorial Assistants: Ella Martin,
Allen Robinson

CONTRIBUTORS
Leigh Adams; Jack Barrington;
Greg Cheetham; Mary-Anne
Danaher; Caroline Digiulio;
Michelle Gorry; Graeme
Haron; How-To Publications;
Robert Johnston; Leta Keens;
Andrew Kemp; Mary Machen;
Alison Magney; Dieter Mylius
(© Parts 1 & 2); Judy Poulos;
Nadia Sbisa; Jane Sheard; Greg
Slater; Hugh Slatyer; Tonia
Todman; Tony Todman; Paul
Urquhart; Colin Try; Christine
Whiston; Ursula Woodhouse

PHOTOGRAPHY
Styling and picture research:
Mary-Anne Danaher; Michelle
Gorry; Sandra Hartley; Wayne
Heeley; Tonia Todman
Photographers (except where
otherwise credited): Andrew
Elton; Simon Kenny; Harm
Mol; Andrew Payne; Vantuan;
David Young

DESIGN AND PRODUCTION
Managers: Sheridan Carter;
Nadia Sbisa
Design and layout: Tara
Barrett; Tracey Burt; Lulu
Dougherty; Monica Kessler-Tay;
Margie Mulray
Finished art: Chris Hatcher,
Steve Joseph

Illustrations: Greg Gaul; Dieter
Mylius; Rod Westblade
Cover design: Frank Pithers

Published by J.B. Fairfax Press
Pty Ltd
80-82 McLachlan Avenue
Rushcutters Bay 2011
Ph: (02) 361 6366

Some of the contents of this
book have been previously
published in other J.B. Fairfax
Press publications.

Easy Home Improvements
Includes Index
ISBN 1 86343 109 8

Formatted by J.B. Fairfax Press
Pty Ltd
Output by Adtype, Sydney
Printed by Toppan Printing Co,
Hong Kong

All care has been taken to
ensure the accuracy of the
information in this book but no
responsibility is accepted for
any errors or omissions.

A.C.N. 003 738 430

NOTE TO READERS

*A well-designed patio can become a room without a roof,
giving you extra space for entertaining and a host of
family activities*

How to Use This Book

Use this general outline in conjunction with the contents list and index to projects and skill classes for a more detailed breakdown of the topics covered in each section of the book.

PART 1
The Basics

Good preparation and planning will help to ensure the success of your DIY home improvements. This section offers advice on setting up a basic tool kit; using and caring for tools; and safe work practices in the home environment.

PART 2
Interior Walls, Windows & Floors

This section combines practical projects with clever and creative ideas for walls, windows and floors. Projects range from installing a dividing wall, a window or new flooring, to making a Roman blind.

PART 3
Storage Solutions

Individual storage needs vary according to lifestyle, number of rooms, amount of exterior space which can be adapted, and the degree to which one is prepared to do a little lateral thinking. Projects range from renovating a second-hand storage cabinet or running-up some fabric shelves, to building an entertainment centre.

PART 4
Kitchen Improvements

Making changes in the kitchen is an extremely rewarding task, especially if those changes make the preparation and serving of food simpler. This section offers guidelines and plans for different kitchen shapes and styles, information on lighting, floors, surfaces, storage and appliances. And there are colour and decorating ideas too.

PART 5
Bathroom Improvements

While the bathroom is not the easiest room to renovate or redecorate, especially if new plumbing is required, there are easy and satisfying ways to make improvements. You can achieve wonders in an old bathroom simply by adding accessories, stencilling a wall border, or repainting.

PART 6
Outdoor Improvements

The 'great outdoors' is a wonderful place for relaxation, whether you have a big garden, a private courtyard, or a small balcony. You don't have to be a keen gardener to enjoy the view or to make the most of what you've got. This section offers advice and ideas as well as projects which range from building a simple timber picket gate through to paving an outdoor area.

ASY HOME IMPROVEMENTS is a hands-on work and ideas book for home renovation and refurbishment. There are practical step-by-step projects, 'how to' skill classes and tips, as well as feature articles in which advice is given on planning and design decisions, budgeting and other practical considerations.

Projects are rated according to skill level required (beginners, average skills, experienced). All materials and special tools needed are listed – as well as the approximate time the project should take (although this will vary from person to person). There are diagrams and illustrations where necessary to help the reader.

Because readers' working conditions and the characteristics of their tools and materials cannot be anticipated here, it is recommended that readers use caution, care and good judgment when following the instructions or procedures outlined in this book. Before starting a project, readers should familiarise themselves with what's involved. This is an essential part of preparing for any project. Readers should also be aware of their own skill level and the instructions and safety precautions associated with the various tools and materials shown. When in doubt, always seek professional advice.

Although an enormous range of work can be done by the home handyperson, some areas are governed by local councils and statutory bodies. These areas vary from region to region. In some cases, it may be that only qualified tradespeople are permitted to do electrical work or plumbing (this is the case, for example, in Australia and New Zealand). For projects involving structural alterations, such as window or wall installation, you may be asked to submit plans for approval, apply for a building permit and pay fees. You must comply with any safety regulations or special legal requirements. Always check with your local council before starting a major project. At the same time, don't forget to stay in your neighbours' good books by keeping them informed, especially if your project will infringe on or disturb their privacy in some way.

Measurements are metric throughout the book. A conversion table (metric to imperial) is included at the back of the book for readers' reference.

CONTENTS

Lifestyle

PART 1

The Basics

Furniture from Country Form

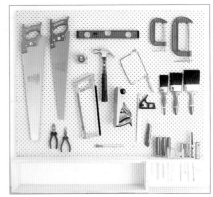

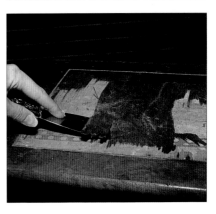

Skill Classes

PART 4 **Kitchen Improvements**

Projects

PART 5 **Bathroom Improvements**

Projects

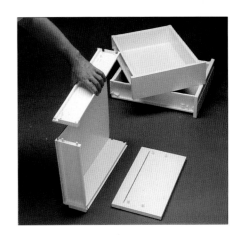

Skill Classes

PART 6 Outdoor Improvements

Projects

Project Ideas

Skill Classes

NOTES

☐ In our concreting projects we recommend that you always reinforce concrete. Reinforcement reduces the risk of cracking and is particularly important on soft subsoils such as clay – especially where these are subject to seasonal shrinkage and movement. On firm subsoils, or in areas of light usage, however, reinforcement is unnecessary and can be omitted.

☐ The use of cellulose fibre reinforced cement sheet (fibre-cement sheet) is recommended in wet areas such as bathrooms. According to the manufacturers this product is immune to water damage and will not rot, and within the normal range of applications the life of the product is limited only by the durability of the supporting structure and fixing materials.

☐ The publisher is not liable in the event of the failure of any product recommended in this book. Any queries should be directed to the manufacturer concerned. Manufacturers can supply comprehensive, detailed fixing instructions for their products if required.

PART 1

The Basics

*A tool carryall is excellent for safe storage and
transport of your tools. It is a practical and easy project for the
new do-it-yourselfer*

Before tackling any kind of home improvement project, check your resources in terms of equipment. Do you have the right tools? Most of the projects in this book require only basic tools, however an amateur carpenter will find that power tools not only make the job easier and quicker, but also much more accurate.

GETTING STARTED

Your tool kit can be added to with every new project – that way all your tools will be used. Avoid cheap tools and always go for quality. Good, albeit expensive, tools should last forever and will be well worth the money. In most instances, very expensive tools or machinery can be hired or borrowed for one-off jobs.

If you already have an extensive collection of tools, make sure they are sharp and ready for use. Old tools can be just as good but may need to be renovated and resharpened.

Tool kit

Following is a list of some of the tools you will need.

Hammer

The hammer should be a claw hammer of light-to-medium weight. This type of hammer is used for driving in nails and stubborn objects. It may have a wooden, fibreglass or steel shaft. Before use, slightly roughen the head of the hammer with some emery cloth to ensure it does not skid off the nails. The claw of the hammer is used for extracting nails.

Saw

A panel saw is the most useful wood or wood-panel cutting saw, usually around 450 mm long, with approximately ten teeth to 25 mm, referred to as 'ten-point'. This saw will cross cut and rip material of most general sizes.

Mitre box

Usually a simple wooden device which enables one to cut timber up to 125 mm wide at the exact angle desired, usually 90° or 45°. More sophisticated examples allow for wider cuts.

Chisels

These can be purchased individually but are best bought in a set. Sets usually comprise three or more. A good starting set would consist of three sizes: 13 mm, 19 mm and 25 mm chisels. Chisels should be of a reasonable quality as they will undergo rough treatment. New chisels generally need to be sharpened before use.

Screwdrivers

Like chisels these can be bought individually, but a set of five containing three widths of slotted and two sizes of Phillips head (crosshead), would be a good starting kit. There are many available but initially three will suffice. If you have to drive or remove many screws, it may be worthwhile investing in a ratchet screwdriver. Electric screwdrivers are also available.

Rule or tape

Most people prefer to use retractable metal tapes, which are available with markings in both metric and imperial units. For some small jobs it may be easier to use a four-fold box rule which folds out to a length of one metre.

Set square (try square)

Used to mark out and check material for square so that projects can be measured accurately.

Smoothing plane

The most popular is the No. 4 smoothing plane with a cast metal body. This plane is about 200 mm long. A good plane is easy and accurate to use and holds its edge well.

Utility knife

For cutting; featuring a fixed, interchangeable or 'snap-off' blade.

Cork block

This inexpensive piece of equipment is most useful when sandpapering. Use it with a sheet of abrasive paper to ensure sanding without causing depressions.

Spirit level

Used for checking the vertical and horizontal planes. This is an essential tool if cupboards, doors and worktops are on the job list. A level of between 450 mm and 900 mm will be most useful for project work.

Files

These are available in many shapes, lengths and grades. Best to start off with a 250 mm general purpose half-round file.

Pinch bar (crowbar)

A useful item to save your back, it can be used to lift heavy items and pull out large nails.

Pliers

General-purpose pliers will grip both flat and small, round objects and usually incorporate a wire cutter. 200 mm combination pliers will handle most jobs. Those with insulated handles are a good idea.

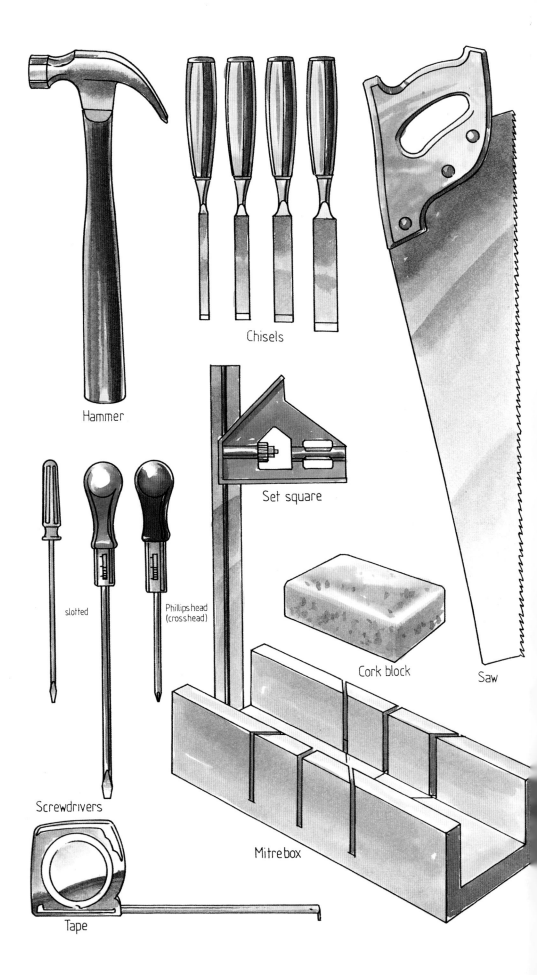

Adjustable spanner
Buy a size suitable for your project, but 200 mm spanners handle most general work.

Clamps
These are your second pair of hands, used to hold timber, clamp joints, etc. They come in various sizes and are commonly used in pairs. Two 200 mm G-clamps are the best to start off with. Pipe or sash clamps/cramps are designed to span large pieces.

Vice
Two types of vice are available. The woodworking vice is permanently bolted to the workbench and sits flush with the benchtop. The jaws of the vice are often 'softened' with either plastic or timber blocks. The other type of vice is an engineer's vice – this is bolted to the top of the workbench. This type is designed for metalwork but, with jaw liners, can be adapted for minor woodwork.

Nail punch
Buy one small and one large for general purpose work.

Hack saw
This is ideal for cutting metal such as bolts, nails, etc. Various tooths are available.

Chalk line
A device that automatically adds chalk to a length of string that can be stretched tight between two points then snapped against the surface where

Hammer

Chisels

Set square

slotted

Phillips head (crosshead)

Cork block

Saw

Screwdrivers

Mitre box

Tape

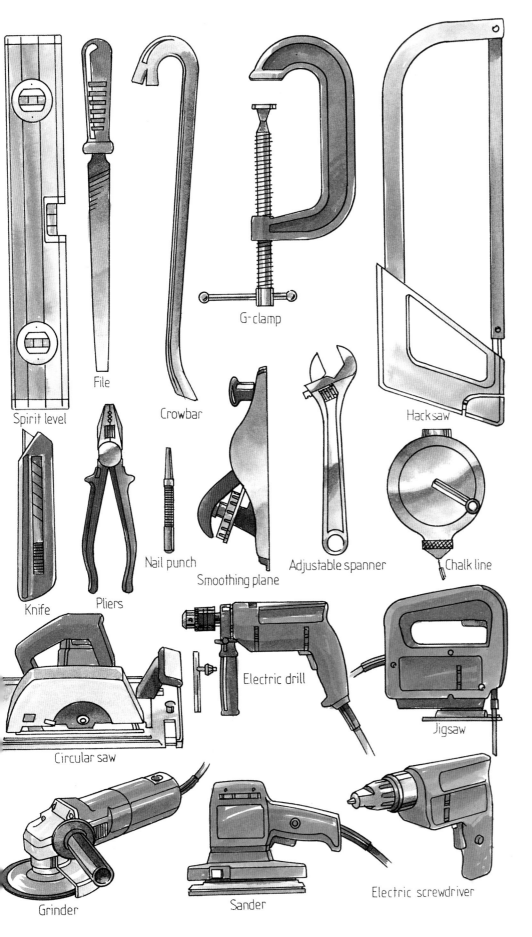

Spirit level

File

Crowbar

G-clamp

Hacksaw

Knife

Pliers

Nail punch

Smoothing plane

Adjustable spanner

Chalk line

Circular saw

Electric drill

Jigsaw

Grinder

Sander

Electric screwdriver

the line is required, leaving a well-defined line.

Oil stone

The combination medium and fine stone is best for keeping chisels and planes sharp. You will also need a small can of oil for oiling the stone. Oil stones should never be used dry. It is recommended that you use light machine oil.

Putty knife

A range of different filling knives for applying fillers, plaster or synthetic wood is available.

Brushes

A small selection of brushes for dusting, touching up and broad-area painting is most useful.

Protection set

Safety is always an issue – a pair of goggles, a face mask and a set of ear defenders or muffs are a worthwhile investment.

TIPSTRIP

USING A SPIRIT LEVEL
A spirit level is used to test the levelness and plumb of any piece of framework. The level has an air bubble inside a sealed glass tube. When the bubble is between two lines at the centre of the tube, the frame is level or plumb, as the case may be. To check the level for accuracy, set it up on a firm base with the bubble at the centre and mark the position of the level on the base. Now reverse the ends of the level and see if the bubble is still centred.

Power tools

Electric drill

A two-speed power drill with a chuck capacity of 10 mm or 13 mm is the most useful. Hammer action, if you can afford it, is also helpful for drilling masonry. The slow speed should be 900 rpm or slower.

Electric screwdriver

Available in 240V and cordless versions. The cordless unit with a rechargeable battery is lightweight, easy to handle and ideal for awkward jobs.

Circular saw

Used to make long, straight cuts. This can be a dangerous tool if not handled correctly, but with care it will cut solid timber and sheet material with ease.

Jigsaw

Ideal for curved work and for cutting holes. Jigsaw blades are available in many grades for cutting wood, plastic and metal.

Sander

Two types are available – orbital and belt. Both types can use different types of abrasive paper to level off and smooth. They can be used for stripping paintwork, but both will leave score marks on the job, so a light rub with hand-held paper is required before painting and oiling.

Grinder

There are two types of grinder: hand-held and bench-mounted. The hand-held unit is very good for cutting and finishing in awkward areas, whereas the bench-mounted unit is designed for sharpening tools and shaping small items.

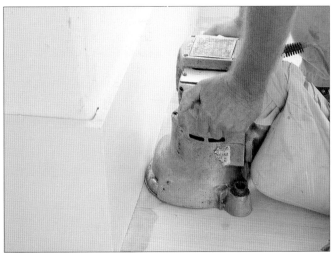

SIMPLE RULES FOR POWER TOOLS

Power tools are a special case safety-wise because accidents tend to occur much more quickly and are often more serious.

☐ Make sure that all power points used are properly earthed, and that all wiring is in top order. If in doubt have an electrician check the circuits.

☐ When using power tools consider using a safety adaptor with RCD protection between the tool and the power outlet so that if an accident occurs the power will be interrupted in less than a heartbeat. (Note: In the Southern Hemisphere a current imbalance interrupter would be used.)

☐ Make sure your power tools are in good condition. Do not use power tools that have exterior covers missing or safety guards removed or inoperable.

☐ Do not overload a power tool – loss of speed is a sign that it cannot cope – and never stall it.

☐ Disconnect the tool from the power source before making adjustments or changing bits and blades.

☐ Beware of any tool grabbing or kicking back. This is always a possibility when drilling thin metal or cutting along a length of timber with a circular saw. Never stand in a position directly behind the saw where the kickback may cause the saw to come into contact with you.

☐ Ensure that extension leads are unrolled entirely when in use as they can heat up considerably if kept in a tight coil.

☐ Keep leads away from cutting blades and be extra careful when using extension leads and power tools near water.

☐ Always allow a tool to stop before putting it down. A coasting tool can grab and come in contact with the operator or a bystander.

☐ Do not block off the ventilation holes or slots in a power tool, even when holding it, as it may overheat. Use the handles provided.

Other useful equipment

For holding work: A portable workbench (e.g. Workmate, Black & Decker).

For bricklaying: Bricklayer's trowel; bolster and club hammer (for cutting bricks and blocks); line pins (to keep courses level); pointing trowel (for finishing off pointing between courses); raking tools or jointer; gauge rod; assortment of buckets, mixing boards and sponges (also see Bricklaying Skill class).

For concreting and plastering: Shovels; screed rail or board (a heavy straightedge used for forming up); a sturdy wheelbarrow; board (sheet of plywood or similar about 1 m square to place the mortar on beside your work); steel float or trowel (for applying plaster and texturing concrete); metal hawk (square sheet metal with handle for carrying plaster); wooden float; tamper/tamping beam and/or garden roller (to compact concrete); buckets; rake (for spreading concrete within formwork) (also see Concreting Skill class)

Tools for hire: Every so often you may need to use specialist equipment, for example, a concrete mixer, light compactor, post-hole borer or stone/ paver splitter. Hiring the equipment will be the most cost-effective solution. Many DIY stores have hire centres, or you can look in the Yellow Pages for local hire shops.

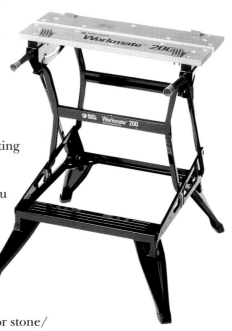

Opposite page: Sanding a timber-strip floor (top); Sanding edges with a disc sander (below) This page: Black & Decker portable workbench (above); A selection of concreting tools (left) – see Concreting Skill class on page 293

Tool care and safety

Having invested in some basic tools for your home improvements, it makes sense to look after them properly.

There is nothing more frustrating than planning a project and getting everything ready, only to discover that your saw needs sharpening and the chisels have chunks missing out of them!

Tools should be stored in a moisture-free place away from curious little fingers. The ideal situation is to have a workroom although most of us have to make do with a corner of the garage. Either way, a pegboard tool storage board and a tool carryall will help you organise your tools efficiently and safely (see Projects 1 and 2).

When doing any handy work make sure the work area is safe. It should be as level as possible and you should not have to stretch for anything – being off balance is dangerous when holding building materials or using tools. Have a first aid kit nearby, just in case. Young children should be kept away from the work area, especially when you are using tools.

Make sure that your clothing is suitable for the job. Wear appropriate face protection in the way of goggles and a breathing mask when working with materials that may chip, splinter, create dangerous dust and odours, or splash or spray. In certain instances ear muffs and gloves are also recommended. Open-toed shoes such as sandals should be barred from all do-it-yourself projects.

A general rule when using most tools is to drive the tool away from you rather than towards you – that way if the tool slips it will be moving away from your body.

Certain tools, such as chisels, must be kept sharp and ready for use. Blunt tools have to be forced to do the job and are more likely to slip and cause injury.

Checklist

☐ Keep all iron and steel surfaces lightly oiled. A wipe-over every now and then with an oily rag will keep these surfaces in good condition. An alternative is to use moisture-excluding sprays or penetrating oils.

☐ Protect all wooden handles from splitting and drying out. The occasional coat of varnish or linseed oil to keep moisture in the timber will help.

☐ Sharpened tools, such as chisels, are best kept in individual leather pouches to protect their edges – and your fingers. If you don't have pouches, hang them by the handle in a position where the cutting

edge will not contact anything else.

☐ Store all screwdrivers, awls, pliers and similar tools in a carryall or similar.

☐ Protect the teeth of saws from other tools. A good method is to use slide-on poster grips as these are self-supporting.

☐ Always store your planes on their sides with the blades retracted.

Holding your work

For projects which involve work on timber and metal you will need somewhere to work and to hold materials down. Comfort and safety are important aspects of organising your home project.

A workbench is ideal if you have the space. It should be sturdy, framed of large-section timbers, and well braced to ensure it doesn't wobble. The top can be made, at least in part, of particle (chip) board or plywood. The front is best made of a more substantial pine or similar, about 200 mm x

75 mm. The timber should not be too hard but solid enough to enable you to hammer and chop without marking the material you are working on. A wood vice or, if you prefer, an engineer's vice can be fitted to the front edge on one end. A portable workbench (e.g. Work-mate, Black & Decker) is also ideal for many home set-ups.

A pair of saw-horses or stools will be most useful for many of the projects in

this book. While making a pair of saw-stools is an interesting exercise, perhaps the first two should be bought, either ready-made or as a kit, so that you will quickly have a suitable surface for working on lengths of timber and panels. Clamps can be used in conjunction with the stools.

Other jobs will require ladders or trestles and these can be bought or hired when necessary. For jobs such as panelling a

staircase a combination ladder will be useful. When using extension ladders on finish work, pad the two top ends well with foam and old cloths to ensure they do not mark the work.

Opposite page: A pair of saw-horses or stools come in handy for a range of home DIY projects This page: Safety should always come first – protective clothing, such as gloves, goggles and facemask, is a wise investment for the home handyperson

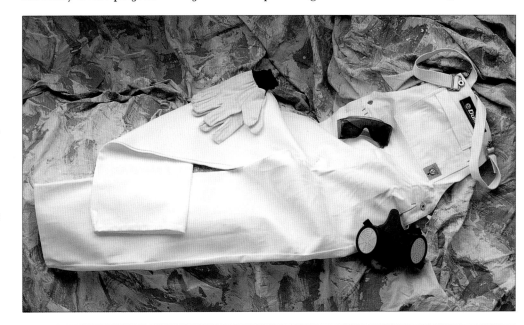

Skill class
Planes and Saws

PLANES

The first thing to remember is that you should never place a plane on its sole (the smooth undersurface out of which the cutting blade projects), as this may damage the blade. Always lay the plane on its side.

When using a plane, make sure your index finger is along the side of the blade, this gives better control. Most planing is done along the grain of the timber, that is, along its length.

Set the blade very fine at first and then adjust it if you need to take more timber off.

When starting to plane, place your weight on the front of the plane, and reverse the weight to the back at the end of the planing. Where possible, planing should extend from end to end of the timber so that the surface does not develop a concave shape.

Sharpening the blades

1   The first stage is the grinding. This is done on a grinding wheel, using water on the wheel to keep the blade cool. The blade is ground to an angle of between 25° and 30°.

2   The second stage is the honing, which is done on an oil-stone with light, clean machine oil. The blade is honed to an angle of between 30° and 35°. When honing, you should move the blade in a figure of eight over the oilstone – this will prevent the stone from wearing down unevenly.

3   After honing, the edge of the blade will have a slight burr on the back. Remove this by lying the blade flat on the stone and rubbing back and forth several times.

SAWS

Saws should always be well main-

tained. Make sure that they are not rusty and that the handle is tightly screwed into the frame. A saw should always be hung up after use to maintain the setting and sharpness of the teeth. Protect the teeth with slide-on poster grips or by slipping over a piece of wood or hose split down the middle.

Sharpen saws frequently. After three or four sharpenings the saw will need to be reset. Setting is the displacement of the teeth out from the main blade. Unless you are an experienced handyperson, it is best to have your saws sharpened and set by a saw doctor.

Tool storage

Tool storage is always a concern, especially when one contemplates the absolute mess that a workshop and workbench can quickly get into with nowhere to put things. A pegboard is simple to make and a low-cost storage solution for all your tools and other bits and pieces.

Project 1

Pegboard

The project involves making a pegboard hanging board with a shelf and screwdriver storage rack, based on the size of half a standard sheet of pegboard. The size of the project can be varied to suit available space.

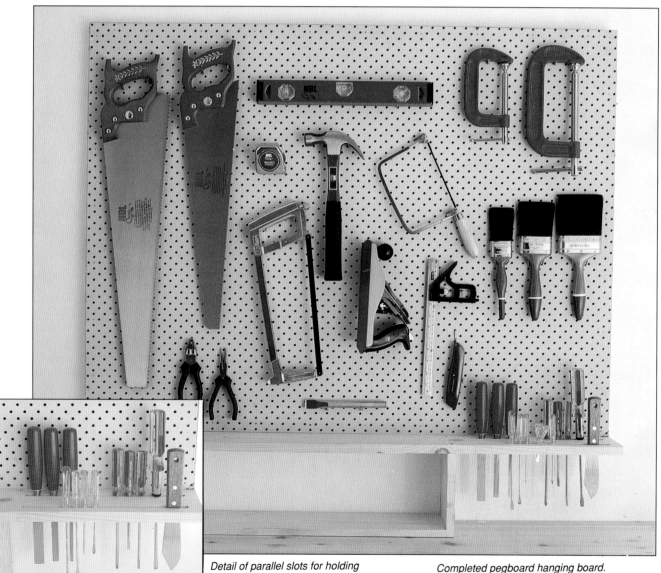

Detail of parallel slots for holding screwdrivers, chisels and putty knife

Completed pegboard hanging board. The shelves can be used for jars and tins of nails and screws

WHAT TO BUY

☐ 1 half-sheet pre-primed 4.8 mm pegboard, 1830 mm x 1220 mm
☐ 50 mm x 25 mm DAR (PAR) spruce or pine, 1 of 4.8 m
☐ 150 mm x 25 mm DAR (PAR) spruce or pine, 1 of 2.4 m
☐ PVA adhesive
☐ handful of 25 mm round wire nails
☐ 17 of 40 mm 8 gauge countersunk screws
☐ 75 mm countersunk wood screws with cup washers for fixing to stud wall; and heavy-duty wallplugs for masonry walls
☐ assortment of pegboard hooks

SPECIAL TOOLS NEEDED

☐ countersinking bit

TIME

One day, plus painting if necessary

STEP BY STEP

1 Carefully check that the piece of pegboard you have is square, and sand the edges smooth. It should also have been cut between the holes (not through the holes).

2 Measure the height, which should be 915 mm, and mark and cut two lengths of 50 mm x 25 mm spruce to this length.

3 Using a small amount of PVA adhesive, nail lengths to the back sides of the pegboard.

4 Measure the distance between the two side battens top and bottom, and cut to length two more lengths of 50 mm x 25 mm spruce.

5 Apply PVA adhesive to each batten and its edges where it butts against the sides. Once again nail in place.

6 Cut to length a piece of 150 mm x 25 mm spruce for the main shelf. This length should be 1220 mm the same as the length of the pegboard frame.

7 Mark out a slot on the right-hand side of this shelf, 19 mm from the front edge and about 12 mm wide. This should stop 25 mm short of the right-hand edge and be 300 mm long.

8 This can then be drilled for a starter hole, and then cut out using the jig saw.

9 A second slot may be cut a further 50 mm back, if desired.

10 The shelf can be screwed to the bottom of the pegboard frame using five 40 mm screws, and PVA adhesive.

11 Cut two side panels for the shelf from the 150 mm x 25 mm spruce, 180 mm deep. Place the two ends together to ensure they are exactly the same length. One piece can be glued and screwed through the left-hand end of the shelf, and the other can be screwed through from the top of the shelf into the end piece, with its outside edge a

distance of 850 mm from the left-hand side.

12 Cut the bottom shelf to length. In this case it should be 812 mm. Glue and screw to the two side panels.

13 The raw timber should be carefully sanded and then coated with two coats of polyurethane.

14 The pegboard itself can be undercoated and painted with a gloss final coat, preferably using a pale colour, so that the outlines of the tools can be easily marked on the surface.

15 You may care to screw (using two screws) several jam jar lids, or similar, to the underside of the bottom shelf for the storage of commonly used items such as screws, nails and pins. These items can be stored in the matching glass containers, which easily screw back into place.

16 Using the 75 mm screws, find the studs and screw the completed project to the wall through the top and bottom battens behind the pegboard.

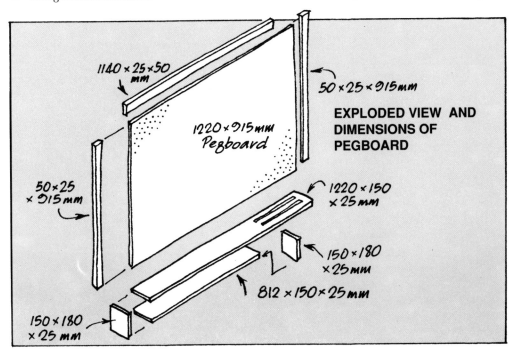

1140 × 25 × 50 mm

50 × 25 × 915 mm

1220 × 915 mm Pegboard

EXPLODED VIEW AND DIMENSIONS OF PEGBOARD

50 × 25 × 915 mm

1220 × 150 × 25 mm

150 × 180 × 25 mm

812 × 150 × 25 mm

150 × 180 × 25 mm

Transporting tools safely
A tool carryall is excellent for the safe storage and transport of your tools and other small items (such as nails, hardware and adhesive) to and from a work area.

Project 2

Tool carryall

The size and style of your carryall will be determined by where it is to be kept, the materials available and what you can carry. It's important that your carryall doesn't become a repository for junk. The carryall shown here is 500 mm long, by the planed width of a 200 mm x 25 mm board (190 mm plus 12 mm for two plywood sides) by 350 mm high.

The completed tool carryall, in raw timber, well-stocked with basic tools

Using a bevel-edged chisel to form slots for tool storage

WHAT TO BUY

Normally a carryall is made of scrap timber left over from other projects or scavenged from elsewhere. However, a nice-looking new one can also be a work of art.

- ☐ 200 mm x 25 mm DAR (PAR) spruce or pine, 1 of 1.2 m
- ☐ 38 mm x 25 mm DAR (PAR) spruce or pine, 1 of 0.6 m
- ☐ 19 mm dowel hardwood, 1 of 0.6 m
- ☐ 600 mm x 400 mm x 6 mm plywood, 1 sheet
- ☐ round head wire nails 50 mm and 30 mm long
- ☐ PVA adhesive

SPECIAL TOOLS NEEDED

- ☐ 19 mm flat bit and electric drill or 19 mm bit and brace

TIME

Two to three hours

STEP BY STEP

1 Prepare a work space and lay out the materials.

2 Square one end of the 200 mm x 25 mm board. Mark off 462 mm, the length of the carryall (500 mm) minus the thicknesses of the two ends (19 mm each). Square this and cut off the base, sawing on the waste side of the line.

3 Similarly, mark and cut off two lengths of 350 mm of the board for the two end panels.

4 On both end panels mark the centre of the hole for the handle halfway between the sides and 40 mm from the top. Bore a 19 mm diameter hole with a flat bit in an electric drill, or a brace and bit. If you only have a smaller bit, you will need to enlarge the hole with a round file. This will add some time to the project and can be quite frustrating.

5 Mark off triangles to be removed from the top ends of the end panels. Measure

50 mm across the top of the end, and 110 mm down the side. Join the two points and cut off. Repeat this for all four top corners of the carryall.

6 Cut two side panels of 500 mm x 180 mm out of the ply.

7 Sand all edges using a sanding block to remove splinters.

8 Apply a bead of PVA adhesive to one bottom end of the base and nail one end of the carryall to this using 50 mm nails. Repeat for the other side.

9 Apply PVA adhesive to the side of the base and 180 mm up the edges of the end panels. Align and nail one plywood side in place using 30 mm nails. Repeat for the other side.

10 Mark and cut to length the 19 mm diameter dowel. It is suggested the dowel protrude at either end a fraction and so is cut to a length of 550 mm. It should be a tight fit with no further fixing required. If loose, it can be held in place with a diagonally driven panel pin joining the dowel and the end panels.

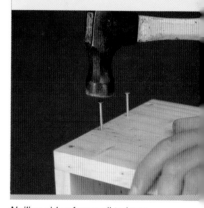

Nailing side of carryall to base

11 Mark and cut the 38 mm x 25 mm spruce (it should be 462 mm long) to fit between the two end panels along the inside top edge of one side. A series of 12 mm holes is drilled in this at 40 or 50 mm centres for storage of screwdrivers and small chisels, and joined 12 mm holes for wider tools such as wide chisels, rasps and files. This can be sanded smooth and fixed in place with PVA adhesive, nails from the ends and the plywood.

12 Your carryall is now complete. Although it is normally left in raw timber it can be painted, stained or clear finished if desired.

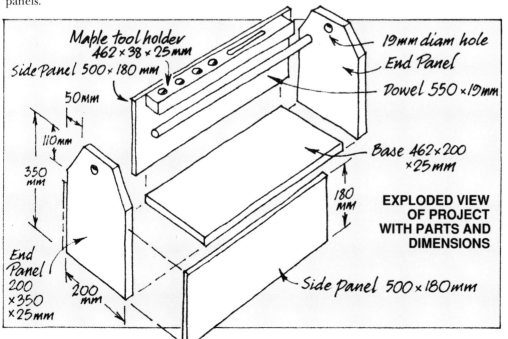

Maple tool holder 462 × 38 × 25 mm
Side Panel 500 × 180 mm
50 mm
110 mm
350 mm
End Panel 200 × 350 × 25 mm
200 mm
19 mm diam hole
End Panel
Dowel 550 × 19 mm
Base 462 × 200 × 25 mm
180 mm

EXPLODED VIEW OF PROJECT WITH PARTS AND DIMENSIONS

Side Panel 500 × 180 mm

PART 2

Interior Walls, Windows & Floors

*Above: Walls and windows need not be boring!
Transform them with pattern and colour to create a
whole new look
Right: Open, airy and full of light - this room's delightful
aspect is achieved by clever use of French doors,
windows and a section of glazed roof*

Walls not only divide up different areas and define the space we live in – they also, quite literally, hold the roof over our heads and act as a major decorating feature in every room. Included here is a feast of inspiring ideas for walls and wallcoverings.

ALL ABOUT WALLS

Clever ideas for the walls around you

Lifestyle

Wallpapered rendered walls with marbled architraves

Some solid internal walls are load bearing – with a structural purpose, to hold up the roof of a building for example – and some are non-load-bearing. They may be there to divide up different areas, and to define interior and exterior space.

Walls are often added or removed in the process of home improvement and to suit a growing family's changing needs. They may be made of stone, brick or block; or can be framed and panelled.

REMOVING WALLS

If a wall is to be removed, it should first be carefully inspected to ensure it is not a structural element supporting another. In this case, if the wall is removed it could cause the structure to collapse. A wall may be holding up a vital section of the roof, an upper floor, or may act as a stiffener for an adjacent wall. The latter is especially important in terrace housing where you have no idea of what structural changes your neighbours have made.

If you don't feel competent enough to check the roofing structure and its support, get in a builder or building consultant to do the job. Before you do any work like this you should also check with your local building authority to ensure that you are allowed to do so.

The versatility of plasterboard can be seen in this open-plan dining area

Floral-print wallpaper and matching drapes create a country-style feel

Opposite: Painted, rendered and set walls with an ornate cornice give this lounge room character

Fibrous plaster walls with border to accent cornice

BUILDING WALLS

New walls are often built to divide large rooms, or are built in the process of wall relocation. Specifically, new walls may be used to divide a new en suite bathroom from a large bedroom, a bar from a lounge, or to divide a dormitory-style bedroom into two smaller, more private units.

When building a new room in this way, it is important that you allow sufficient light and ventilation for the purpose of the room so that the two divided areas still comply with any building regulations. Generally, 'habitable' rooms require window glass equal to at least 10 per cent of the floor area, and one half of that should afford good ventilation.

MASONRY WALLS

Masonry walls are common in older full-brick buildings, but they are not so easily replaced once removed. Masonry walls are heavy (at least 0.25 tonnes to the square metre) and need correct support. They cannot just be built on an existing floor, but need to be taken to ground on a footing or a proper structural support such as a beam. An engineer should be commissioned to work out the minimum support needed in this case.

FRAMED WALLS

Timber-framed walls are more common than masonry walls. Most home handypersons would build a timber-framed wall, which is then lined both sides with any number of materials. Most frames are 75 mm or 100 mm thick, with the lining adding a further 10 mm to 25 mm both sides. This should be taken into account when measuring up as 120 mm is an appreciable amount to lose in dividing spaces.

The frame is normally built to sit on the solid floor (not on the carpet) and fixed to the ceiling joists above. If the roof framing is of a truss type, the connection to the bottom binder of the roof truss should be flexible to allow for movement; the wall should not be a tight fit.

When building a new frame wall, it is a good opportunity to install extra services. A new switch layout, concealed telephone intercom wiring, or extra plumbing services can easily be incorporated into the wall.

OTHER WALLS

There are other types of walls which you can build. Glass-block walls, for example, are designed to allow maximum light through. These can be heavy and you may need advice from an engineer about suspended locations. Glass blocks are also available in acrylic,

which are much lighter. Normally suppliers have detailed installation instructions for all of these.

Interior fixed glazing in either clear or obscured glass can also be used. There is no reason why office partitioning systems cannot also be used to divide rooms. These are generally metal-framed and modular and are best installed by the manufacturers.

If the 95 mm minimum wall thickness of a framed wall is excessive, another option is to use tongued and grooved particle (chip)board of 19 mm thickness. This can be held bottom and top by fixed skirtings and covings

and, as long as the occasional vertical joint is not annoying, can provide a strong yet thin wall. Services are difficult to locate in this type of wall.

WALL FINISHES

Once a wall has been built it can be finished in a myriad of ways. Painting and wallpapering on plasterboard or fibrous plaster are major possibilities, but other options exist. Decorative paint techniques, such as sponging and ragging, are far more interesting than plain, painted walls. Walls may be covered in fabrics and heavily textured weaves. Paintable fibreglass texture wall coverings are available.

Imitation suede is popular as are hessian finishes and cork tiles. In bathrooms, tiles are commonly used; but in other areas ceramic tiles, slate, marble, and granite are all possibilities. If you have lightweight walls but like the brick look, it is possible to adhere brick wafers to the wall to give a solid brick appearance.

Other possibilities are timber panelling, which comes in a great variety of tonings and profiles; laminated sheets; and various plain and textured wallboards and vinyl linings.

The variety and possibilities are only limited by your imagination.

Opposite: Sunny wallpapered bedroom walls with matching panels in doors to robe, hall and en suite

Open-plan living achieved by removing wall sections. Note the top of the wall in place to cover beam, and small nib walls for structural stability

Changing needs

Somehow there never seems to be enough space at home, especially where children are concerned. Changing needs often demand extra space and new interior layouts – how often have you wished you could push the walls apart just a fraction, add an extra room or wave a magic wand and conjure up more storage space?

Project 1

Dividing wall

A wall frame is made of a number of parts. The main parts are plates, studs, heads, noggings, lintels and bracing.

This project consists of building a wall to divide a storage/pantry area from a dining room. It is 3.0 m long by the standard 2.4 m high. There is a doorway at one end to take a standard door. The wall framing must be solid, to provide fixing support for plasterboard on both sides as well as the door and door frame.

■ **PLATES**

Head (top) plate: The head plate forms the top of the wall. In this case, it supports no load other than wall linings.

Sole (bottom) plate: The sole plate forms the bottom edge of the wall frame, and is supported by the floor frame.

Plates can be trenched to about 10 mm to allow for any difference in thickness. This is measured from the outside face of the plate to leave a uniform thickness on each plate. This is not necessary when plates are machine-gauged to a uniform thickness by the timber supplier.

■ **STUDS:** Studs are the vertical members between plates and can be spaced at 450 mm or 600 mm centres. To determine the length of the studs, measure the ceiling height and subtract the thicknesses of the plates.

■ **HEAD:** The door head is a horizontal short member above the door, which in this case is not load bearing. If a head is load bearing, a lintel may be needed.

Completed wall covered in painted plasterboard with skirtings and architraves in place

4 Mark in the position of studs at the ends then space out and mark the studs at 450 mm centres. Allow for the thickness of the studs (50 mm). On these faces, mark which is the head and sole plate, and which way up they are to go.

5 Measure the depth of the trenches or housings in the head and sole plates, and gauge them ready for cutting. The measurement should be taken from the top side of the head plate and bottom side of the sole plate. A maximum of 10 mm should be removed. A marking gauge can be used to mark the depth.

6 Cut along the marks of the stud housings down to the gauged mark, then chisel out the housings with a 19 mm or 25 mm chisel and wooden mallet. Chisel from the centre of the housing towards the cuts, or from the edge to the centre. They can then be smoothed with a coarse rasp (make sure it has a handle). This whole procedure can be made easier with a power circular saw where the depth of cut is adjusted to a maximum of 10 mm and a series of parallel cuts are made between the marked housings. The residue left can be smoothed with the rasp if necessary. Professional frame carpenters use a radial-arm saw – this option is normally unavailable to home handypersons.

■ **NOGGINGS:** The studs in each wall are stiffened by the addition of noggings closely fitted between the studs. Noggings are usually the same size as the studs. They are placed approximately halfway between head and sole plates in walls up to 2700 mm in height.

■ **BRACING:** Occasionally walls must be stiffened against distortion by using diagonal bracing. This, however, is not common on interior dividing walls. The most effective angle for a brace is 45°. Bracing may be of timber or metal. Metal bracing should run in opposite directions.

■ **LINTELS:** Occasionally, where openings occur in the interior wall framing which also supports a roof, the load over the opening may be supported by a lintel.

STEP BY STEP

1 The wall will be built as one unit, and the studs will be housed into the head and sole plates. When completed it will be tilted into position and secured. It may be wise to make the frame about 10 mm short at the top to allow for wall variations and manoeuvring when putting in position.

2 Lay out two straight timber lengths for plates on stools and hold them together with clamps. Mark and square the length, in this case 3000 mm minus 10 mm for ease of installation. Therefore total length will be 2990 mm. Cut to length.

3 Mark the position for the door opening. The sole plate is left running through the door opening. This portion of the sole plate is not cut out until the wall is permanently fixed in position.

Nailing noggings to studs

Securing bottom plate to floor along string line

31

Trueing studs prior to fixing to wall

7 Now calculate the length of the studs. The length will be 2400 mm minus an allowance for fitting of 10 mm, minus the remaining thickness of the two plates, which will be 40 mm each. The total length of the studs therefore is 2310 mm.

8 Cut one stud to length then lay it between the head and sole plate on the floor. Check for total height to verify that all the measurements are correct.

9 If the measurements are correct, cut the remaining five studs to length.

10 Mark the door heads to provide an opening of 2100 mm in height on the two straightest studs. The

mark will actually be 2060 mm from the base of the stud to allow for the thickness of the housed bottom plate. Mark a width of 50 mm, ready for housing in the head of the door, then cut and chisel out the housing.

11 Now assemble the wall frames. Lay out the plates and studs on the floor as close as possible to where the wall frame is to go. Lay all the round edges of the studs the same way up.

12 Nail the plates to the studs with two nails at each joint. This is easier with two people, one at each end.

13 Cut to length the head over the door opening, which should be 900 mm plus

10 mm each end – that is, a total of 920 mm. Fit the head into the housings and nail into place.

14 The noggings should be fixed with their centres about halfway between floor and ceiling. The noggings are fixed in a straight line or staggered. The noggings should not coincide with plasterboard joins.

15 To fix the noggings, measure the length between studs and cut to length. Nail the noggings to the studs from each side along that line, stepping alternate noggings above and below the line.

16 Cut and fit a short stud between head and head plate. This is about 210 mm long, and may possibly be an offcut from one of the plates, or from the noggings.

17 Square up the wall frame by making the two diagonals equal by measuring with a steel tape. The diagonal should measure approximately 3842 mm. If the diagonals are not equal, adjust as necessary and then secure with a temporary diagonal brace.

18 Carefully mark the position of the frame on the floor. It is worth double-checking this measurement. When satisfied, drive a 100 mm nail partly into the floor near both ends of the marked line to prevent the bottom plate of the frame from skidding beyond that point. Enlist some help when tilting frames into position to ensure a safe operation.

19 When the frame has been stood upright, secure with a temporary nail into the wall until a more permanent fixing is made.

20 The frame must now be trued accurately in a number of steps.

21 Each end of the frame should be temporarily fixed to the floor on the mark previously made. It may be necessary to remove the temporary nail holding the frame to the wall to get it into the right position.

22 Straighten the sole plate. Stretch a string line packed out from the sole plate using blocks of equal thickness. Align the sole plate to this and nail through into the joists if possible. If your wall is parallel to the joists, it may be worth installing a joist under the floor directly below the new wall.

23 True the vertical of the two walls by using a plumb bob or a long level, then hold the frame in the vertical position with two nails. Place 'packing' between the existing walls and the new wall, and permanently nail the wall in place. On a brick wall three masonry bolts would be suitable. Suitable packing in this case would be plywood, fibre cement or hardboard offcuts.

24 Check alignment of the head plate to a string line as for sole. Fix it to ceiling joists.

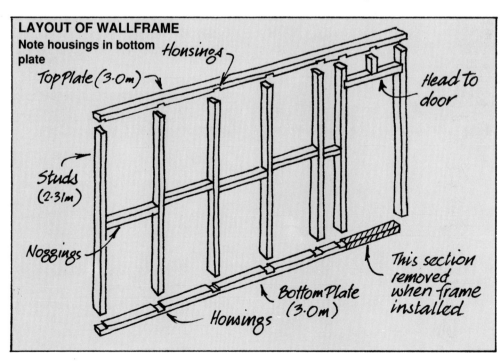

LAYOUT OF WALLFRAME
Note housings in bottom plate
Housings
TopPlate (3·0m)
Head to door
Studs (2·31m)
Noggings
BottomPlate (3·0m)
Housings
This section removed when frame installed

Finishing off
*Our interior dividing wall, made from a framework of timber
(see Project 1) has been built and is already in place. This frame is
now ready to be lined (faced with plasterboard on both sides), finished
off, and to have a door installed in it.*

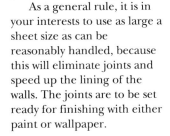

Plasterboard and cornices

The wall is 3.0 m long by the standard 2.4 m high. We have allowed for a doorway at one end to take a standard door.

We will fix 10 mm tapered-edge plasterboard to both sides; the joint to the ceiling will be finished without a cornice. Cornice-fixing details follow this basic plasterboard fixing guide.

As a general rule, it is in your interests to use as large a sheet size as can be reasonably handled, because this will eliminate joints and speed up the lining of the walls. The joints are to be set ready for finishing with either paint or wallpaper.

STEP BY STEP

1 Ensure that the walls are true and straight. Hold a long straight edge over the face of the studs and ensure there are no ridges or hollows. If a stud needs to be cut or straightened, use fish plates to secure the cut. Otherwise the studs will need to be shaved or packed to compensate.

2 Make sure that there are no nails or other protuberances from the face of the studs.

3 Any plumbing or wiring must be installed in the wall cavity before the plasterboard is fixed.

4 Plasterboard can be fixed horizontally when using tapered-edge plasterboard.

5 Mark the sheets to the correct size. The first sheet will only run as far as the door, so is cut 2050 mm. Mark the line to be cut on the face of the smaller sheet.

6 Cut the sheet of plasterboard to size. This is most easily done using a sharp, short-bladed utility knife. Run the knife along the marked line using a straight edge of sufficient length. The board is then snapped back along this cut; the sheet will break and only be hinged by its rear paper.

7 Cut through the rear paper face, from the rear, to separate the two sheets.

8 Place two offcuts of 10 mm plasterboard on the floor at the base of the wall to automatically give the required gap to the floor.

Top: Using utility knife to cut plasterboard

Plasterboard adhered and nailed in place

Applying jointing cement and bottom tape to recessed sheet joint

9 Apply the plasterboard adhesive to the studs so that they will not coincide with the nailing positions of the sheets. The adhesive should be applied in dobs about the size of a 10p or 10 cent coin.

10 Fit the plasterboard to the wall and secure with galvanised plasterboard nails. Nailing should be at every stud. The sheets should be nailed about 12 mm from the edge and again in the centre of the sheet on each stud. Double-nail with the second nail about 60-75 mm away from the first to properly secure the wall. The manufacturers recommend that you don't nail to the noggings.

11 The second sheet will need to be fitted around the door and over its top. This should be carefully measured, and marked on the face of the sheet.

12 To cut a rectangle out of a corner of the board, the first shorter cut can be made with a panel saw, and the second cut with the utility knife – snapping the sheet as before.

13 When cut, fit the second sheet over the first. Manoeuvring the sheet into position in a tight space can be tricky and it is important that it is lifted straight without skewing, as this may damage adjacent wall linings

and the corners of the sheet itself. A second person would certainly be a help!

14 When the sheet is in position, adhere and nail it in place as before.

15 Cut a narrow strip and fit in place down the remaining stud at the door, to even out the face for future application of the architraves of the door.

16 Now the joints are ready to be set for a smooth finish. Firstly ensure there is no

dust or other contaminants on the sheets by wiping them over with a damp cloth.

17 Apply self-adhesive scrim tape to the joint and firm it in place as you go.

18 This tape is then covered with a good layer of jointing plaster applied with the filling knife to a width of about 100 mm to 150 mm. This should be finished to the level of the surrounding plasterboard, and not be built up to a higher level.

19 Similarly the joint to the ceiling must be taped and set but in this case using an internal corner finishing tool. The tape is firmly pushed into the corner, and for each layer of plaster applied to the face of the plasterboard, a layer of finishing plaster is applied to the corner and worked in position using the corner finishing tool.

20 After 24 hours, when the first application of jointing plaster is dry, the second can be applied, slightly wider to say 200 mm, being careful to

apply it as smoothly to the level of plasterboard as possible.

21 This is also left to dry, and the final application of jointing plaster is applied in a broad band about 250 mm in width to achieve a completely smooth joint that is completely flush with the plasterboard surrounds. For an even finer edge, it can be gently brushed with a damp brush to 'feather' the edge.

FINISHING THE WALL

Having finished the plasterwork, the wall can be prepared for painting or wallpapering. If you are using natural timber skirting boards it may be worthwhile to fix them after the wall has been painted.

The paper face of plasterboard is quite absorbent, and the jointing cement will have a different suction to the face of the boards. It is recommended that you first seal the surface with a wallboard sealer, which

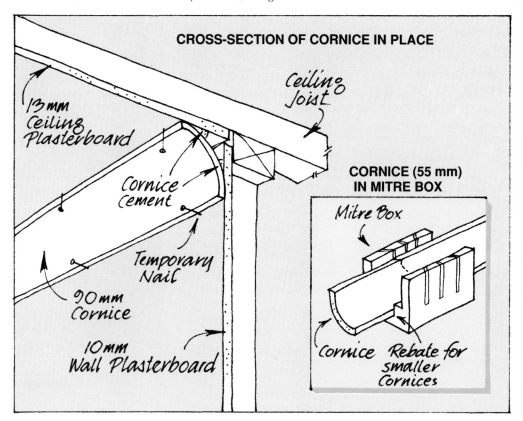

CROSS-SECTION OF CORNICE IN PLACE

Ceiling Joist

13 mm Ceiling Plasterboard

Cornice Cement

Temporary Nail

90 mm Cornice

10 mm Wall Plasterboard

CORNICE (55 mm) IN MITRE BOX

Mitre Box

Cornice Rebate for smaller Cornices

may be either acrylic or oil based.

Sealers are simply painted or rolled on. Allow to dry between 4 and 24 hours depending on the product used. At this stage the wall may be papered or painted. Our example was painted using two coats of a quality water-based, low-sheen vinyl paint. The edges and cutting-in were done with a 50 mm brush, and the wall then generally coated with a roller (fine-to-medium nap). Painting walls with oil-based paints is more involved and the clean-up is nowhere near as easy.

For wallpapering, the surface is coated with size, and then papered with any of the vast range of papers on the market. For first-time wallpapers, pre-pasted paper is easiest to use.

Coat the skirting boards and the architraves around the door with a coat of polyurethane. When dry, fix the skirting boards firstly to the doorway, and then around the bottom of the floor. Skirting boards are scribed rather than mitred into the corners. They can be nailed to the base of the wall because there is a structural timber member, the sole plate, behind there. When fixed, the nails can be punched below the surface, and the holes filled with a matching wood-stopping compound. The final coat of polyurethane is applied to finish off the room.

CORNICES

A cornice is a continuous horizontal plaster moulding, often quite ornate and decorative, at the joint of wall and ceiling.

1 If cornices are to be fitted to the ceiling and wall junction, mark down the wall in several places along its length, and join the marks to indicate where the bottom of the cornice will be.

2 Measure the lengths of the cornice required. It is a good idea to cut the long length about 3 mm oversize so that it can be snapped into position, forming a tight joint.

3 Use a mitre box to cut a mitre at both ends of the long and short lengths. Make sure that the mitre runs the correct way – the two lengths should be a mirror image of each other. Where the cornice needs to be joined, cut the mitres before they are cut to length. This will allow you more choices in case of an error.

4 Install the shorter lengths first.

5 Mix the cornice plaster with water to a creamy consistency. The mixture is useable for about 30 minutes.

6 Butter 10 mm beads of cornice plaster on the back of the cornice edges. Apply cornice plaster to one length at a time, and fix that length in place. On a hot day it may be worth slightly dampening the cornice where the plaster is applied to stop it drying out too quickly.

7 Put each short piece in position and hold in place using some temporary nails; if in doubt about their holding in place, use galvanised nails about 25 mm in from the edge nailed into the frame.

8 When in place, butter the long length and, bending slightly, 'snap' it into place. Once again hold it firmly in place with galvanised nails.

9 As the cornice plaster goes off rather quickly, it is important to clean off all excess plaster at the earliest possible time.

10 When set, apply finishing plaster to the mitres. Finish off the joint with a light brush-over with a damp brush to smooth the joint.

11 Remove all temporary nails. Apply a second coat of filler to the mitres and joints as well as to the nail holes. Use the damp brush again for a feather edge.

12 When all is set, a light sanding using #150 grade paper with a float on the flat areas and by hand on the curved, will leave a surface ready for sealing for paint or wallpaper.

One of the most attractive feature walls is one lined with a beautifully grained and coloured species of timber. Solid timber panelling is available in many species, all of which have their own charm. The timbers may be local or imported.

Project 3

Timber panelling

Panelling is normally solid timber, but a large range of decorative plywoods and other boards are available, with exotic species of timber in veneer form. The price for all types of panelling will vary greatly, depending mainly on the species and thickness of timber used.

The profile may be shiplap, where one board overlaps another, or be tongue and grooved (t & g), where each board has a milled tongue which fits into the groove of the next board. These are often milled to give a V-joint. Some shiplap profiles also feature t & g grooves for secret fixing or reversal of the timber to provide a t & g finish.

Our project is the timber panelling of a staircase. The staircase has four risers to a landing and then a further nine risers to the upstairs area. The timber selected for the panelling is Western red cedar. However, any other timber can be used. The profile is a 150 mm shiplap suitable for secret nailing. Because of the profile the effective cover is only 133 mm.

Timber feature wall

WHAT TO BUY

☐ 150 mm x 12 mm shiplap Western red cedar
or cladding 150 linear m

SPECIAL TOOLS NEEDED

☐ sliding bevel

TIME

Timber panelling – two weekends
Trim and finishing – one weekend

Additional noggings ready to be fixed to frame

STEP BY STEP

1 Before putting up panelling it is essential to ensure that the wall is plumb and straight. Timber panelling that is 12 mm thick will follow any irregularities in the wall. If the wall is irregular, you may need to build and fix a frame to provide a plumb and straight base (see Tipstrip, next page).

2 Timber panelling must be properly supported to avoid distortion or breakage. Intermediate noggings should be fitted between timber studs so that the maximum unsupported length of the panel is 600 mm.

3 Panelling must be straight to look effective! We will start over the doorway, and work down the stairs. Once the wall has been checked and prepared as necessary, it is time to mark in a true vertical line near one corner of the wall. Unless the adjoining wall is perfectly true and plumb, this mark should be slightly less than the width of the panelling timber profile. This allows the board to be scribed to the corner.

4 Using a long level or a plumb line, mark a true vertical on each nogging from this mark.

5 Temporarily, fix the panel along the vertical line, with the tongue facing away from the wall. Two panel pins only

partly driven should be plenty.

6 Transfer the profile of the wall onto the panel, by running a short offcut down the wall together with a sharp pencil marking the outline of the wall on the timber length that was fixed temporarily. Extract the nails, and the board can then be taken away and planed to the marked line, which is the exact shape that will fit the adjacent wall.

7 The first panel can then be nailed to the wall. Most profiles are milled to allow for secret nailing, so that nail heads are not visible. Use only fine panel pins to avoid the problem of timber splitting, and place the nail

where the next panel will cover the nail head.

8 With all panelling, it is wise to hammer the nail only to within about 3 mm of the surface, after which the nail should be driven with the aid of a nail punch. Western red

cedar marks easily and hammer marks all over the wall are most unattractive.

9 The next length will only need to be cut to length. It is then fitted with its grooves properly engaged in the tongue of the first panel. This

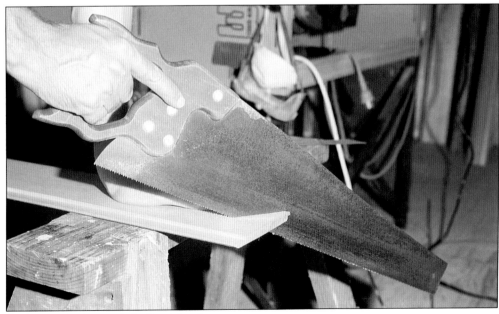

Cutting panels at an angle for the staircase

■ Where walls are not suitable to have the timber applied directly due to irregularities or bowing or hollows, a separate frame will need to be made first. This frame is called the ground. Grounds can be fabricated and fixed to the wall, or can be built directly onto the wall. They are normally made of 50 mm x 25 mm softwood. The important dimension is the thickness, as this ensures a smooth wall. Grounds can be nailed to the studs of timber-framed walls or can be stuck or fixed with frame fixings to brickwork. If the walls are uneven, it may be necessary to pack behind them to bring them level.

■ If you wish to fix the timber panelling in the horizontal plane or even diagonally, the battens will have to be repositioned to ensure that adequate fixing is available. Horizontal panelling can be directly attached to the framework of the house, as studs occur every 450 mm or 500 mm.

■ Traditionally, timber panelling was fixed to frames by nailing directly. Some timber suppliers strongly suggest both nailing and gluing with a good-quality wallboard adhesive for the best results.

■ If using plywood, a variety of finishes and colours are available. Fixing plywood is very similar, with similar requirements for support. Plywood for walls usually has a regular or random-groove pattern, and the nails are easily disguised if hammered in the grooves.

can be tight at times, and you may need to tap the board into place. If you just use a hammer, the timber edge will be crushed and distorted, and the next panel will be difficult to fit. Tapping into place is best done using an offcut of the panel, and snapping it in half along its grain. This will give you a grooved half that can be fitted over the tongue and used as a hammering block. It will not damage the delicate edges of the panelling.

10 Slowly begin fixing the panelling to the wall, checking every two or three boards to make sure that the panelling is still truly vertical.

11 After six lengths of panelling are fitted over the door, the next will need to be cut out around the door. Cut a board to the total height of

Panel moved to show nailing position for 'secret nailing'

Using level to plumb panels

floor to ceiling, and then hold it against the door and mark off the top of the jamb. Fit another small offcut into the tongue of the board last fitted and mark the width of the cut on the offcut. This

can be accurately transferred to the new length you are preparing.

12 To cut the section out, use your panel saw and cut along the grain first. This is called ripping. Do this gently as timbers with a well-defined grain can easily split along the grain rather than the mark if the saw is forced. At the marked end, cut off across the grain.

13 When fitting this panel take extra care to get the board truly plumb.

14 The following panels start going down the stairs, and each will be longer than the preceding one. To get the angle right, set a sliding bevel permanently to the angle between the top of the stair string and a true vertical. This technique will always give you the right angle at which to mark and cut the bottom of each panel. As you proceed down the stairs, you will need a ladder to reach the higher areas to effectively nail the timber in position. A small extension ladder is ideal, together with a ladder leveller so that you can use it on the stairs. Each top point of the ladder should be well wrapped in foam rubber, and then in an old cloth. This way you can work safely without marking the panelling with the ladder. Don't balance the ladder on boxes or bricks – they are not safe.

15 When you are about two or three boards from the end of the wall, put them into position, without nailing. You will have to measure the final board to trim it to shape. This is easiest when the adjacent boards are not fixed. In some cases it may be necessary to round off the back of the final board so that it can be slipped into the corner.

16 When the panel is an exact fit, fix all the last panels into position. This includes those on opposite walls.

17 There will be one external angle on the landing. This can be dressed by using a specially moulded corner piece in the same timber.

18 At this stage, it is time to start applying all the trim pieces such as architraves around the door, beads to cover joints between balustrading bottom rails and panelling, and to the stair strings where necessary.

19 It is also time to apply the brackets to fix the handrail section. These cannot be supported by the timber panelling, and must be fixed through to the studs behind the panelling.

20 Finishing of timber panelling is up to you. Most people prefer to use low-sheen finishes and these can be achieved using the various finishing oils on the market. If the panelling is likely to undergo frequent handling, a polyurethane will be the easiest surface to wipe down. Regardless of which is chosen for the panelling, the staircase and strings should be coated in a hard-wearing finish such as polyurethane because of the wear it will be subjected to.

Lifestyle

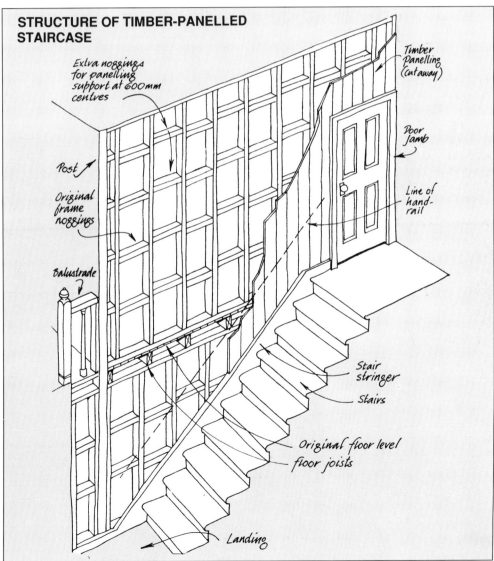

STRUCTURE OF TIMBER-PANELLED STAIRCASE

Extra noggings for panelling support at 600mm centres

Timber Panelling (cutaway)

Post

Original frame noggings

Balustrade

Door Jamb

Line of hand-rail

Stair stringer

Stairs

Original floor level
floor joists

Landing

Windows are a major visual feature of the modern house, they are also its eyes – imparting style, character and personality while providing good ventilation and light.

LET IN THE LIGHT
Bright ideas for light and shade

Australian Colonial Federation style windows to a dining room

This skylight opens out and brightens up an otherwise dark and featureless hallway

Natural light is let in by modern glazed doors, louvred side and fan light, and a skylight

Opposite: Lounge with French doors and windows with colonial glazing bars, and featuring a section of glazed roof

French leadlight doors are a feature of this living area, adding their own distinctive, very decorative character

Openings in houses may be voids, doors or windows. Voids tend to be in areas where security is not a consideration, such as between rooms in an open-plan living area. Doors provide a means of access and security to the building. Windows, however, are designed to provide daylight and a means of ventilation. They should also provide a view, but still allow for privacy when required.

The difficulty in placing windows is that the best position for maximum daylight may not coincide with the best view, or best ventilation possible. Compromises are inevitable. The light admitted will depend not only on position but also on the type of glass used, the reflection from walls, floor and ceilings; and the sun control treatment used.

GLASS

Glass in most instances will be clear. However, for areas such as bathrooms, glass is available in various levels of obscurity, or it may be tinted. The range of solar and reflective glasses, although expensive, may be used to control solar radiation. Safety glass should be used around sliding doors and floor-level glazing panels.

WINDOWS

There are many types of windows, each with their advantages and disadvantages.

Fixed windows: Don't have any opening sashes. They are not normally used as the only window in a room.

Timber sash (box-framed) windows: The old traditional windows where the sashes slide up and down, and are counter-balanced by weights.

Casement windows: Style where the sash is hinged on the vertical framing members.

Double-hung windows: The modern equivalent of the old timber sash window. Both top and bottom open to allow convection movement of air.

Sliding windows: Commonly aluminium, where one half slides past the other fixed half. This allows large, open areas.

Awning (top-hung) windows: Style where the sash is hinged to the top horizontal member and opens out. They may be left open in the rain, but allow only limited air circulation.

Sashless windows: Glass without a frame, various styles but mainly for commercial purposes.

Frame materials may be timber, aluminium, steel or PVC. The choice will be based on the style of house, exposure, availability, and maintenance requirements.

LEADLIGHTS

An attractive alternative is leadlight or stained glass. These are available as 'standard' panels, or a leadlight or stained glass panel can be commissioned from an artist. Imitation leadlighting with surface-applied lead and a stain wash to the glass is also available.

GLASS BRICKS

Glass bricks are a way of providing obscured filtered light into areas such as stairwells and bathrooms. Their installation is exacting, and allowance must be made for expansion and contraction.

PATIO DOORS

Patio doors are an extension of multiple windows, and in many homes may be a combination of normal opening floor-to-ceiling windows, together with fixed sashes. For ventilation in humid situations, banks of louvres may be used.

CONSERVATORIES

Conservatories are a popular extension of patio doors, where the roof or part of the roof is also glazed. It is important to use a proprietary system and keep the pitch correct, to achieve adequate waterproofing.

SKYLIGHTS

Where rooms are enclosed and don't have their own window, a common option is that of a skylight or roof 'window'. They are effective together with a lightwell, and are available in vented or unvented styles.

Attic room with both dormer window and a double-glazed roof window

Barrel lights may have curved glass and glazing bars and can be made to cover entire rooms. It is important in this case to watch the heat gain through the glazing – many people find air-conditioning a necessity after installation.

SHADING

Shading of windows is possible in many ways. Most effective are external methods such as awnings, external blinds and louvres or shutters. Also effective are solar films. On the interior, heat can be controlled with reflective blinds and a range of venetians, blinds, and even curtains.

A rather beautiful entrance, with its timber-strip floor, well-chosen antiques and understated decor, is highlighted even more by a large skylight

Skylights and roof windows can help to transform any room, especially those with little access to natural light.

Project 4

Installing a skylight

STEP BY STEP

1 The size of a skylight is based on the floor area of the area to be lit. It is generally recommended that the skylight be at least 10 per cent of the floor area. In this case the skylight will be 800 mm x 800 mm.

2 Order the skylight, specifying size, roof type, the shape required, and if any accessories, such as diffusers or solar control features are required.

3 Climb into the roof space to decide where the skylight is to go.

4 Remove tiles and sarking felt in the area where the skylight is to be installed. Treat the tiles carefully as some will be needed later. Stack them to one side.

5 Carefully mark on the rafters and battens where the skylight is to go. Make a 50 mm allowance top and bottom of the rafter for the trimmers which are needed to frame the cut-out hole. This should be done with reference to the ceiling and where the lightwell is to go. Also take note of any wires, pipes, roof ridges or valleys that may affect the installation, or will require moving.

The project is to install a skylight in a concrete tile roof to provide a lightwell for maximum lighting in an enclosed kitchen. The skylight will be 800 mm square so will need a rafter cut, and the lightwell is to be painted white for maximum natural light.

Completed skylight in kitchen

44

Tiles removed from roof

6 Cut the battens flush with the rafters, and nail any loose trimmed battens to the rafters. Make sure no battens run across the area in which the skylight is to be installed.

7 There is a bend in the tray of the skylight and this should be in line with the bottom edge of the batten.

8 As this is a wide model, it will be necessary to saw through one rafter at the top and bottom of the cut-out. Do this carefully to the marks, making sure you have made an allowance for the thickness of the trimmer top and bottom.

9 Cut two trimmers to length, top and bottom, to secure the cut rafter. The trimmer should be a tight fit between the two adjacent rafters. Measure the trimmer directly. When nailing it in place ensure that it is completely square to the rafter and truly horizontal using a level. A short length of rafter will be needed between the trimmers to allow for the width of the skylight.

10 Remove the internal catches that hold the dome of the skylight to its base. In most cases these will be internal toggle catches.

11 Place the base over the opening. Make sure that the joint where the flashing joins onto the base is supported by a tile.

12 Secure the anchoring straps of the base to rafters by nails or screws.

13 Make sure that all the folds and channels on the base have not been deformed as this could affect the waterproofing of the skylight, especially in high winds.

14 Re-lay the tiles to within 50 mm of the vertical side upstands of the base. (To do this with terracotta tiles it may be necessary to remove the lugs from the underside of the tiles.)

15 Dress the lead flashing over the lower tiles. In high-exposure areas, point up with cement mortar between the lead and tiles. This should not, however, normally be necessary.

16 As we are also fitting a lightwell it may be easier to leave the dome until the lightwell is installed. Usually the dome would be fitted into position as recommended by the manufacturer and the toggles replaced and firmly sealed from the inside.

17 The lightwell can be flared to be wider at the ceiling than at the skylight. This will give a better distribution of light in the room. However, keep the lightwell between the matching ceiling joists and expand it in the other direction, otherwise large trimming joists will be needed to support the ceiling

Trimmers installed and battens secured

adequately – especially if the ceiling is a large one.

18 Measure down to the ceiling where it is to be cut. Mark on the ceiling rafters the position of the lightwell. Drive a nail through the ceiling lining to mark each corner of the lightwell on the underside of the ceiling

where the cuts are to be made.

19 Make sure that there are no electric wires, telephone wires or plumbing pipes in the lightwell area before cutting.

20 Mark out the rectangle to be cut on the ceiling on the room side.

45

Dressing lead to the tiles

Base of skylight and tiles back in place

21 Cut the ceiling lining to the marks with a panel saw. As it is plaster it should be easy to cut but, if working from below, wear goggles and a face mask to protect the eyes and breathing passages against plaster dust.

22 Install the trimming joists for the ceiling, once again making sure that the opening is framed square.

23 The simplest method of lightwell construction, where the distance between roof rafter and ceiling joist is not great, is to make the well out of chipboard or medium density fibreboard. This is carefully marked out to the shape required, and prefabricated using adhesive and nailing, before being fitted.

24 The lightwell is then lifted into place from the underside of the ceiling, and nailed in place.

25 Finish the lightwell with a timber trim to cover the joint to the ceiling.

Inserting prefabricated lightwell

26 As an alternative, the lightwell can be framed between the roof rafters and the ceiling joists. This is best made of 75 mm x 38 mm softwood framing. The job will be greatly simplified with the use of nail plates to enable you to build the box on top of the ceiling joists, and directly under the roof rafters. You will, however, find that due to the construction of the roof they will be offset by the thickness of a roof rafter. Remember to design the framing with corners so that you have something to fix the lining of the lightwell to. When the frame is secure the lightwell can be lined. It is best to use a 'warm' material as this will have greater resistance to condensation. Timber linings are excellent, but foil-backed plasterboard, particle (chip) board or plywood would also suffice. A high level of finish is not required to the lightwell if it is hidden behind a diffuser. However, if there is no diffuser, greater care will be needed in finishing off.

27 Finish the interior of the lightwell with two or three coats of white vinyl paint.

28 A diffuser panel can be loosely fitted on top of neat timber battens nailed to the sides of the lightwell, flush to 50 mm from the ceiling level. These should be installed prepainted.

29 Fit the diffuser by passing it up at an angle and twisting it and lowering it into position.

Nailing cleats for a neat lightwell to ceiling joist

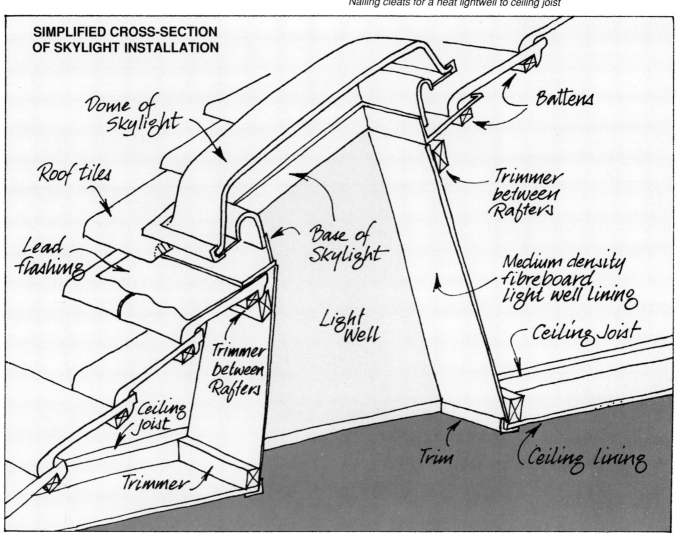

SIMPLIFIED CROSS-SECTION OF SKYLIGHT INSTALLATION

Dome of Skylight

Roof tiles

Lead flashing

Trimmer between Rafters

Ceiling Joist

Trimmer

Base of Skylight

Light Well

Battens

Trimmer between Rafters

Medium density fibreboard light well lining

Ceiling Joist

Trim

Ceiling Lining

One of the more noticeable features of modern houses is the way they have been opened up by incorporating a much greater window area. Today, homemakers have a more acute awareness of the great outdoors, a desire for more natural light, and a realisation that correctly designed and placed windows increase the efficiency of winter heating.

Project 5

Installing a window

Many people have in fact devalued their home by installing modern windows with very little regard to the period or style of the rest of the building. Larger windows can be made in many different styles and materials. They should be compatible with what is already in place, and are not always a lot more expensive.

This particular project involves the installation of a window in a downstairs brick-veneer wall, that is, one with a timber structural frame, and a veneer of single-skin brickwork on the exterior. A second storey is being supported by the timber frame. The window is a cedar frame with a brand name aluminium sashless horizontal sliding system, using 6 mm thick glass. The size of the window is 950 mm high by 880 mm wide.

There has been a popular move to upgrade the home by increasing the number and areas of windows facing the sun – to allow winter light and warmth to enter, while keeping the summer sun out. Larger windows may also be desirable to make the most of an outdoor view, whether it is of your garden or a more distant vista.

Completed window installation. Note storm mould finishing window to brick joint

Stegbar and Sydney Window Installation

48

Timber framing removed and prop support in place

WHAT TO BUY

- [ ] new window, 950 mm high by 880 mm wide, cedar frame with aluminium sashless horizontal sliding operating system with 6 mm thick glass
- [ ] galvanised steel lintel, 75 mm x 10 mm bar
- [ ] flashing for top and bottom of window; aluminium core flashing is easiest to mould, and the width should be 300 mm wide. It can always be trimmed if needed

SPECIAL TOOLS NEEDED

- [ ] 2 to 4 props
- [ ] 2 kg club hammer
- [ ] bolster
- [ ] plugging chisel
- [ ] bricklaying tools – shovel, bricklayer's trowel, level

TIME

One weekend, once you are organised. Any longer and you will have a waterproofing and security problem. Make an early start!

STEP BY STEP

1 The first step is to decide on the style of window suitable for the house. The new window should match the existing windows, while providing the amount of extra light required.

2 Our window is 880 mm wide and 950 mm high, of cedar construction.

3 When you have your window, take the exact outside dimensions, for your mark-out. Our window is 880 mm wide so the opening size will need to be 890 mm horizontally to allow for fitting and squaring. The height of the window is 950 mm, so the opening size should be 960 mm to 970 mm on the inside. This should be the quoted opening size. Allow for the new lintel or window head. On the outside, as well as allowing for the lintel thickness (10 mm), allow for the sill bricks. The sill brick will take a height of about 1.5 bricks. Therefore the exterior opening will be about 1065 mm in height.

4 The opening sizes of the window should be roughly marked on the inside. The marking is not critical on the external wall as you will be removing and replacing brickwork to suit the window anyway, and this can be done in relation to the internal timber-frame opening.

5 Start by removing the wall lining on the inside to expose the area where the window is to go. It should be removed floor to ceiling, and well past the opening to allow you to work on the frame. Patching smaller strips of linings will be frustrating anyway. You can now see the frame and mark exactly on the frame where the window is to be fitted.

6 As the frame is holding up an upper floor and framing, it is important that these joists be supported before you start working. This can be done with the use of a prop for a small opening (in our case) or two if the opening is larger. It is firmly placed on a sole plate of solid timber, and firmly screwed up to a temporary 75 mm x 100 mm timber beam.

7 Remove any noggings or

Timber frame prepared for window, and bricks laid ready to accept window. Note interior prop holding upper floor framing

49

studs that are in the way, but save them if possible as they will be suitable for the altered framing. Remove all nails. Push any wiring to one side to give a clear working area.

8 Cut two timber studs to suit. Measure and mark where the bottom of the window head will be on both studs, and make a second mark 50 mm above this. Square lines across the broad face of the stud. Place the studs on your saw stools; saw 5-10 mm depth along each of the four lines, and then chisel out the timber between the cuts. These are called housings. Now fix the two studs either side of the window opening, with the housings facing towards each other, nailing into both head and sole plates. On a small window, single studs would be adequate but if larger openings are required,

secondary 'jack' studs will be needed to support the larger lintel.

9 Cut and install a sill plate for the bottom of the window. Don't forget to allow for the gaps. Make sure it is installed dead level. Then cut and fix a short jack stud in the centre of the opening under the sill plate.

10 Across the top, install the head into the housing previously prepared, and install a small packer between the head plate and frame head to complete the inside frame.

11 Start knocking out bricks on the exterior. If the brickwork is sound, and the joints solid, an opening of 900 mm will most likely be self-supporting. If it does collapse it will be in the form of a triangle of full

In large openings an angle lintel is used to take the weight over the greater span

unsupported bricks. Where joints are weak, a 'needle' is needed about halfway between the extremities of the window, and above where the top of the lintel will be. Needles are made of at least 100 mm x 125 mm timber and held both inside and out by props. Once supported the rest of the brickwork can be removed safely.

12 Bricks are knocked out using a club hammer and bolster. Work from the top and centre of the window opening to the outside edge, and leave a saw-tooth arrangement of bricks, wider than the window, to allow the neat finishing of brickwork to the window edge.

13 Remove the bottom 38 mm of vertical joints

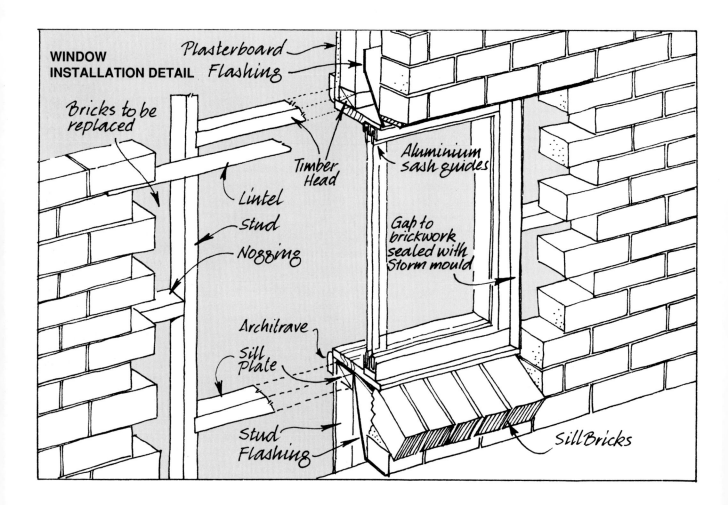

WINDOW INSTALLATION DETAIL

Plasterboard
Flashing
Bricks to be replaced
Timber Head
Aluminium sash guides
Lintel
Stud
Nogging
Gap to brickwork sealed with Storm mould
Architrave
Sill Plate
Stud Flashing
Sill Bricks

(perpends) between the bricks over where the lintel is to go with a plugging chisel. These act as weep holes for the top flashing.

14 Once the first full row at the top of the opening is exposed, the top flashing from the timber frame over the top of the lintel can be installed, prior to the lintel being put in place. Fix the flashing 150 mm above the top of the window to studs or lintel if high enough.

15 The steel lintel can now be put in place and is a further protection against brickwork collapse. Be careful that the flashing is not damaged or caught up. It must have a bearing of about 150 mm both sides.

16 If necessary, the lintel can be further supported halfway along its length by a prop at a slight angle.

17 The wall can now be bricked up to the exact outside dimensions of the window opening, finishing with a plumb neat finish to both sides of the opening, and within one horizontal course of bricks to the underside of the sill. The sill bricks are installed later.

18 It's now time to fit the bottom flashing to the window, if one is not already provided. This runs under the window sill and turns up inside about 12 mm, and on the outside is wide enough in one piece to preferably lap into the mortar joint one brick course below the sill. It should be slightly wider at the sides so that it can be turned up at the edges. In our case, the flashing was installed directly under the sill bricks.

19 Fit the window in the opening and check for fit. You should have about 5 mm space to either side of the window for packing and adjustment. Make sure the flashing is not caught up.

Flashing and first sill brick in place. Storm moulding is added after sill bricks

20 Check that the window sitting on the sill framing is truly horizontal. Align it so that the internal edge of the window frame overhangs sufficiently to cover the lining, which in most cases is 10 mm. This allows a good finish for the architraves. Some joiners take a slight angled shaving off the outside edge of the reveal to provide a tighter fit for the architrave.

21 Now check that the vertical is plumb, and use packing between the house frame and the window frame for any adjustments. Pack the other side as well. The packing shouldn't be too tight as you may bend the frame out of shape and the window will bind.

22 Make sure the window is not twisted, otherwise the sashes won't operate correctly. Then nail in place to the timber frame using galvanised nails to hold everything in place.

23 Dress the flashings into place. Now install the sill

bricks on a drier mortar bed to get the fall with the flashing in place under the sill bricks. The bricks must be cut with the bolster and hammer, and are fitted to within about 10 mm from the underside of the timber. Regardless of where the flashings are, if water is trapped it has to be able to flow out of the cavity. Allow for weep holes to the underside of the sill mortar joints so that water can flow out from the flashing.

24 Seal the gap between brickwork and timber window with non-hardening mastic.

25 Replace linings to the inside, and fill and sand all joints as described in the plasterboard section (see Project 2).

26 Fix architraves for a professional finish.

T I P S T R I P

■ Windows are sold in a number of standard sizes. Off-the-shelf windows are often available for immediate delivery. In window sizes there are generally three sizes. One is the open glass area, the second is the actual window size, and the third, the opening size. It is the last figure you are interested in, as it gives you the dimensions for marking out the project. If you want to match brick sizes you will have to work in multiples of 240 mm or 120 mm. You can also work to stud sizes, which will be at either 450 mm centres or in more recent homes, 600 mm.

■ Aluminium windows should be ordered with reveals already fixed. These are the planed timber frames around the aluminium frames, and provide the necessary depth of total frame to take up the thickness of the house frame, the cavity and a small section of the brickwork. The reveals are normally planed softwood ready for staining or painting.

■ Lintels vary in size depending on the span of the opening. Openings greater than 1200 mm will generally require an angle, rather than a flat bar (see illustration). Further, when working on large openings, ensure that the whole job has been checked by a structural engineer who will be able to design the size of the lintel, the internal lintel and the needles to support brickwork.

Fabric, pelmets and blinds
Dressed windows, in the form of curtains, elaborate drapes and blinds, are probably the most decorative type of fabric use in the home. Large or small areas of attractively used fabric can quickly transform a room – so look upon window dressing as interior decorating, as well as a practical essential.

Project 6

Window dressing
Three projects in one

FABRIC

Don't have high expectations of fabrics that were never intended for anything other than their specific purpose. So very often a fabric is chosen on the emotional basis of 'I just have to have it!'

Fabric should first of all be chosen for weight, weave and, sensibly, cost. Then isolate the colours, pattern and texture or sheen that appeals most to you. Generally, the more the fabric will be handled or sat on, the sturdier it has to be. No sensible person would upholster the family room sofa in a lightweight chintz, because chintz is not hardwearing, has a processed wax surface which does not take kindly to soiling, and creases quite easily! Having said that, chintz is one of the most universally appealing fabrics. It is usually beautifully coloured or designed, with

Classic swags and tails work well with tall windows and ceilings, and can be ideal positioned over the top of French windows

great lustre and presence – when used suitably in curtains, bedspreads and cushions it is simply wonderful. In the same way, don't use a heavy linen for your sheer bedroom curtains, or attempt to sew it into loose covers on your lightweight home sewing machine. It's a beautiful and enduring fabric, but is also heavy and sometimes difficult to handle expertly. You will find many different combinations of man-made fibres in fabrics today, and a wonderful assortment of weights of natural fabrics – mostly linen, cotton and, to a large extent, wool for upholstery. Both types have benefits, so be guided by the manufacturer's instructions, your colour preferences and

your budget. So, in brief, fabrics have definite purposes, and to ask more of a fabric than is sensible can become a big problem – both financially and aesthetically. Seek advice from the trained assistant in your fabric shop, and also observe what fabrics designers favour when decorating.

FABRIC CALCULATIONS

When calculating the number of metres required, always measure at least twice and take the process slowly and carefully. If possible, get someone else to check your measurements and allowances. Be sure to allow for matching patterns in printed fabrics, and don't be frugal with hems and good-

quality lining. Remember, curtains are a focal point in a room and if they delight the eye you'll be happy to live with them until they wear out. If they irritate you for some reason – too short, wrong colour, too skimpy – you'll be constantly reminded of your mistakes!

FABRIC SHRINKAGE

Most natural fibres will shrink, so be aware of the manufacturer's instructions about cleaning fabrics. All lined items should be dry-cleaned. At best, when washing curtains do them by hand, do not crease unduly or allow to soak for long periods of time. Allow them to hang straight rather than creased over a line.

TIE BANDS

A tie band is a simple corded tassel, or an elaborate padded and plaited tie band – the widest choice of options is available here to the home decorator. Tie bands are at once practical and visually exciting. They hold curtains back to allow light through, they create a line to open curtains that is decorative and controlled, and allow you to adjust your curtains to be

fuller and softer should your decor demand this.
Tie bands are generally straight, or can be slightly curved. A brown paper pattern cut and adjusted for your situation will help you achieve your ideal tie band. Brass hooks can be purchased that screw onto the wall – simply tuck the curtains behind them – or create your

own straight pieces of fabric from curtain scraps. Experiment with fabric borders, padded tie bands, fabric with bias binding edges for emphasis, satin ribbons on sheer fabrics, or elaborate tie bands trimmed with luxurious fringing and gimp braids (upholstery braids, usually vertically woven, often using two or three colours).

1 Strips of padded fabric plaited to make a tie band. Attach small curtain rings at each end to hook

2 A purchased tassel and card used as a tie band

3 A stylish brass curtain band – available at curtain shops – screws into the wall. Simply tuck the curtain behind the curved 'arm'

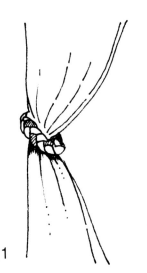

1

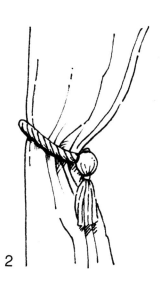

2

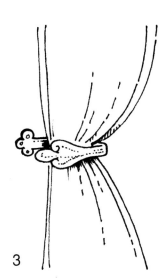

3

SWAG PELMETS

Formal swag pelmets are draped pieces of fabric which, when attached to a pelmet support board, become a classic draped pelmet. They hang free of the curtain and usually add a classical, ornate appearance to windows.

Here are some rules to remember with swag trimmings: they look best on tall windows in rooms with high ceilings, so be sure that you don't over-design your room; consider your fabric requirements (swag curtains can take up large amounts of fabric, and this can become a budget-breaker) – plain calico or home-spun fabric is one idea, as the old principle of using fabric generously applies well here. Generous amounts of inexpensive fabric look wonderful next to skimpy quantities of expensive fabric.

STEP BY STEP

Fabric: The main fabric for the swag is cut on the bias. Allow one-and-a-half times the finished width, which will be the length of the curtain track plus seam allowances, by two-and-a-half times the finished depth, plus hems. Join fabrics as shown, to create a piece large enough, prior to cutting out the swag. It will make your task simpler if you create a paper pattern of your swag shape. Working on a large, flat surface, cut out the lining first, then use this piece as a template to cut the main fabric piece. With right sides facing, stitch lining piece and main piece together around curved edge only.

Clip seam, turn to right side, press. Pin lining and main fabric pieces together around remaining edges, stitch to secure, neatening edges as you go.

Cut a piece of fabric, probably from scraps, that measures the finished width of the swag, plus seam allowances. Mark the centre, and the finished width. Allowing the straight piece of fabric to lie close to the edge of your worktable, secure it to the table surface. Match 'C' of swag to centre of secured fabric, allowing swag piece to hang over edge of table. Working upwards from 'A', fold in rough pleats until you reach 'B'. Adjust these folds or pleats until you are satisfied with the way they lie and their evenness. Repeat for the other side, pleating from 'E' up to 'D'. When you are satisfied with the lie of the pleats and that the width of the swag matches your straight fabric strip, pin and stitch the pleats to the fabric strip. Trim this fabric strip back to 3 cm in depth.

It is important to estimate fabric quantities accurately; to cut the fabric correctly; and to observe bias cut sections, as these need to fall and drape in deep folds.

Swags: Swags need to be in proportion to the completed length of your curtains. As a guide to depths of finished swags, reckon on the swag finishing at one sixth to one eighth of the window height.

Tails with even vertical folds: Tails are generally a third to one-half the height of the window but, again, proportion is important and you are the best judge of what suits your particular window size. The length of the short inner vertical edge is again up to you but a third to one-half of the outside length is a good starting point.

The width of the finished tail can be estimated by pleating brown paper to approximate the desired size. Use this measurement as the width of the top edge of the tails. Your template should look like a triangle with the inner top corner cut away. When purchasing lining fabric, remember that it will be seen when the tail is pleated. The colour and texture of the lining is important, and can become an added decorative note. Cut out lining piece, then, using this shape as a pattern, cut main fabric piece.

With right sides facing, stitch lining and main fabric tail pieces together, leaving top edge open. Trim corners, clip seams for ease and turn to right side. Press. Following the instructions for pleating the swag, cut a scrap of fabric the finished width of the pleated tail, plus seam allowances. Pleat tail into this width and, when satisfied with lie and evenness, stitch to scrap strip. Trim scrap strip to 3 cm depth. Repeat for matching tail or tails.

Support Board: The most secure way to affix swags and tails is to a support board cut to the width of the curtain track, and to a depth that

SWAG PATTERN

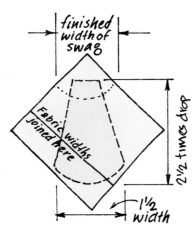

How to plan and measure your swag pattern

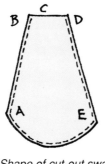

Shape of cut-out swag

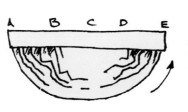

Completed swag with strip of fabric applied ready for attachment to support board

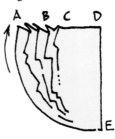

Pleating the sides of the swag

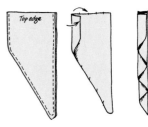

Pattern and how to pleat tails

allows the swag and tails to hang free of the curtains. Cover the board with fabric, secured with tacks, glue or staples, and secure the board to the wall with L-shaped brackets at either end. Tack the top tails and then the top of the swag into place along the top of this board.

Fixing to the support board: First you must bind the edges of the swag and tails with a flap of fabric that finishes at the same depth as the support board. Cut fabric pieces the length of the finished swag and tails plus seam allowances; with right sides facing, stitch one long side of binding strip to swag and each tail piece.

Press 1 cm to wrong side of remaining long side. Fold binding strip to have right sides facing, stitch short ends, fold binding strip to its right side. Press. Hand or machine stitch to previous row of stitching. You now have a flap that is the length and depth of the support board.

Gentle colours coordinating in matched fabrics bring a restful feeling to a bedroom. The tailored pelmet and tie-backs are trimmed with matching braid

TAILORED PELMETS

These decorative elements have outgrown their stuffy and slightly old-fashioned image of the past. They can now, with clever choices and use of fabric, totally complement what is really a plain set of curtains, and transform a room into a well-thought-out home decorator's triumph.

Some are shaped, others are simple gathered valances or short frills matching the curtains. Others are padded, and some are swags of matching fabric. There are many options available, and most are easy for the home decorator to achieve. Most pelmets depend on a support board being fixed to the wall either side of the curtains. Be sure that you allow sufficient room for the curtains to bunch together when open.

Simple trimmed padded pelmets are a tailored trim for simple pleated curtains. You will need a support board as described in the Step by Step for Swag Pelmets – again, long enough to allow the pelmet to hang free of the curtain at the front and at the side return area.

Fix this to the wall with L-shaped brackets. Be sure to allow space for the curtains to bunch up when open, and do not position the brackets so as to interfere with this bunching.

In general, pelmets are of the same fabric as the curtains, often with complementary braid trimming. They are stiffened with interfacing, and lined.

STEP BY STEP

Generally pelmet depth is one-eighth of the overall drop of the curtains, plus about 20 cm for hems and upper turnover allowances. Width is the length of the support board plus the distance from the front of the support board to the wall, plus seam allowances.

Decide how you wish the pattern in your fabric to run, and cut and join pieces to achieve this if necessary. Cut out a lining piece the same size as the main fabric piece.

Iron on interfacing to the back of the main fabric piece. With right sides facing and raw edges matching, stitch around all edges of main pelmet piece and lining, leaving a small opening for turning. Turn, press. Stitch one row of Velcro to the top side of the pelmet by hand, or by machine if corresponding trim on the right side of the pelmet conceals this stitching. Trim front of pelmet if desired. Glue or staple opposite Velcro strip to front and side edges of support board. Secure pelmet to edge of board by pressing Velcro bands together.

BEAUTIFUL BLINDS

Blinds have travelled a long way from their origins as the gauze window protectors of elaborate drapes and furnishings in grand houses. Modern blinds can be totally functional and unobtrusive, or unashamedly ornate and extravagant.

ROMAN BLINDS

These blinds are tailored and neat looking, economical in their use of fabric and regarded as being quite simple to make. There is less sewing in this style of blind than, say, a festoon blind, and they lend themselves to stripes or evenly printed geometric fabrics very well.

STEP BY STEP

The blind is traditionally fitted inside the window frame, and has a series of cords that are pulled or released to raise and lower the blind. These cords are held together and are wound around a metal cleat that has been fastened to the window frame. The best cord is a fine nylon cord that is flexible and not more than 6-8 mm thick.

The cord runs through a series of metal cording rings screwed into the back of timber support laths that are inserted through sewn tucks in the blind (see our illustration for the positions of these elements). To line or not to line – this is the question! Some fabrics simply have to be lined, especially those with strong patterns, or those blinds that have to block out most of the light. Interfacing is ironed on to the back of the main fabric piece and this in itself will block out most of the light and, providing your hems are neat and evenly stitched, may be all you need.

Should you decide that lining is the only way for you to go, cut your lining piece 5 cm smaller all round than your main blind piece. Position the lining on the wrong side of the main piece, fold in your 5 cm-deep hems, stitch, then treat this piece as one layer of fabric. Fabric requirements will depend on how many pleats you desire, and the depth of the timber laths you use. The basic size of the blind is calculated thus: The width of the window frame (inner or wherever you wish the blind to sit) plus the depth. Add 5 cm hems to the sides and lower edge, plus 30 cm in length for folding over the top timber support lath. Add to this figure approximately 12 cm for each lath pocket you decide to have. The best way to calculate their distance apart is to divide the length of the window into sixths or eighths, allowing room at the very top of the blind for the folds to bunch when the blind is pulled up.

Again, the easiest way to calculate all this is to make a pattern of the blind from brown paper, creasing in the folds, hems and the area folded over the top support lath. It is easy to re-crease the paper until you are satisfied with the spacing and length. Remember that, ideally, when the blind is fully down it should lie flat – with no remaining folds.

AUSTRIAN BLINDS

These blinds are delightfully stylish, can look dramatic or feminine, and are remarkably easy to make. They usually work well on their own, but can be complemented by side drapes that are not pulled closed. Austrian blinds can be made in sheer fabric, and indeed, this is their ideal weight of fabric, as they originally were intended to allow light through, but to give some sense of privacy to the room. These blinds are permanently ruched from top to base in vertical rows, creating crescents of curved fabric, held in place by integral rows of cording rings on the reverse side. They pull up and are released by fine cording threaded through these rings.

ROLLER BLINDS

Roller blinds are a traditional, simple form of window trimming that can be made at home. They are backed with a firm, iron-on interfacing or bonding fabric and usually have some form of trimming at the lower edge. They are fixed to a support lath or roller, and are secured to brackets set into the window frame. They are most suitable where light has to be eliminated; where decorative details are not demanded and simplicity is the key; and where space for curtains is not available. Often they fit behind curtains most unobtrusively, as they roll up neatly and do not create bulk.

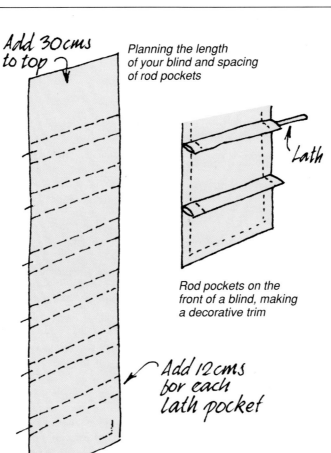

Add 30cms to top

Planning the length of your blind and spacing of rod pockets

Lath

Rod pockets on the front of a blind, making a decorative trim

Add 12cms for each lath pocket

Add 5cms for hem to sides and bottom

A classic Roman blind leaves the area around a window free of clutter. These blinds are ideal for tailored or masculine rooms, and can show off bold-patterned fabric beautifully

TIPSTRIP

■ Decide what your budget, colour scheme and abilities are in creating your own interiors. If you decide that the simplest drapes are all you can achieve, don't attempt elaborate and complicated versions. Either save up for professional assistance, or talk yourself into tackling the simpler version. Expensive fabric in the hands of a novice can be money thrown away. If your heart is set on the elaborate, compromise by making the lining, hanging it as curtains and perhaps trimming it with a pretty tie band. Then, when your budget allows, go to a professional curtainmaker for the longed-for curtains.

■ Stick to your colour scheme. Carry swatches around with you as well as your paint colour, carpet or rug colours, and an idea of the size and scale of your room. Don't settle for a colour unless you have looked at it in the room to be decorated or painted – remember the light in that room is the only light that matters when matching colours.

■ Don't overwhelm a room with drapes and curtains. You are the best judge of what you want, and personal taste has a lot to do with the limits here. Proportion is important – again, you will be the best judge of this.

■ Don't skimp on fabric. Use generous amounts of inexpensive fabric – even calico – in preference to using expensive fabric frugally.

There is nothing quite like a well-designed and well-made leadlight window. Pinpoints of light and flashes of colour can transform a boring window with a poor view, into a major feature. Leadlighting is one of those projects that should not perhaps be undertaken as a one-off project.

Lovely Leadlights

Enhancing your view

Above: Entrance showing front door with leadlight panels, and leadlight porthole
Left: Detail of porthole

The equipment necessary to get started on your own leadlight project involves considerable expense – but the materials that you buy will provide lots of bits and pieces for later projects.

In the case of this kitchen, new leadlight was installed to obscure the view – a neighbour's rooftop. The new leadlight was carefully made to match the existing leadlight

Hallway fan lights as leadlight panels

Leadlight for landing

Leadlighting is an art as much as a trade. The effectiveness of the window depends on the design and colour section as much as workmanship. If you are keen to learn how to leadlight, consider joining a leadlighting class, where equipment and materials will be available for a reasonable cost. Having someone point out the steps as you work can be a great help to the beginner.

Project 7

Leadlight porthole

STEP BY STEP

NOTE: When working with lead make sure that you clean your hands before breaking for meals. Washing hands thoroughly after leaving the workshop should be automatic as lead is an accumulative poison.

1   Set up an area to work in that is flat and will not damage the glass. A workbench with a particle (chip) board top is ideal. A felt covering will prevent scratching to the glass. As work progresses the surface should be frequently vacuumed of glass splinters as these may damage or break glass being cut.

2   Finalise your design. This is often the slowest part of the job, but many books on the subject have a number of designs that can be used or adapted. Try to avoid designs where tight curves or sharp internal corners need to be cut, because you probably won't be successful. Plain shapes with relatively simple curves are easiest to cut and lead up.

3   Once the miniature design is finished, make several copies and colour them in with the colours you've selected. It may be worthwhile trying several combinations of colours to get the leadlight just right.

The project featured is not the easiest leadlighting project to start off with, but will give an indication of what is achievable in this medium. There is a wide lead edge, and three sizes of thin lead for effect.

Hold them in place in the position they are to go, in a variety of light conditions.

4   Measure the window. In this case, it is a 415 mm circular window. Deduct half the width of the lead (came), in this case about 7 mm, plus an additional 3 mm from the circle all round to allow for fitting. Large 'H' section lead is used on edges to allow for trimming should the pattern slightly 'grow' while being made. Therefore the pattern (cartoon) size is finalised at 400 mm in diameter.

5   Transfer your design to the full pattern size and make a full-scale drawing of the window. Do it in pencil first to ensure it is right. Then finally draw it in heavy felt pen to leave a line about 1.5 mm thick between the glass pieces. This automatically makes an allowance for the wall thickness of the lead section.

6   Make a couple of copies of the pattern, so that they can be used for numbering glass pieces, or cut into individual pieces and used as templates for cutting the glass (if you find that easiest), or if one gets damaged or torn.

The completed project in place

7   Mount your main cartoon on a piece of particle (chip) board or similar, with plenty of room to work around the edges of the design. Normally, two battens are fixed to the board against which you can work. In the case of this circular design, mark out and cut a panel to fit against the battens, and mark out and cut a semicircle to hold the lead in place. In this example, glass was used as the panel, but you can use thin plywood as well.

8   Choose the glass for each shape according to the colours worked out; buy it and have it ready to start. Similarly, have the lead ready as well as horseshoe nails and all other needs.

9   Cut the first piece of glass to size. This should be a piece of scrap just for practice. Start the cut a small distance in from the edge of the glass. Apply steady pressure without stopping, and hold the cutter close to 90°. Draw it towards you, and let it roll over the

WHAT TO BUY

- [ ] 15 mm 'H' section round lead cames for edges
- [ ] 4.2 mm, 5.2 mm and 5.5 mm 'H' section round lead cames for internal edges
- [ ] glass as selected – in this case German machine antique glass was used in green, blue/grey, pink, mauve and clear, with roundels in pink
- [ ] 50/50 solder stick
- [ ] horseshoe nails
- [ ] flux
- [ ] leadlighting cement
- [ ] whiting
- [ ] stove black

SPECIAL TOOLS NEEDED

Leadlighting requires specialised equipment. Making your existing tools do the job will not produce the best results. One idea is to join a class and use equipment available. However, if you do decide to invest in the right tools, here are some that should be considered. These tools are generally only available from stained glass materials suppliers

- [ ] ordinary steel wheel cutter
- [ ] good-quality tungsten carbide glass cutter if using selenium oxide glass. If not self-lubricating, organise a small container to hold the lubricant – a mixture of light oil and kerosene
- [ ] glass pliers
- [ ] cut running pliers
- [ ] grozing pliers
- [ ] electric soldering iron, 80 watt with 'hook nose' tip
- [ ] lead vice and pliers
- [ ] lathekin
- [ ] lead knife, such as Don Carlos pattern
- [ ] wire brush

TIME

Two or three weekends construction time; many hours planning and design

---

edge near you.

10 To break the glass, hold it vertically and place your two index fingers under either side of the cut, and your thumbs on top of the glass – the knuckles should be touching. Rotate both hands down, or clockwise and anticlockwise, and the glass should break and 'run' along your score line. Shake off any glass splinters.

11 If the glass will not break itself, lightly tap under the score line with the hammer on the non-cutting end of the glass cutter. Hold the glass close to the score line to avoid breakage.

12 If you are still unsuccessful using fingers, you may have to invest in a pair of 'cut running pliers', to do the job. When cutting thin strips it may be necessary to use grozing pliers to grip the narrow side, or you may injure your hand if you slip. Glass cut in this way will never be as neat as when it is cut by running.

13 When cutting the glass for the actual leadlight, mark out from the cartoon directly or from the cut-out pieces. Cut the large pieces first as the offcuts may then be used for smaller pieces of the same colour. Aim at being economical within reason.

14 Once cut, hold each piece against your pattern and make sure it fits between the inked-in lines. If it overlaps it will need trimming with the grozing pliers. If it is too small it will need to be recut.

15 Generally leadlighters like to cut all the glass pieces to shape before starting the leading. The pieces can be laid on the spare cartoon, or each piece can be numbered on the face side with a corresponding number on the spare cartoon. The pieces can be carefully laid in a box until ready for use.

16 Before lead can be used it must be stretched, and this is done with a lead vice and pliers. This must be done with care so that when applying pressure the lead does not snap and you end up on the floor. Once stretched, the channels of the lead may need to be opened using a lathekin. In some areas you may be able to purchase pre-stretched lead.

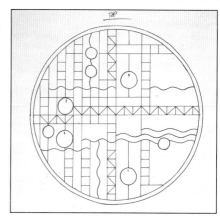

Template of leadlight porthole

Drawing of porthole showing different colour sections of leadlight

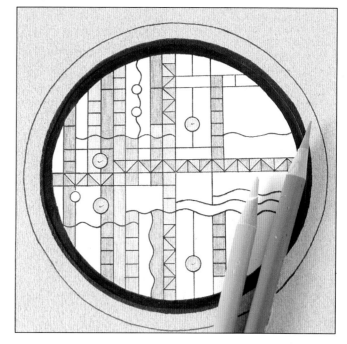

17 Cut off the two damaged ends of the lead, and then cut sufficient length off the wider lead to place around the semicircle defined by the cut panel. The lead is cut using a sharp lead knife, in a rocking motion. The other half of the perimeter is the last piece in the jigsaw to be fitted at the end.

18 Select the piece of glass for the starting point. On our circle it can just about be anywhere on the bottom perimeter, but where successive pieces can be installed easily. The best place would be in the middle.

19 This particular window was made by building up from the bottom filling in all the lower area, and then working up the centre and out to the sides, one at a time.

20 Insert the first piece of glass, gently tapping it into place with the wooden end of the lead knife, and hold it in place with horseshoe nails,

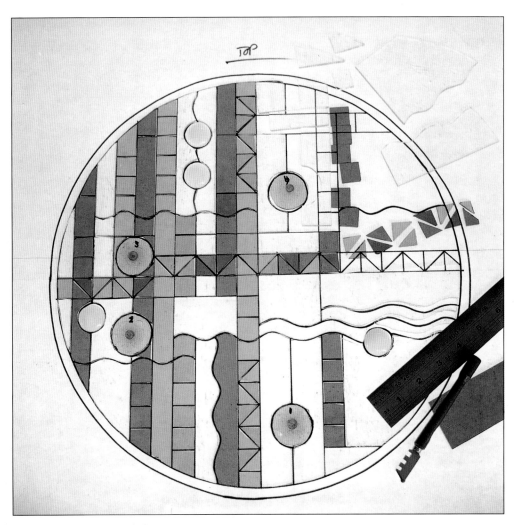

Cut glass for leadlight porthole

TIPSTRIP

■ When starting to cut the glass it is probably wise to practise a little first. A good-quality tungsten cutter is recommended. Cutting is normally done by drawing the cutter at a steep angle towards you so it makes a good hissing sound as it scores the glass. Some people prefer to push the cutter in a near vertical position. Try both methods a number of times to find which method you prefer.

■ On a square or rectangular job the starting point is normally a corner. You can then work out from the corner and gradually build the pattern in a fan shape. Bear in mind that you can't insert glass into pockets that are surrounded by lead.

flat side of nails against the glass. Cut a length of the internal (thinner) lead slightly longer than the edge to be joined, and insert the adjoining glass into the lead. Hold in place using the horseshoe nails again. Mark the joint of the two glass pieces on the lead, getting the angle right, and remove the lead. Make another mark just back from this first one, and cut the lead slightly short. This allows for the next lead, which crosses the first one, to sit properly with an accurate joint that will be easy to solder. Slowly continue in this fashion, fanning out across the window, building up the leadlight.

21 Always hold each new piece or section with the

horseshoe nails. Never use the nails against the lead as they will cause irreparable damage with the lead being so soft. When the entire light has been made, the final outside wider came is fitted in place. You are now ready to solder the joints. Measure the panel for size and square the corners if applicable.

22 Just before soldering, ensure that no flanges from the lead are bent onto the glass or out of shape, because once soldered they will be set.

23 Soldering is done with an 80 watt iron, as this heats up quickly. Lower wattage irons can be used, but may be a little slower. The easiest tip to use is a 'hook nose' or angled tip, as shown opposite.

The tip should be properly tinned before use. Soldering must be carried out in the presence of flux, which removes oxide from the surface of the lead, and provides a good surface for the solder to adhere to. Solid flux is easiest to clean up afterwards, so is recommended. Rub the flux over the joint to be soldered.

24 Start soldering at the furthest point away from where you are standing. Hold the iron close to the lead, and take a small blob of solder from the stick. Place this on the joint. This should run onto the joint, and when the iron is removed will soon set. Use a little at a time, you can always add more if the joint looks scantly soldered.

25 When all the joints are soldered, take a wire brush and brush off all traces of flux on the window. Any solder spilt on the glass or lead should peel off as well.

26 Turn the window over, together with the base as the window is still not strong. Repeat the soldering on the back side. Once again, remove the leftover flux.

27 It's now time to putty the window. It must be done in one sitting, as otherwise it will set and leave oil stains. Use pre-prepared leadlighting cement, which has been made with carbon black. Wear old clothes as this is a messy job. Force the cement under the lead flanges with whatever you find easiest, thumbs or the lathekin. Do not press down too hard on the glass as the panels can break very easily. Excess cement can be removed by carefully scraping with the lathekin or by using a horseshoe nail alongside the lead. The cement will come away.

28 At this stage sprinkle whiting over the surface of the whole window and scrub vigorously to clean the window. Don't press too hard, as the whole window is still a little soft and may distort. Repeat the process on the other side.

29 Let the window stand, rather than lie, for a few days to allow the cement to harden. After three or so days, decide whether you would like a grey or black finish. If grey, simply polish the window with a bristle brush. If you want the lead to be black, apply some well-mixed stove black with a brush. After a few minutes, when the solvent has evaporated, polish with a brush once again. Now install the window in the frame prepared.

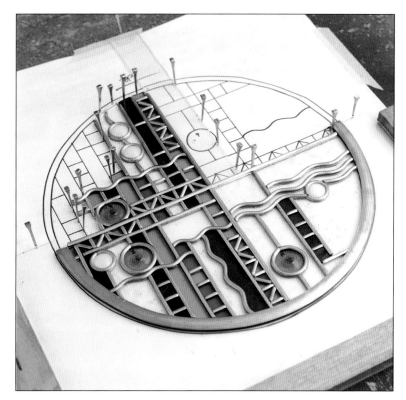

Assembling the glass pieces and lead, filling design from bottom

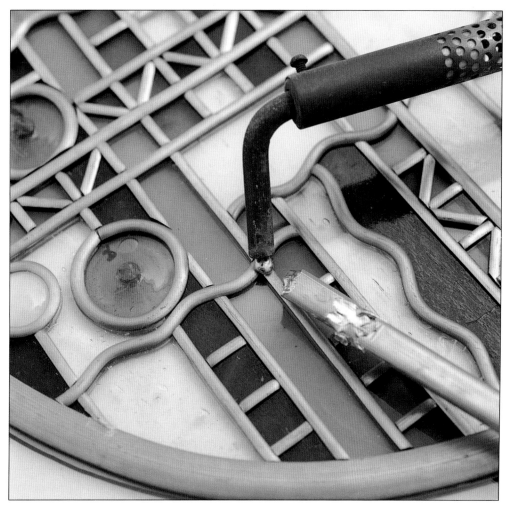

Soldering lead joints with 'hook nose' soldering iron

Choosing the right floor and floorcovering is an important aspect of furnishing your home – it is not only one of the most dominant decorative surfaces, it will also claim a large proportion of your furnishing budget.

THE PERFECT FLOOR

An important aspect of furnishing your home

The type and quality of the floorcovering you choose should be appropriate for each room, just as the right colour and design are important. Poor quality flooring, ill-suited to the requirements of the room, will wear out quickly and end up costing you a lot more in the long run.

Cork floor for kitchen/dining area

FLOOR CONSTRUCTION MATERIALS

Concrete: An artificial rock which is normally on the ground in homes, but in certain instances may be suspended. 'Slab on ground' refers to concrete laid on a membrane directly onto prepared foundation soil. Raft slabs are designed to float on poor foundation soils. Good drainage is essential. A suspended concrete floor refers to concrete supported off the ground on a base structure. Concrete is rigid and offers good thermal mass and soundproofing.

Timber: This is still the most commonly used material for domestic floors built on honeycomb walls. It may be a strip floor of individual solid timber boards, or a sheet material such as particle (chip) board or plywood. Timber provides a more resilient floor, but must be properly ventilated underneath to prevent moisture and rot problems. Tempered particle (chip) board is resistant to

moisture and therefore especially suitable for wet areas.

Brick: Mainly used in the province of alternative builders; also used as paving.

UNDERLAYS

Many flooring finishes are not fixed directly to the main structural floor but to an underlay to ensure that the type of floor has no effect on the final finish. Common materials used as underlays are plywood for rigid and resilient tiles, hardboard for resilient tiles, and various applied materials, usually where rigid floor finishes are applied to non-rigid floor structures. Floor levelling compounds are also available.

FLOOR FINISHES

Coatings: Timber structural floors can be sanded and finished with clear finishes, but other structural floor materials are normally covered.

Resilient tiles: These include studded rubber, vinyl in many variations, cork and cork composite,

Lifestyle

Dining/family room with herringbone pattern block parquetry floor

Terracotta and ceramic tiles. Note the correct grout joints

and linoleum. They are available in many colours and easy to keep looking good.

Sheet materials: These include sheet vinyls and linoleum, otherwise similar to tiles.

Parquetry: Consists of small timber strips or blocks, laid in various patterns, adhered to the floor and then clear finished. They are also now available in loose-lay interlocking tiles. Parquetry must be kept dry, or it will buckle.

Ceramic and quarry tiles: Now popular in most rooms of the house. The choice is from among ceramic, monocottura (single-fired), extruded quarry and terracotta tiles, available in various glaze levels and as non-slip tiles. They must be isolated from movement by slip joints or flexible

adhesives, and have allowances made for expansion and contraction.

Stone: Most commonly used are slate and quartzite. More prestige materials increasing in popularity are marble, travertine and granite. They are all rigid and require a rigid subfloor.

Carpet: Commonplace in most homes. Now choices include not only woven styles and patterns, but also materials such as wools, nylons, acrylics and other man-made fibres, as well as blends for all applications. It is important to match the expected traffic of the carpet to the carpet's classification.

Polished hardwood timber-strip floor

Light vinyl floor with dark accent tiles

Sanding and sealing your timber floor
One of the simplest and most attractive floors is the polished timber-strip floor. In many a renovation or restoration, old floors of hard-to-get and well-seasoned timbers can be exposed, and brought to light in all their original glory by careful sanding and clear finishing.

Project 8

Timber-strip floor

This project involves sanding and sealing a timber-strip floor. Sanding floors properly is not easy and the equipment used is heavy and powerful, requiring a certain amount of strength to operate efficiently. There will be occasions, especially with problem floors, when even the most diehard do-it-yourselfer should seek professional help and advice.

For a new room, or when replacing a floor, there is nothing quite like a timber-strip floor. It's not an easy project, but is well worth the effort – even if you hire a professional to do it.

STEP BY STEP

1   The first step is to decide whether or not the floor is worth doing; if it is badly damaged it will never look good. This investigation should also include checking under the floor to ensure that there is adequate ventilation. If the ventilation is poor, the floor will need improvement before work on the surface begins.

2   The floor should be cordonned off from the time work starts to stop any possible staining, dirt or other contaminants affecting the floor.

3   Any tacks from old carpet should be removed. Any old accumulations of adhesive

Finished timber-strip floor. Detail: Applying coating on timber using a lamb's wool pad

WHAT TO BUY

☐ polyurethane finish
☐ 1 litre solvent

SPECIAL TOOLS NEEDED

☐ nail punch (3 mm)
☐ drum sander (hire)
☐ disc sander (designed for flooring; also hired)
☐ lamb's wool pad and long-handled extension
☐ 50 mm or 75 mm brush
☐ face mask and cartridge suitable for hydrocarbons
☐ hand-sanding float

TIME

Two weekends, on and off. The final sanding and first coating should be on the same day to protect the newly sanded surface from accidental staining.

---

should be scraped off as far as possible.

4 All nails should be punched to about 3 mm below the surface.

5 Sanding can now commence. The procedure will depend on the state of the floor. The sander should initially be fitted with a coarse grade abrasive, about #40 grade. This will level and cut into the floor. Normally three passes are made across the floor. The first at 45° to the direction of the floorboards. At no time should the machine be stationary while the drum is revolving as this will cause a 'stop mark' or depression on the floor.

6 The second pass is at right angles to the first.

7 Clean the floor and vacuum, especially around the nail holes. Any splits, small depressions and nail holes should be stopped (filled) at this stage with a good-quality wood filler. Fill the holes well.

8 When the cleaning and filling work is dry, the final cut with the coarse abrasive can be carried out parallel to the floorboards.

9 The areas close to the walls or skirtings that cannot be reached by the drum sander need to be sanded carefully with the disc sander. Progress should be slow and careful as swirl marks are easily made. Any inaccessible areas will have to be scraped level or planed by hand.

10 The sanding belt now needs to be replaced with one of #80 to #120 grade, and the same three passes are made to remove all scratch marks. This should leave a smooth surface suitable for coating. Once again, the edges need to be carefully sanded with the disc sander, using #120 to #150 grade abrasive. Check for nails before sanding with fine papers. On completion sweep up the dust and vacuum thoroughly.

11 Apply the first coat of sealer once the sanded area has been cleaned. Brush around the perimeter, and follow this by using a lamb's wool pad to apply the finish

over the broad floor areas. This is made easier if the pad is on an extension handle. When the surface is dry, lightly sand it by hand using a float. An alternative is a short-to-medium nap roller.

12 Apply a second coat, allow it to dry and then sand it again. The final coat must be carefully applied. Shut all windows and doors to ensure that no dust or wind-blown matter can land and settle on the finish coat.

TIPSTRIP

In the past it was often suggested that the grain of the timber be filled. However, with modern finishes and the timber species commonly used, this is not necessary.

MOUTH AND NOSE MASK

It is wise to wear a mouth and nose mask capable of filtering hydrocarbons when applying polyurethane sealers, as the odour can be overpowering. For the first coat, leave the windows and doors open to allow for better ventilation.

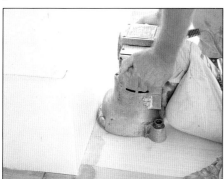

Sanding edges with a disc sander Below: Sanding machine on final pass

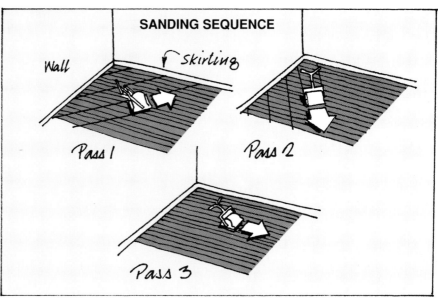

SANDING SEQUENCE

Wall — Skirting

Pass 1

Pass 2

Pass 3

Slate floor for a family room
Slate has enjoyed great popularity with home improvers for many years, because of its toughness and range of natural earthy colours, which can vary from soft green to deep purple, mottled brown and dark charcoal.

Project 9

Slate floor

The choice of slate is usually made against other hard floorcoverings such as quarry or monocottura (single-fired) tiles, ceramic floor tiles, and other natural stones such as quartzite, marble, sandstone or granite. Slate is unique in that it is naturally a highly laminated rock and the working of this material differs in some ways to most of the other tiling materials.

Slates are available in a range of sizes, colours and durabilities and are highly regarded for their heat retention properties in passive solar houses.

The colouring of slates is due to the mineral content, and is essentially non-fading. The multicoloured slates are also coloured by weathering along the lamination planes – this may wear off over time in heavy traffic areas unless protected.

Most multicoloured slates are available in sawn edge. These have a neater appearance than the guillotine-edge style.

The project is to apply slate to a family room, where its lasting strength will provide good service. We have chosen to use attractive 300 mm x 200 mm brown multicoloured slates. The floor at present is a timber-based particle (chip) board floor. The floor area is 5.2 m x 3.6 m. It runs into a kitchen, which will also be done in slate.

Dark, multicoloured slate floor in open-plan dining/kitchen/family area

The Slate People

WHAT TO BUY

Slate is commonly sold by the square metre (sq.m). To get the area of a room in square metres simply measure the length and width of the room then multiply the measurements.

If the tiles will be bought on a per-piece basis, take the dimensions of each tile and add 6 mm to the dimensions for the joint – then calculate the number required for the whole area. This quantity is for a total area of approximately 19 sq.m, or 320 individual tiles.

- ☐ slates (see above)
- ☐ sufficient hessian and bitumen underlay for the floor area
- ☐ slate-laying adhesive (enough for a cover of 19 sq. m – preferable to cement mortar)

SPECIAL TOOLS NEEDED

- ☐ string line and pins (or bricks) for setting out
- ☐ straight edge for aligning
- ☐ builder's square, which can be made up in large sizes in timber using the 3:4:5 Pythagoras rule
- ☐ selection of buckets for dry-mix and fully prepared adhesive
- ☐ hammer, wooden-handled, for help in bedding tiles
- ☐ sponge and scouring pads for cleaning of work
- ☐ trowel for spreading adhesive, usually with 12 mm notches

STEP BY STEP

1 Slate must be laid on a firm base that will support it. Timber floors present a problem in that timber and particle (chip) board expand during humid periods, and shrink during drier times. Timber floors can be prepared in several ways. Care should be taken with all the procedures however, bearing in mind that timber or particle (chip) board is not the best base material for slate.

2 A number of slate suppliers have specially developed membrane systems available for the installation of slate on a timber floor. The one used here is the hessian and bitumen method and will provide the necessary 'slip' joint between the rigid tiles and the timber.

3 Clean the floor thoroughly, and punch any protruding nails below the surface.

4 Tack the hessian to the floor and apply the bitumen material to the rate specified by the manufacturer. Ensure it is well worked through the hessian, and achieves good contact with the floor. The hessian acts as reinforcement in the bitumen.

5 Allow to dry overnight.

6 Now the tiling can be laid out. As slates are more difficult to trim than normal tiles, we have laid them against two walls that are at right angles (checked using the 3:4:5 rule). Dry-lay a row of tiles along the two walls. Ensure that the cuts required at the ends of the row are greater than 50 mm, as smaller cuts result in very brittle pieces of slate that are difficult to bed (see Skill class on page 236). The rest of the room can then be squared from these rows. Also remember that slates should not be butted up hard against each other, but should have a 6 mm grouting gap to allow for any thermal movement in either the slate or the surface on which it is laid.

7 Slates are not uniform in thickness. It makes the job much easier if they are sorted into similar relative thicknesses before even mixing the mortar. If, for instance, four separate piles were made, each with tiles of a similar thickness, they can be used in rank of thickness, on mortar beds of constant thickness. If you use the thickest tiles first, the mortar bed can gradually be increased for the thinner tiles as the job progresses.

8 It may be that some of the slates are slightly bowed. If so, they should be laid with the bow up. If they are laid the other way up it is difficult to provide a strong enough edge-bearing for the tile, and with time it will tend to loosen.

9 If you are a first-time slate layer it is probably easier, though more expensive, to use a proprietary adhesive and to follow the instructions closely. Most adhesives are cement based with a fine aggregate, together with workability additives and bonding agents already included. These provide a reasonable working time, so that you have more time to

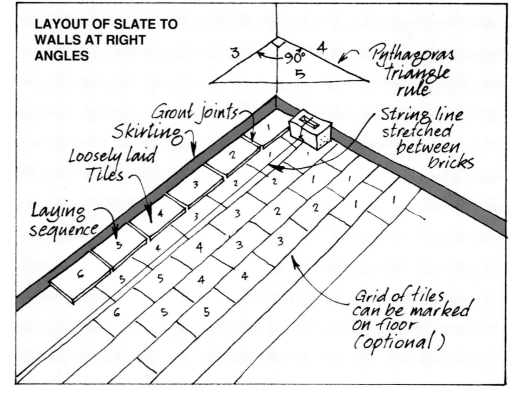

LAYOUT OF SLATE TO WALLS AT RIGHT ANGLES

Pythagoras triangle rule

String line stretched between bricks

Grout joints

Skirting

Loosely laid Tiles

Laying sequence

Grid of tiles can be marked on floor (optional)

Underlay hessian and bitumen

Laying down of slate in adhesive

Grouting the joints

carry out adjustments and take levels. All are water mixable and washable while wet.

10 Once you are happy with the design and layout, the adhesive can be mixed. Bear in mind that many of the proprietary brand mixtures require you to leave the mix standing for up to 15 minutes before use. Most mixes remain workable for around 2 hours in the summer and 3 hours in the winter. After this period of time the adhesive should be discarded.

11 Mix enough adhesive for about 1-2 sq.m at a time and finish this amount of tiling before mixing more. This will easily be worked in the time spans available. Spread the adhesive over the area where you intend to start the tiling, and notch it using a 12 mm notched trowel.

12 Place the tile in the right position and gently rock it into position. The slate should be manoeuvred from the centre, and the gentle back-and-forward rocking should force most of the air out from underneath the tile. The final positioning can be done using the wooden handle of a hammer, tapping the tile only near the centre. It helps if the other hand is placed on the tile, as this provides shock absorption so that the tile doesn't just rock

around its spot and actually loosen the bond.

13 Every now and again remove a tile that has been properly laid, just to monitor that the bedding is covering the whole of the back of the tile, and that the consistency of the mortar is correct, with minimal air holes.

14 When you are happy with one tile, proceed to the next.

15 Once about a metre square of tiles has been laid, it is time to clean off any excess mortar or adhesive, before it sets and stains the tile. This is best done with a damp sponge and frequent changes of water. The sponge should only be damp and must be used gently, otherwise the mortar may be pulled out of the joints, which will stain the slate further. Remove as much as possible with the sponge; the rest can be removed by a scouring pad at the end of a day's work. The aim is not to have to take any remedial action such as acid washing at a later date, as acids can affect the colour of the slate.

16 The tiles should be left for at least 24 hours before they are grouted.

17 The grout is usually the same mix as was used for laying. Once again, make sure you clean the tiles thoroughly to prevent

stubborn stains.

18 Once you have grouted the tiles, allow a further 24 hours to pass before walking on the tiled area.

19 Slates are normally sealed on interior surfaces. Premature sealing, or sealing while there is any moisture in the slate or in the mortar, may lead to a milky stain forming. This is a white soluble salt that can badly stain the tiles as it forms when water evaporates from the surface. All evaporation must have stopped before you begin sealing or the moisture and any salt will be trapped. At worst, the salt can effect a slow break-down in the entire slate finish.

20 Sealing is done with either an acrylic or polyurethane coating system. Acrylic is easier as it is water based. It is not advisable to use any products other than those specifically designed for use on slates. Our coloured slates rely in part on the colour of the weathering bands, and should be thoroughly brushed to remove any excess powder, which could cause the sealer to fail. Application can be carried out by sponge. Refer to the directions on the manufacturer's container when recoating or for any other special requirements.

One of the most successful types of floorcovering for a kitchen is cork tiling. The colour of cork is fairly neutral and these days can be natural, stained, or dyed to various colours. The finish applied is easy to care for, and the job can be done by any handyperson.

Project 10

Cork tile floor

Cork is available in 4.5 mm or 6 mm thickness. For a kitchen or any heavy-traffic area, the thicker cork should be used. Cork is also available pre-finished or natural. Natural cork has to be completely coated when laid on the floor. This is preferable as the coating will form a seamless finish which is highly resistant to penetration by liquids.

Our project kitchen and family room is a large area, just under 50 sq. m. The original floor is structural plywood. There are three steps between the kitchen and family areas, which will be edged with light-coloured seasoned hardwood as a wearing edge.

Finished cork floor with steps to kitchen area

STEP BY STEP

FAMILY ROOM

1 A timber floor to be covered in cork must be well ventilated. The surface coating acts as a vapour barrier upwards, and moisture in the floor or subfloor will cause failure of the floor or premature rot to the underside.

2 Check the floor for level. Any undulations should be sanded out, or in very bad cases a floor-levelling compound could be used.

3 Make sure all nails are well-nailed down. There should be no protruding heads.

4 If skirting is not already there, and is wanted, install it securely to the wall.

5 The floor should be sanded to ensure there are no local projections or loose areas. This can be done by a professional sanding company, or with care you could do it yourself. (See Project 8 on sanding a timber-strip floor.)

6 Sweep the floor, then thoroughly vacuum it to ensure that no foreign matter or dust remains.

7 Bring all the underlay into the room and, if packaged up, open and stand or lay the hardboard underlay around the room for at least 24 hours to acclimatise the underlay to the room. Make sure that air can circulate freely around the sheets.

8 Fix a hardwood or similar edge nosing to the tread edge of the steps. It must be rebated to allow for depth of underlay, plus the thickness of the cork. It could be milled to shape by your local timber merchant. If you have access to a saw bench or router the strips could be prepared at home. Glue and nail the strips in place.

9 Lay out the underlay, smooth side up, across the existing flooring. The sheets should not run in the same direction as the grain of the floor. It is also important to stagger the joints, and not to allow any joints in the hardboard to coincide with joints in the flooring. Leave half-millimetre joints between the sheets.

10 Apply a panel adhesive from a cartridge gun following the manufacturer's recommendations, to ensure that there is no drumminess or movement between the timber floor and the underlay.

11 Fix the hardboard with special underlay nails. This is a tedious job, as each sheet should be fixed every 75 mm around its perimeter, and at 150 mm centres over the rest of the sheet. This means you will use 91 nails per sheet. Ensure the nails are driven to just beneath the surface. An alternative would be to hire a nail gun, and to use staples to fix the sheets. This is a lot easier on the hands.

12 Apply strips of hardboard to the tread surfaces of the steps. The risers of the steps do not need an underlay.

13 Sand all the joints in the hardboard smooth and, again, ensure that all nails are below the surface. Depending on the adhesive used for the cork, the sanded areas may need to be sealed first.

14 Thoroughly vacuum the floor.

15 Mark out the floor. It is normal to divide it into quarters, roughly in the centre. To find the centre of the room, mark in two lines each drawn between the centre points of opposite

walls. The easiest way to do this is to use a chalkline. Stretch it between the walls, and give the line a flick. The chalk will mark the exact line you need: where they cross is the centre.

16 The angle at which they cross should be checked to ensure that it is a right angle. You may have a builder's square, or you could use the Pythagoras 3:4:5 rule to ensure a right angle.

17 Next dry-lay a row of cork tiles to the skirting wall to see how they work out when they reach the wall. Adjust the starting point to allow a small cut from the edge of the perimeter tiles, in case of irregularities in the walls.

18 Then lift up the tiles, and apply a latex cork adhesive with a fine notched applicator.

19 Aim to do only one quarter of the floor at a time, as defined by the lines. In fact, in large areas aim at completing one quarter a session or a day, as laying cork can be backbreaking work.

20 Work a maximum of 1 m at a time. If you do more, you run the risk of the adhesive skinning, and not adhering properly to the tiles.

21 Lay the first tile straight down without sliding it in place. Take great care in

WHAT TO BUY

- ☐ 50 sq. m of cork tiles, including an allowance for waste
- ☐ 50 sq. m of hardboard underlay – say 40 sheets of 1200 mm x 900 mm
- ☐ 3 kg underlay nails or staples if power equipment is available
- ☐ 75 mm x 50 mm hardwood DAR (PAR), 3 of 2.4 m
- ☐ 20 cartridges of panel adhesive and gun
- ☐ 30 litres of latex adhesive
- ☐ 120 litres of polyurethane finish in gloss
- ☐ 1 litre of solvent for cleaning the finish
- ☐ sandpaper and float, or orbital sander

SPECIAL TOOLS NEEDED

- ☐ adhesive applicators, 3 mm notched trowels
- ☐ paint brushes
- ☐ paint roller and extension
- ☐ vacuum cleaner
- ☐ chalkline
- ☐ power stapler (if desired)

HIRE

- ☐ sander for smoothing floor

TIME

Four full weekends

The underlay is fixed across the floor and joints are staggered

Cork tiles bedded in adhesive

Marking tile to be cut

Coating the cork tiles with a roller

aligning it properly. All tiles should be laid without sliding them in place.

22 Lay the following tiles in the form of triangles towards the corner, butting each one against its neighbours.

23 When you reach a wall, tiles will need to be cut. To mark the exact shape required, place a full tile over the last full tile laid in that row, and place another full tile over that. The top tile can then be slid against the wall or skirting. Use a pencil to mark a line on the lower tile, which corresponds to where the tile should be cut.

24 Cut the tile with a straight edge and a sharp utility knife. If you end up with a rough edge, you may need to lightly sand the edge.

25 Finish one quarter at a time, and clean excess adhesive off the floor as you go so that you will be able to continue from where you left off the following day.

26 Clean all applicators ready for the next day's work.

27 Repeat these steps for all other sections, until the floor is finished.

KITCHEN

28 Repeat the above steps in the adjoining kitchen in the same way. The steps will need all cut tiles, and the cork will need to be measured individually. Apply the tread tiles first, then the riser tiles.

29 When the cork is down but before it is finished, it is important to avoid staining the floor with food, drinks or paint, or even stains from dirt or building debris carried underfoot. It is safest to keep traffic off the floor.

30 Once the tiles are set (leave overnight), the floor will need to be sanded to remove any high spots, or to level where the thickness of tiles was not exactly the same. (Some variation in thickness is not uncommon.) You can have the floor professionally

sanded to level the joints, or do it yourself with an orbital sander or hand-float. It is a slow job – you must take care not to sand grooves or depressions into the floor. Use #120 grade paper. The dust generated is unbelievable and you should wear a mask with a fine particle filter for breathing.

31 Vacuum floor again.

32 You are now ready to coat the floor. For your breathing protection, obtain a cartridge rated for protection against hydrocarbon fumes, because the odour of many of the coatings is overpowering.

33 Open windows and provide good ventilation through the room. Close doors to other areas of the house.

34 Apply the first coat of polyurethane by brushing around the perimeter. Use a roller on an extension rod for the main body of the floor. The roller should have a medium nap.

35 Once dry, sand smooth with #120 paper and vacuum once again.

36 Apply the second coat of polyurethane as before. You start getting a shine with this coat.

37 Give the floor a last final light sand and vacuum up the dust carefully.

38 Close the windows to provide still, dustless air. Apply the final coat with brush and roller, and let this cure for at least 24 hours before light traffic, and three or four days before normal traffic is let on the floor.

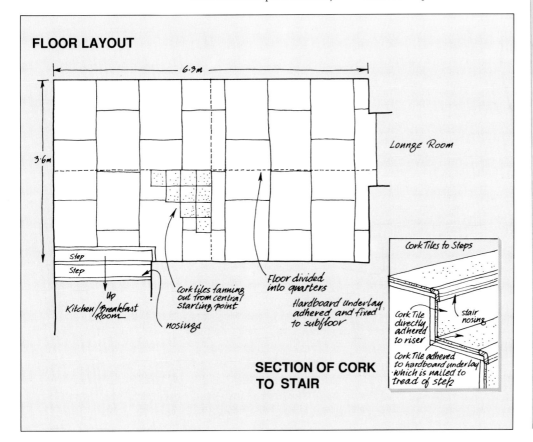

FLOOR LAYOUT

6.3 m

3.6 m

Lounge Room

Step

Step

Up

Kitchen/Breakfast Room

Cork tiles fanning out from central starting point

nosings

Floor divided into quarters

Hardboard underlay adhered and fixed to subfloor

SECTION OF CORK TO STAIR

Cork Tiles to Steps

stair nosing

Cork Tile directly adhered to riser

Cork Tile adhered to hardboard underlay which is nailed to tread of step

Rugs can be a unique and complementary part of your total design scheme, adding colour, accent and life. In fact, a rug is often the decorating accessory which pulls a whole room together. It is a versatile design element, easily moved around, practical yet full of creative possibilities.

RAVISHING RUGS
Traditional and contemporary

Your rug may be there to add atmosphere and comfort to a hard, cold floor surface, or to provide cheerful (and cheap) relief from unsightly patches of stained or worn-out carpet. A well-chosen rug will dress up a plain carpet, and protect it, especially in heavy traffic areas such as halls and corridors.

Rugs are available to suit every budget. They can be bought as part of a quick, on-the-cheap home improvement project, or as part of a more long-term financial investment. Although most rugs are imported, the industry is highly competitive and there's always room for a bargain.

RUG TYPES
Aside from the traditional types of rug – there are basically two types: flat weave (where the surface looks similar to a piece of cloth) and tufted (where the surface is raised into a cut or looped pile) – there is a wide range of contemporary rugs available in all price brackets and designs. Those made by individual craft makers, rather than by carpet manufacturers, are a particularly exciting alternative, especially if you want something of lasting value for your wall or floor.

Rag, braided and hooked rugs are also part of a thriving cottage industry tradition, and will add a warm, cosy look and splash of colour and texture to your living room. Why not recycle your scraps of suede, string, silk, cotton and wool by making your own homemade version?

DHURRIES: Dhurries are flat-woven pure wool rugs available in a fantastic range of colours from pastel to bright, usually geometric designs, stripes and simple borders. They are extremely versatile, reasonably priced and very hard-wearing. Dhurries can be used either for formal lounge areas, or for the more relaxed, casual environment of the family room. They are at home on hard timber or tile floors, as well as on the more luxurious backdrop of wall-to-wall body carpet.

CUSTOM-MADE HANDTUFTED PURE WOOL RUGS: This style of rug comes in a wealth of different styles from very traditional through to ultra-modern – they can be made to custom size, shape, colour and design and are very versatile despite their formal, rich character. These high-quality rugs are hand-made from the finest blend of New Zealand and Scottish wool yarns – single strand, which gives the rug a tight, dense, velvet-like appearance. They can also be made in a loop pile, offering a more informal, dense look.

A rug which is uniquely yours can be specially designed to extend a room's decoration onto the floor as an integral part of your total design theme.

KELIMS: Kelims are wonderful old weaves (30 -40 years) from Southern Russia (Karabagh) and Yugoslavia – their most distinctive feature being very decorative and

stylised geometric designs, which make them suitable for interiors that are rich in colour, shapes and style. Kelims can look highly individual and different, and are handwoven in pure wool (woolweft on wool warp) to last.

PORTUGUESE NEEDLEPOINT RUGS: These luxurious, hand-made rugs come in many decorative styles – mainly floral for very refined decoration. They are hard-wearing, and will go well in any room. The coarser weave looks wonderful with a simple, more rustic decorative scheme which highlights textures; the fine weave suits a more delicate interior style. These rugs offer tremendous character and flair, and can successfully pull many design elements in a room together.

Robyn Cosgrove Rugs

Picture Key
1 Blue and white striped Dhurry
2 Kelim from Yugoslavia
3 Dhurry
4 Custom-made handtufted rug
5 Portuguese needlepoint rug
6 Kelim from Yugoslavia

PART 3

Storage Solutions

Above: Everything that opens and shuts
for bookworms and TV buffs . . .
Right: A country-style kitchen with storage
features to match

When you can barely see into your wardrobe for clothes, your desk for paperwork, or your children's rooms for the layers of 'mess', you know you have a problem – mess has a mind of its own. It's time to roll up your sleeves and get started!

GETTING STARTED

Storage is often the last thing on the home-maker's list of priorities, and yet this practical and decorative aspect of home improvements is just as important as colour and furnishings to the way you use and enjoy your home.

All too often a simple task such as ironing a shirt can turn into a nightmare when the ironing board is stored at the rear of a cupboard cluttered with mops and pails, a carton of bottles put aside for recycling and the overflowing washing basket! Higgledy-piggledy storage may sound like fun, but the truth is, it is as inefficient as it is infuriating. Good storage is a question of balance – a way of dealing with (and finding) everything you use on a day-to-day basis (as well as the 101 items you use occasionally!).

Careful clutter notwithstanding, homes where there is a sense of order and a feeling of space are the easiest and most attractive to live in. It sounds simple, but careful planning and forethought will help you beat the mess and achieve this aim.

Assess the mess

Step number one is to take a pen, a piece of paper and a ruthless, assessing eye on a tour around the place. In each room, what is the nature of the storage problem? In the kitchen, are there too few cupboards? In the bedroom, is there too little hanging space? In the bathroom, are the towels taking over? In the children's room, are obsolete possessions still taking up valuable floor and wardrobe space? Is there a lot of 'dead' space around the place? For instance, are the beds high off the floor? This allows for under-bed storage or the construction of simple drawers.

Are your walls bereft of shelving, hooks and built-in cupboards? That's more dead space you can turn to your advantage. Have you thought of going up to the attic? Under the stairs? Excavating under the ground floor? Would renovations help? Additional rooms or an additional storey? Or would the mess just grow in proportion to the amount of space available to it? If the truthful answer to that last question is 'yes' then you know you need to take an even firmer grip on a deteriorating situation!

A plan of attack

Step number two is to sit down with the family, pen and paper in hand, and start making lists. Each family member should have something to contribute to the overall plan. Next, take those lists and massage and bully them into a single, workable concept. Sometimes it is useful to start with a very general list.

❏ Areas to be tackled
❏ Aspects to be retained
❏ Areas for renovation
❏ New possibilities for existing space

Swept-bare, possession-free living has romantic appeal, but the reality is that people like to surround themselves with all sorts of objects in order to live. Homes are the natural repository for these items.

IKEA

IKEA

Country Form

Clockwise from top right: A modern living room with freestanding units to suit; Sideboard for storage and display; Country-style kitchen; Wardrobe with stackable wire baskets; Family entertainment centre; Brightly coloured plastic storage boxes on castors – just keep stacking as you need more storage!

Board games supplied by Toyworld

Stack 'N' Store. Woollen jumpers from Benetton

Country Form

- ❏ Budgetary allocations
- ❏ Design aspects
- ❏ Built-ins versus freestanding, modular or knockdown units
- ❏ Items requiring specialist storage

A checklist made up of questions can be very helpful.

- ❏ Is there a single room or area which could be made into a storage-only room?
- ❏ What extra space can you utilise for storage?
- ❏ Do certain items need to be stored in particular rooms?
- ❏ Is there storage space for sports and hobby equipment?
- ❏ Are there some items you need but can never find?
- ❏ Do you need somewhere to put things you want to keep but not necessarily look at constantly, such as souvenirs from holidays, letters, and treasured collections?
- ❏ Are there some items you use more often in summer or in winter, so that you can organise storage on a seasonal basis?
- ❏ Do some of your possessions suffer from the way they are stored, such as:
  - tools that get rusty
  - clothes that get crumpled
  - fragile things that get broken
  - papers that get muddled?
- ❏ How much can you spend on storage?
- ❏ Will the storage facilities you plan increase the value of your house or apartment?

The weeding-out process

It goes without saying that any genuine reappraisal of your storage needs ruthlessness. It makes no sense to invest in a fabulous new storage unit only to transfer years of accumulated bric-a-brac onto its shelves. The third step in the grand plan is a weeding-out process; going through those untidy drawers and bulging cupboards to 'rationalise' their contents.

Be constructive. Think about recycling out-of-date or ill-fitting shoes and clothes, stacks of old magazines and newspapers. Consider a garage sale to rid yourself of saleable items and get rid of the rest.

SORT PILE: Things you want but have nowhere to keep. Put these things into bags or boxes and leave them for a while. The longer you leave the sort pile, the less you miss whatever is in it! Finally, your dread of sorting it will outweigh the dread of throwing it away. After taking out the things you really do need, it's two bags down and one box to go!

CHARITY PILE: Things that are still repairable or useful (to someone else), clothes and accessories – anything that can be used by someone or could raise money for a good cause.

JUNK PILE: Things that are broken, outdated, out of style, ugly, useless or mouldy – get rid of them, they are junk!

A room-by-room appraisal

Once you have a workable plan the next stage is to consider the specific requirements of each room. It goes without saying that certain parts of the home are natural storage areas, but also pay attention to the areas you may not have thought of, such as hallways, under the stairs, or up in the roof. Refer to the relevant sections in this book to help you with your room-by-room appraisal – you'll be amazed at just how simple a solution can be!

Winning the space race

Re-evaluating your existing space in terms of storage is imperative for the eventual

Tailor your storage units to suit a room's character and purpose

Country Form

Ornate freestanding wooden units with a limed finish

success of the storage system you choose. Try to think in terms of wall space. Objects at floor level, and thus in full view, take up more space and lead to a cluttered look. By moving items up off the floor and onto the walls, rooms will suddenly appear larger.

Streamlining is indeed the answer to most storage problems – the right storage will enable you to enjoy your possessions more and to indulge in the fine art of display. Remember that off-the-shelf units are customised by the addition of your own precious possessions, and this important designer aspect should be borne in mind throughout the various stages of planning.

A question of style

The possibilities for storage systems are as varied as those for every other type of household furnishing. Thus the final and arguably the most exciting part of your storage strategy is its overall design. Pay attention to:
❑ the age and architectural features of your home or apartment
❑ the style of existing furnishings
❑ personal design preferences
❑ the sorts of items to be stored/displayed
❑ future flexibility
❑ DIY potential

You can choose from a unit which will create visual impact in your home, or opt for something which will merge with the walls. Don't forget that large-scale storage units alter the proportions of a room and can be used to highlight or downplay architectural features such as windows or fireplaces.

Broadly speaking, the types of unit and system available fit into three designer categories: contemporary, classical and country – all of which have very specific characteristics. Contemporary design focuses on clean, uncluttered lines and makes use of materials such as tubular steel, glass, and lacquer/laminate finishes. Classical design features darker timbers and finishes, with traditional cabinet features and lines; whereas the country look features lighter timbers such as pine, slightly naive styling and a notable absence of fussy detail.

Again, you can create any of these looks by using a series of individual components. Buy ready-made units or, particularly in the case of kitchen storage, have something built to suit.

Don't overlook the importance of custom-

finishing your storage system. Colour – in the form of stains, stencils and painted finishes – can have a remarkable effect, and even simple additions such as new handles or door knobs can create just the effect you have been looking for.

A flexible future

The final point to take into consideration in your storage strategy is planning for the future. No matter how much storage you provide now, there will come a time in the future when it will need to be reviewed. This is where the wonderful flexibility offered by modular systems comes into its own, especially when planning for the needs of a growing family.

Take care not to lock yourself into a specialised system which can't be changed. Instead, try to aim for something which can be altered if necessary, added to or moved to another part of the house. Even custom-built units can be designed to include adjustable features with the potential for expansion.

If buying units for a child's room, think ahead to the time when a desk will be needed, and make sure there is room in the plan for such an addition. If installing a new kitchen, make provision for features such as an internal racking system which can be added as your budget allows.

Finally, remember that good storage will add enormously to the value of your home. A well-planned kitchen, effective wardrobes and cupboards in bedrooms, good use of space under the stairs and in hallways, are just the thing to strike the right chord with potential buyers, as well as simplifying life for you and your family.

With all of its pots, pans, bags of groceries and delicious comforting aromas, the kitchen is the heart of the home. But it does have a dual role to play: it has to be efficient yet comfortable and inviting.

IN THE KITCHEN

Planning a kitchen may seem daunting at first, but most of the important decisions will be common-sense ones. Then you can spend time on the fun things like colour schemes and the overall 'look'.

Practical storage need not interfere with the visual aspect of your kitchen design and can often enhance many features. The kitchen is the main working area of your home and must be compatible with your lifestyle as well as easy to clean and maintain.

Whether your kitchen is modern, country style or industrial high-tech in character, planning how it will work is the top priority. Kitchens tend to operate around three main activity centres: the stove, the sink and large storage areas, including the pantry and refrigerator. Ideally, the total distance between these areas should be between 3.5 m and 7 m for effective work efficiency (often referred to as the work triangle).

Work centres

❑ The main food preparation area is usually the worktop or bench space between the sink and the stove – this area should be large enough to prepare a meal on. If possible, the pantry or food storage area and any tall storage units should not interrupt the worktop space. Try to avoid gaps between appliances and units as this wastes space and makes cleaning difficult.

❑ The sink should be close to storage cupboards or shelves that house everyday crockery, cutlery, pots and glassware. Avoid plumbing a sink in a corner and allow space for a dishwasher and waste disposal unit if required. Consider draining baskets and a chopping board that fits over the sink if space is limited.

❑ Ovens and cooktops (hobs) are often separated today – both should be located near the sink so that steaming pots and pans can be carried easily. A centre island, which may house the cooktop (hob), can shorten the distance between major appliances and offer extra storage space. Avoid situating the cooktop (hob) in a corner – it should be well away from a wall cupboard or a window with curtains because of the fire danger. Large, deep pan drawers installed near the oven and cooktop (hob) are an advantage.

❑ Another cooking appliance that has become part of today's working kitchen is the microwave oven.

Consider positioning it for ease of use and allow clearance space for opening the oven door. Even if you don't have a microwave oven, it is wise to think about the space it *would* occupy (Who knows what you may receive for Christmas next year!)

Space to bake

For baking enthusiasts, here

Above top: Wall-mounted plate rack
Above: Pot drawers

Country Form

Styling: Michelle Gorry   Saucepans from Made Where

Clockwise from left: Pull-out pantry; Pale apricot kitchen; Appliance centre
Clockwise from right: Wine storage under breakfast bar; Stainless steel grid; Contemporary kitchen complete with shelf for microwave oven

Modern, country-style or industrial high-tech kitchen? Planning how it will work is the top priority.

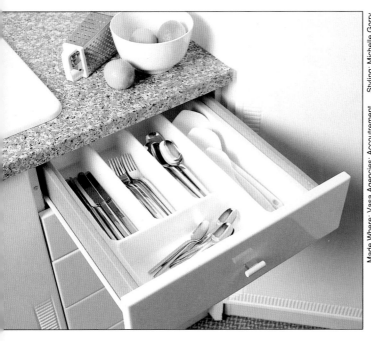

Cutlery drawer

Styling: Michelle Gorry

are some ideas for a wonderful kitchen area that tells the story of baking:

❏ A marble worktop for rolling dough and whisking egg whites

❏ Cupboards that open to reveal a pull-out filing device for baking trays and muffin pans: each tray stands

vertically side by side (no more unstacking trays searching for the right size)

❏ Shallow drawers for cutters, rolling pins, piping bags and all manner of accoutrements

❏ An extension table or a fold-away shelf for an electric mixer, slightly lower than worktop height for easy viewing

Made Where; Vasa Agencies; Accoutrement   Styling: Michelle Gorry

❏ A simple stand for a recipe book

❏ Measuring jugs, scales and an assortment of pans stacked neatly in overhead cupboards

❏ A stainless steel artist's ruler attached to a pull-out drawer for measuring pans and pastry

❏ A swing-out cupboard for drying home-made pastry

❏ A wall-mounted microwave oven on a swing-out bracket

❏ A telephone extension close by to avoid flour-coated telephone calls!

No excuses now if the cake doesn't rise!

Behind closed doors

Cupboard storage ideas are only as limited as your imagination.

❏ Glass doors can often be incorporated into cupboard design – these are generally at eye level to show off colour-coordinated china and glassware.

❏ Plastic-coated wire baskets are popular for storing numerous items from pots to vegetables.

❏ A tea-towel rack may be useful in a small narrow space.

❏ Storage units under the sink are useful for dishcloths, detergents, brushes and scourers. These units can be small baskets or swing-out compartments.

❏ Many kitchen designs now incorporate a fridge or a dishwasher behind a cupboard door – uniformity can easily be achieved with this clever design idea. When planning kitchen cupboard storage, consider items that are in constant use, those used from time to time and items that can be relegated to top cupboards or difficult corners. Make sure all your cupboards open in the most convenient way.

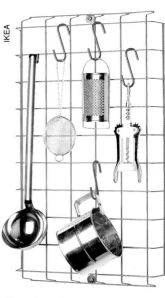

IKEA

Utensils rack

Drawing the line

Deep pan drawers are specially designed to hold saucepans, colanders and sieves, making them easily accessible. Very wide deep drawers can be useful for plastic containers. Shallow drawers are handy for cutlery and rolls of plastic wrap, aluminium foil and paper. Moulded plastic trays can assist with storing cutlery. Consider whether or not you require the space to store tea towels, tablecloths and napkins in the kitchen. Very small drawers can be used to store spices, balls of string, matches and piping tubes or other small items. Positioning

Country-style kitchen

Zuhause; Vasa Agencies; Made Where; Accoutrement

Carousel cupboard

Country Form

QUICK-FIX PROJECT
Storage racks on pantry doors
Why not make useful space of the inside of doors? It's easy to do with these purchased plastic shelves that screw onto the door.

Be sure to calculate the position of shelves so that they don't bump into existing shelves when the door is closed. Add another shelf under the sink for soap, brushes and cleansers.

drawers near the cooktop (hob) is often sensible for storing those indispensable items that you may need close at hand: thermometers, spatulas, ladles, tongs, timers, brushes, skewers, string and pot holders.

All drawers should run smoothly on runners.

Just hanging around

It is surprising what can be stored in overhead space if you are lacking floor or cupboard space. Plastic-coated or plated wire racks hung from the ceiling or the wall are useful for storage and display of pots and skillets. These should be hung within reach but above head height. A stainless steel wall rack can house cooking utensils and bottles of frequently used spices, oils and vinegars.

Generally this is situated near the cooktop (hob).

❑ Place hooks on the underside of shelves to hang cups, or hang a spice rack wherever it is most convenient. Tie up bunches of herbs and hang them from a shelf or curtain rail. A suspended plate rack is a solution for drainage and display. Decorative plates can be attractive when hung on a bare wall. Using a little imagination you can achieve very practical *and* attractive solutions.

Cost and practicality

Open shelving is one solution to low-cost storage. This need not lack style. Inexpensive glass jars containing ingredients can be very

The pantry

The old tradition of larder or pantry which predated refrigeration has not outlived its usefulness for food storage.

If your kitchen is large enough, a walk-in cupboard makes practical use of space. Heavy items can be stored on lower shelves or on the floor; regularly used items at eye level and items used occasionally on the top shelves. If you are fortunate enough, the room could be converted to a cool room for storage of fruit, vegetables and dairy products.

❑ A corner pantry is a clever way to utilise corner space, and carousel attachments and pull-out baskets allow easy access to deep corners. Door clearance is an important point to consider with cupboards and pantries. Varying shelf heights are sensible for ease of viewing items.

❑ Consider your regular shopping items and allow space for each item. Lower levels of the pantry can incorporate pull-out fittings, racks for spices, bottles and cans and trays for loose packets. Plastic storage bins can be fitted onto runners to utilise the top space of a deep cupboard. See-through glass or plastic jars or canisters of varying heights will keep food fresh and storage tidy. Wire baskets fitted into a drawer mechanism are an excellent idea for vegetable storage. Make use of wasted space on the back of pantry doors, with easily attached hooks, small storage baskets and racks.

A charming, old-fashioned pantry

Styling: Michelle Gorry

Country Form; Zuhause; Country Trader; Gallerie Nomart; Accoutrement; Appley Hoare Antiques

This country-style kitchen features built-in storage units in keeping with its rustic character

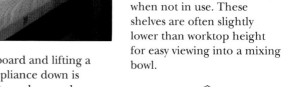

Vegetable basket

attractive in line. Colour-coordinate your plates and glassware, and use shelving to display much loved items. Keep cookery books where they will be used. Anything that you may want to hide away can be curtained off or placed in inexpensive plastic tubs fixed on runners (colour-coordinated of course!).

QUICK-FIX PROJECT
Sideboard drawer divider
Are your heirlooms in a clutter? Consider dividing your sideboard drawer into made-to-measure sections to neatly contain its contents. First measure your drawer and cutlery, then draw up a plan of how best to divide up the drawer, allowing room for candles, bottle openers, carving knives and similar dining room needs. The sections are cut from plywood strips of a suitable height, then all are nailed or glued together to create a lift-in/lift-out drawer divider. Line the bottom of the drawer with a layer of fine batting or felt before fitting in the divider.

❏ A noticeboard is helpful to leave messages on and keep favourite recipes at hand.
❏ A magnetic strip can be attached quite simply to the wall near the cooktop (hob) for safe storage of knives.

Storing small appliances
How many times do you think about baking a cake or preparing fresh fruit juice, but the thought of rummaging in the back of a

top cupboard and lifting a heavy appliance down is enough to make you change your mind?
❏ A sensible idea to consider, if space permits, is an appliance cupboard. This is generally a narrow cupboard situated above the worktop, allowing you to use the appliances and store them at the correct height. A concertina door that folds as it opens is a space-saving option.
❏ Another option is to have

fitted a pull-out shelf that actually extends your worktop space for an electric mixer or food processor, or a fold-away mixer shelf that stows the mixer in the cupboard below the worktop when not in use. These shelves are often slightly lower than worktop height for easy viewing into a mixing bowl.

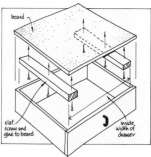

QUICK-FIX PROJECT
Kid's cooking drawer
Make a handy activity top to fit your kitchen drawers – your child will have a special worktop for painting or cutting out, or for assisting the master chef at those critical moments.

GREEN TIP
❏ **Pull-out bins encourage recyc-**ling of waste products like glass, metals, plastics and foodstuffs. Some units have a chute situated near the sink to place waste products into the bin, so the cupboard need only be opened to empty the bin.
❏ **Recycle your glass jars as canisters: paint the lids a colour that coordinates with your kitchen.**

Wall-mounted kitchen cabinet

Keep your good china, glassware and other kitchenware close at hand in this clever kitchen cabinet.

STEP BY STEP

Except for the gateleg and the dropleaf, this cabinet is made out of softwood (pine).
Note: All joints to be drilled, glued and screwed throughout assembly.

1 Cutting out: Cut out all the components (sides, shelves, cleat, bottom trim, support flange, support, gateleg, dropleaf). Use a saw to cut the steps on shelf sides, and a jigsaw to cut the gateleg and table top to the radii shown.

2 Shelf unit: Start by fastening the batten/cleat to the under-side back edge of the top shelf. Saw 19 mm off the depth of the bottom shelf. Assemble the shelves and sides and complete with the bottom trim, flush with the bottom of the sides.

3 Gateleg: Screw through the back of the support flange into the back edge of the softwood support, using four screws evenly spaced. To allow the gateleg to swing freely, saw 12 mm off its top edge for all but the front 100 mm. Using the 400 mm length of piano hinge-ing, screw the gateleg to the front edge of the support (see illustration). Drill through the

support flange and screw the whole support structure to the wall with the table top at table height (see illustration detail).

4 Finishing off: Sit the shelving unit on top of the gateleg and screw through the cleat to wall-mount the unit. Screw through the bottom shelf into the top of the support. Use the 1100 mm length of piano hinge-ing to fix the dropleaf to the front trim (see detail). Finish with paint.

MATERIALS

ITEM	DIMENSIONS (mm)	QUANTITY
sides	1900 x 290 x 19 thick	2
shelves	3600 x 290 x 19 thick	3
batten/cleat	1200 x 90 x 19 thick	1
bottom trim	1200 x 40 x 19 thick	1
support flange	450 x 70 x 19 thick	1
support	450 x 240 x 19 thick	1
gateleg, high-density particle (chip) board	450 x 410 x 18 thick	1
dropleaf, high-density particle (chip) board	1200 x 600 x 18 thick	1
400 mm piano hingeing	400	
1100 mm piano hingeing	1100	
35 mm countersunk screws	35	
piano hinge screws		
PVA adhesive		
paint		

SPECIAL TOOLS
jigsaw

TIME
One weekend

SKILL CLASS
Using an electric drill

❏ When you are using an electric drill, make sure that you don't overload the motor by applying too much pressure.

❏ Always make sure that you are drilling square to the work surface. A simple way to do this is to align the drill bit with a try square placed on its edge. If the hole has to be at right angles to the timber, such as for dowels, use a dowelling jig.

❏ The best method for absolute accuracy is to use a drill stand into which the drill is clamped – make sure that you get one which will take your drill.

The art of renovation is not limited to demolishing walls and raising the roof. Recycling should always be a priority and small-scale renovation projects offer great scope to the homemaker who likes to be creative.

NEW LOOKS FOR OLD

Many storage items lend themselves perfectly to renovation – so why not trade new looks for old?

When you're considering storage, don't make the mistake of thinking that the only way to improve the situation is to start again. Firstly, it is not always the most practical solution. Secondly, the constraints of budget rarely allow such luxury, and thirdly, in the interests of the planet, recycling should always be a priority.

A great many storage items have potentially exciting DIY possibilities. Take that battered tin trunk in the garage, for example, or that chest of drawers in the children's room that has seen better days. These are just some of the storage items lurking in your home which can easily and effectively be given a whole new lease of life.

In fact, once you start looking at old pieces of furniture you'll soon begin to realise that they simply don't make them like that any more! The high cost of materials and labour today has led to various manufacturing shortcuts and, despite the greater range offered, it has also led to the demise (in all but the most finely crafted furniture) of the cupboard that closes perfectly and the drawer that glides securely shut.

This is where recycling can be a real plus in so many ways.

Timber is a rapidly diminishing resource – why not help protect the world's dwindling forests by retaining existing timber pieces and revamping or renovating them? After all, one of the beauties of timber is its durability, and this alone is reason enough to roll up your sleeves and start being resourceful with what you already have.

Talking timber

The inherent beauty of timber, together with its practicality, has meant that it has always been our most basic building material. Throughout the years it has been fashioned into an enormous range of furniture, of which storage items are amongst the most common.

There are two ways to tackle the task of renovating timber storage pieces.
❏ Restoration – a process whereby the style of the piece is retained and its original finish restored.
❏ Revamping – whereby the original form of the item is retained but its finish and character is completely altered.

Why not renovate that old, wonderfully roomy wardrobe you inherited from your great aunt?

It may not fit in with the rest of your furnishings yet – but it will with a little work and decorating flair.

Workbench from Country Form

Above: A revamped industrial workbench used for storage and display
Right: This old, galvanised tin has been painted in an interesting way to give it a new lease of life

Restoring an object or an item of furniture is a classic form of recycling – and you can be experimental and creative at the same time. Why not stand back and reconsider your junk? You could be in for a pleasant surprise.

Left: This kitchen sideboard is excellent for storage and display of crockery and lends a rustic character to the room
Below: This second-hand shop bargain was restored by stripping back and staining (see Project 2, Storage cabinet)

Kitchen safe from Country Form

Country Form

Tin from Country Form

Clockwise from left:
A wooden cabinet restored to make the most of the woodgrain and positioned in the room to contrast with stained timber wall panelling; Old cane suitcases revived by spray-painting; An old kitchen safe as is, used as a cabinet for storing crockery

89

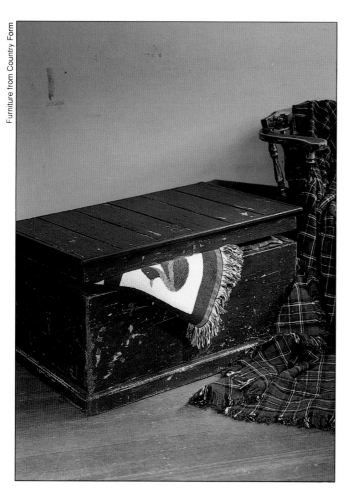

Furniture from Country Form

This timber chest has been painted green over the original paint and then rubbed back

Restoration

The revival of interest in old-style, antique or rustic 'cottage' furniture has meant that pieces such as country-style dressers and chests of drawers are becoming harder and harder to find. All the more reason then to 'rescue' one you stumble across, tucked away in a second-hand store (or your garage!).

There are two ways of

tackling the restoration of timber furniture: chemical stripping and sanding.

Chemical stripping

Because of the popularity of styles characterised by their rough-hewn or hand-crafted appearance, it is no longer necessary to achieve a flawless finish. This has made it a great deal easier for the DIY enthusiast. If your preference still tends towards a surface free of any traces of old paint, varnishes and stains, you may have to consider having the piece professionally stripped. This is the most effective way of getting back to the raw timber beneath; it is also the most practical way of dealing with larger pieces.

An acid bath is the most common method used and the item to be stripped is literally dipped into the stripping solution to remove accumulated surface coatings.

If you are working with a small item such as a timber chest, it is possible to strip the timber by hand. There are many commercial preparations available for these small-scale projects, but remember it is still a time-consuming and rather messy task. For this reason alone, it is important that you have some idea of the timber underneath before you go to the trouble of stripping it back. The craftsmanship and/or detailing of the piece itself will very often give you a clue. If you are in any doubt,

GREEN TIP

The safest and cheapest way of stripping paint is dry scraping, but it is slow work and only suitable for small areas. Use a two-bladed scraper, with a serrated and a plain blade, to speed things up.
❏ Score the surface lightly using the blade with the serrated edge.
❏ Remove the paint with the plain edge. Be careful not to scratch or score the wood.

test-sample a small area at the back or side before you commence work. The experts do not recommend that either timber veneers or particle (chip) board items be caustic-stripped.

Sanding

Sanding is the other method used to remove accumulated layers on timber surfaces. It is hard work but rewarding, and the effects will be most gratifying.

Start with a coarse grade of sandpaper graduating to finer grains as the sanding proceeds. Once the timber has been reduced to its (nearly) original state, the process of filling and smoothing must be tackled. Whatever finish you are to apply, be it natural or a painted one, it is important that the surface you are working on is as clean and free of imperfections as possible. Paint, wax or sealants will not adhere to dusty, damp or grimy surfaces.

SKILL CLASS
Paint stripping

It is not necessary to strip paint just because the surface has been painted a number of times. A good number of coats will provide more protection. On the other hand, badly blistered or peeling paint will need to be stripped. If this is confined to isolated areas, strip the faulty area only.
❏ Scraping paint is best done with a scraper used in conjunction with heat, either from a blowlamp or electric heat gun or stripper (both of which can be hired). Play the heat source back and forward across the surface so that the paint is melted without damaging the timber surface.
❏ Chemical paint stripping has a number of advantages. There is no likelihood of damaging the timber, particularly important if you intend to stain it afterwards. Chemical stripping has the added advantage that you can work close to glass panels, such as those in old doors.

If you are going to strip paint from metal, make sure the stripper is suitable first, as some chemicals may etch the surface of the metal. Always read the information on the tin before buying.

Apply the stripper and wait for the chemical action to take place. Remove the old paint with a scraper for wide surfaces and a shave hook for mouldings.

After stripping, clean down the surface with turpentine (white spirit) or white vinegar to neutralise any chemical residue.

If you are looking for a natural finish there is a number of options available. Before deciding, give some thought to where the piece will go. A soft beeswax finish, for example, is inappropriate for a child's room where it will be subjected to harsh wear and tear and possible spills. The glow of a beeswax finish is better suited to a storage item which will be on display perhaps in the living room or hallway.

For a harder wearing natural-look finish, there are various other options available. Restored timbers can be oiled, varnished or finished with one of the many commercially available timber sealants. You can opt for low or high sheen, remembering that a low-sheen finish tends to show fewer marks. Most major manufacturers of timber finishes also offer brochures with detailed advice on their products. Make sure you are fully informed about a product before using it.

Revamping

A smooth timber surface provides the ultimate bare canvas for a whole range of exciting decorative painted finishes which can completely alter the character of a piece and even totally disguise the fact that it is made of timber at all. These finishes are ideal for lower quality timbers and timber veneers, and old pieces which have been sanded back to the bare wood.

Painted finishes

Painted finishes are currently enjoying a renewed popularity. A standard painted finish is one where colour is applied to a surface to either create contrast or to help an item blend with the existing surroundings. A decorative painted finish, on the other hand, can achieve an extraordinary range of

special effects, adding another dimension to painted surfaces. Some even go as far as to deceive the eye altogether.

Apart from their good looks, the other appeal of painted finishes is that anyone can master them. The techniques are quite straightforward. Have all the necessary materials to hand and make sure you have practised the chosen technique on a piece of card or board before beginning work.

The decorative painted techniques you will find useful for revamping include dragging, rag-rolling, sponging and stippling.

Inside out

Whether you are restoring or revamping, don't forget the inside of that wardrobe or chest. Renovation applies equally to the interior of storage units, since very often existing space is ill-used or wasted altogether.

Built-in units are the prime candidates for the wardrobe crush, and the easiest way to resolve this is to revamp the interior with an internal racking system of some kind. The most effective of these are the wire basket systems which are available in various sizes and stack into a lightweight frame which is fitted into your existing cupboards or wardrobes. By flat-stacking items such as shoes, jumpers, underwear or towels, you'll free up space for hanging clothes or for storing taller items.

The same principle applies to your kitchen cabinets. You might not be in the market for a new kitchen, but by revamping the interior space you already have, you can sometimes double your existing storage potential. Look for units to make drawers more efficient, corner units for those hard-to-get-at and all too often

wasted areas, and racks to hang brooms and mops, thus freeing floor space in larger cupboards.

Simple additions too can make a world of difference. Adjustable shelving, for example. A cavernous cupboard will, in fact, contain less than a smaller, efficiently outfitted one. All you need is one of the many racking systems available, or a set of additional shelves precut to the desired size. This is an ideal weekend project for the home handyperson.

Specialist storage shops and kitchen specialists will provide a plethora of ideas and inspiration as will commercial storage outlets. The systems designed for use in offices, factories and shops can work just as effectively in your home and are very adaptable.

A long narrow cupboard with a blue duck stencil pattern on the door

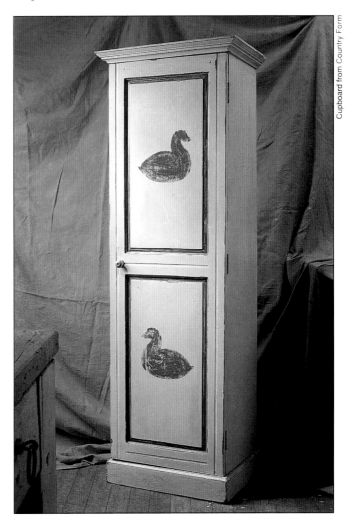

Cupboard from Country Form

SKILL CLASS
Painted finishes and special effects

Rag rolling

This is considered a basic technique. The effect is achieved by lifting some of the topcoat of colour from the basecoat (usually a lighter shade such as cream or a pastel) with a scrunched-up rag which has been soaked in solvent. A random textured effect is created as the lighter basecoat is revealed beneath the darker topcoat.

❏ Working on a clean, dry surface, apply the basecoat and allow it to dry. Apply the topcoat sparingly. It can be thinned to achieve the desired translucence.

❏ Using the solvent-dipped rag scrunched into a sausage shape, simply roll lightly across the freshly painted surface, removing as much of the topcoat as you can to create the desired effect. The action is rather like rolling pastry with a rolling pin.

❏ Work on a small area at a time and discard the rag for a fresh piece once it has become too loaded with paint. Work in strips for ease of application and uniformity.

❏ When dry, apply a coat of clear polyurethane for protection.

Dragging

This method is similar to that for rag rolling except that a wide brush is the tool used and this is literally dragged vertically over a wash of colour. The effect achieved is one of even texture. It is important to work with a topcoat that has been thinned down to the correct consistency. Oil-based paints are ideal because they don't dry as quickly and will not run.

❏ The project is best tackled by two people – one applying the strip of colour wash, the other dragging the brush down the wet surface.

❏ Work around vertical lines. Begin dragging where a natural vertical exists, for example, on a drawer or cupboard door.

❏ Clean the brush on a rag after every few dragging strokes and clean excess paint off the surface before it has a chance to accumulate and dry.

❏ A coat of clear polyurethane should be added for protection once the surface is completely dry.

Sponging and stippling

The techniques used for these effects are similar – one uses a sponge, the other a stiff, circular stippling brush – but the results are quite different. Sponging a colour onto a washed surface achieves a soft, country-style look, whereas stippling gives a more controlled effect. Both are ideal for medium-sized pieces such as a timber chest, a bedside table or corner cabinet. Polyurethane can be used to protect the finish.

Special effects

A close relation to painted finishes are the special effects which can be achieved with paint. Some of the most popular include stencilling, decoupage and trompe l'oeil finishes such as marbling. A little more

Sponging

precision is required with these techniques but the results can be sensational.

The sorts of items suitable for stencilling or some form of faux finish include smaller chests of drawers, timber trunks or chests, bedside cabinets, spice racks and so on. A variety of surfaces can be worked on: prepared timber, old or new, is ideal but metal and even glass can also be decorated this way.

Stencilling

Stencils are most often applied as a border and provide an ideal embellishment for ordinary storage items. You can customise a chest of drawers, for example, by adding a simple floral or geometric motif to the top and bottom of each drawer, or to the corners of cupboards on a bedside cabinet.

❏ When applying stencils, which you can either create yourself or buy ready-made in kit form, it is important to fix the stencil in place – masking tape is ideal – and apply the paint carefully to prevent it running underneath. The paint

Stencilling

needs to be just the right consistency. It is wise to experiment on a piece of old timber or card first.

❑ Apply the paint with a circular stencil brush, using a dabbing motion and working from the sides to the centre of the stencil. Make sure all gaps are filled with colour, leave to dry for a few minutes then carefully remove.

❑ Wipe any excess paint from the stencil before applying to the next area.

❑ If you plan to work with more than one colour, complete the first colour before adding the second or third.

If you are anxious to practise the technique before tackling a large item, try your hand on something small and easy to handle such as an old cutlery storage box, which is practical as well as pretty.

Decoupage

This is a delightful effect and one ideally suited to old travelling trunks, even old suitcases, toy boxes and so on. It's fun and easy to do and the results are very individual.

The technique involves cutting out motifs and gluing them to a surface to form either a pattern or picture. You can use just about any image that takes your fancy. A collection of old birthday cards, for example, would be a superb way to cheer up a toy box. You can opt for an all-over effect, or create a pattern inside the lid of a chest or just on the corners. Make sure the working surface is clean and dry before fixing the images with a strong paper glue or woodworking adhesive. The more coats the better, as the cut-outs then disappear into the thickness of the varnish and give a smooth surface (lightly sand between each coat).

Marbling

This is the method whereby timber (usually) is made to look like marble. The effects can be quite dramatic and wonderfully deceiving. It is an excellent device for an otherwise plain

built-in. As with all these techniques it is important to practise first so that you are reasonably familiar with the method before commencing work on a piece of furniture.

❑ To achieve a marbled effect, apply a series of vein-type patterns in dark shades over a light gloss basecoat to resemble the veiny effect of marble. Use a feather to create a marbled effect: apply vein-type lines with a deliberate wriggly movement so that the edges are slightly blurred. Use the lighter contrasting shade for larger veins, the darker for the smaller ones. You can also gently sponge vein lines to further soften the effect. Highlights can be added later.

 GREEN TIP
❑ **Wrap containers of leftover paint and turpentine (white spirit) before putting them in your bin.**
❑ **Choose water-based paints over oil-based whenever possible.**
❑ **Clean your brushes away from drains.**

Right: A stencilled tin chest

Stencilled bread bin and wall border

Project 2
Storage cabinet

French polishing is a skilled craft but, using proprietary solutions, it can be tackled by anyone with patience for that special piece of furniture that is beau but not faux.

STEP BY STEP

1 Remove broken latch and strip wood veneer off top panels.

2 Rub down timber with methylated spirits using steel wool to remove lacquer.

3 Sand all areas with medium-grade paper to remove minor blemishes. (Note that we wanted to retain an antique quality so not all marks were removed.)

4 Wipe down all surfaces with a damp cloth to remove any dust and loose particles.

Above left: Stripping wood veneer off top panel
Left: Using steel wool and methylated spirits to remove lacquer

5 Cut new wood veneer panels to size and iron onto surface or glue plain veneer panels with thixotropic contact adhesive (this will allow slight repositioning). Allow panels to adhere.

6 Apply stain to all areas of timber and new wood veneer and allow to dry overnight.

7 Prepare polishing pad by taking a wad of cotton wool (the size of an egg) and fitting it snugly into a piece of cloth. Create an egg-like shape and twist cloth tightly behind pad.

8 Dip cotton pad into proprietary French polish solution or shellac mixture and apply sparingly in long, sweeping movements. Cover entire area and allow to dry for at least ten minutes before applying second coat. As many coats as desired can be applied, depending upon the gloss finish preferred.

9 Select and attach new latch for cabinet door.

Above: Sanding down
Below: Wiping down with a damp cloth

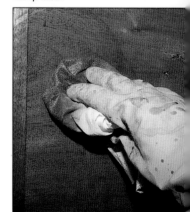

MATERIALS

ITEM	QUANTITY
sandpaper	4 sheets
steel wool	1 packet
methylated spirits	1 can
stain	1 bottle
cotton wool (medicinal type)	20 cm x 20 cm square
lint-free cloth	1 piece
iron-on wood veneer or plain veneer panels and thixotropic contact adhesive to glue	1 packet
proprietary French polish or shellac mixture (part shellac, part methylated spirits)	
new latch	

SPECIAL TOOLS
paint scraper
hammer and chisel (for hard-to-get-at places)

TIME
One weekend

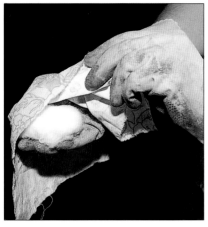

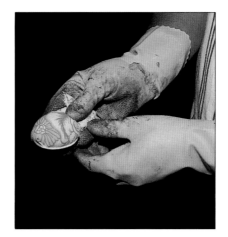

Preparing the polishing pad

Attaching the new latch

SKILL CLASS
Plugging a wall

To fix brackets or other items to a brick or masonry wall it is necessary to drill and plug the wall.

PLASTIC PLUG

PLASTIC PLUG

WOODEN PLUG

Plastic plugs are preferable for a screw fixing and a wooden plug 10 mm to 12 mm in diameter is suitable when a nail fixing is adopted. To select a plastic plug, first determine the gauge of the screw to be used and select a suitable one from the range of plugs usually available in hardware stores. The length of the screw should then be equal to the length of the plug plus the thickness of the item to be fixed.

To drill the wall you will require an electric drill, preferably a hammer drill, and a masonry bit the correct size to suit the plug. Mark the position of the plug on the wall with a cross, this will allow you to note

if the hole drifts off-centre. Place a mark on the masonry bit to indicate the depth of the hole equal to the length of the plug, plus about 10 mm.

Hold the drilling machine square to the face of the wall and commence drilling, first pressing lightly until the hole is seen to be started in the correct position. Press firmly on the drill to keep it cutting and not just rubbing in the hole (this will blunt the drill), and continue until the required depth is reached. Clear the waste dust from the hole and drive the plug into the hole until it is flush with the surface.

Hold the item to be fixed in position, enter the screw into the plug and tighten securely. Note: When fixing into soft plastered walls make sure that the plug is long enough to

penetrate sufficiently into the firm masonry below. Most importantly, beware of drilling into a water pipe or electric cable that could be bedded just below the surface.

Clever ways to recycle

Just because a piece of furniture looks old and shabby, it does not mean it has to stay this way or be discarded.

Old or antique furniture was usually made from quality timber and had a craftsman-like finish. Furniture makers of yesteryear had time to create well-designed pieces that were both functional and very stylish. These qualities alone make furniture recycling a worthwhile exercise.

Modern lifestyles and changing needs also demand a practical and often ingenious approach to home furnishing, especially where storage is concerned. When you are on a shoestring budget and have minimal or odd spaces to play with, you need to carefully assess how and where a piece of furniture will fit in. So find yourself some wonderful, old or down-at-heel treasure and start by analysing its potential.

Does it have 'good bones'? Look beyond the shabby outward appearance of an object for fresh new refurbishing ideas – for example, the basic bookcase. It may be covered with peeling paint, look uninteresting and, as it stands, certainly wouldn't fit in with a fresh, bright furnishing look. However, once it has been repaired, stripped and perhaps stained or repainted, there are many decorative and practical ways of using it.

You could fix it to a wall above floor level and make a set of feature shelves; use it as a bedhead or a room divider; fit it into or in front of a no-longer-used doorway to display a treasured collection; place it in the garage for extra tool storage; cut it into two lower units and seal it with paint to make an accessible pot-plant stand; or stand it in a hanging-only cupboard as storage for folded clothes and shoes. Your once-shabby bookcase can be transformed in even more subtle ways by covering it completely with wallpaper or fabric to blend in with the rest of your decor. The list goes on – and this was only a humble bookcase!

Once you enter into the spirit of searching for unwanted treasures, you will begin to see possibilities in just about any piece of furniture. But beware, it's important to recognise the strengths and weaknesses of your 'find'.

Thinking about buying and refurbishing an old cupboard? There are many real advantages in doing-up an old cupboard: good-quality timber and workmanship, spacious deep drawers and generous hanging capacity, for example. There are, alas, some potential drawbacks.

❑ Is the timber used heavily lacquered? This may be a real problem to strip and restain; in this case you may be forced to paint over the lacquer.

❑ Is it solid and free of insect attack? Look for tell-tale small holes and piles of sawdust. Professional fumigation may be required, or treatment with woodworm fluid and polish to restore the surface.

❑ Does it have door hinges and locks? These can be replaced but often not cheaply. Quality brass fittings can be expensive at retail outlets, so shop around. Brass restoration experts often have oddments available, and are well worth visiting.

❑ Do the drawers run smoothly? You may need to

QUICK-FIX PROJECT
Tin chest
A rummage in the garden shed revealed this charming, well-shaped old tin trunk patiently awaiting its chance for a new life. It was not rusty and only needed a sanding back to prepare it for a coat of paint. Undercoat and paint suitable for painting metal were used, and the pattern was created using a commercial stencil and spray paints. Most commercial stencils have simple-to-follow instructions on the packaging. When using spray paints to stencil, instead of brushes, use a piece of cardboard as a screen to prevent excess spray paint escaping and drifting, to land where it's not needed!

replace the drawer runners or use sandpaper to smooth off damp-swollen timber.

❏ Can you get the cupboard through the door when moving it to its new address? If the tape measure says this is not to be, is it possible to unscrew parts of the cupboard and reassemble it once moved?

Visit auctions, fairs, church bazaars and garage sales. Check the newspaper often for auctions of office furniture (you'll be surprised by the variety *and*

the bargains!). Two second-hand identical filing cabinets, perhaps repainted then set apart by about 1.5 m with a wide softwood table top resting across the tops, make a fine desk. If no old table top is available, consider buying a new one from contemporary knockdown furniture suppliers.

Remember that storage opportunities often present themselves in obscure and unpredictable ways. To help you with your treasure hunt, consider how different pieces of furniture can be adapted.

❏ Tables may have legs shortened to become casual occasional tables. They are perfect for stencilling or covering with fabric, and are a natural for a simple paint-over.

❏ Strongly woven baskets provide all sorts of storage possibilities: paint them, line them with fabric, stack lidded baskets, or use them in rows on open shelves for kitchen storage. Flat baskets with rims can become excellent trays. Old cane laundry baskets make ideal toy storage and can easily become a decorative feature when cleverly coloured. A deep, strongly woven basket with handles can be both stylish and practical when filled with wood ready for an open fire. Leave it outside under shelter for wood storage all year round, and carry it in when the weather sends smoke signals.

❏ Old luggage can provide

QUICK-FIX PROJECT
Creative wine storage
Out-of-use fireplaces can provide an ideal place for wine storage. Fireplaces are cool, in a fixed and unobtrusive spot, and easily accessible. To create your own wine storage area, stack up hexagonal terracotta drainage pipes to fit within the fireplace opening, being sure to have your lowest layer of pipes spread completely across the base of the hearth – this will prevent the pipes from 'spreading' once they become heavier with wine bottles.

decorative storage. Paint tin trunks, restain old leather luggage or refurbish a truly authentic hat-box.

❏ Boxes of all sorts and sizes can become amusing and talked-about storage containers (or articles). Old wooden ammunition boxes, biscuit tins, sturdy paper cartons and slatted pine fruit boxes can be painted or decoupaged, and even shoe boxes made from very firm cardboard can be covered with fabric to become a practical and attractive storage container.

❏ Picture frames can be used as notice-board surrounds.

❏ Small wooden safety ladders, providing they have a flat top, can become ideal bedside tables. Single-sided old ladders

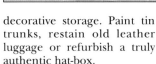

QUICK-FIX PROJECT
Brass luggage rack
A brass railway carriage luggage rack attached to the bathroom wall is an unexpected storage fitting. Replacing books with attractively folded towels is an option if long visits to the bathroom need to be discouraged!

with frame and rungs of dowel can become discussion pieces when used as towel racks in a kitchen – lean them against a wall and you instantly have storage for six or so towels.

❏ Storage is an essential element in any household, but don't be bogged down by the expected or expensive solutions. The whimsical, achievable, recycled, amusing and unexpected alternatives are just waiting to be discovered.

Finishing Touches

That great second-hand find isn't finished until you've added the decorative touches. If it's flair or dash you want, fittings like knobs and latches can really add that 'je ne sais quoi' to an otherwise quite ordinary piece.

A 'finishing touch' is quite literally that – whether you add bold red plastic knobs to a chest of drawers in a brightly coloured children's room, or install a very classy brass latch on a restored, natural-finish timber chest.

Decorative fittings are many-splendoured things and come in a vast range of different styles, colours and textures. Naturally, the style you choose will reflect the character of the piece itself, or even a room's general theme, personality or colour scheme. A modern piece often demands a modern treatment – for example, a smooth rounded style with no sharp edges, made from metal or plastic. This type of fitting is easy to clean and designed for safety.

A country-style piece often suits the more textured look of wood grain, which can be clear-stained or lightly oiled or waxed. You may decide to paint a wooden knob to match the overall finish of a piece, or even hand-paint or stencil on a design for that extra-special treatment.

If your piece is a genuine antique, you should enhance its distinctive style and character by selecting the appropriate fittings.

A selection of brass and chrome door knobs and latches

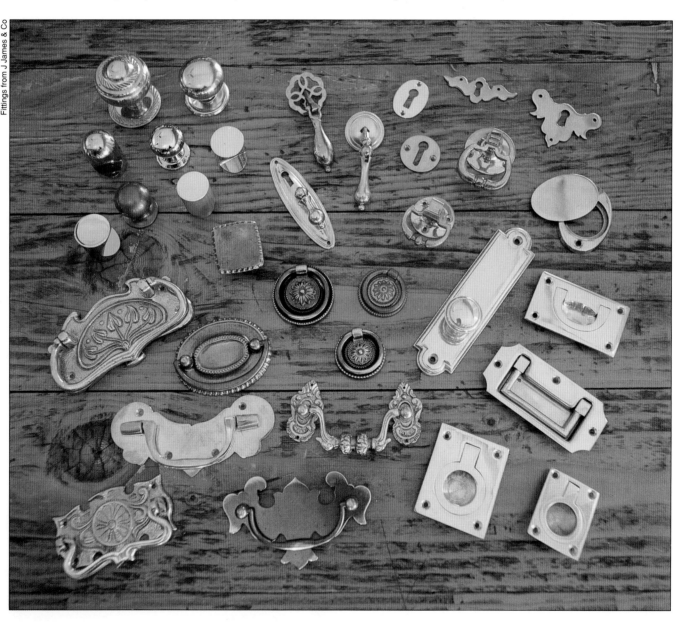

Fittings from J James & Co

NAILS

For accurate, well-finished work, nails alone do not normally make a strong enough joint. However, if the nails are angled in opposition to each other, a reasonable joint can be made. When used in conjunction with one of the modern woodworking adhesives, a very strong joint can be achieved.

When nailing two pieces of wood together, nail the smaller to the larger. Avoid nailing into hardwoods altogether: if you must, drill a pilot hole first, slightly smaller than the shank of the nail.

Removing nails

The claw hammer is used to remove partially driven nails. To avoid damaging the surface of the wood, place a small offcut under the hammer head before you start levering. Extract nails with a number of pulls rather than trying to do the job in one.

Use pincers to remove small nails and pins which are difficult to grip with the claw hammer, (e.g. nail without a head).

If a nail is impossible to remove, punch it below the surface of the wood and use filler to cover the hole, or carefully chip away some of the wood around the head until you can get a grip on the nail head with a pair of pincers.

Using a hammer

Take a firm grip at the end of the handle and form your arm into a right-angle, looking straight down on the work as you do so. Start the nail by tapping it lightly, keeping your wrist controlled but flexible and letting the hammer head do the work. Increase the power of your stroke slightly as the nail goes in but at no time let your arm waver – if you do, you will either miss or bend the nail. On well-finished work, remember not to drive nails right in – leave a bit protruding for the hammer and nail punch to finish off.

Use nails about 3 times as long as the workpiece. Always nail smaller to larger.

On rough work, clench nailed joints are much stronger.

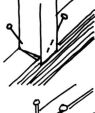

Skew-nailing is one of the best ways of securing a housing joint.

When nailing into end-grain, drive in nails at opposing angles.

Driving more than one nail along the same grain line risks splitting the wood.

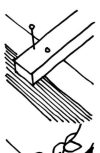

Nail small battens overlength to avoid splitting the ends. Saw or plane off the excess.

Small nails can be positioned with the aid of a cardboard holder.

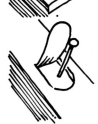

Secret nailing. Prise up a sliver of timber with a chisel. Glue down after nailing.

SCREWS
Drilling screw holes

All screws must have pilot holes made before they can be driven home. For screws smaller than No. 6 gauge (3.5 mm) into softwood, make these with a bradawl. Drive it into the wood with its chisel point across the grain, to avoid splitting.

Screws larger than No. 6 gauge into hardwood and screws into softwood need two holes – one for the thread (the pilot hole) and one for the shank (the clearance hole). These must be made with a drill and bit.

When drilling pilot holes, mark the required depth on the drill bit with a piece of masking tape. This will tell you when to stop and cannot damage the workpiece should you overdrill.

As with nailing, where two pieces of wood are to be fixed together, screw the smaller to the larger. Drill the clearance hole right through the smaller piece so it is pulled down tight as the screw is driven home. If the clearance hole goes only part of the way through you will find it very hard to pull the top piece of wood down tight and may risk breaking or damaging the screw. Brute force should never be used – it indicates that either the thread hole or the shank hole is too small.

Driving screws

Always make sure that the tip of your screwdriver is in good condition and that it fits exactly into the slot in the screw head. A blade which is too narrow or rounded damages the slot, while too wide a blade damages the wood as the screw goes in.

As a time-saving alternative to the conventional screwdriver, a pump-action screwdriver works by converting downward movement of the sliding handle into rotation of the tip. So, simply by pushing hard, the screw is driven very quickly in or out of the wood (depending on the setting of the ratchet). Take extra care when using a pump-action screwdriver that it does not slip and cause you an injury.

Countersinking

Countersinking is normally the easiest way of recessing screw heads flush with, or below the surface of the wood. The recess is made with a countersink bit after the clearance hole has been drilled, to the same depth as the countersunk screw head. Take particular care if you are countersinking with a power drill or the recess may accidentally become too large.

For some screw sizes, special bits are available to drill the thread hole, shank hole and countersink recess in one operation. Care should be taken, however, as they break easily.

Common types and uses

Countersunk screw: Used for general woodwork. The head sinks in flush with or slightly below the wood surface.

Crosshead screw: Used for general woodwork, but needs a special screwdriver which does not slip from the head.

Countersunk roundhead (raised head): Used for fixing door-handle plates and other decorative fittings with countersunk holes. The head is designed to be seen.

Roundhead screw: Used for fixing hardware fittings without countersunk holes.

Mirror (dome) screw: Used for fixing mirrors and bathroom fittings. The chromed cap threads into the screw head to hide the screw. Do not over-tighten.

Coach (or hexagon) head screw: Used for fixing heavy constructions together and heavy equipment to timbers. Tighten with a spanner.

Invisible (dowel) screw: Used for invisible joining of two pieces of timber.

Self-tapping (panel) screw: Used for fixing thin sheets of metal and plastic. Cuts its own thread as it is screwed in. Various types of head are available.

Particle (chip) board screw: Used for securing particle (chip) board and its derivatives.

Shelve it, stack it, stow it, store it! Shelving is one of the easiest and most versatile ways of dealing with domestic clutter. Place items on view or design a system to hide them away.

SHELVING IT

Good storage, as much as having good installations to handle it, is a state of mind and relates to a very human desire to put things away or hoard. Before choosing a suitable storage system for your lifestyle, there are a couple of points you should consider.

❑ Do you want to conceal things or display them? Most household items are well hidden away in cupboards and nooks, whereas some items, like collectables or ornaments, are possessions you would like to see.

❑ How often will you be using the stored items? Many seasonal items such as summer/winter clothes, blankets and eiderdowns, fans, portable heaters and Christmas decorations are likely to be used only at a certain time of the year.

Items used more frequently include tools, hobby equipment and clothes.

Things used daily must be stored in a handy place. These include cooking equipment, crockery, cutlery and glassware, daily clothes and shoes, toys, cleaning materials, study materials, videos, tapes, records and CDs, linen and so on. Books should be stored where they are easily accessible and away from any damp.

Most household items fit best in square and rectangular storage systems. Make sure you are happy and comfortable with the way your system works.

Shelving

The possibilities in shelving are enormous. Not only can you put objects on top of shelves but, with rails and hooks, the underside can also be utilised.

One of the most versatile installations is adjustable shelving for storage of just about anything. This type of shelving can cover a whole wall, or just a section of a wall. It can be fixed to timber-framed or brick walls.

Bookcases

Bookcases are a special form of shelving, and are always a point of interest in the home. Like shelving, bookcases come in various styles. To define where shelving stops and bookcases start is perhaps best done by examining what is on the shelves.

Alcoves

Look at wasted corners around the house. A popular storage idea for years has been to fit out the space between projections such as fireplaces and piers. The possibilities are endless. One such solution is to convert an alcove into two-tier hanging space in a bedroom, thus relieving the pressure on your everyday wardrobe. See Project 3 (Framing up an alcove).

In other rooms alcoves can house shelving for books or treasures; they can include built-in loudspeakers which otherwise take up floor or shelf space; they can

Above: Bookshelves in the television/reading room with a pull-out swivel television, a shelf underneath for the VCR and cupboard doors that open out with pull-out trays for storage of video tapes. Glass cupboard doors protect a collection of old, rare books
Right: High-tech combination of desk and shelves with rubber caps that 'grab' the wall

FREEDOM

Shelving is the staple of the storage system – it comes in all shapes, sizes and styles.

Clockwise from bottom left: Compact study/work area features a desk with pull-out leaf and a cupboard above for storage of stationery and books; Adjustable shelves in a kitchen cupboard with alcove shelves for display; Shelf unit used as a room divider; Shelf built in over a doorway for convenient storage of a television and VCR; Decorative wooden wall shelves for toiletries

Assess what you want in terms of materials for shelves and consider how you will attach them to the wall.

101

Wardrobes and built-ins

These days wardrobes are generally built-in, with sliding doors which include a full height mirror. These built-ins are an integral part of the house.

The fit-out of wardrobes has gone beyond a few drawers, some hanging space and shelves. Now wardrobe companies will supply a whole system that includes ample drawers, shelves and hanging space, often on several levels. Manufacturers also include wire basket storage systems which may be wheeled or fixed and are usually stackable; shoe storage; pull-out extra towel rails; tie and belt racks. Normally, the wardrobe will be internally lit, with an automatic switch, and may also include a dressing table-cum-mirror arrangement. The whole unit may even be built across the entrance to an otherwise poky en-suite or dressing room. Many are built of predrilled vertical members,

allowing the fittings to be changed to an infinite number of combinations as needs change, or as you accumulate more possessions.

Cabinets and cupboards

The ultimate in the furniture maker's art is that of attractive display cabinets. Often cabinets do not make best use of the space they occupy, but then that is not their primary function.

Cabinets would be amongst the most expensive forms of storage in that often solid wood is used, great detail in workmanship is displayed, and areas of glass, also expensive, abound. The level of finish is usually much better than that of the average built-in, with the fit of doors and attention to detail superior.

Cabinets are most often chosen to store and display collections of china, porcelain, art objects, crystal, and just about anything else of value. Because of the display aspect of cabinets, the contents are normally not crammed in as in other storage units.

incorporate a small bar refrigerator, or a wine rack, or wood storage for the fireplace, or they can be converted into a linen cupboard.

Alcoves are common in many rooms, especially in older homes. They can be considered as the inside space of a cabinet or cupboard, ready to be fitted out in whatever manner is appropriate for your storage needs. It is a simple matter to mount a series of shelves in the space, in any of the methods described elsewhere in this book. This makes ideal storage for ornaments, books, games, pottery – even an open bar. It is also possible to include glass shelving for display purposes. The alcove may also have glass doors on its front face for protection against dust.

An alcove can simply have a door or doors fitted to the front to allow upright storage of vacuum cleaners, brooms, hanging clothes, or the like. Some converted alcoves have sophisticated architectural storage features, incorporating room themes such as arches, window

designs, corbelling or other features.

The trick with fitting out any alcove or similar area is to avoid building a second hefty frame which will eat up potential storage space. Thin jambs on either side, or sleek thin brackets should be sufficient.

It is important that the weight on the shelves can be adequately supported by the support or bracketing provided. The walls should be sound enough to take screws into timber studs, or to be plugged for fixing to masonry or plastered walls. Another problem, especially in older homes, is that of working around ornate skirtings and cornices. There may even be picture rails, dado panels, rails and vents that have to be taken into account. However, with care, you can work around all these features without destroying them (perhaps they could even be extended through the alcove fit-out as a continuation of the room's ornamentation).

IKEA

SKILL CLASS
Easy ways to go up the wall

A number of materials can be used for shelving. Our table on types of shelving provides a list of those in common use, with a suggested maximum span or bracket spacing for average loading.

SHELF (STAYED) BRACKETS

For supporting heavy loads, sometimes called gallows brackets. Welded steel brackets for shelving up to 300 mm wide can be purchased ready-made, or they can be constructed from timber to suit shelving up to any reasonable width (say 600 mm).

❏ To fix brackets to the wall, select a suitable spacing so as not to exceed the maximum span for the type of shelving to be used (see table).

❏ Strike a level line at the required height of the shelf.

❏ For timber-framed structures, brackets must be fastened to a solid stud using 12- or 14-gauge screws; on brick or masonry walls, drill and plug the wall for a screw fixing or, alternatively, a suitable masonry bolt will provide even more secure fixing for very heavy loads.

SHELF SUPPORTS

These are a simple method of providing support for adjustable shelving within a cabinet or wall unit. A series of holes to fit the pin of the shelf support, usually 5 mm to 6.5 mm in diameter, are drilled into the side members. Supports of metal, or coloured or clear plastic come in a variety of patterns. It is essential that all of the holes are drilled at the same height within the unit. On a piece of firm timber, approximately 40 mm x 10 mm, mark out and drill the holes at the required spacing. Clamp this jig to the side members where holes are required, keeping the bottom to a fixed line marked on each member. Drill the holes to the depth required, using a depth-stop on the drill bit.

SHELF BRACKETS

For average loads. Available in galvanised steel or pressed metal in a variety of sizes to suit shelving up to 300 mm wide of solid timber, plywood or particle (chip) board. Again, strike a level line to indicate the height of the shelf and fix the brackets to this line with 10- or 12-gauge screws.

TIMBER BATTENS/CLEATS

Where the end of a shelf butts up to a side wall, a timber batten/cleat can provide adequate support.

❏ Cut the batten/cleat from approximately 50 mm x 25 mm DAR (PAR) timber and mark a level line at the height of the shelf.

❏ Drill and plug the wall and secure the batten/cleat with 10- or 12-gauge screws.

METAL STANDARDS AND BRACKETS

Slotted metal uprights and adjustable brackets provide adjustable shelving for average loads. Shelving is usually of 16 mm melamine-faced particle (chip) board or MDF in a variety of colours and widths from 150 mm to 300 mm. The shelves can also be of glass.

❏ To set up the system, select a suitable spacing for the uprights and locate secure fixing points on the wall. Strike a vertical line at each position and mark lightly. Mark the height to the bottom of the first upright and from this point level across and mark a point for the next and any subsequent ones. Using suitable screws, often provided with the system, fix the uprights to the wall at the positions marked.

❏ The brackets can now be fixed in the desired positions by means of two lugs which engage into the slots in the uprights.

LADDER BRACKET

The ladder bracket is a convenient way of giving support to multiple shelving where fixing points for other types of brackets or battens/cleats are not available. The brackets can be made to any depth up to 450 mm for the storage of linen and so on, or 600 mm if part of the space is to be used for the hanging of clothes. Brackets can be made from 50 mm x 25 mm DAR (PAR) timber, and consist of uprights and intermediate rails spaced as required for the shelving. They are preferably dowelled together, and need only be nailed to the side walls as a complete unit at, say, four or five fixing points wherever they can be found.

TYPES OF SHELVING		
Material	Finished thickness (mm)	Maximum span (mm)
solid dressed (planed) timber	19	900
solid dressed (planed) timber	31	1350
structural plywood	17	900
particle (chip) board	18	700
melamine-faced particle (chip) board	16	600
sheet glass		

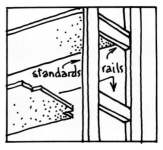

LADDER BRACKET (for multiple shelving)

SLOTTED STANDARD (with adjustable brackets)

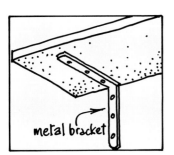

METAL BRACKET
(galvanised steel or pressed metal types)

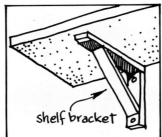

SHELF BRACKET
(for heavy loading timber or metal types)

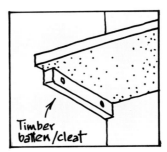

TIMBER BATTEN/CLEAT
(metal standards and brackets)

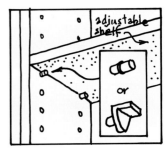

SHELF SUPPORT
(for adjustable shelving within units)

Project 3

TT

Framing up an alcove

Alcoves offer the perfect opportunity to make the most of otherwise small and cramped spaces.

This particular project is in a bedroom, where a solitary alcove originally made the room appear strangely offset. The space was used as additional hanging space for good clothes on two levels, as well as shoe and dress jewellery storage. The top hanging level is for seasonal or infrequently used clothes, and the lower provides ready access for more popular items. The idea was also to use two standard off-the-shelf doors to enclose the area.

STEP BY STEP

1 Firstly, measure up the space accurately so that you can draw a plan of the project. In this case, the alcove is 1380 mm wide, by a total of 2985 mm high. The total available depth is 440 mm. The alcove has an ornate cornice and an older style but plain 170 mm-high timber skirting. The floor is carpeted.

2 The fitting-out involves fixing two doors to jambs, and the installation of two rail supports to carry the two levels of clothing rails at 1740 mm and 2790 mm from the floor.

Cut the two side frames (jambs) to size (in this case, standard 75 mm x 25 mm stock without a rebate was used). The thickness of the jamb is the same as the bottom skirting, so will sit on top. The jambs must be notched to a depth of 25 mm between 1500 mm and 1570 mm, and between 2550 mm and 2620 mm from the base to house the front rail supports. When the jambs are completed, they can be screwed to plugged walls or, if timber studs, to the timber frame.

3 To plug the wall, drill holes about 10 mm diameter with a tungsten-carbide tipped masonry bit in a hammer drill set on slow speed and hammer action. They should be in the middle of the jambs so that the plug is covered by the jamb. Smaller plugs can be used for finer work. Drive a soft piece of timber into each hole – then the nails or screws can be driven

in. This is a traditional method of plugging. Heavy-duty wall plugs or frame fixings (screws with integral plugs) can also be used and don't require such a large drill.

4 When secure, cut the two front rails of 75 mm x 25 mm timber to length and nail to the housings in the jambs. After marking with a spirit level, nail a similar pair at the same height to the rear wall, once again plugging the wall if necessary. This provides the basic structure for the storage space.

5 Cut 16 mm plastic-covered steel rods to length 1400 mm to fit between the front face of the rail support and the rear wall (hold in place using simple saddle clips). Purpose-made brass or other rail holders can also be used if preferred. Both rails are spaced with their centres at 295 mm from the side walls.

6 Lay a 1380 mm x 240 mm piece of 19 mm particle (chip) board across the skirtings to act as a shoe shelf. This should be painted with an undercoat and

MATERIALS

ITEM	DIMENSIONS (mm)	QUANTITY
softwood (pine or similar)	75 x 25	2 lengths (3.0 m), 4 lengths (1.5 m)
softwood (pine or similar)	50 x 25	1 length (1.5 m)
particle (chip) board	1500 x 240 x 19 thick 1500 x 650 x 15 thick	1 length 1 length
hollow core doors	size to fit	2
plastic-covered steel rod or similar	16 diameter	4 (400 mm)
saddle clips		8
butt hinges	75	3 per door
knobs		2
roller catches		2
aluminium strips	1.5 x 25 (600)	3 lengths
rubber doorstops		6
nails, screws and wall fixings as necessary		
undercoat and oil-based paint to finish		

SPECIAL TOOLS
hammer drill
jigsaw

TIME
Two weekends

finished with two coats of oil-based paint.

7 The doors now need to be fitted, one at a time. Butt hinges give the required clearance when the leaves are parallel and the door closed and therefore need to be let into the door and jamb. To fit the butt hinges to the doors, mark the position of the hinges on each door edge, one 150 mm from the top, one 200 mm from the bottom and one in the middle. Use a sharp chisel to remove a small amount of timber – just enough to allow the hinge flap to sit neat and flush in the door edge – then insert two screws for each hinge. It is best to predrill slightly with a smaller diameter drill bit before driving in the screws.

8 Support each door on small wedges to give the correct clearance over the carpeted floor, and mark in the position of the hinges on the jamb. Chisel out enough of the jamb to allow the hinge flap to fit flush as well, then hold the door in place and mark and drill the screw holes to get the screws started. Hang the door by inserting a screw, top and bottom. Before putting in all screws, make sure that the door closes properly and is correctly aligned. If not, make adjustments until it is right, using an adjacent screw hole.

Repeat this procedure for the other door. When both doors have been fitted, check that they have sufficient clearance, and that the meeting of the two door edges is parallel and neat. The meeting stiles may need to be slightly bevelled to the rear if the fit is close, to allow the doors to shut. When all is well, insert the remaining screws in both doors. Fit the decorative knobs of your choice to the doors.

Fit two catches and keepers to the central rail support and to each door and block them out so that the doors will fit flush across their face.

9 The doors are only 2350 mm high, thus leaving a gap above of about 630 mm, which is filled using a sheet of 15 mm particle (chip) board. But first fix a small batten/cleat of 50 mm x 25 mm timber to the door jambs above each door by screwing in place, 15 mm in from the front.

The particle (chip) board must be cut to suit the cornice profile. A handy tool for this job is a profile gauge. Otherwise, make a cardboard template to suit the cornice and then transpose this onto the two top corners of the particle (chip) board as a cutting guide.

10 When ready, nail or screw the particle (chip) board to the battens/cleats and finish flush with the jamb. Punch and fill any nail holes, then seal and undercoat using oil-based paints to stop the grain rising. Finish the doors similarly with an oil-based undercoat and top coats.

11 All remaining surfaces should be prepared for painting by lightly sanding and dusting down before the interior is painted out. For a finishing touch, a wallpaper strip was added around the room just under the cornice, thus marrying the infilled alcove to the rest of the room.

12 For storage of earrings, screw three 600 mm-long rails of 25 mm x 1.5 mm aluminium to the inside face of one of the doors, using rubber doorstops as spacers. (See Quick-fix project on page 139.)

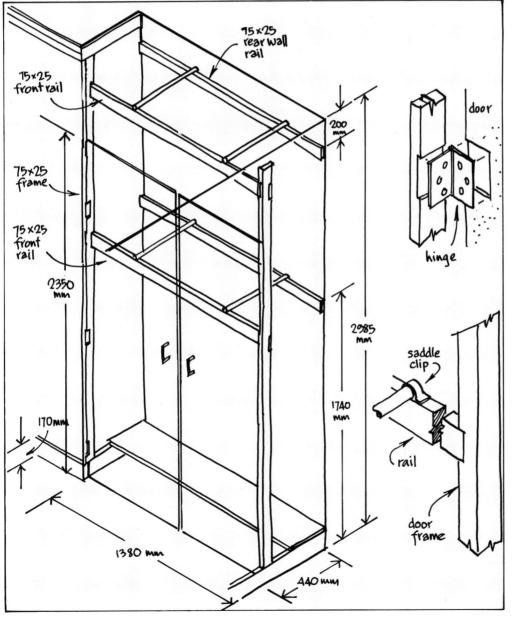

The living room is usually the room most on show to visitors – it is, in many ways, your indoor home entertainment area. Make your storage system visually appealing, easily accessible and compatible with your lifestyle.

LIVING SPACES

Your furniture and especially your storage units should be as visually appealing as possible, yet still comfortable and user-friendly.

To establish your storage needs, consider who will be using the room and what its main function will be. Do you want permanently fixed storage or do you want to rearrange the room from time to time? Is there a natural focus in the room? Could a collection of objects or a large piece of furniture – such as a bookcase, cabinet or wall unit – be incorporated to display a prized collection? Is the living area mainly a family room?

Also consider how well any new storage units will fit into your living room. Ask yourself:
❑ Is it the right size?
❑ Does it harmonise with other elements in the room? Functional furniture, such as the television and stereo system, is best kept behind closed doors in a unit or cabinet, or at least in a part of the room where it will be relatively safe from the children's occasional rough and tumble. Treasured items, on the other hand, should be on display. Your antiques, for example, could be a focal point in a glass-fronted cabinet or Georgian chest-on-chest. Books are classic adornments and may range from your toddler's picture books to large-format coffee table books.

The three basic types of

storage to choose from are freestanding, movable furniture (sideboards, chest, cabinets, bookcases and industrial shelving); built-in shelves and cupboards; and modular units. Modular units are specifically designed to fit flush against the wall or to form a solid dividing unit. Keep the finish simple and continue any moulding of baseboards across the top and bottom of new fittings to maintain a regular appearance in the room. A wall unit is certainly a neat solution for both storage and display. In large rooms, a modular unit could be freestanding; in a townhouse, built-in shelving and cupboards can exploit otherwise wasted space.

The most practical style of shelving unit has cupboards below and a deep shelf at waist height. The cupboards could be deep enough to hold a filing cabinet if the room doubles as a study, and a television set could be fitted on a tray for easy viewing.

Adjustable shelving is an added benefit if you have lots of books and collectables. Avoid placing bookshelves near fireplaces or in direct sunlight. Valuable books should be protected behind glass.

Glass shelving is ideal for contemporary homes or where light is at a premium.

Records, cassettes and CDs need support at regular intervals. For convenience, short but deep stackable cubes are perfect.

Clockwise from bottom left (page 106):
Shelves built into a staircase wall; Built-in cupboards with glass doors for display and storage of ornaments, glass and silverware; Portable wine storage next to an ornamental fireplace

Clockwise from right: High-tech portable entertainment centre; Wooden storage unit; Freestanding unit for multipurpose storage; Adjustable bookshelves

Modularack

FREEDOM

FREEDOM

FREEDOM

FREEDOM

Living room, lounge, parlour, salon, drawing room, front room – the variety of names given to living rooms reflects a variety of uses. Generally, they can be divided into two distinct types of room: a formal setting for use only when entertaining, and the more relaxed centre for family life.

Entertainment centre

This modular stereo and home entertainment centre can easily be expanded or adapted to suit your needs. It has been cleverly designed to accommodate equipment as well as an extensive collection of CDs, records, videos and cassettes.

The project consists of three units which have a total width of just over 1500 mm. Although the centre is modular, it is also relatively low level, and a single top and kickboard draws all three units together.

The centre is built on a slight plinth, and involves a minimum of carpentry complications. Commercial connection fittings have been used – these are strong and save the otherwise extensive dowelling and gluing procedures; they have the added benefit of being easy to dismantle. The main cabinet is built of veneered particle (chip) board, edge-veneered on the front, with solid cabinet timber drawer fronts, kickboard and top edging.

Note: Cabinet timber refers to any fine-quality, dressed (planed) furniture-grade timber of your choice.

STEP BY STEP

Buy all the materials, and have them ready for use. Treat the veneered board with care to avoid damage. If possible, make the total number of units you require at once. This will make the process much faster as you can set up a mini production line.

1 Mark out the sides of the cabinet on the particle (chip) board sheets. The depth of all sides, bottoms, shelves and the top is 400 mm, so cut the particle (chip) board into 400 mm-wide strips for convenience. The sides are 825 mm high. Cut the particle (chip) board sheets with a circular saw for the best results. When cutting with a circular saw, put the best side face down, as the saw 'cuts up' and gives a very clean edge on the underside. To guide the saw, clamp a straightedge on the panel to be cut, allowing for the distance between the saw base edge and the blade. Use scraps of softwood to protect the board when clamping. Once all the sheets have been cut, cut a small 40 mm deep x 70 mm notch out of the bottom front of each panel to later accommodate the kickboard.

2 Before proceeding any further, mark on the inside cabinet the position of the shelves and the tops of the shelf supports. The basic positions of the spacing used in this project are (from the top):

19 mm – underside of top frame
170 mm – top of top shelf
189 mm – underside of top shelf, shelf support
350 mm – top of middle shelf
369 mm – underside of middle shelf, shelf support
731 mm – top of bottom shelf
750 mm – underside of bottom shelf
825 mm – base of side

The tops of the drawer guides can also be marked where applicable. For example, in the unit with just one middle drawer, mark the top of the guide at 120 mm above the

MATERIALS

Quantities are for building three units. This can be varied for more or less units. This project was made using 19 mm particle (chip) board but 16 mm thick board can also be used with the necessary adjustments to dimensions.

ITEM	DIMENSIONS (mm)	QUANTITY
hardwood-veneered particle (chip) board – cabinet	1220 x 2440 x 19	2 sheets
plywood – backs and drawer bottoms	1220 x 2440 x 3	1 sheet
cabinet timber DAR (PAR) – drawer fronts for large drawers	200 x 25	1 length (1 m)
cabinet timber DAR (PAR) – front top member of cabinet, kickboard and drawer fronts for small drawers	100 x 25	2 lengths (1.5 m) 1 length (2.1 m)
cabinet timber DAR (PAR) – rear top of cabinet	75 x 25	1 length (1.5 m)
cabinet timber DAR (PAR) – edging of the top	25 x 25	1 length (1.8 m) 2 lengths (0.6 m)
cabinet timber DAR (PAR) – large drawer sides and backs	150 x 19	1 length (2.7 m)
cabinet timber DAR (PAR) – small drawer sides and backs	75 x 19	1 length (2.4 m)
cabinet timber DAR (PAR) – drawer guides	12 x 25	2 lengths (2.4 m)
cabinet timber glazing bead – optional	12 x 19	2 lengths (3.6 m)
cabinet timber DAR (PAR) – shelf battens/cleats	12 x 12	1 length (2.4 m)
iron-on veneer to suit		8 m
connection fittings		24 in total (8 per unit)
double-headed connecting screws		8
handles to suit		6
record dividers (optional)		
stain and polyurethane finish as required		

SPECIAL TOOLS
This project could be built using hand tools, but power tools will save you a lot of time.
circular saw (with a fine-cutting tungsten-carbide tip blade)
router
jigsaw
power drill
sash cramps (optional)

TIME
Three or four weekends, depending on finish

Ironing on veneer

Drawer ready to be assembled

Fixing top drawer on guides

shelf immediately below it. This gives a 1 mm clearance between the drawer bottom and the shelf.

3 Cut to length the shelf supports and drawer guides and fix in place. The shelf supports in this case were simply 12 mm x 12 mm cabinet timber strips cut to 350 mm (that is, 50 mm short of the front) and at 45°, and glued and nailed in place. An alternative would be to drill holes and use plastic or metal shelf supports instead. If the shelves were to be housed in the sides, the housings should be routed or cut out to a depth of 5 mm at this stage.

4 The drawer guides are 19 mm x 12 mm cabinet timber cut to 385 mm, and must be accurately glued and nailed (or screwed) to the sides. (You may prefer to fit the drawer guides when the drawers are ready, to double-check that the position is right.)

5 Mark and cut out the bottom shelf, 400 mm deep by 462 mm wide. When finished this will give a total width of 500 mm for the whole unit.

6 Mark and cut rear and front top members of cabinet from

75 mm x 25 mm and 100 mm x 25 mm cabinet timber. These are also 462 mm long.

7 The bottom shelf and the two top framing members can be fixed to each side using connection fittings. These consist of male and female blocks which are screwed to the underside of the horizontal members and the corresponding position on the sides. When brought together, the coarse joining screw draws the two pieces tightly together. In all, eight connectors are needed for each cabinet.

Once in place, the position on the sides is easily marked by aligning the horizontal members with the sides. When these are set up, they can be assembled and dismantled if necessary.

8 Cut the backs to size – slightly less than the width and height of the cabinet to ensure that they are not seen. It is important to have good access to the rear of the stereo components for connecting, and good air circulation for cooling. For this reason, large neat holes are cut in the rear ply. They roughly follow the opening size, but the corners are rounded. Lightly nail the

backs to the rear of each cabinet, carefully aligning the cabinet to ensure that all corners are completely square. This may be temporary only to allow for dismantling and staining (see step 15). The plywood will act as a brace and stiffen up the cabinet. The bottom shelf can now also be drilled for the record dividers.

9 Screw a piece of 100 mm x 25 mm cabinet timber to the rear top framing member of one of the cabinets. This accommodates a four- or six-outlet electrical power board into which all the appliances can be plugged (so that only one electrical lead runs down to the power point).

10 The front edges of the particle (chip) board cabinets can now be covered in iron-on veneer to hide the end grain. The veneer strips are normally about 2-3 mm wider than necessary; cut them to length first. Heat up the edge of the particle (chip) board by running a hot iron along it over a piece of brown paper. Then place veneer on the edge and repeat the procedure. Follow along with a soft piece of timber to ensure good adhesion to the particle (chip) board. Any spots

that fail to adhere can be reheated and stuck again. Trim off excess veneer with a utility knife and sand the edges smooth.

Now cut the intermediate shelves 462 mm wide out of the 400 mm particle (chip) board panels. The front edge of these also needs to be edge-veneered to match the rest of the cabinet. The whole cabinet is now ready for sanding and finishing, which happens in a few steps time.

11 The next job is to make the drawers. These are perhaps the most difficult part of the project, even though they are not dovetailed and otherwise avoid tricky joinery. Power tools were used to minimise the time and work involved. Prefabricated drawers can also be used, with some adjustment made to the size of the whole unit for the correct fitting.

There are two drawer sizes, the larger size for compact discs and video tapes, and the smaller size for audio cassettes.

❏ Large-sized drawers: The fronts of the two larger drawers are made of 200 mm x 25 mm cabinet timber cut down to 158 mm exactly. This will give about a 1 mm clearance top and bottom between the shelves. The sides and back are made of 150 mm x 19 mm cabinet timber, which finishes at 141 mm x 12 mm. The back is cut down to 130 mm.

Groove the drawer front and sides between 7 mm and 10 mm to accept the 3 mm plywood drawer bottom. This is easiest to do with a power saw with a tungsten-tipped blade set to a shallow depth (about 5 mm). Also groove the sides between 99 mm and 119 mm on the outside to accept the drawer guides already fixed to the cabinet. This channel is easiest to cut with a router and a 12 mm straight bit (set to cut 8 mm deep).

Rebate the drawer front on the back edges to accept the sides. The depth is 12 mm, the same as the thickness of the sides, and is designed to enable the side to be nailed into the end grain of the front, rather than nailing through the front. This groove should only go high enough to accommodate the side, thus leaving the top continuous.

Assemble each drawer with 25 mm panel pins and adhesive. Fit the back of the drawer above the bottom groove to allow the plywood bottom to be slid in place once the drawer has been constructed. Cut the drawer bottom to suit, slide it in position and nail the back of the bottom to the back of the drawer using small flat-head (roundhead) nails.

If not done previously, fit the drawer guides into the cabinet, and try each drawer to ensure it runs smoothly. If necessary, adjust the guides to suit.

❏ Small-sized drawers: The cassette drawers are construc-

ted in a similar way using the smaller sized timbers.

12 The insides of the drawers can be fitted with dividers if desired. The cassette drawer will hold three cassettes across with a little extra space for head cleaning or other equipment. The CD drawer also holds three CDs across.

13 The table top to cover all three units is made of the same veneered particle (chip) board, but in this case is edged with 25 mm x 25 mm dressed (planed) timber of the same species. Apply the edging to the front edge and sides, and mitre it to the corners. This involves accurately cutting a 45° angle at the two front corners so that when assembled, the timber will show no end grain. Glue and nail the edging to the edge of the particle (chip) board, and punch and fill the nails. Use sash cramps to help hold the edge in place if necessary. For a more decorative effect, the edge can be routed to any number of edge treatments to match existing furniture, or to

simply round off the exposed edge. In this case, a rounding-over bit was used.

14 Fashion the front kickboard out of 100 mm x 25 mm cabinet timber, cut down to 70 mm, and screw-fix along the top of the kickboard with brown snap-on screw covers to hide the screw heads.

15 At this stage all the components are ready for finishing. To do this, it is best to totally dismantle the units, identifying each piece so that you know which unit it came from. Take each piece individually and carefully sand the edges and face using #120 paper. Remove all splinters, irregularities and pencil marks, being careful not to sand through the veneer. If staining, carefully apply the stain to all visible faces, wiping off any excess (follow the instructions on the tin).

16 Reassemble each unit, permanently nailing on backs and keeping the top, drawers and kickboard separate. Apply the recommended number of

finishing coats – in this case, a furniture-grade polyurethane was used.

17 When dry, the units can be joined using double-headed screw connectors – this will ensure they stay together and in alignment. Hold the cabinets together with a clamp while drilling for connectors, using scraps of softwood to protect the finish. The top can then be fixed to the units by screwing from the underside of the top framing members into the table top. Drill the holes in the cabinets slightly oversize, so that they will accommodate any slight movement in the top. Fix the kickboard to the rebate.

18 Fit the drawer-pulls or handles to the drawers. If the handles you are using are fixed from the inside, fit a little block under the fixing screws in the drawer bottom to ensure that cassettes or CDs do not get damaged by being in contact with the fixings. As an alternative, recess fixings into the drawer fronts by counter-boring.

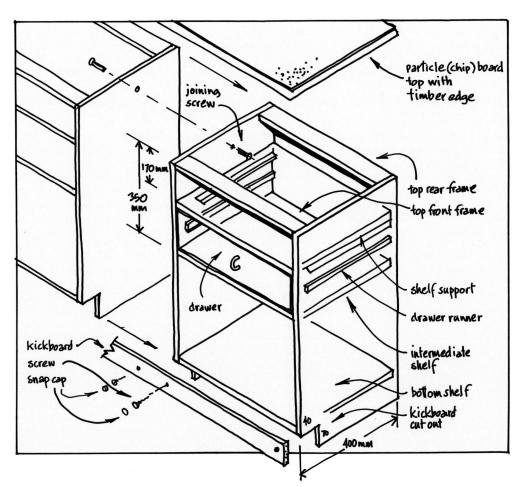

Flexibility is the key to successful storage in double-duty rooms and multipurpose areas. This need not result in makeshift mayhem. These stylish space-savers have been designed to make the most of in-between areas.

MULTIPURPOSE AREAS

There are so many ways to keep things in order and easily accessible – be inventive and resourceful with every little space you have.

Entrances

One area which needs to be flexible is the hallway, and as this is where visitors gain their first impressions, it is logical to give thought to its design and fittings. If possible, there should be at least one chair and a table large enough to take parcels, letters, magazines, a telephone, message pads and directories. A long, stepped bookcase can combine all three functions of table, seating and storage. Install handy hooks on the wall for coats and scarves, and a stand for umbrellas (a revamped Victorian hallstand can make an interesting talking-point).

In long or large corridors, there are obvious places for fitting in extra storage: for example, walls can be lined with units to take any excess household paraphernalia. China and glassware should be safely stored on the top shelf.

Wall-mounted fittings will occupy less space than freestanding pieces of furniture, and you may be able to use irregularities in the shape of the room to create an alcove with shelving for books, or, with the addition of sliding doors and some hooks or rails, a small cupboard for outdoor gear.

Thought should also be given to entrances at the back of the house. In many houses this is the service entry and, as such, there needs to be provision for the storage of prams, baskets, sporting equipment, outdoor toys, wet-weather gear or maybe even gardening implements.

Again, heavy-duty hooks hammered or screwed into solid walls could carry many of these items. One idea is to hang fishing rods, complete with reels, horizontally above doors – this way they become a decorative addition as well.

Study/guest room

Another room which often does double duty is the study/guest room. Storage can be organised to take up little space to enable the inclusion of a sofa bed or divan and a decent-sized desk. Whether you are using a whole room, or part of one, try to fit in the maximum amount of storage. An easily accessible filing system to keep papers and correspondence in some logical order should be a priority. Remember that items which are frequently used should be kept within easy reach.

Open shelving can be installed on the walls above or behind the desk. Deep drawers in desks, cupboards or wall units can be used for suspension files. A common practice is to use a laminate-finished desk surface to span a pair of two-drawer filing cabinets. This combines work space and storage in one.

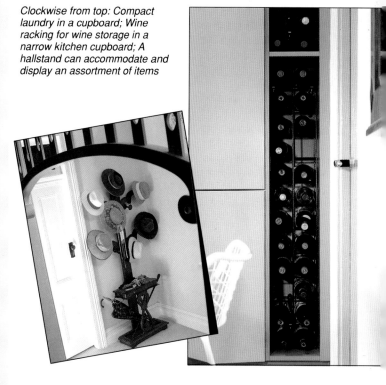

Clockwise from top: Compact laundry in a cupboard; Wine racking for wine storage in a narrow kitchen cupboard; A hallstand can accommodate and display an assortment of items

Stack 'N' Store. Props from Derek Scott, Sandy de Beyer

Linen cupboard for storage of bath towels, blankets and assorted linen

Full-length sliding doors or screens will allow you to close off the work area and to use the room for other purposes.

Books are an important part of any study and have certain storage requirements. They can deteriorate in areas of high humidity, gather dust and will turn yellow if exposed to direct sunlight. Books can be quite heavy, so ensure shelving is strong enough to hold their weight. Adjustable shelving will accommodate almost any type of tome, be it a directory, journal, coffee table book or large folder.

Bookshelves can be custom-built and cover a wall or walls to frame a sofa or stretch up and around doors and windows, giving a sense of perspective to the room. When guests come to stay it is easy to hide the working spaces and shelves of textbooks with a series of pull-up blinds (see Quick-fix project). These can be dropped down for the duration of the stay and then raised for work to begin again. If the room is not big enough for a full-sized bed, consider a sofa bed. For

simple convenience put a couple of brass hooks on the back of the door for hanging clothes or, even better, why not try your hand at making fabric shelves (Project 5, opposite page).

It is not only the study where a desk may be needed: it can be useful to have a pull-out desk or a flap at the end of a workbench in the kitchen for writing lists, or resting a recipe book on.

QUICK-FIX PROJECT
Pull-up blinds
The principle of these blinds is an old and good one. The front of the shelves is covered with fabric cut and sewn to fit the dimensions of the shelves. At evenly spaced intervals up the inside, casings are stitched across the blind, through which thin timber battens/cleats are slotted. Metal eye hooks are screwed into these battens/cleats through the fabric in straight rows up the back of the blind, about 35 cm in from the edge of the blind and in the centre. The top of the fabric is tacked onto a timber batten/cleat, which is then screwed onto the outside top front of the shelves. Screw one more eyehook into the supporting bracket at the top of each row of hooks. Cords are fastened to the lowest hook in each row, then threaded through the eyehooks, taken to one side and fastened onto a cleat. The blind moves up and down by pulling or releasing the cords.

Clever cupboards

If you do not have enough floor space to designate to utility areas like the laundry, there are simple but effective ways to disguise utilitarian facilities in your living spaces. Any long cupboard space can be used for brooms, mops, vacuum cleaners and outdoor gear. With a laundry, all you need is space for a washing machine, dryer and a wash tub or sink. The area does not need to be large, indeed a laundry works most efficiently when the spaces between equipment is not great (see Project 10, Laundry in a cupboard). Other space-saving possibilities include hanging canvas laundry bags or fabric shelves, cupboard doors that fold down to become table surfaces, and a fold-away ironing board. For another clever cupboard idea, see our Sewing centre project (Project 6).

Under the stairs, up in the attic

It can be useful to take a fresh look at spaces that have never been used before for

Understair storage

storage. Stairs are an example. The understairs area is popular for storage, especially in small terrace houses, as it is often already partly enclosed and is surprisingly large. This area is easily converted into storage for luggage, sports equipment, firewood, wine, linen, and so on. The trick is to make sure that items stored at the rear, which is often over a metre from the front, are still accessible. Here, a good idea is to build a

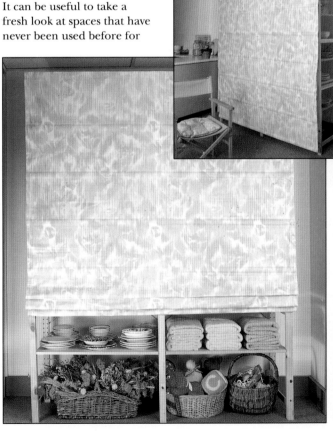

Fabric shelves

These fabric shelves are ideal for a dual-purpose room which is short on space.

STEP BY STEP

1 With right sides facing, stitch stripe print pieces together along short edges to form one long strip. Press seam open. Press under 1 cm at remaining short edges, top-stitch and edgestitch to finish.

2 Fold strip every 30 cm to form five double-thickness open-backed shelves, with four single-thickness backs in between. Press.

3 With right sides facing, pin one small check print square to top, back and lower edges of one shelf side. 1 cm seam allowance at front edge of square will extend past finished shelf front. Clipping into corners, stitch around top, back and lower edges to form shelf side. Press. Repeat for other seven squares to form entire shelf unit.

4 With right sides facing, pin one large check print piece to side of shelf unit around front, back and lower edges. Large check print piece will extend 31 cm above top of shelf unit to form top hanging section. Clipping into corners, stitch around front, back and lower edges to enclose all seam allowances. Trim seams and turn to right side. Press. Repeat for other side.

5 With right sides facing, stitch top edges of large check print pieces together to form top hanging section. Press seam open.

6 With right sides facing, stitch small check print rectangle to top hanging section along front edge. Clipping into corners, stitch side edges of rectangle to side edges of top shelf, enclosing all seam allowances. Trim seams, turn to right side. Press.

7 Press under 1 cm along back edges of top hanging section to enclose remaining seam allowances. Slipstitch together to finish.

8 Insert five rectangles of hardboard into open backs of shelves to complete shelf unit. Top hanging section should then be suspended from an appropriate wall bracket.

Open up your attic for extra storage

series of wheeled trolleys that roll into the space, are covered by attractive false panelling and, when something is needed, can be wheeled out and are easily accessible.

Gaining access to the attic can be as simple as installing a ladder – a range of practical attic ladders is available commercially. They are simple to pull down and store in the attic space themselves.

Underfloor storage

While it cannot be recommended to completely fill the subfloor area of the house with storage, because of ventilation, there is nevertheless plenty of scope for some storage there. It may not even have to be accessible through the tiny side door either. Items stored underfloor could include wine with access via a hatch or trapdoor or, more popularly, floor safes for valuables, covered by a rug or, better still, carpet tiles.

MATERIALS

ITEM	QUANTITY
115 cm wide large check print cotton fabric	2 m
115 cm wide stripe print cotton fabric	2.20 m
115 cm wide small check print cotton fabric	1.50 m
rectangles of hardboard (39 cm x 29 cm)	5

PATTERN

Cut two rectangles of large check print 152 cm x 32 cm for outside panels and top. Cut two rectangles of stripe print 212 cm x 42 cm for shelves and back. Cut eight squares of small check print 32 cm x 32 cm for inside panels, and cut one rectangle of small check print 62 cm x 32 cm for inside top. 1 cm seams allowed.

Project 6

Sewing centre

This neat fold-away sewing centre has ample storage for not only a sewing machine, but also an overlocker, shelves of patterns, sewing accessories and other odds and ends.

This clever cupboard idea is based on a simple upright cabinet that takes no more room than a bookcase, and folds away in one or two easy steps.

The overall cupboard is 1070 mm wide as built (to fit in a corner) by 2070 mm high, and is a total of only about 350 mm deep with the doors shut. When open it reveals seven shelves for storage, and a sewing table 1220 mm x 600 mm. Our project was made from 19 mm particle (chip) board, but the sizes can easily be adjusted to other commonly available board thickness. It is made by simple carpentry, with no complex joints involved, and is finished with plastic laminate sheet glued to the particle (chip) board.

STEP BY STEP

You will need a considerable amount of room to build the unit, as the components are fairly large. It will be built on its face and then turned over.

1   Start by building the plinth on which the unit stands. This is made of 19 mm particle (chip) board which will be laminated later, with other surfaces. The size of the base is 1058 mm wide by 285 mm deep by 160 mm high. Cut two pieces of particle (chip) board 1058 mm x 160 mm, and three at 247 mm x 160 mm. Glue and nail (or screw) the base together, with one of the shorter pieces nailed as a centre support or stiffener.

2   Measure and cut the two side panels. They are 311 mm wide by 1910 mm high. Put the two sides together, and mark on each the position of shelves. The sequence from the top of the cabinet to the top of each shelf is 245 mm, 425 mm, 615 mm, 920 mm, 1315 mm and 1685 mm. Square across each piece at this level.

3   Measure and cut the top and bottom, both 311 mm wide by 1020 mm long. Cut the back out of hardboard to the size 1910 mm x 1058 mm. This forms the basis of the carcase. Also measure and cut six shelves out of the 19 mm particle (chip) board, each 225 mm wide by 1020 mm long.

4   Assemble the main outside of the carcase (face down) by gluing and nailing (or screwing) the sides to the top and bottom. Use PVA adhesive and 50 mm thin bullet-head nails.

While the cabinet is in this position, glue and nail or screw the shelves where marked. On the outside of each panel, draw a line corresponding with the half thickness of the shelves to give you a nailing guide. From the top, these lines would be at 254 mm, 434 mm, 624 mm, 929 mm, 1324 mm and 1694 mm. When nailing the shelves in position, align them to the upturned back of the cabinet for a well-aligned joint.

5   When all the shelves are in position, nail the back onto the cabinet with small flat-head (roundhead) nails, ensuring that the cabinet is held square. The hardboard will act as sheet bracing.

6   It is necessary to install a 50 mm x 25 mm softwood support to the underside of the shelf to be laminated; the table will be hinged to this shelf at 1295 mm from the top. Glue and screw the support from the particle (chip) board into the side grain of the softwood, which itself is secured to the sides of the cabinet by screwing or nailing and gluing. This will stop the shelf from bending with the considerable weights that will be placed on it. Similarly, screw a 75 mm x 25 mm batten/cleat to the underside of the top of the cabinet, 16 mm in from the front. Once the softwood front

MATERIALS

ITEM	DIMENSIONS (mm)	QUANTITY
particle (chip) board:		
– sides, shelves and plinth	2400 x 1200 x 19 thick	2 sheets
– front doors (prefinished and cut to size)	2100 x 600 x 19 thick	2 sheets
– table top	1220 x 600 x 19 thick	1 sheet
hardboard	1200 x 2100 x 3 thick	1 sheet
softwood DAR (PAR):		
– table leg	150 x 25	1 length (0.9 m)
– top and rear batten/cleat	75 x 25	2 lengths (1.2 m)
– shelf support	50 x 25	1 length (1.2 m)
– cabinet edging	25 x 25	2 lengths (2.1 m)
		1 length (2.4 m)
polyurethane (gloss)		
laminate	2100 x 650	1 sheet
	1220 x 900	1 sheet
matching laminate edging		4.8 m
iron-on edge veneer		6 m
cam-type sash lock		1
small magnetic catches		4
piano hingeing (600 mm)		1 length
butt hinge (75 mm)		1
overlay hinges for 19 mm doors (3 left-hand/3 right-hand)		6
door knobs of your choice		2
self-adhesive rubber doorstops (10 mm)		2
adhesive, nails and screws to suit		

SPECIAL TOOLS

laminate knife (double-sided, tungsten-tipped scriber)
laminate trimmer (router with laminate trimming bits) or a selection of flat files (coarse to fine)

TIME

Three weekends

edges are installed, this will be 35 mm back from the front. This panel is designed to take the cam-type sash lock that will hold the table in a vertical position when the cabinet is closed up.

7 Also cut to length a 75 mm x 25 mm length of softwood to make the batten/cleat, which is fixed to the top back of the cabinet to act as an anchor that can be screwed to the wall. The two sides are trimmed off at 45°. Screw the batten/cleat to the cabinet from the underside of the top panel into the side grain of the timber.

8 The entire interior of the cabinet and the shelves can now be coated with polyurethane to give an easy-care, hard-wearing surface. Gloss was chosen as this also brings out the cork-like texture of the particle (chip) board. Give the whole at least two, preferably three, coats. Do not coat the front edge of the shelves or the top surface of the shelf that will be laminated (see below).

9 The next task is to cut out the table top to the size 1218 mm x 598 mm. The width can be increased or decreased if desired, but the height must remain at 1218 mm to fit inside the cabinet, unless the shelf heights are also adjusted. Once the table top is cut out it is ready for laminating, which will bring the total size to 1220 mm x 600 mm.

10 The first surface to laminate will be the exposed side of the cupboard (you may find it easiest to have the cabinet laying on its opposite side for this).

Laminating with plastics should be done carefully as the materials are relatively expensive. Cut the laminate to about 2 mm oversize all the way round (this allows accurate trimming when the laminate is fully glued) using a laminate knife. This is run along a straight edge repeatedly (front and back) until a sufficiently deep groove is cut for the sheet to be easily snapped.

11 Cut a series of dowels or thin scrap timber strips to lay across the worktop to separate the laminate from the particle (chip) board while it is adjusted into place. Make sure both laminate and particle (chip) board are dust free, then evenly spread a thin layer of contact adhesive (using the supplied applicator) on the laminate and then on the particle (chip)

board. Being a contact adhesive, it works best when it is just dry. Test this with the back of your hand in one or two spots. The adhesive will also look dull rather than wet.

When tack free, lay the previously cut dowels on the side about 300 mm apart, and then position the plastic laminate on the dowels. Get the laminate into the right position, then remove the dowels one by one from one end, gently pressing the laminate into position.

12 Once the sheet is down, ensure a good bond by hammering with a block of softwood over the entire surface. Pay special attention to the edges for a permanent bond. The edges can then be trimmed at a right angle to the face of the laminate and flush with the edge using a metal file.

The file must only be used pushing down on the laminate, never pulling up, as this may break the bond, which takes several days to reach its maximum strength. If you have access to one, a laminate trimmer or a router with a laminate trimming bit and pilot will save hours of work.

Repeat this with the other side if necessary. Also apply laminate to the exposed faces of the base unit. Where two faces of laminate meet, it is wise to file the joint at roughly 45° or 60° to remove the sharp edge. This will leave the typical dark edge line that is a feature of trimmed laminates. Once again, this can easily be done with a laminate trimming bit.

13 The shelf at 1295 mm from the top is also laminated on its top and front edge as it will undergo much harsh treatment (this shelf is the table extension onto which the sewing machine and any other bits and pieces are pushed). Cut the front edge strip to size (wide in height but in this case accurate in length), and glue it into place. Trim to a flat surface with the top of the shelf.

The laminate for the shelf has to be cut to fit exactly to the back edge and the two sides. The front edge can hang over by 2 mm to allow trimming to size when it is glued. Glue the laminate as before and when in place finish it off at 45° to 60° to the edge with a file or a laminate trimmer.

14 The final laminating job is that of the table top and edges. This needs to have all four edges laminated first, and then the top laminated to finish over the edges. It is also finished at 45° to give a safe smooth working surface and edge.

15 The dressed (planed) 25 mm x 25 mm front softwood edgings are actually dressed (planed) to 19 mm x 19 mm and can be glued and nailed (or screwed) to the front edge of the particle (chip) board to give an attractive finished appearance. As they will be butting against your new laminate on the outside faces, precoat them with polyurethane to avoid accidentally getting any coating on the new laminate.

16 To attach the table leg to the table, screw it to the underside of the table with the butt hinge. It is important that the flap of the hinge faces towards the cupboard so that when the table is raised, the leg will automatically fold against the bottom of the table. If correctly cut, the top of the table will be at 760 mm, which is normally a comfortable height to work at.

17 Fix the table top to the left side of the cupboard with a continuous piano hinge, screwed first to the table edge, and then to the shelf.

18 Fix the self-adhesive door-stops to the top shelf to soften the contact between table top and cabinet when the unit is closed. Also fit the cam-type sash lock to the top batten/cleat and the catch to the underside of the outer table edge. Check that it is in the correct position with the table up.

19 Fit lengths of the iron-on edge veneer to the front of the particle (chip) board shelves for a professional finish. This is applied with a household iron set on high – the adhesive on the edging will be melted. Finish the bond by running over the edging with a soft timber block while the adhesive is cooling. Then trim the edges flush with the top and bottom of each shelf.

20 The final major components needed to finish the unit are the doors. The right door is 524 mm wide x 1910 mm in height, and the left is 534 mm, with the leading edge rebated 10 mm to define the joint and to hide any slight irregularity that may result in the fitting.

21 Each door is fixed with three overlay hinges. These are semi-concealed and easy to install. The top and bottom hinges will need to be slightly let into the door to allow the hinge to sit flush with the top and bottom of the door. Cut an angled slot halfway down the door to accommodate the middle hinge. Each door will take one of one hand, and two of the other hand hinges.

22 Mark the position of the hinge screw holes on the door, and lightly predrill the screw hole. Similar predrilling should be done on the cabinet edge – this will ensure that the screws enter straight. It also helps to get the screws started through the laminate.

23 Fit the small magnetic catches to the top and bottom of the cabinet and fit the knobs to the doors. If desired, a power point can be added to the inside face of the cabinet above the laminated shelf.

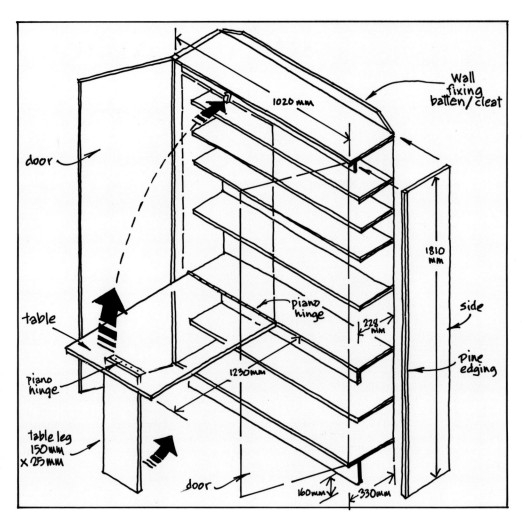

Skill Class
Dowel joints

This type of joint is used to join pieces of timber together side by side to increase the overall width – such as may be necessary for timber shelves. Dowels can only be used if the timber is thicker than 12 mm – any less, and there is not enough room to insert the dowels. Dowelling is a simple and concealed method of making a strong edge joint.

❑ Once the joint is planed true, square pencil lines across the edges to mark the position of the dowels. Separate the timber and use a gauge from the face side of each board, set to half the timber thickness, to mark at each pencil line. The point of intersection is the position of the dowel centre.

❑ Bore holes for the dowels, standing at the end of the work to make sure the drill is perpendicular to the timber. Now slightly countersink the holes. Make sure that the dowel length is slightly shorter than the combined depth of the holes, with the ends bevelled. Finally, run a saw kerf along the dowel if not already grooved.

❑ To assemble the joint, put adhesive into the holes and glue onto the dowels, then knock the dowels into the holes in one of the timber pieces. Clean off any surplus adhesive and then add the other piece of timber and lightly cramp together.

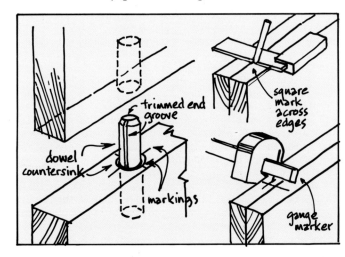

In Easy Reach

Designing to the correct dimensions for effective and comfortable use is a science in itself. It is called ergonomics. Today it is a fundamental part of designing the environments people work in.

When you start planning a project, you will already have a general idea of the size you want a structure to be and how it will fit in. Before you can make actual construction plans, you need to determine the exact dimensions of your project.

This is the science of anthropometry, which is concerned with the measurement of the human body. A lot of research has been carried out throughout the world to compile average body sizes and these measurements are used to achieve the correct relationship between people and their working environment. This means designing or selecting furniture and storage facilities that are best suited to your use.

The reason why kitchen worktops or benches are usually 900 mm high is because that height is best suited to most people when standing. The typical depth of 600 mm enables everything on the bench to be within reach. Tables and desks are usually set at 750 mm because that height suits the mean dimensions of the adult human body.

The accompanying dia-grams show average European dimensions. When you are planning to build something, use these dimensions as a guide.

When designing for storage shelves or fittings, allow the maximum dimensions for the items to be stored, such as large books and folders, computer disks or music tapes.

If you are designing a study desk, you may want to allow for a set of filing cabinets under it. These will vary in size so that you will need to check the actual dimensions.

It is likely that you will not have enough room for every-thing to be stored within convenient reach of the main work area. Decide which items you are going to need on a regular basis and place these close to the work level. Long-term storage, such as old reference books or files, can be stored higher up.

TIPSTRIP

ODD SPACES
Consider the amount of space wasted, or perhaps made unusable by such things as the placing of light switches, windows and, worst of all, the swing of doors.
❏ Switches should be placed close to a door on the lock side so that they are easily operated and also so they take least room away from wall areas.
❏ Doors travel through quite an arc, and in small homes, cavity sliding door units may be a useful option to increase usable room area.
❏ Glassed areas can take up a lot of wall space which would otherwise be used for storage.

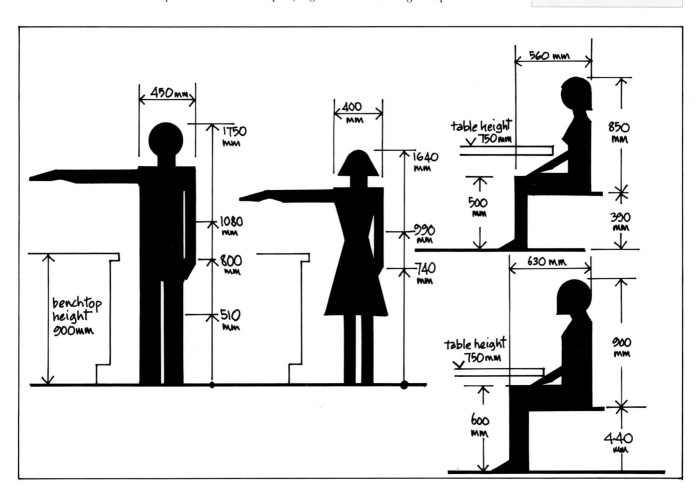

The cosy book-lined study of past generations is rapidly changing into the home office of today. Even if you just want a little office space for family records and financial matters – it pays to organise it properly to suit the job at hand.

HOME OFFICE

Although a 'study' conjures up a very different image from that of a 'home office', it is used for the same activities: paperwork, reading, study, peace and quiet, household accounts, correspondence, and so on. A home office, however, suggests something more streamlined and modern (and possibly even profitable!).

Efficient storage is an essential and integral part of a well-organised home office or study. Your work area needs to be thoughtfully planned around the type of work you do. For example, if you are involved with design and drawing work, you will need a lot of deep desk space, pin-up space on the walls and cardboard tubes for storage of drawing paper. Make a list of the items you use regularly when working. For example:

❏ pens and pencils
❏ paper and other stationery items
❏ telephone
❏ desk lamp
❏ calculator
❏ filing trays
❏ suspension (hanging) files
❏ typewriter/computer keyboard and screen
❏ waste-paper basket
❏ personal mementos
❏ reference books

Remember that items should be easy to locate, see and reach. Fitted coordinated storage units are neater than freestanding ones.

Office equipment

Today's high-tech communication equipment – mobile telephones, answering machines, personal computers and printers, modems and facsimile machines – all allow home-based workers to communicate easily with clients or head office.

Consider the location of the equipment you will need, both now and in the future. Location of computers and peripheral equipment is important not only because of limitations on the length of leads from the computer and the printer, but also because of the large number of power and data leads which will hang about. One way to free-up your work surface is to install a duct at the back of the desk or clip the cables under the desk with holes in the top through which the cables can be drawn.

Don't forget the need for storing boxes of computer and photocopying paper and other bulk supplies.

Storage solutions

A home office may lack sufficient floor space to accommodate a large desk, or enough wall space to locate all the shelves and cupboards you need. Our Deskmate (Project 7) and Window storage box (Project 8) projects are simple and quick to make and can be finished to suit your office/ study design.

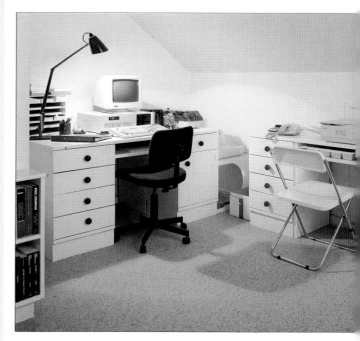

Above: This home office is the result of an attic/loft conversion and has everything in easy reach

Below: Study area in the den

Clockwise from left:
A workspace for a small home business dealing in dried flowers and pot pourri; High-tech office furniture – smart and easy to adjust for changing storage needs; Small office area with a bookcase, desk and return; Desk accessories; Home office with a view

A home office is for paper work, concentration and private retreat, so locate it in the quietest part of your home.

Study and computer centre

The work area of your home office/study must be designed for working in comfort with everything in easy reach and at the right height.

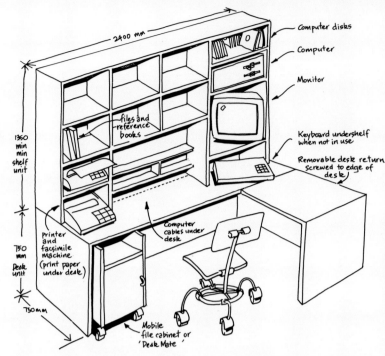

- 2400 mm
- Computer disks
- Computer
- Monitor
- 1350 min min shelf unit
- files and reference books
- Keyboard undershelf when not in use
- Removable desk return screwed to edge of desk
- 750 mm Desk unit
- printer and facsimile machine (print paper under desk)
- Computer cables under desk
- 750 mm
- Mobile file cabinet or 'Desk Mate'

LARGE COMPUTER AREA

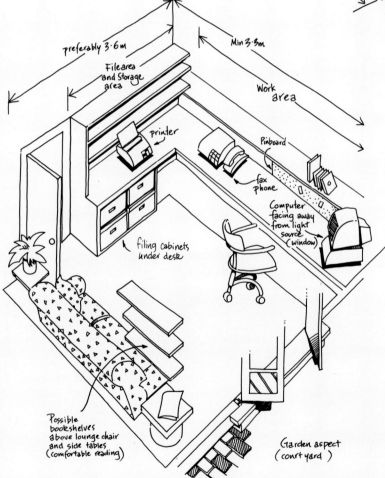

- preferably 3.6m
- Min 3.3m
- File area and Storage area
- Work area
- printer
- Pinboard
- fax Phone
- Computer facing away from light source (window)
- filing cabinets under desk
- Possible bookshelves above lounge chair and side tables (comfortable reading)
- Garden aspect (courtyard)

HOME OFFICE PLAN

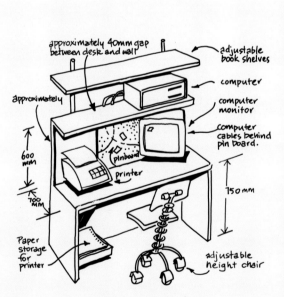

- approximately 40mm gap between desk and wall
- adjustable book shelves
- computer
- computer monitor
- computer cables behind pin board.
- approximately
- 600 mm
- 700 mm
- Pinboard
- printer
- 750 mm
- Paper storage for printer
- adjustable height chair

SMALL COMPUTER CENTRE

Project 7

TT

Deskmate

A deskmate is a mobile storage cabinet which is stored out of the way under a desk and rolled out when needed.

There is a number of different configurations ranging from simple storage of paper, envelopes and a few files you may be working on, to a deskmate which can store a printer on the top with the paper feeding from the shelf at the back.

STEP BY STEP

1 Follow the cutting diagram for cutting out the panels. It is best to mark out one panel at a time and cut this out before cutting the next. This will ensure that you set the panels at the correct size. Remember the saying 'Measure twice, cut once'.

The side, bottom, middle and back panels should be cut first. Mark out the size of the panel, ensuring the sides are perpendicular to each other by using a try square. Use a timber batten/cleat as a guide for the power saw to run along. This will result in a much cleaner job. Measure your saw to find the distance from the guide fence to the side of the blade teeth. Mark this distance from the line you are to cut and temporarily fix the batten/cleat in position with small nails.

2 Fix these main panels with PVA adhesive and nails, checking that the panels are square as you proceed. Once these panels are nailed in place, fix screws as well, about 50 mm from corners and edges. Drill pilot holes smaller than the screw shaft and countersink the

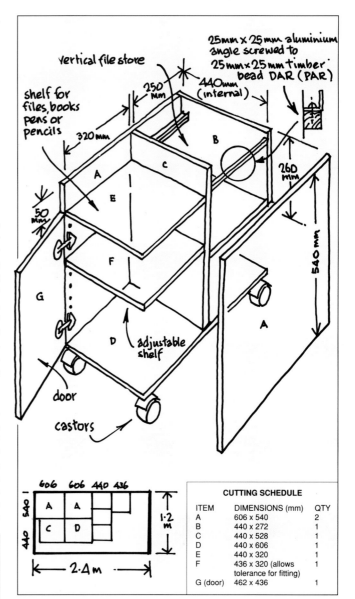

vertical file store

shelf for files, books pens or pencils

adjustable shelf

door

castors

25mm x 25mm aluminium angle screwed to 25mm x 25mm timber bead DAR (PAR)

CUTTING SCHEDULE		
ITEM	DIMENSIONS (mm)	QTY
A	606 x 540	2
B	440 x 272	1
C	440 x 528	1
D	440 x 606	1
E	440 x 320	1
F	436 x 320 (allows tolerance for fitting)	1
G (door)	462 x 436	1

hole so that the end of the screw finishes below the face of the panels.

3 At this point you should check the dimensions for the remaining panels in case the first panels are a different size to the cutting diagram. This is particularly important for the door panel, which should be check-measured and cut after the main panels are fixed together. Fix the door hinges following the manufacturer's instructions. The hinges allow final adjustment of the door panel by turning grub screws on the face of the hinges.

4 All that remains is to fix the timber battens/cleats, aluminium angle and the castors to the bottom.

5 When the unit is complete, use a fine sandpaper to rub down the edges then undercoat. Leave to dry, following the instructions on the paint tin. Use an oil-based paint for the final coats (this will resist abrasions more easily). Paint two coats, sanding down with wet and dry sandpaper between coats.

TIP: Nailing provides a handy way to hold panels together while the adhesive sets and you drive the screws. But don't rely on nails alone for strength.

MATERIALS

ITEM	DIMENSIONS (mm)	QUANTITY
medium-density fibreboard (MDF)	2.4 m x 1.2 m x 12 thick	1 sheet
timber batten/cleat (DAR/PAR)	25 x 25	1
aluminium angle	25 x 25	1
PVA adhesive		
particle (chip) board screws		
25 mm twisted-shank nails		
hinges for particle (chip) board doors		2
castors		4
all-purpose undercoat and oil-based paint for finishing		

SPECIAL TOOLS
hand-saw and power saw
electric drill
hammer and screwdriver

TIME
Allow 4 hours to construct and another two days for the painting (one coat of undercoat and two finishing coats).

Window storage box

This very simple box with its hinged-top lid panels is ideal for storing items such as copier or computer paper, old job files and children's artistic endeavours.

The box used here is 2.4 m long to suit the standard length of MDF board, but could be shorter. The completed box can be positioned under a window and finished off with cushions, or placed anywhere in your office or study, depending on layout, so that it doubles as a piece of furniture.

STEP BY STEP

1 Follow the cutting diagram for cutting out the panels. Use a guide batten/cleat for the power saw, as described for Project 7 (Deskmate). Start by cutting out the front, back and two end panels together with the plywood base.

2 Apply adhesive to the edges of the panels and nail together. Once the side and end panels are nailed together, and before the adhesive has dried, glue and nail the base plywood panel in place with panel pins. Make sure that the corners are square before nailing the base in place. Now screw the panels near each corner.

3 Turn the partly completed box over and check-measure for the centre panel and top lid

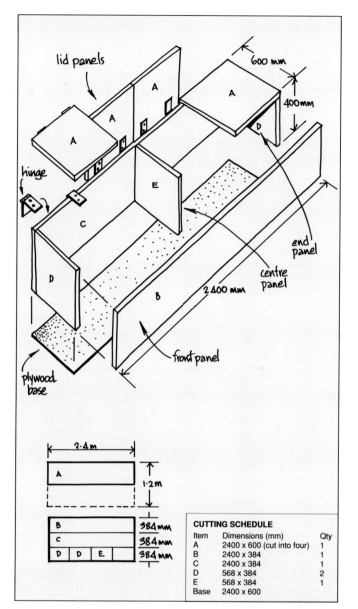

CUTTING SCHEDULE

Item	Dimensions (mm)	Qty
A	2400 x 600 (cut into four)	1
B	2400 x 384	1
C	2400 x 384	1
D	568 x 384	2
E	568 x 384	1
Base	2400 x 600	

panels. Cut the centre panel and nail and screw in place. Fix the hinges to the lid panels and set in place.

4 All that remains is to sand down the edges of the panels, undercoat and finish.

TIP: Nailing provides a handy way to hold panels together while the adhesive sets and you drive the screws. But don't rely on nails alone for strength.

MATERIALS

ITEM	DIMENSIONS (mm)	QUANTITY
medium-density fibreboard (MDF)	2.4 x 1.2 x 16 thick	2 sheets
plywood	2.4 x 0.9 x 4 thick	1 sheet
PVA adhesive		
particle (chip) board screws		
25 mm twisted-shank nails		
panel pins		
hinges for particle (chip) board doors		8
all-purpose undercoat and oil-based paint for finishing		

SPECIAL TOOLS
handsaw and power saw
electric drill
hammer and screwdriver

TIME
Allow 6 hours to construct and another two days for the painting (one coat of undercoat and two finishing coats).

GREEN TIP

Paper recycling bin or box
One storage article that deserves the little space it takes up in every room or every second room is the paper recycling bin or box. It's not until you start recycling old newspapers, magazines and junk mail that you notice the vast quantity of paper waste created in an average week. It is quite staggering. Re-use your paper as much as possible before disposing of it. If your community does not yet have collection days or recycling depots, make a fuss until they start.

SKILL CLASS

MORTISE AND TENON

This joint is quite commonly used. It is used for joining timber together at right angles to each other, and basically consists of a recess (the mortise) in one piece and the tenon (cut to fit into the mortise) at the end of the other piece (see illustration).

PLAIN GLUED JOINTS

Where glue is to be relied on solely for the joint bond, the edges need to be accurately planed. Relying on cramps to close up gaps between the edges

of the timber is not enough.

❏ For a straight edge to the timber, use a long plane such as a jointing plane, which will give a straighter edge than a smoothing plane.

❏ The best method is to remove shavings from the middle until the plane ceases to cut, and then take a couple of shavings right through. In this way, the edge is first made slightly hollow, and then this is corrected when the final shavings are taken off. Generally, this method will work well for joints up to 900 mm long.

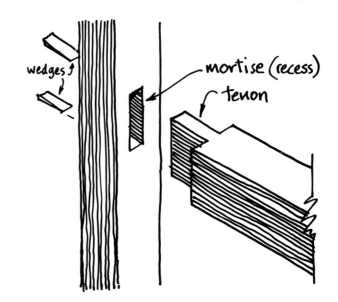

Making a shooting board

Use a shooting board with a hand plane for accurate planing work. Used with a jack or jointer plane, it is ideal for accurate planing of end grain or the edges of long thin panels. The shooting board consists of two boards, which guide the plane, and a stop, which holds the timber in place. The timber for the shooting board should be about 1 m long and made out of straight seasoned hardwood, although plywood will do. Glue and nail the boards to timber spacers and punch the nails when you have finished.

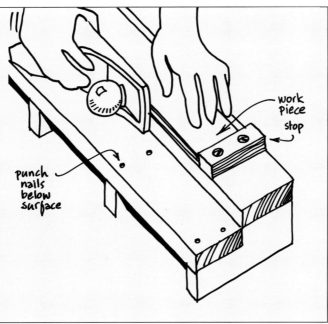

USING A HANDSAW

❏ When holding a saw, extend the index finger down the side of the handle – this provides some lateral restraint on the saw.

TIPSTRIP

NAILING NEAR EDGES OF TIMBER
Whenever nailing near the edge of a piece of timber, always drill a pilot hole for each nail slightly smaller in diameter than the nail. This will prevent splitting of the timber.

❏ When starting a cut, place your thumb as a guide beside the saw blade, which is on the waste side of the cutting line. Make the first few strokes backward, leaving the thumb against the blade until the cut is well under way.

USING A CIRCULAR SAW

The circular saw is generally used by all tradespeople for a variety of uses. It can be used for crosscutting and ripcutting as well as rebating and grooving, by adjusting the blade depth.

❏ Make sure that the saw motor is not overloaded. The

saw blade should be running at full speed before it comes into contact with the timber.

❏ Never start the motor when the blade is in contact with timber.

❏ When in use, ease the saw forward slowly and smoothly without too much forward pressure, which will strain the motor.

❏ If the motor speed drops, ease back and let the motor speed come back up before continuing.

❏ Always set the saw blade so that its teeth just penetrate the other side of the timber.

TIPSTRIP

SMOOTH-CUTTING TIMBER
When timber is cut with a saw it will leave a slightly rough edge. The following method of cutting timber with a sharp edge is commonly used in cabinet joints.
❏ After marking the cut, scribe the mark line with a sharp chisel several times to make an incision in the timber face.
❏ Next, use the chisel to cut a small sloping groove on the waste side of the cut – this groove will provide a channel in which the saw can run.
Note: This method will give you an accurate cut and a sharp edge.

❏ If you are cutting large panels of timber or sheets of particle (chip) board, use a timber batten/cleat, or a narrow offcut as a guide for the edge of the power saw to run along. This will give a straight edge and a much cleaner job.

Measure your saw to find the distance from the edge of the sole plate to the side of the blade teeth. Mark this distance from the line you are to cut and temporarily fix the batten/cleat in position with small nails or clamps.

123

When you next look around your home thinking that you couldn't swing a cat let alone put away your record collection, think again. Even the smallest studio flat has storage potential. You can make your tiny corner of the city a more spacious and pleasant place to live.

TIGHT CORNERS

Finding somewhere reasonably central at a price you can afford, especially if you are single, often means sacrificing the luxury of space. This usually means living in a one-bedroom flat or a studio apartment where storage space and the most efficient use of your living space is of paramount importance. Not for you the convenience of the loft space where those unused belongings lurk out of sight and out of mind. What you have, you use – and it has to be on hand, but not under your feet.

Kitchen

Unless you're very lucky, the one room in the house where you are very unlikely to have a lot of space to spare is the kitchen. Think in terms of the room's volume and not the floor area. If you're leading a busy lifestyle, there are going to be things you need every day and those things that you don't – make sure everyday items are easily accessible.

❏ Cupboards and shelves should be built up to the ceiling, allowing work areas to be placed at a convenient height for food preparation.

❏ Even in a very tight space, storage can still be used as a decorative feature. An old-fashioned dresser will add character to your kitchen and is an excellent way to show off your crockery and glassware.

❏ Every wall space is a potential storage area – attach a mesh rack to the wall and use hooks to hang bulky items such as ladles and colanders; hang pots and pans from a sturdy ceiling rack; a wall-mounted spice rack above your worktop may do wonders for your cooking! Racks and hooks can also be used in a small hallway to hang up coats, scarves, hats and umbrellas.

❏ Another storage idea that can grow as you need it is a modular vegetable rack – fill it with all your favourites!

❏ Shelving should be deep enough to store large casseroles and the like – but not so deep that you lose things!

❏ Sharp kitchen knives can be stuck to the wall using a magnetic knife rack – make sure it is safely located away from little fingers!

Bathroom

How many times have you felt your bathroom has been invaded by the shampoo bottles from outer space? You know what it's like – all those bottles of shampoo, last year's suntan lotion and a doctor's cabinet of 'flu remedies that you're loath to chuck out!

❏ Install a shelf above the bath (along its length) or, alternatively, install several smaller shelves above the bath taps. Another solution is to have small shelves fitted into the angle of two walls.

❏ A multi-tiered trolley for bathtime essentials is movable and adaptable.

❏ Hooks are another quick-fix solution for hanging towels, clothes and pot plants.

Above: Entrance/hallway
Right: Office/study in a cupboard

This small but well-designed inner-city apartment is full of clever, space-saving storage solutions.

*Clockwise from top left:
Pull-out drawers under
window seating in living
area; Compact kitchen;
Pull-out bedside table
and drawers in bedroom;
Bedroom wall cabinets;
Floor to ceiling wardrobe
and shelving system;
Bathroom*

Styling: Michelle Gorry
Graheme McIntosh, Interior
Design Consultant

Props courtesy of: Private
Collection, Made Where;
Sandy de Beyer; Les Olivades;
Made in Japan; In Residence;
Version; The Annexe; The
Dressing Room; Mary Lou's
Linen and Bathroom Shoppe

Multipurpose mezzanine

The living room is often the most important room in a flat and in many cases also doubles up as a bedroom. Put yourself up on the shelf by building a mezzanine floor! This idea requires a fairly large room with highish ceilings. A mezzanine is easy and cheap to build, can make a very attractive feature and, most importantly, can be a real selling point when you decide to sell. It is quite simply the most space-saving thing you could hope to have – even the steps up to it form an eye-catching tiered storage space perfect for storing all your documents and files in attractive stackable boxes. Underneath can become a cosy spot to place the sofa or a desk. Otherwise you can devote the whole space to storage – it is the ideal place to put your hi-fi, television and video and the like.

Dual-purpose bed

Of course, not everyone has the possibility of building a mezzanine, so now is the time to start thinking about a dual-purpose sofa bed or divan. It's a worthwhile investment –

QUICK-FIX PROJECT
Stackable cane suitcases
What could be more attractively practical than a stack of cane suitcases? These were purchased at a low-price home-decorating chain store, then painted inside and out with gloss spray paint.
To dress up your suitcases, simply line the lid base and inner lower part of each with polyester batting, gluing the edges to secure. Cover the wadding again with fabric pieces, turning under

after all, there's no point having more space to move around in if you can't even get up in the morning! Divan drawers are excellent for storing spare blankets and out-of-season clothes.

Revamping junk

❏ Do up a second-hand blanket box – it can double as a coffee or bedside table or sit at the end of your bed.

the outer edges of fabric to neaten. Glue to secure. Glue braid over edges, and trim as you wish. The fabric lining will mean that the suitcases remain dust free and insect-proof, and

❏ Revamp an old wardrobe or cupboard and put shelves inside to double your storage space. Install a shoe rack and wire baskets in the bottom too.

Wall-to-wall shelving

The classic solution for storage problems is wall-to-wall shelving. Break up the monotony with recesses for your collectables, ornaments and pot plants. The shelves can be of different sizes and strengths according to what you want to store on them.

Freestanding pluses

Freestanding storage units such as desks and worktops, drawers and cupboards can be used as room dividers or as island units. One plus is that you can rearrange the room whenever you feel like a change, or take the units with you when you move on. Built-in cupboards can be tailored to suit your needs but they *are* permanent fixtures – you'll need to weigh up the pros and cons of fixed versus freestanding storage units.

can be used to store woollens and household linen. Just for good measure, place some pot pourri sachets and mothballs in the bottom.

Divan bed in a teenager's sitting room

Cane chests

Fabric pouches for general storage

Under-the-bed storage drawer

Children always seem to need more storage than anyone else in the home! Although it's worth remembering that storage alone doesn't tidy the room. This portable drawer on castors slides neatly away into whatever space is available.

The measurements given for this project may not suit the space you have under your bed. Adapt the design and measure for your own sizes, remembering to consider the height of the castors in the overall height. You may decide to make two smaller boxes instead of one large box.

STEP BY STEP

1 Cut all pieces to precise sizes required.

2 Glue and nail front to sides.

3 Glue and nail back to sides.

4 Glue and nail supports between front and back at each side and one in the middle, level with lower edges so the 70 mm dimension is horizontal.

5 Nail through side panels into supports.

6 Screw castors onto supports at each corner so that they do not swivel beyond the outer edges of the drawer.

7 Cut base to specified size and drop into frame.

MATERIALS

ITEM	DIMENSIONS (mm)	QUANTITY
front and back, softwood DAR (PAR)	1220 x 240 x 20 thick	2
sides, softwood DAR (PAR)	765 x 240 x 20 thick	2
supports, softwood DAR (PAR)	765 x 70 x 20 thick	3
base, ply or softwood DAR (PAR)	1180 x 765 x 15 thick	1
castors and screws as required		2 pairs
panel pins		
PVA adhesive		

SPECIAL TOOLS
saw

TIME
2-3 hours

QUICK-FIX PROJECT
Blanket box
This once shabby old toy box has been transformed into a very attractive blanket box for storage purposes. It has been lined and covered with medium thickness quilter's wadding, then the fabric of our choice. All pieces were cut to size, allowing for turn-unders and overlaps. The edges were stapled, glued or held with decorative upholstery tacks. Woven braid covers some overlapped areas inside, for example where the lining meets the exterior fabric. A length of fine chain with an eyehook (screweye) at each end attaches the lid to the inside of the box, and prevents it flipping open too far. New handles were added.

For an area that is used several times a week and is always hard at work to keep you looking your best, the laundry is often sadly neglected. Pay it a little attention, too, and solve those washday blues at the same time.

WASHDAY BLUES

To get the most space and ease out of your laundry, first consider its layout and be critical about its shortcomings. Many householders have no choice but to incorporate the laundry into the bathroom or kitchen, so the laundry basket, peg bag, sink unit, bucket, washing machine, dryer, detergents and all the rest of it has to be fitted in as unobtrusively as possible. Your laundry may even be positioned in a narrow passageway or back corner. Don't despair – well-thought-out planning doesn't require a lot of space.

If your appliances rest on the floor, take full advantage of any unused wall space above by fixing a full-length cupboard along the wall. The deeper the better – you can always use the extra room for safe storage of cleaning solutions and spare light bulbs. By building an enclosed cupboard around your washing machine and dryer you can hide them away while at the same time creating valuable worktop space for folding and sorting.

If you have enough room, also allow space for an airing cupboard – it will prove to be an invaluable in-between storage area. A fold-away ironing board attached to the wall also saves space and eliminates the often awkward storage of a traditional freestanding one. Don't forget about stackable wire baskets, racks and hooks – they take up very little room and provide handy extra storage.

Stacking your front-loading washing machine and dryer will help create immediate space (see Project 10, Laundry in a cupboard). If possible, try to leave some room between them for a pull-out shelf to rest your laundry basket on, or for folding clothes. Stacking your appliances may also free you of space to build a tall side-cupboard, which is sometimes easier to access than the high mounted type of cupboard. Shallow, wire pull-drawers are excellent for storing sewing utensils for on-the-spot repairs. Install a wire rack or hanging rails for hanging ironed shirts and other clothes.

If space isn't a problem, include built-in bins for dirty clothes so that the whites can be separated from the coloureds. Two more bins for clean clothes will complete the set, one for clothes which need to be folded and the other for those to be ironed. A stylish choice of cane baskets can also be a help here. Cane baskets last virtually forever and are highly portable and environmentally friendly.

If your laundry is confined to a small, awkward space, why not hide your appliances behind bifold doors, louvres, Roman blinds or curtains? Or convert space in an alcove or under a stairway into a new laundry.

Just make sure you take into account electrical outlets

Clockwise from top:
From house to line – a colourful set of cane baskets and a pegbag are all you need;
Foldaway ironing centre;
Laundry behind bifold doors;
Laundry shelving – the wall has been opened up and narrow shelves fitted in between noggings

Whitegoods supplied by Hoover

and the surrounding floor covering (carpets do not sit well with washing spills). With small laundries try and keep things sleek and simple – the less cluttered it is the more organised you'll feel.

If you are lucky enough to have a small room devoted to it or have space to spare, think about turning your laundry into a multipurpose utility room packed with convenience. Wouldn't it be nice to have a complete sewing and mending centre close at hand? Or a room you can count on for 101 tasks, from polishing your shoes or silver to fixing that broken lamp?

Transforming your laundry can often be as simple as installing additional cupboards and shelving where space permits. See-through wire baskets, too, are readily found and slide easily under countertops. Drying racks can double as an extra space for ironed clothes. Use the worktop as a desk and sewing area, positioned by a sunny window if possible. Sewing enthusiasts will appreciate the convenience of having a walled pegboard to keep thread and scissors.

With so many practical storage options, it's easy to get carried away. But don't forget about the finishing touches. A friendly, warm colour scheme and comfortable chair or stool will make all the difference in turning your utility room into an area you'll enjoy using.

Clockwise from top: Utility room – an area for soiled clothes and clothes drying, mending/sewing centre ; Handy attachment for drying smalls and delicates; Detail of mending/sewing centre showing drawers for storage of sewing materials and a self-charging vacuum for picking up stray threads

The value of a good utility room has to be experienced to be appreciated: it is an area set aside for 101 different jobs.

Laundry in a cupboard

Although this project was built in a specific location, it incorporates many options and can easily be modified to suit individual needs and available space.

In this case, a laundry, including the washing machine, a dryer, a laundry tub/sink and the dirty clothes basket, was installed in one section of a large built-in area (to a depth of 850 mm) in the family room. The front of the built-in has a series of off-the-shelf, floor-to-ceiling wardrobe doors hinged as pairs. Choose ready-made doors in the closest size and adapt frame sizes to suit. The dryer was mounted over the washing machine on its own support provision. Inside, three shelves were installed adjacent to and above the dryer.

MATERIALS

ITEM	DIMENSIONS (mm)	QUANTITY
doors	2340 x 620 x 35 thick	2
door frames (not rebated)	75 x 38	2 (2.4 m) 1 (1.5 m)
hinges	75 butt	6
brackets	125 x 150 100 x 125	4 4
particle (chip) board	2440 x 1220 x 15 thick 25 x 25	offcuts or 1 sheet
battens/cleats, softwood (DAR/PAR)		1 length (3.6 m)
vents to suit		2 exterior 2 interior
washing machine stop cocks		1 set
washing machine standpipe		1 set
ceramic tiles, wall tiling adhesive and grout		3 sq m
oil-based sealer and water-based paint to finish		

SPECIAL TOOLS
tile cutter and grouting tool
router

TIME
Approximately two weekends

STEP BY STEP

1 Measure up the area accurately, including ceiling height, depth of cupboard and location of any power points. Note sizes of facilities to be built in.
In this project:

❏ washing machine (620 mm wide x 720 mm needed from rear wall x 1100 mm high)

❏ dryer (620 mm wide x 520 mm deep x 720 mm high)

❏ laundry tub/sink (680 mm wide x 420 mm deep x 890 mm high)

Make a sketch of the project including sizes and notes as to what will happen where.

2 Organise to have a plumber install hot and cold water supply as well as adequate drainage for both the automatic washing machine and the tub/sink.

3 Have the power point changed to a double power outlet that can take the load of both the washing machine and the dryer operating simultaneously. If you want lighting installed, this can be done at the same time. A further requirement if operating a dryer is to provide ventilation to the outside of the wall to expel humidity.

4 Once all the plumbing and wiring have been installed, the walls can be made good. (In this case, the right and rear walls were plastered and simply needed filling where the chasing was done, to get back to a good surface.)

5 Install two high vents to allow good air flow through the space, especially when the dryer is being used. Vents can be installed by removing three bricks from the exterior of the house. This is most easily done by drilling a series of closely spaced holes into the mortar. Use a hammer drill set on low speed with a 10 mm tungsten carbide masonry bit. The remaining mortar can be removed with a plugging chisel. Take care to prevent debris from falling into the wall cavity.

6 Cut a similar hole inside to coincide with the outside. The outside can then have a terra-

cover the installation and cement them in place. The cowling will cover most of the ragged edges.

8 It is important to install the shelving before the doors, as the framing and doors will only hinder working in a tight space. The shelves are all made of 15 mm particle (chip) board. Cut the first shelf (top) to 1615 mm x 760 mm. This shelf is full width at 1615 mm and is positioned at a height of 2110 mm from the floor and held up by battens/cleats screwed to the walls. Masonry walls will have to be plugged. This involves predrilling with a masonry bit, inserting a plastic plug and then screwing into that. The timber should also be primed before installation for maximum protection in case of high humidity in the laundry. As this shelf is spanning a distance greater than 1600 mm across the front, otherwise unsupported, a structural member (or beam) needs to be installed to ensure the shelf does not sag. This is best done with a similar length of 75 mm x 25 mm timber, glued and screwed on edge to the underside of the

shelf with 50 mm x No. 8 gauge screws. The shelf and lintel should be primed ready for painting.

9 Cut the second shelf smaller, 980 mm wide by 250 mm deep, with a return coming out the left-hand side, 780 mm x 250 mm. Fix the shelf at 1810 mm from the floor on 150 mm x 125 mm brackets fixed to the wall by screwing as before. Once again, the shelf should then be primed. The third shelf is the smallest at 980 mm wide and 150 mm deep, with a return of 780 mm out of the left wall. Fix the shelf 1510 mm from the floor on 100 mm x 125 mm brackets.

10 The opening to the laundry cupboard is defined by a light timber casing with a horizontal timber member, which comes down about 110 mm from the ceiling, installed over the top of the doors. Finish this either with some leftover particle (chip) board (painted), or plasterboard. A 90 mm plain cornice can then be installed to finish the built-in laundry to the ceiling.

11 The door frames are rebated 12 mm deep to receive the doors. The width of the rebate must be at least equal to the thickness of the door, plus 3 mm for clearance. The frames are made up as a set: the vertical side frames and the top frame. They are made up with a temporary diagonal brace and spacer at the bottom to maintain the correct width. The frame is nailed together before installation.

12 The door frames can now be prepared. The length of the side frame is set out to the height of the door plus top and bottom clearance. Top clearance is 2 mm and bottom clearance 10 mm. The width is set out as the width of the two doors plus 5 mm to allow for clearances. In this case, mark 1245 mm centrally onto the top frame, and square across. Line up short piece of frame material to the rebate, and mark the top frame each side for the width of the housing. This can then be cut to size, and the housing cut with a saw and chisel. Also cut a bottom brace and nail together the jambs, holding them square. A bottom

cotta vent/airbrick to match the brickwork, or perhaps better still a brass mesh vent or plastic-coated airbrick, which allows good air circulation. If it is an exposed wall, a hooded vent may be required. Set the vent/airbrick in place using a mortar mix to match the colour of the exterior – use a 1:1:6 cement, lime and sand mix. Use two half-bricks to fill in around the vents. Install plaster vents with flyscreens on the inside, using a cornice cement, and fill to finish neatly to the internal render.

7 If you are required to have power ventilation, arrange to install a power point high on the wall – this will make it easier for you to install a plug-in type extractor fan. Once again, a large hole will have to be made in the brick and the internal skin to fit the fan. Most through-wall fans are made with an outside cowling that will shed water, and have an integral duct that is adaptable to most common wall thicknesses. There are also various ducting kits available. When in place, cut the bricks around the outside to

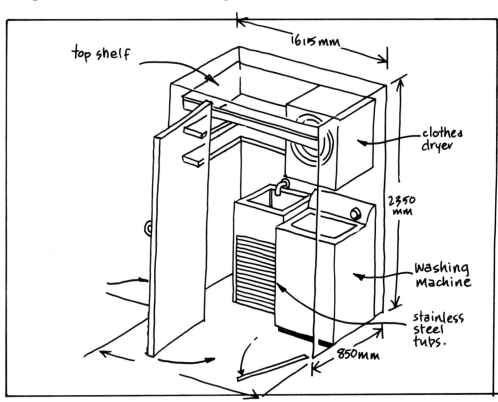

spreader, fitting 1245 mm exactly between the rebates, may help.

13 Check the floor across the opening for level. It normally would be level – if it is out then that amount will have to be cut from the bottom of the appropriate side frame to compensate. The top frame should always be level.

14 Stand the frames in the opening and lightly drive a small wedge directly over the side frames to hold in place. Make sure the frames are plumb, and then pack between the light timber casing and one frame near the bottom (suitable packing includes offcuts of plywood or hardboard) and nail the frame to the stud. Continue packing and nailing that frame at the top and up the sides, making sure it remains straight and plumb. Repeat this on the other frame, making sure the width between the rebates remains constant. Don't nail the top frame to the house. When fixed, remove spreader and brace.

15 The doors will be held with ordinary steel butt hinges. Before fitting the door, give both the bottom and top edges a good coat of primer and/or undercoat to seal them – this protects the door against delamination.

Stand one door in the opening and make sure it fits with adequate clearance. For a good tight fit, the side of the

door that is not fixed to the jamb may need to be bevelled slightly so that it will clear the neighbouring door when closing. Stand the door in the opening and use a spacer at the top for the right clearance, and then wedge underneath to hold the door in place. The hinges are fitted 150 mm down from the top and 200 mm up from the bottom, and one half way. Mark the position and size of the hinges on the jamb and the door using the hinge as a template. Use a sharp chisel to check out/recess the door and the jamb for the hinge, and fix the hinge flap to the door with two screws. It is a good idea to drill a small pilot hole for the screws, to make sure they go in squarely. Fit the other flap into the check-out on the jamb, and screw in securely. Make sure the door works properly without any hindrance before putting in all the screws. Make any necessary minor adjustments then insert the remaining screws.

Repeat this process for the other door.

16 The entire interior can now be painted. It is suggested that the walls first be cleaned down with sugar soap or similar, and then prepared using a universal oil-based sealer. This can then be coated with a water-based paint for an easy-care surface.

17 The doors and shelves should be painted with an oil-based system as oil-based paints have a better abrasion resist-

ance, and are also easier to clean. Undercoat the doors and shelves, and then apply two coats of finish over the top, sanding lightly between coats.

18 Have a plumber install the tub/sink and secure it to the wall in the correct position, allowing room for the washing machine. The tiling can then be done (up to a height of 1365 mm) around the washing machine and tub/sink and over the upturned lip of the bowl. Install the tiles in a thin bed of wall tiling adhesive, applied with a 4.5 mm notched trowel as in the manufacturer's instructions. Allow 24 hours for

Laundry in a cupboard – behind closed doors

the tiles to set then fill the joints with grout so that they shed water more effectively.

19 For the finishing touches fit selected knobs to the doors, and top and bottom catches to hold the doors shut. When this is done you can connect the washing machine, and hang the dryer on its supports.

SKILL CLASS
Housed joints

This joint is used mainly for fixing shelves to the vertical divisions. In the simplest type, the groove is taken right across the timber where it is exposed at both edges. A stopped housed joint entails stopping the housing from the face of the timber so that it is concealed when put together.

❏ To make a simple housed joint, mark the position of the joint deeply with a sharp chisel or knife and square, with two

lines equal to the depth of the shelf thickness.

❏ On the groove side of each line, cut a sloping channel with a chisel – this provides a guide for cutting with a tenon saw.

❏ Remove the waste timber in the groove with a chisel and then finish off with a hand router. Alternatively, all the waste can be removed with an electric router. The router ensures that the depth of the housing is constant.

tenon saw

mark sloping channels

chisel out waste

Bathrooms are common storage trouble spots that seem to get very messy, very quickly. These days there are lots of bright ideas for bathroom storage that utilise every bit of available space.

BATHROOMS

Building a vanity unit around a pedestal basin will help disguise any unsightly pipework while creating extra shelf and cupboard space. Lining the area inside with waterproof shelving paper will help to guard against moisture and possible water leaks. Plastic baskets are readily available and are good for keeping various bathroom items such as stray plasters and razor blades. When choosing a basin, look for one that has an extra wide rim and, of course, recesses for soap. Pick the one as large as your basin space will accommodate.

Mirrored medicine cabinets are a time-favoured bathroom accoutrement, and with good reason. Positioned above the basin they provide easy reach for everyday toiletries and medicines, which are neatly hidden away. Open shelves are another option. Painted wood or melamine-coated particle (chip) board are a sensible choice of material, and while glass is an attractive alternative it must be forever wiped and kept clean. Plastic-coated wire-rack units are a good, economical shelving solution, and work particularly well in a smaller bathroom where heavy wood cupboards may be too overpowering. Whatever cupboards or shelving units you choose, make sure that fragile bottles are not where they can fall and break and that all medicines, detergents

and poisons are either locked up or kept well out of the reach of children.

Make the most of generous bathtub rims by keeping soap dishes, shampoos, or a stack of folded handtowels along the surface. Bathtubs come in a reasonable selection of colours, shapes and sizes – if you opt for a larger, oversized tub, remember that it will be more costly to fill. In terms of space, freestanding tubs make little difference, and traditional cast iron ones can look quite charming in a more rustic-looking bathroom.

More economical than baths, showers can be bought as ready-made cubicles, custom-built, or incorporated into your existing bath. Ready-made cubicles come in a variety of styles, and some come with built-in towel racks and shampoo shelves. A better idea might be a custom-built tiled alcove. Just make sure you include a good shower curtain or glass/plastic screen. If you integrate your bath and shower, be sure you have a flat-bottomed bath (the wider the better) and add nonslip mats to the surface.

Invest some time and take pride in your bathroom's decor. A visit to your local bathroom showroom will give you an array of ideas on bathroom design, fittings and accessories. Soap dishes, towel rails, toothbrush-holders, waste bins and laundry baskets can be

Clockwise from top: Wall cabinets and cabinets under vanity; Heated towel rack; Wire basket for towel storage; Toiletries organiser drawer

Styling: Michelle Gorry   Mary Lou's Linen and Bathroom Shoppe

FREEDOM

Project 11
Towel rack

This easy-to-make towel rack is one simple but effective storage solution for your bathroom.

STEP BY STEP

1 Cut out the particle (chip) board sides. Mark and then cut out the semicircular curve at the end of each side piece (each curve should have a 100 mm radius) using a jigsaw.

2 Apply iron-on edging strip to sides.

3 Measure up, mark out and drill holes for the dowel rails. Before drilling laminate you should punch a starting point with a centre punch. Drill, glue and screw the four lengths of dowel in place as indicated (see illustration), using screw caps to conceal the screw heads.

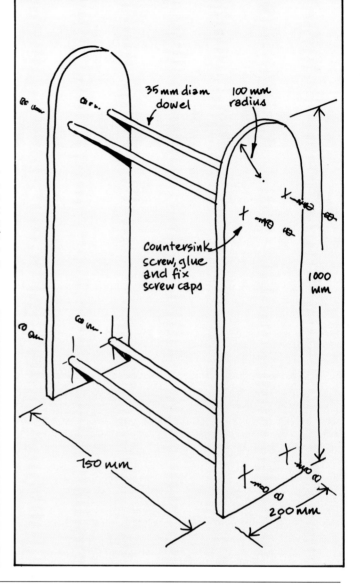

MATERIALS

ITEM	DIMENSIONS (mm)	QUANTITY
plastic-laminated particle (chip) board for sides	1000 x 200 x 16 thick	2 sheets
dowel (rails)	750 x 35 diameter	4 lengths
iron-on edging strip	to cover 16 mm edge	5 m
screws		8
screw caps		8
waterproof adhesive		

SPECIAL TOOLS
jigsaw
electric drill

TIME
One or two days

---

practical as well as adding a nice finishing touch. Introduce an accent colour and buy your accessories in a coordinating range. Towel and magazine racks are also a useful addition, and can create lots of storage room. Mirrors are ideal for a smaller bathroom as they create the illusion of spaciousness.

Bathroom shelves

There is usually little call for extensive storage in bathrooms other than a place to hide the extra shampoo, cleaners and soaps. If you have a vanity unit this may well be adequate, but if you simply have a pedestal basin, you may wish to install a couple of small shelves underneath, cut to fit around the pedestal, with a little curtain across the front to hide the contents. This is easily done with a small rail of chrome or stainless steel tube made up to approximate the shape of the basin and screwed to the wall. The curtain, or curtain rings, can then be fed onto this and be opened and closed as with normal curtains.

Shelving with pull-down laundry cupboard in en suite

Bathside trolley

Relax in the bath after a long day with everything to hand on your own bathside trolley.

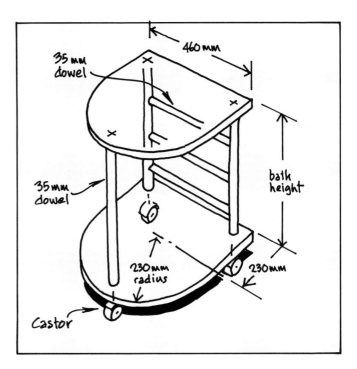

STEP BY STEP

1 Mark out then cut two semicircular shapes on each piece of 16 mm plastic-laminated particle (chip) board using a jigsaw. Each curve should have a 230 mm radius and an additional 230 mm depth at the straight edges.

2 Cover the exposed end-grain edges with iron-on edging strip.

3 Cut the three 35 mm dowels to match the height of your bath, taking into account the height of the castors and the two semicircular shelves.

4 Mark out, drill and insert three 400 mm lengths of 25 mm dowel horizontally to a depth of 20 mm between two of the 35 mm dowels to make the back leg structure.

5 Mark out, drill and insert screws through the two shelves into the ends of the three dowels. To conceal their heads in the top shelf of the trolley, use white sleeves and screw caps. Fit the conical sleeve over the screw when inserting and clipping the cap in place, after you have driven the screw home.

6 Screw the castors in place.

MATERIALS

ITEM	DIMENSIONS (mm)	QUANTITY
plastic-laminated particle (chip) board for shelves	460 x 460 x 16 thick	2 sheets
dowel (for legs)	35	3
dowel (for rails)	400 x 25	3
iron-on edging strip		
50 mm particle (chip) board screws		
conical white sleeves and screw caps		
castors		2 pairs

SPECIAL TOOLS
jigsaw
electric drill

TIME
One day

Wall (mirrored) cabinets and cupboards under vanity and full length of wall

Bedrooms seem to thrive on clutter! The good news is that a little creativity can go a long way. There are numerous things you can do to create more storage space and make for a more comfortable environment in the process.

BEDROOMS

The area around the bed holds several storage possibilities. A bedside table is a must; make sure you have plenty of room for an alarm clock, reading lamp, books and a telephone if you have a bedroom extension. Fabric draped over an old side-table is a quick and economical way to create a bedside table. It may, however, be worth your while to fully utilise the space below in the form of a low-lying bookcase, particularly if you're an avid reader.

Bedheads bring an attractive element to an otherwise little-used area of potential space behind the bed. You can buy several variations of modular units, and most come with matching bedside tables and frames. For the DIY enthusiast, bedheads can also be custom-made to match your specific requirements. Whatever you choose, remember to consider your lighting needs. Overhead and track lighting can add another dimension to your decor while freeing potential space. Adjustable and reading lights are practical choices for a bedside table because they occupy less space than traditional lamps.

And don't forget about the space under the bed. Retrieve those lost tennis shoes, and utilise the area to store out-of-season belongings using stackable boxes (hat, blanket and even shoe boxes). Bed frames with pull-out drawers are ideal, but empty suitcases can also do the same job. Storage trays on wheels are another good idea and let you get at your clothes easily (see Project 9, Under-the-bed storage drawer). If you have some space at the foot of your bed, an old wooden chest or tin trunk can find a home here easily and create lots of storage space.

To get the most out of freestanding wardrobes, try installing hooks or tie/scarf racks inside the doors. The real advantage with freestanding furniture is its portability – it can be moved around as you wish to suit your changing needs and circumstances.

Built-ins are perfect for awkward or unused spaces. They can be expensive, but perhaps well worth the investment, renovation time or storage space saved. A good idea to try: with the bed across the corner, build a triangular-shaped cupboard behind it to store infrequently used items. Build adjoining bedside tables along the same angle as the bed, and continue (if desired) with a two-tiered shelf of the same height along the walls. Or try a built-in couch with storage space incorporated secretly underneath. The possibilities are endless, but remember to keep built-ins as simple as possible and neutral in colour to match the walls.

If you are blessed with walk-in cupboard space, consider adding a built-in wardrobe.

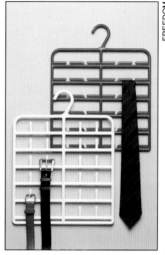

Above: Tie/belt rack
Right: Wardrobe with stackable wire baskets
Below: Natural-finish trundle bed and bookshelves

Stack 'N' Store, Woollen jumpers from Benetton

FREEDOM

Built-in cupboards and drawers can be custom-made to suit your needs.

FREEDOM

To 'customise' storage units, you can change the handles and paint the doors, or replace them with mirrored ones to increase the feeling of light and space.

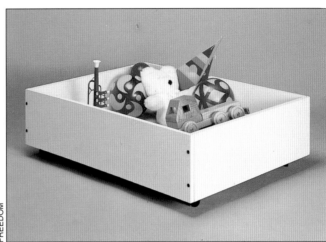

FREEDOM

Clockwise from top right: Toy box on wheels for under-the-bed storage; Floor to ceiling cabinets; Bright, portable and stackable storage; Robe savers; Built-in wardrobe

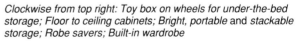

IKEA

Handbag tidy

Always losing your handbag under a pile of clothes? Instead, why not put it away in your own handbag tidy?

STEP BY STEP

1 With right sides facing, stitch front and back print fabric panels together along top short edges. Press seam open. Repeat for plain fabric (lining) panels.

2 With right sides facing, stitch print and plain fabric panels together down long sides. Turn to right side. Press.

3 With print side uppermost, fold over hanger at seam line between front and back panels. Pin through all thicknesses and stitch from side to side 4 cm down from fold, to enclose hanger bar.

4 With right sides facing, stitch front and back print fabric panels together along bottom short edges. Press seam open. Turn to right side. Press matching plain fabric lining seams under 1 cm and slipstitch together to finish.

5 Mark four sections 48 cm deep on the front panel and four sections 30 cm deep on the back panel. Pin through all thicknesses matching marked lines and stitch from side to side to form four open-sided pockets.

MATERIALS

ITEM	QUANTITY
115 cm wide print cotton fabric	2 m
115 cm wide plain cotton fabric	2 m
coathanger	1

PATTERN
Cut one rectangle of print fabric 198 cm x 42 cm and one rectangle of plain fabric 198 cm x 42 cm for front panel. Cut one rectangle of print fabric 126 cm x 42 cm and one rectangle of plain fabric 126 cm x 42 cm for back panel. 1 cm seams allowed.

IKEA

Simple storage for the nursery

Remember to assess your storage needs first, then plan, build or buy accordingly. Start by asking yourself a few pertinent questions. Do you prefer your clothes folded or hung up? Just how long is your longest dress or pair of trousers? Maybe you want to include a space for jewellery, perfume and toiletries. Be sure to take into account your height so that objects are not out of reach.

A few more things to remember: cubby holes are the best way to store folded articles of clothing. If you choose drawers, it's a good idea to include several shallow ones as well as a variation of depths. Wire storage units are good because you can see what's inside them. Clear perspex on sliding drawers may cost a bit more, but is worth the investment, particularly if you have a lot of clothes. And when buying or building a wardrobe, remember that laminates are a good choice, but wood veneer is not good near a bathroom where steam can get at it.

Nursery
A baby's bedroom should be planned with the same regard as any aspect of your new child's life – with an eye towards the future. A nursery should also revolve around the child's immediate needs: nursing, feeding, changing. If you succumb to buying charming but impractical baby furniture, try and choose a piece that can be adapted or used elsewhere later on. A good chest of drawers or changing table will usually suffice. Paint the furniture white or a pastel colour, and adorn it with playful handles, knobs and decals (transfers). You can also add a padded, waterproof mat on the top for changing. As for the baby's stuffed animals, toys and knick-knacks, it's best to show them off rather than try and store them neatly away.

Under-fives
Cute as they are, little children can create a storage nightmare. They are an active, inquisitive bunch, and their bedroom will reflect their changing needs. They require masses of equipment,

A growing child needs a range of storage accessories

most of which are vital at one stage of growth and redundant at another. In terms of storage, expandable and adjustable units are the most sensible option. They should be safe and durable, and all handles and shelves should be low enough for your child to reach.

In the average toddler's room, you will find nappies, a changing table, a bottom seat, a nappy bucket; a chest of drawers choking with singlets, tops, bottoms, booties, all-in-one suits, a woolly dressing gown, hats; soft toys, mobiles, blocks, a little blackboard; a night light, sheets and blankets; books of all shapes and sizes – the list never ends.

One storage item that is truly vital when young children are around is your basic mothproofed chest or box/boxes. Store as you go along, washing and putting aside clothing or equipment for the next baby – your own, your sister's or your friends'!

Books and toys are the other major storage problem in a young child's room. Putting things out of sight for a while (perhaps in an attractive storage box) is a

good trick with under twos – they think the toys are brand new when re-presented!

The over twos get more sentimentally attached to things as a rule and like familiar things around them. An attractive toy box (make sure the lid cannot drop suddenly and that the box has good ventilation) and a bookshelf that displays books rather than stores them, spine to the forefront, are both practical and decorating assets. Remember that a bed and desk will subsequently take the place of the cot and changing area. Also, bright colours may win out over pastels.

School-age child

Once your child starts school, his or her storage needs will change. A desk with drawers is needed to take the increasing amounts of paperwork that the child needs or wants to keep.

A cork pin-up board also becomes a storage point for favourite pieces of memorabilia, school notices, sports notices, ribbons, badges and those all-important stickers. Rather here than on the fridge or underfoot.

Wardrobe needs are more sophisticated now, with more hanging space needed (see Project 3, Framing up an alcove); shoe storage becomes more important, as do bookshelves.

Bunk beds are good in a shared room situation, and many incorporate desks and storage units. Privacy becomes increasingly vital to a child, so provide some storage that can be locked, and give the child a key (keep a spare to cover the inevitable, tragic loss!).

Young children are avid collectors, so make sure you have a good collection of glass jars, baskets, boxes and tins. A toy box will continue to be invaluable for storage of sports or hobby-related equipment.

Stackable wire baskets for toy storage

QUICK-FIX PROJECT
Earring racks
Install as many of these racks as your accessories require. Measure inside your cupboard doors to establish the length of each rack. The racks are made of narrow strip steel and are held away from the door at each end by screwing through a rubber doorstop. Drill a hole at the ends of each rack the size of the diameter of the screw for the door stop. Cover each rack with adhesive electrical tape, then screw through the doorstops to the cupboard doors. Scarves can be draped over these racks, and belts can be hung from them after fastening the buckle.

A teenager's room needs to accommodate many different interests

Teenagers

Like it or not, a teenager's bedroom often becomes their favourite habitat, and what once sufficed as a perfectly acceptable chest of drawers is now suddenly 'childish'. Don't despair. In fact, it is probably not such a bad idea to think about renovating a little or investing in some new furniture. A teenager's bedroom often becomes a spare or guest bedroom, eventually, so it might be worth decorating now with that end in mind.

Angular built-ins are a smart idea, and custom-built shelves can house stereo equipment, records, books, magazines and photo albums. Narrow shelves are handy for tapes and books. Divan or sofa beds serve a dual purpose as they can be used for sleeping or sitting – they are ideal, as a teenager's bedroom is also a focal point for visiting friends.

GREEN TIP

Mothproofing
❏ **Place muslin bags, each containing 50 g of ground cloves, cinnamon, black pepper and orris root, among the clothes.**
❏ **Place lavender in gauze sachets between the layers and folds of clothing.**

Storing your clothes

Keeping clothes, shoes, hats or bed linen for long periods of time requires more than simply making sure they are clean.

Store your best linen in blue tissue paper away from light

Fabric needs room to breathe or the fibres will deteriorate. Linen, for example, needs to be kept in a cool place and preferably on slatted shelves to allow the air to circulate around the garment. When hanging your clothes, it is a good idea to separate weekend gear from the less worn outfits. It's also advisable to cover full-sleeved garments with short plastic covers so that the sleeves do not crease.

❏ Do not hang knitted or jersey clothes as they will stretch. Instead, fold them carefully and pack them in a suitcase, drawer or on a shelf; sweaters shouldn't be squashed into drawers as this can also ruin the fibres and may result in permanent creasing. Light-coloured jumpers should be stored in plastic bags to prevent fading. This is also an excellent way to re-use plastic bags.

❏ When folding jumpers, lay the garment face down, fold one side and arm to the middle, fold the arm back down on itself and repeat with the other side. Fold the sweater in two, taking the top down to the bottom with the sleeves inside the fold.

❏ Shirts should be hung on coathangers. If it is necessary to fold and pack them, button the shirt to the top to prevent creasing and to stop the collar from being distorted, lay the shirt face down, turn both sides into the middle, fold in the sleeves (in line with the body) and turn the tail up then fold the bottom up to the collar.

❏ Trousers should be folded along the crease and stored on hangers. To protect against a hanging mark, tape cardboard or wrap a piece of clean cloth around the hanger as padding. Evening gowns should hang inside out to keep them clean. For skirts, sew bias binding

(cloth binding tape) loops on to the inside of waistbands and hang on coathangers; pleats should be tacked in place.

❏ An important factor for proper hanging is that coathangers should fit the garment exactly, spanning the width of the shoulders, and the back should support the neck of the garment. Never use wire hangers.

❏ Leather and suede should be shaken well before being stored so that creases do not set into the garment. They should also be hung in plastic bags.

❏ Furs need to be hung in a well-ventilated and cold place, or stored in sealed plastic bags containing moth repellent.

❏ Precious garments such as bridal and christening gowns, veils or damask table cloths should be completely wrapped in blue tissue paper (to keep moisture out) and stored in a box.

❏ Boots and shoes should be kept on racks so that they are tidy, but also to prevent them from scratching or marking each other. A shoe rack can be easily attached to the inside of a wardrobe. To keep their shape, boots should be filled with tissue paper or newspaper. Galoshes or gumboots can be punctured at the top of the rubber of each boot and hung with string on a hook.

❏ Store bed linen in large plastic bags and keep it on top of a wardrobe, at the foot of a bed in a blanket, or under the bed so it doesn't get too squashed.

❏ Do not store linen in an airing cupboard for long periods as the humidity can damage the fibres.

❏ Accessories can be easily kept in baskets decorated with large bows on shelves in the dressing room. Another idea is to use small decorating hooks, linked by stencilled ribbon and bows, to hang hair accessories, scarves and jewellery – creating a pretty effect in the bedroom.

Project 14

Storage bed-end

Make this fun shelf unit for the end of the bed for your bedtime books and bits and pieces or for toy storage in a child's room.

The size and layout of the shelves and storage recesses can be to any design you choose as long as there is enough room for the bed and pillow to rest against the bed-end.

Our bed-end is for a bed which is accessible from both sides, that is, not placed lengthways against a wall. The two side shelf units are separate so that you can leave these out or change them to suit your particular needs, such as making a larger shelf unit on one side of the bed only, with perhaps a desk space as well.

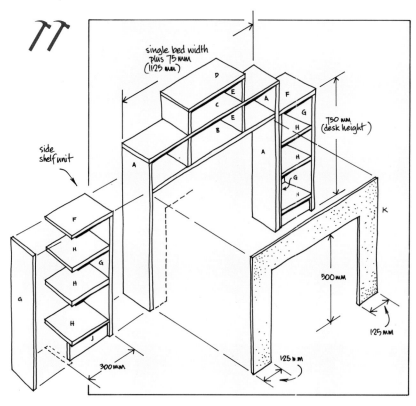

MATERIALS

ITEM	DIMENSIONS (mm)	QUANTITY
medium-density fibreboard (MDF)	2.4 x 1.2 m x 16 thick 1.8 x 0.9 m x 16 thick	1 sheet 1 sheet
PVA adhesive		
adjustable shelf supports – these come in a variety of types and materials, from brass to plastic		
particle (chip) board screws		
25 mm twisted-shank nails		
panel pins		
all-purpose undercoat and oil-based gloss paint for finishing		

SPECIAL TOOLS
handsaw and power saw
electric drill
hammer and screwdriver
square

TIME
Allow about 8 hours to construct and another two days for the painting (one coat of undercoat and two finishing coats).

STEP BY STEP

1 Follow the cutting diagram for cutting out the panels. Use a guide batten/cleat for the power saw, as described for Project 7 (Deskmate). Start by cutting the main side and top panels (A, B and C) and panel K, which fixes to the end of the bed and acts as a bracing panel. When you have cut each panel, check that the corners are square.

2 Apply adhesive to the edges of the panels and nail together, starting with panels A and K, followed by B and C. At this point you are able to measure for panels E and D. Cut these panels and nail or screw and glue in position, making sure that they are square.

3 The side shelf units are made as separate units which are screwed to each side of the main bed-end. Cut the side panels (G) together with the bottom and top panels (F and H). Drill blind holes into the side panels for the adjustable shelf supports at about 50 mm apart. Now glue and nail these panels together.

Fix the skirting panel (J) in place and make sure the unit is square. It is a good idea to use a piece of offcut timber as a temporary brace at the back until the adhesive is dry and you have finished screwing the panels together. Check-measure and cut the shelf panels (H) ready to fit into place.

4 When you have completed the nailing and gluing, drill-pilot and countersink holes for the screws near each corner. Apply a little adhesive to each screw and screw into place.

5 When complete, use a fine sandpaper to rub down the edges then paint with undercoat. Leave to dry according to the instructions on the paint tin.

Use an oil-based gloss paint for the final coats. This will resist abrasions more easily. Paint on two coats, remembering to sand down with wet and dry sandpaper between coats.

TIP: Nailing provides a handy way to hold panels together while the adhesive sets and you drive the screws. But don't rely on nails alone for strength.

CUTTING SCHEDULE

Item	Dimensions (mm)	Quantity
A	934 x 250	2
B	1093 x 250	1
C	1125 x 250	1
D	625 x 250	1
E	184 x 250	5
F	300 x 250	2
G	734 x 250	4
H	268 x 240	6
J	268 x 100	2
K	dimensions indicated	1

Don't despair when you look at the jumble of tools, gardening equipment, outdoor furniture and all the junk you've accumulated over the years. Ingenuity is the name of the game when it comes to organising outdoor storage areas.

OUTDOOR STORAGE

Storage aids for outdoor areas come in all shapes and forms: rope, nails, screws and hooks; lengths of metal fencing; pieces of timber; metal brackets; door knobs; bricks. You'd be surprised how many things can be useful. Now take stock of your surroundings. The empty overhead and wall space in the garage or carport, the cellar or basement area (see our special Cellar project) and even the nooks and crannies are begging to be used as repositories.

❏ When neither garage nor under-house space is available, a timber or metal garden shed or even a gazebo or a child's play house can provide excellent storage for garden equipment, furniture and tools.

❏ Less elaborate outdoor storage may take the form of a simple cupboard, suitably waterproofed with a sloping roof, built against the wall of the house.

❏ An unsightly water tank or rubbish bin can be stored away and hidden behind slatted timber or latticework panels.

❏ In an outdoor living area, such as a patio or even a conservatory, a long timber seat with a waterproofed, hinged lid could disguise a storage box for garden tools and cushions. Similar seats could be built in a gazebo or as part of a barbecue area.

❏ Cupboards elevated off the ground beside a built-in barbecue can be used to house firewood, extra crockery and a variety of other articles.

❏ Outdoor furniture, a portable barbecue and cushions can be tucked away neatly in an unobtrusive cupboard built against a fence or a wall.

Garage/carport

The garage and, to a lesser extent, the carport have enormous potential for storage, particularly if they have pitched roofs. Think of all that wasted space above the car and how it could be used to store any number of bulky items, from bicycles to boats, from bags to blankets. Often, there will be enough space to add wall shelving or cupboards too. If you do intend to store anything in the carport, consider security and weatherproofing carefully. With suitable insulation, waterproofing and electric wiring you may be able to turn a no-longer-used garage into a home office, a studio, a child's playroom or a fully-equipped workroom.

Garden sheds

Where space permits, a garden shed is one of the most practical solutions to outdoor storage and many of the garden sheds today are designed to be aesthetically pleasing as well.

Prefabricated, lock-up sheds are available in a variety of sizes and styles, with hinged or sliding doors. They are easy for the competent

Top: Garden/tool shed with a variety of storage units – old bookcases, cupboard and shelf unit with a worktop, wall-mounted board for tools and a full-length louvre-door cupboard
Right: Garden/tool shed (exterior view)

Make sure your storage areas are well lit for easy location of items.

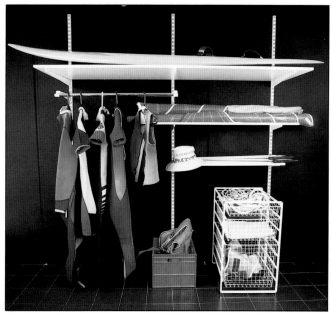

Clockwise from top: Wooden pegs and tray for easy storage of ski equipment; Timber cupboard with sloping roof for storing firewood and an assortment of outdoor equipment; Metal adjustable shelving; Rubbish bin and hot water cylinder hidden from view by latticework panels

One of life's frustrating moments is to be halfway through a job and unable to find an essential tool: every tool should have its place.

TIPSTRIP

HANDY STORAGE

❏ Epoxy-coated steel baskets, drawers and cubes provide great storage on or under shelves, either free-standing or on drawer glides in frames with castors.

❏ Any type of storage unit on castors will save time and effort. An old tea trolley tucked under a worktop or bench can be used to wheel things around; timber boxes can have castors attached to make them mobile.

❏ Plastic bins or cardboard boxes in various sizes stacked on shelves can be a neat way of storing any number of items, from sports equipment to seasonal clothes to old books and toys.

❏ Sealed rubbish bins also rate well as storage receptacles. Note, however, that deep bins can be a handicap if you want to fish something out from the bottom.

❏ If there is sufficient space, you could add tall but narrow vertical cupboards for long-handled tools, a lawn mower or sporting gear such as skis and fishing rods. The advantage of having cupboards is that you can lock the doors for safety and security and they will protect goods from dust and moisture. Sliding doors save space.

❏ A timber rack with dowelling pegs or blocks of timber at the top and a wooden tray at the bottom can be made to support skis or any tall sporting equipment.

❏ Cupboards with shelves or drawers placed underneath or above a worktop provide dust-free storage. Old cupboards picked up at a junkyard or retrieved from a kitchen renovation are worth considering for this job.

❏ Safety is always important; any poisonous substances should be locked in an overhead cupboard.

A garden hoserack with real character

home handyperson to install – with a little help.

Most steel-framed sheds come without floors. Ideally, they should be placed on a concrete slab, but specially treated timber decking or pavers can be used. If a shed is raised off the ground, it may be necessary to install some sort of access ramp for large articles such as a lawnmower or a wheelbarrow. Some steel-framed garden sheds come with freestanding shelves and other accessories as optional extras (in this type of shed the walls are usually not strong enough to take heavy weights). Alternatively, you can build your own timber frame within the shed and use this to support shelves on the walls.

Attractively designed rustic timber garden sheds, complete with their own floors, come in kit form in all shapes, sizes and styles – some even with windows and verandas, giving them the look of a mini house.

The more elaborate model with windows may become a workroom, a garden potting centre with worktops, shelves and cupboards – or even a cosy retreat from the daily grind.

Wall storage

While overhead storage has merit when space is at a premium, it is best used for articles which are not needed too often. Wall storage, on the other hand, is more practical for everyday use.
❏ The home handyperson can set up a great work area in an adequately sized garage by putting in a worktop (or an old kitchen table will do) at the far end, with storage space above and on side walls.
❏ Shelves can be wall-mounted, freestanding or hanging. As a rule of thumb, the length of a timber shelf should never be more than 1.2 m for light loads and 800 mm for heavier loads. A good depth for a shelf is around 300 mm.
❏ In a timber-framed garage, simple shallow timber shelves can be built between the studs to hold, for example, jars and boxes of nails, tins of paint or garden products. Make sure that any area where you store tins of paint or any other type of chemical can be locked.

An old bookcase makes a useful freestanding storage unit. Timber shelves can also be hung by rope, which is knotted under each shelf for stability and attached to the rafters or joists with strong hooks. Alternatively, lengths of timber shelving can be placed on bricks or concrete blocks laid on the floor.
❏ Adjustable metal track shelving in different configurations can be fitted to walls. Track shelving can also be used to hold bicycles. Simply set up the tracks as directed for the shelving system, and mount them to wall studs which will support the weight of the bicycle. Pad the brackets to prevent scratching the top tube, and adjust them to the correct height for hanging the bicycle (also see Project 15, Bicycle rack).
❏ A pegboard attached to the wall, complete with pegs and hooks for hanging, is an efficient way to hold tools and garden equipment. More upmarket is a metal louvre-panel system which has louvres designed to support various-sized plastic storage containers.

❏ Magnetic bars screwed to the wall are excellent for storage of metal tools.
❏ Hooks can be used to hang anything from a ladder to a bicycle in either a vertical or horizontal position. Two large hooks side by side are ideal for holding garden hoses or lengths of rope.
❏ Never underestimate the humble nail, which can be hammered into the wall or into a piece of board to support a variety of items including tools, garden equipment, and brooms and sporting equipment, such as tennis and squash racquets.
❏ For safety, sharp tools should be kept up high, out of the reach of children. Outlining the shape of each tool with a felt tip pen on the board will make it easy for you to return tools to their correct place after use.
❏ Coat hooks, shelf brackets, door and drawer knobs, and wooden pegs or dowels glued into predrilled holes can all be used for hanging various articles.

Cane basket for storing firewood undercover just outside the back door

Sturdy bicycle rack

This bicycle rack is a great idea for storing your bicycle and forms the base frame for overhead storage racks.

About 4.2 m of 75 mm x 38 mm, and 1 m of 75 mm x 25 mm building grade timber is all it takes to build this project.

STEP BY STEP

1 Assemble the bicycle rack by nailing or bolting the brace between the two pairs of uprights. You may need to adjust the dimensions to fit the space and your bicycles. The uprights should overlap the ceiling joists by 75 mm.

2 Cut a 25 mm notch in both ends of the hangers 50-75 mm from the end of the boards. Nail or screw to the end of the rack (see illustration).

3 Slip top of uprights over the ceiling joist and nail or bolt in place.

MATERIALS

ITEM	DIMENSIONS (mm)	QUANTITY
uprights	900 x 75 x 38 (according to available height)	4
brace	600 x 75 x 38 (to match your joists)	1
hangers	450 x 75 x 25	2
flat-head (roundhead) nails	65	
bolts/screws (optional)	6 (minimum diameter)	

SPECIAL TOOLS
electric drill

TIME
3-4 hours

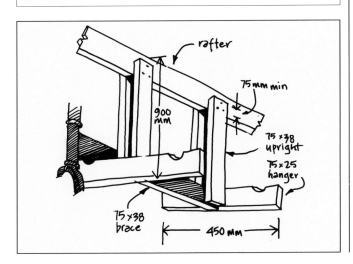

rafter

75 mm min

900 mm

75 x 38 upright

75 x 25 hanger

75 x 38 brace

450 MM

Overhead storage

Overhead storage can be as simple as using the existing rafters and beams to hold solid items like rolled-up rugs or surfboards, or as sophisticated as installing an electric chain block system to hoist up the family dinghy. When planning overhead storage in a garage, make sure there is adequate headroom – a sensible height for most overhead storage is around 2 m.

❑ Pulley systems. One of the problems of overhead storage is accessibility, which can be a real worry if items are super heavy. This is where pulley systems come into their own. To get cumbersome articles up and out of the way, chain-block or rope-block (block and tackle) systems can be used. Working on a ratchet, the chain block system levers the item up to the required position where it remains stable without having to be secured.

The less sophisticated rope block system works on the pulley principle where the item is winched up and secured by ropes when it is in position. This is easy for the home handyperson to install, and can be used to hold in place anything from a ladder to a canoe.

Awning pulley systems should be used for reasonably

Wire plant holder

light articles only, but can be quite handy if you want to get things up and out of the way without having to use a ladder.

❑ A wooden platform under the joists is another simple method of holding goods. Simply screw or nail shelving to the bottom of the joists and, hey presto, you have a ready-made basket.

❑ Alternatively, screw or nail a large timber shelf to the top of the joists, or suspend a timber platform by ropes or chains from the rafters.

❑ You could also build a tall, solid timber platform on legs for storage at the far end of the garage, high enough off the ground to enable the bonnet of the car to nuzzle in underneath.

❑ Looking for something simpler? A hammock strung across the rafters by hooks is ideal for storing lightweight articles up high.

❑ Firmly anchored hooks are another easy and inexpensive way to hold items overhead. Butchers' hooks hung over the beams and joists will support quite heavy weights. Sturdy plastic-coated hooks can be used to hold bicycles.

Overhead storage rack

And you thought your garage couldn't hold another thing! Just look up – it's nearly that easy to make this suspended storage unit.

The closer this rack is positioned to a side wall, the greater its load-bearing potential for storing all of those bulky extras.

STEP BY STEP

1 Assemble two or more shelf support units, following the instructions given in Project 15 (Bicycle rack). The distance between the uprights should not exceed 1200 mm.

2 Attach the shelf support units to ceiling joist as shown. The distance between the vertical support units should not be greater than 900 mm.

3 Nail or bolt 150 mm x 75 mm boards to the brace as shown.

MATERIALS		
ITEM	DIMENSIONS (mm)	QUANTITY
uprights	900 x 75 x 38	12
braces	1000 x 75 x 38	3
boards	1600 x 150 x 25	6
flat-head (roundhead) nails	65	
bolts/screws (optional)	6 diameter	

SPECIAL TOOLS
electric drill

TIME
One day

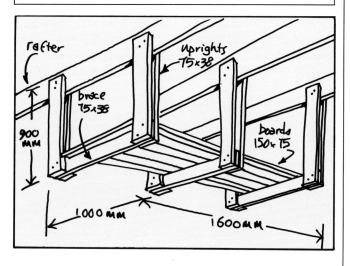

The Cellar

Depending on its size, condition and accessibility, a cellar has the potential to hold almost anything.

Older houses often have nonhabitable cellars which have traditionally been used for coal and junk – but with careful thought and planning they can be transformed quite cheaply into efficient and capacious storerooms. Some of the best uses for the cellar are:

❑ Wine and food – the cool conditions suit wine perfectly and will help a freezer to run more efficiently.

❑ Tools and decorating or building materials. If there is room, the cellar may also form a convenient workshop.

❑ Long-term storage of little-used items (such as holiday luggage or seasonal sports equipment).

Practical considerations

A dry, clean, well-ventilated cellar with a solid floor and the walls in good condition can be treated as an extension of the house as far as providing safe storage is concerned. It will be colder than elsewhere indoors, but you might even consider extending the heating system into the cellar if cool storage (such as for wine) is not important. Any suspicion of damp, however, and you are immediately limited as to what you can store in contact with the floor or walls; broadly, only items made of plastics, glass, noncorroding metals such as copper, aluminium and galvanised steel, and preservative-treated timber. Rodents and other pests are another point to watch out for, especially if the floor is bare earth.

The usage will also depend on how easy it is to get into the cellar and whether or not there is enough headroom. Cellars with steep steps and low ceilings are not ideal for manoeuvring heavy, bulky objects in and out of! For the same reason, it makes sense to keep things which you will need frequently near the door. Shallow shelves and wall-mounted hooks, racks and brackets which do not restrict access are best here. Use the hidden depths for storing items that will receive less regular visits.

Surveying the possibilities

To give yourself a clear picture of the potential, work through the points below and check what needs to be done to make the best use of the space.

❑ **Construction:** A cellar may be completely below ground or may be partly above and partly below ground level (semi-basement). The latter type often has a window, exterior hatch or grille, whereas a below-ground cellar will probably have little or no ventilation or natural light. Extra lighting is fairly simple to arrange, but ventilation may be tricky.

❑ **Damp:** This is a major consideration since it restricts what can be stored without damage. Test for damp with a meter (available in DIY outlets and builders'

merchants) or call in a specialist firm for an estimate. If you test after a spell of dry weather and find no signs of damp, don't assume that this automatically gives the all clear – check again after a period of rain.

Walls can be damp-proofed with chemicals or physically with rendering and waterproof panelling. Both really mean calling in the professionals and can be expensive. There is also some risk that physical treatment may force damp to rise into the room above if there is no damp-proof course (DPC).

Bare earth floors are never completely dry, but can be screeded with concrete incorporating a plastic damp-proof membrane (DPM) if there is sufficient headroom to permit the build-up in level (see below).

❏ **Ventilation:** A good airflow is important if the cellar doubles as a workshop, and is essential if you will be using solvents which give off harmful vapours. In any case, ventilation prevents mustiness and helps to control damp and associated problems to some extent. Airbricks can be

installed if any of the cellar walls are above ground, whereas an extractor fan (controlled by a humidity detector if desired) can be fitted through a wall or window, but will have to be ducted into a below-ground cellar.

❏ **Cleanliness:** General junk and coal are the usual obstacles. Junk can be sorted and disposed of as required; anything useful can be rehoused in the cellar afterwards in a more orderly way. Removing coal is a bigger task – even if there is

This cellar, or semibasement, has been converted into a very comfortable granny flat

very little left, the dust has usually impregnated all the surfaces. The only solution is rubble sacks, a shovel, old clothes, a dust mask, an industrial vacuum cleaner and time and energy. When you have removed as much as possible, follow up by cleaning and painting.

❏ **Lighting and power:** Storage is only efficient if you can see what you are looking for, and most cellars are lit by a single bulb or nothing at all. Adding fluorescent lighting coupled with white walls will give the best illumination of all areas. If you are in any doubt about what is involved, contact a qualified electrician.

If there is no existing light point to extend from, a separate 20 amp radial circuit from the consumer unit (which is often conveniently sited in the cellar) is the best solution. This can provide power as well, with the lighting being taken via a 5 amp fused connection unit. Another option is to run a 5 amp fused spur from the power circuit in the room above, making sure that by doing so you do not exceed the maximum floor area that the circuit can serve: 100 sq m for ring circuits; 50 sq m for 30 amp radial circuits. The light switch should be close to, but just inside, the door so that it can be turned on without entering the cellar, but cannot inadvertently be switched on from outside and left on unnoticed.

A separate spur will be needed for power outlets. This should be RCD-protected if you intend using power tools.

❏ **Access:** This may be via a trapdoor in the floor, a door under the stairs, or a full-height door (in the case of a semibasement cellar). Access determines what can be stored according to its size, weight and regularity of use, so think about improvements like rehanging a door the other way round to make it easier to open. Where access is restricted, storage can be arranged around the door so that it can be used like a cupboard.

❏ **Headroom:** Most cellars are below habitable height (2.3 m), but this only means that they must not be used as

living areas. If the headroom is less than your own height, the usage is broadly determined by how low you are prepared to stoop. If the floor joists above are exposed, this may make all the difference through being able to stand full-height at intervals between them.

One way to increase headroom may be to excavate the floor, but seek professional advice first to check if this will leave adequate support for the house walls and foundations.

❏ **Size:** Together with headroom, this is the factor that most determines how useful the cellar is – obviously, the bigger the better. If the cellar is 2.4 m or more in width, you can significantly increase the wall storage space by partially dividing it along its length with a racking system.

❏ **Floor:** A smooth, dry floor helps to keep the cellar clean and gives more flexibility as to what can be stored on it. Simple ways to provide hard-standing are to lay paving slabs on a bed of sand around the walls, or to section off these areas with timber and cast strips of concrete. In this way you will not reduce the headroom of the standing area in the middle, and at the same time you will also help to lessen the stooping distance.

❏ **Walls:** These form a large, useful and easily accessible area. Providing the walls are sound, shelves and cupboards can be fixed to them for a variety of storage. Any timber in contact with the masonry should be well soaked with preservative unless it is pretreated (e.g. Tanalised), and you should leave an air gap behind any cupboard units with a back by mounting them on battens/cleats or simply threading spacers

(such as rubber doorstops) on to the mounting screws.

In some cellars the inner 'walls' will be formed by brick pillars supporting the floor above. The gaps between these should not be filled in completely, as they provide essential airflow under the house, although you can still fix things across them.

❏ **Ceiling:** Open joists provide a wealth of hanging space for lightweight items in areas where headroom is not a problem. If the floor above is made of bare boards, panels of fibreboard stapled to the underside will help provide a degree of insulation from noise and dust – especially if the cellar is to double as a workshop. They can also be painted white to reflect light better.

Fitting out

Plan the layout of the cellar with storage systems that suit the items to be kept there, making full use of walls (and open ceilings) as hanging space and providing shelving of different depths. Site storage for long items such as timber opposite the door for easy access and removal.

In an area like this, appearance doesn't matter, so using what you have to hand or can salvage is the key to successful low-cost storage. Because of this, the following suggestions can only provide useful guidelines.

Remember that any storage is only as efficient as the ability to see what is stored, and this is doubly

important in a confined space. Don't make shelves and cupboards too deep, and help to identify small objects by using transparent containers or clear labelling; once an item is hidden by something in front of it, it is effectively 'lost'. Use self-adhesive labels and a marker pen for large unidentifiable boxes and a plastic lettering system (such as Dymo) for smaller containers in regular use.

Saving on the cost of materials by using up offcuts and 'recycled' timber salvaged from builders' skips is ideal, since looks will be relatively unimportant. But make sure that it is free from rot and insect attack.

❏ **Back-to-back racks:** You can add 'wall' space, if the floor width is 2.4 m or more, by erecting a simple floor-to-ceiling stud framework to divide part of the cellar lengthways and provide the storage area of two walls. Use straight, knot-free 50 mm x 50 mm DAR (PAR) softwood – there is no need to line the frame, because cladding means extra work and materials and will cut out light and ventilation, as well as making fixing to the studs more difficult.

In all cases, fix a length of timber to the floor so that you can screw the bottoms of the studs to it. If the frame runs parallel to open ceiling joists, align the floor timber with the closest joist, so you can screw the top of each stud to the side of it. To strengthen this joist, fix bracing between it and the adjacent joists. Alternatively insert cross-braces between two joists and screw the studs to the braces instead. If the framework runs at right-

For wine buffs – the cellar is an ideal place for storing wine, and lots of it . . .

angles to the joists, screw one stud to each joist. No bracing is necessary. If the ceiling is lined, fix a 50 mm x 50 mm beam to the surface, screwing through it into the joists, and attach the studs to this.

Attach shelf brackets or adjustable shelving supports to both sides of the studs. Aligning the shelves back-to-back like this provides deep shelving that can be reached from both sides; cut notches in the backs of each shelf so that they fit over the studs and span the centre gap. If you can't align the shelves, a batten/cleat along the back of the shelf will prevent things from rolling or being pushed off it. Horizontal battens/cleats can also be screwed part way up the studs to provide bracing and can be fitted with hooks or drilled for dowels to provide hanging space for tools.

❑ **Using alcoves:** These are a ready-made storage area. If there is a fireplace in the room above, the supporting brickwork will probably create three alcoves that can be fitted out with floor-to-ceiling shelves resting on battens/cleats. Doors can be hung on vertical battens/cleats to close off the space, but ensure that there is some ventilation behind them. Louvre doors are especially suitable.

❑ **Using benching:** A horizontal surface fixed around the walls both provides storage in its own right and forms a useful worktop – where space permits, it could even be an unusual venue for an electric train! Suitable dimensions are a height of 900 mm with a depth of 600 mm, and you should use timber at least 20 mm thick, such as old floorboards. Provide support every 900 mm on a 50 mm x 50 mm bearer fixed front to back, with one end set into the brickwork and the front end supported on an upright post.

Shelving above the benching can be of different depths – deep shelves high up for large items and shallow shelves lower down for small ones, so that they restrict the bench space as little as possible. Make sure, however, that the deep shelves are far enough back from the front of the benching to prevent a head-on collision when you bend forwards.

Benching is an obvious place to store tools. Particle (chip) board or MDF panels supported on the back of the benching can be fitted with clips and hooks to store handtools just where they will be needed. By making the boards detachable they can be transferred easily (with help) to other working areas. Use each tool as a template to draw around its outline – to keep it in the right place and to spot what has been borrowed!

Pull-out storage under the benching is best for anything other than large items, since the area at the back is difficult to reach. An old chest of drawers makes an excellent storage unit, but you may need to reinforce the drawer bases with strips of plywood glued underneath, before storing heavy things in them.

Shelving supported on the upright posts can hold plastic storage crates (inserted lengthways front to back). In this case, you will need a second set of uprights, screwed to the wall, to carry cross-bearers for the shelving. Space the shelves to give just sufficient clearance to move the crates in and out so as to keep out dust, especially if the benching above will be used as a workbench.

Another form of pull-out storage is a wine rack; this should stand on the floor so as to minimise vibration of the contents. Also on the floor, a tea-chest is ideal for storing 'useful' offcuts of timber and the like. Cut a piece of 12 mm plywood to the size of the base and nail this to two timber bearers. Stand the tea-chest on this for additional support and to allow air to circulate beneath it. Castors could be fitted to the bearers to allow it to be pulled out easily.

❑ **Racking:** Long items such as timber are efficiently stored on ladder racks, on which they are accessible from the end and side. Construct the ladder sections from 50 mm x 50 mm DAR (PAR) softwood and secure them to the wall and ceiling. Space the 'rungs' at intervals to suit the sizes of timber that you expect to store (not forgetting sheet materials), and position the racks at 900 mm intervals so as to support timber of this length or over. Anything shorter than that can be kept in the offcut tea-chest. Two stout angle brackets screwed to the front of the uprights will support a ladder – again in a position where it can easily be carried through the doorway. Good access is the key to successful storage.

In emergencies

❑ Ensure that there is a clear route to isolating switches and valves for mains services (electricity, water and gas) and that nothing can be stored in front of them.

PART 4

Kitchen Improvements

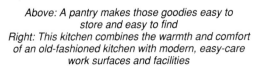

*Above: A pantry makes those goodies easy to
store and easy to find
Right: This kitchen combines the warmth and comfort
of an old-fashioned kitchen with modern, easy-care
work surfaces and facilities*

You need more than money to create a kitchen that looks good and works well. Far more important is a sense of how you actually want your kitchen to work, plus a knowledge of basic planning principles.

THE KITCHEN PLAN

The layout of the room, rather than its size, has an enormous impact on its level of efficiency. It's worth taking your time over the planning stage to avoid what could prove to be costly and annoying mistakes.

There is no right or wrong design for a kitchen; if it suits the way you operate, then that's absolutely fine.

Before you call in a kitchen company, architect, designer or builder, it's worth thinking about how you want the kitchen to be used; probably not a subject you've given much thought to up until now.

Obviously its basic functions are in the cooking and serving of meals, and the cleaning up afterwards. However, the way all that works for you is a fairly complex matter, so first ask yourself the following questions:

❏ How many family members use the kitchen?
❏ Will more than one person be cooking in it at a time?
❏ What do you all like and dislike about your present kitchen?
❏ What is your idea of the ultimate kitchen?
❏ Do you eat in the kitchen, and if so, just for quick snacks or for sit-down meals?
❏ What eating facilities are needed: a table, a breakfast bar, or a fold-down table?
❏ Do you need a serving hatch through to the dining room?
❏ Is the kitchen the social centre of the house?
❏ What activities take place in the kitchen apart from food preparation and eating hot meals?
❏ Do the children do their homework or watch television in there?
❏ Do you want a casual sitting area for friends?
❏ Do you eat a lot of frozen food; in other words, do you need a separate freezer?
❏ Does it necessarily have to be in the kitchen?
❏ How much food and equipment do you keep in the kitchen?
❏ Will cutlery and crockery be kept in the kitchen or dining room?
❏ How much worktop do you need?
❏ Is your present kitchen big enough?
❏ Can you take in extra space from adjoining areas or rooms?
❏ Do you need to add an extension to your house to accommodate the new kitchen?
❏ Could you remove a wall or two between your current kitchen and an adjoining room?
❏ Could you re-site the kitchen in another room?
❏ What sort of power do you use for cooking?
❏ Do you need to change your power supplies?
❏ Are these changes vital, or would you be just as satisfied with another arrangement?
❏ Do you have enough power points for all your small appliances?
❏ How much money do you have to spend on your new kitchen?
❏ Will you have to borrow money?
❏ Are you thinking of moving within the next few years? If so, don't overspend. A sound investment would be to build a kitchen that costs no more than 10 per cent of the current resale value of your house.

These are the basics – from there you must think about materials you want to use in the kitchen, the look you are hoping to achieve, as well as more practical aspects such as lighting, waste disposal and ventilation. You'll find information on those things later in this section.

For the layout of your new kitchen, many people find it useful to draw up an accurate scale floor plan of the room on graph paper, and then make scale cut-outs of all appliances (with allowances for pipes, wires and ventilation). They can then be moved around on the plan, until you find the most suitable set-up for your needs. If you find it hard to visualise on paper, you can do the same thing in the actual kitchen, using masking tape to show where cupboards and appliances will go.

A modern country look – this kitchen features attractive and practical storage areas

The eat-in kitchen

The most informal arrangement, the eat-in kitchen can fit into almost any shaped room as long as it's not too small.

A great benefit of this layout is that the cook need never feel left out from what's going on at the table. On the down side of things it is impossible to close the door on kitchen mess.

The most usual configuration is to have a single-line or L-shaped kitchen, with the table in the middle of the room. When not in use, it can double as extra workspace, acting as an island in the room. You must be sure to leave at least one metre around the perimeter of the table to accommodate chairs. If space is a problem, consider having benches instead of chairs; they are not as flexible, but take up less room.

Another possibility, in a narrower room, is to have a single-line arrangement with the table against the opposite wall. Make sure, if there are overhead cupboards or shelves on this wall, that they are not directly above the chairs.

With both these types of eat-in kitchen, try to find a dining table that complements the overall design of the room. For instance, in a country-style kitchen, you could choose an old scrubbed pine table; in a modern setting a simple ash or marble-topped table may be more appropriate. In many kitchens, there's not the space for a proper table; the dining part of the room, then, may be a peninsula unit, or small return at the end of a sweep of worktop.

You may need to look for fold-up chairs, which can be stored away neatly when not in use, or stools, which can tuck away under the bar. Another possibility is to have a breakfast bar running along the length of the room in a narrow single-line kitchen. If space is at a premium, the bar can be hinged so that it folds down against the wall when it is not being used.

In a really tiny kitchen, the top drawer in a bank of drawers can conceal a pull-out table, which can also be used as extra worktop space when necessary.

A spacious L-shaped eat-in kitchen

Poggenpohl – Kitchen Architecture

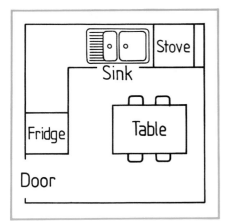

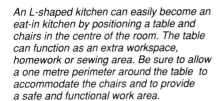

An L-shaped kitchen can easily become an eat-in kitchen by positioning a table and chairs in the centre of the room. The table can function as an extra workspace, homework or sewing area. Be sure to allow a one metre perimeter around the table to accommodate the chairs and to provide a safe and functional work area.

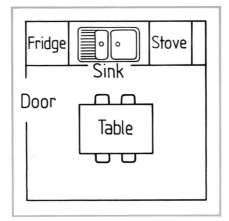

Single-line kitchens maximise space and allow room for a dining area. If the bench area of the kitchen is inadequate the table can be used as an extra work surface. As with all eat-in kitchens, allow for the traffic flow by positioning the table and chairs so that at least one person can be working in the kitchen while others are seated.

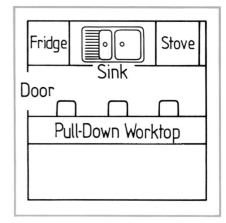

When space is a problem a pull-down hinged surface can be incorporated into a single-line kitchen to create an eating area or extra worktop. Stools or folding chairs are best as they can be removed when the worktop is folded away, to increase the floor space. This handy work surface, when in use, creates a flexible galley-style kitchen.

THE WORK TRIANGLE

It's been around for years, and although cliched, the so-called work triangle is a good starting point in the planning of your kitchen. In essence, it's a way of organising elements so that the room can be used in the most efficient way.

Admittedly, not everyone demands the same thing from a kitchen, and with technological advances such as the microwave oven and dishwasher, priorities have changed over the years and the kitchen in general is used in a different way. However, the basic principles still apply.

The three major items in the kitchen are cooker, sink and refrigerator. These should be placed in a triangle, with the sink as the pivot point. Ideally, the triangle should be equilateral with sides of no less than 1.2 m, otherwise you will feel too cramped. Likewise, they should be no more than a couple of metres apart to avoid unnecessary walking.

If you decide on a cooktop (hob) and wall oven, and perhaps a microwave, it's not always possible to group them together in the work triangle. In that case, it's probably a good idea to have the cooktop (hob) in the triangle, with the wall oven built into a bank of cupboards. The microwave oven, which doesn't take up much room, can be placed on the worktop, mounted on a swivelling wall bracket, or built into a bank of cupboards. Remember to have it at a low enough level so that all the family can use it.

Another consideration is the dishwasher — even if you don't plan to install one straight away it's a good idea to make provision for one. That way, later plumbing and installation costs can be minimised. Ideally, it should be placed near the sink, within easy reach of cupboards in which crockery and glassware are stored.

For safety, the triangle should not be interrupted by a doorway; someone racing in unexpectedly could easily cause an accident.

Between each of the three appliances there should be sufficient work surface for preparing and cleaning up after meals. A set down space of at least half a metre should be allocated beside the refrigerator and stove for safety as well as convenience.

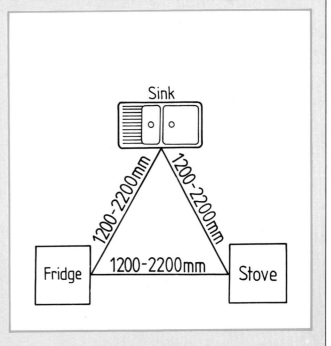

The L-shaped kitchen

This configuration is suitable for virtually all types of rooms, except for particularly narrow ones, or those with lots of doors.

It's often used to create a kitchen in the corner of an open-plan living room, or in a large combined kitchen/dining room.

In almost every case, the L-shaped kitchen can include an eating area, even if it's only in the form of a breakfast bar; generally, though, there's room here for a table. Of course, it's a very sociable set-up, ideal for relaxed entertaining and family meals, enabling the cook to join in conversation without feeling excluded. It's also an adaptable arrangement, which should easily be able to accommodate two cooks at a time, and one in which through traffic is generally not a problem.

There are several possible configurations for the L-shaped kitchen. It can run along two adjacent walls, meeting in the corner – this is particularly suitable in the case of a large eat-in kitchen. Another possibility is that all appliances run along one arm of the 'L', with the other arm forming a peninsula unit or divider between the kitchen and the living or dining area.

The temptation, if the room is very large, is to make the sides of the 'L' extra long, stretching out the work triangle. The message is to keep the work triangle fairly compact, but separated by reasonable stretches of worktop to ensure that the main working area doesn't get too congested. In order to gain a convenient sweep of unbroken workspace, the refrigerator and tall cupboards can be placed at either end of the two arms of the 'L', or at one end of the long arm. As in all other types of kitchen, the refrigerator should be placed in the most convenient position

The L-shape is a very sociable set-up.

for family members to use without getting in the cook's way.

Planning of the kitchen should include provision for a convenient setdown area near the stove, pantry or refrigerator, so that food can be moved safely and easily from one area to another.

Lighting is often a problem in the L-shaped kitchen, as a large proportion of worktop is likely to be away from the window. For this reason, leave the window uncluttered to maximise light during the day, and carefully plan overall and spot lighting so the kitchen is well lit at night.

WORKING WITH THE PROFESSIONALS

The first thing to do is to ask around amongst friends for recommendations of architects, kitchen specialists, interior designers and builders. Also, look in design magazines to find the names of people or companies whose work you admire. Make sure whoever you choose is qualified to do the job.

Obtain quotes from at least three builders to compare prices. Beware of the difference between a firm quote – a fixed price – and an estimate, which is just an educated guess at the final cost.

The cheapest quote is not necessarily the one you should choose; ask to see an example of the builder's work, and try to talk to previous clients.

Be specific when you're asking for quotes; put in as many details as possible. For instance, if you want a particular laminate, say so; otherwise the builder will almost certainly price the job on the cheapest available material. Even so, when the work is finished, you can expect a price variation of anything up to 15 per cent on your original quote.

The work done by builders, kitchen companies, interior designers and architects varies enormously. Clarify exactly what can be expected of them – will they be supervising the job, for example, or merely drawing up plans.

Ask for a written work schedule from the builder, and don't be satisfied with 'about 10 days'. Insist on details such as 'removing existing kitchen – one man, one day; electrical work – one man, half a day'. Find out how the builder wants to be paid; the usual way is at the completion of each stage. This is where the work schedule comes in handy. Some small businesses, however, do not have the cash flow to buy materials without being paid up front.

Find out about professional fees. Are they a flat fee, or a percentage of the cost of the job? Make sure you find this out before the work starts, so that you don't have any nasty surprises later on.

Find out how many men will be permanently on site, and what they expect working hours to be.

Establish the order of work; find out, for instance, whether the plumber can come early if the electrician fails to turn up on time.

Ask the builder to give you a completion date, and have a penalty clause written into the contract making the builder liable for any unacceptable delays. He cannot be held responsible for acts of God, for unforeseen situations such as a major damp problem, or for any change of mind you may have.

Clarify the day-to-day arrangements the builder has; where he will store his material (you don't want him blocking access to your garage); what access there is to the site – if it's through the house, make sure the floors are protected; whether he will use your bathroom and telephone, or make his own arrangements. Always add a final stage to the building schedule, relating to making good, detail work and clearing up. This will give the builder the incentive not to abandon you at an awkward moment. It could include such things as rehanging doors which do not open properly or repairing faulty switches.

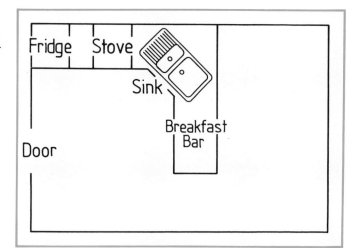

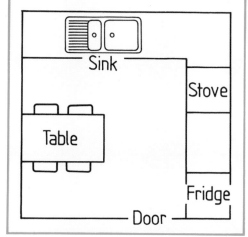

Right: The breakfast bar can double as a room divider

Far right: The L-shape is particularly suitable as an eat-in kitchen

Several possible configurations exist for the L-shaped kitchen. It can run along two adjacent walls, meeting in the corner – this is particularly suitable in the case of a large eat-in kitchen. Another possibility is that all appliances run along one arm of the 'L', with the other arm forming a peninsula unit or divider between the kitchen, living or dining area.

Right: The compact work area of this L-shaped kitchen includes modern appliances and a breakfast bar

IKEA

IKEA

The U-shaped kitchen

With cabinets and appliances running in an unbroken line around three counters, the U-shape is generally considered to be the most workable kitchen design.

To create an efficient work triangle in a U-shaped kitchen, awkwardly positioned doorways are more of a problem than the actual size of the room. In the true U-shape, the line of work surfaces is uninterrupted by doors, so that the cook is undisturbed by family members continually tramping through the work area.

A small kitchen can happily accommodate a U-shape, although it is important that the floor space between the two arms be at least 1.5 m, and preferably 1.8 m if there is

likely to be more than one person working in there at any one time.

A large U-shape can, admittedly, offer a large expanse of worktop, but, unless you're careful, it can also create an elongated work triangle. It's best to confine the triangle to the base of the 'U', unless you want the walking you do in the kitchen to contribute significantly to your overall exercise program!

Apart from considering the work triangle, it's also important to consider plumbing requirements –

keeping changes to original plumbing to a minimum. You will also have to think about access to gas and electricity, and the need to allow enough room for all doors to open comfortably.

The most common configuration is to have the sink at the base of the 'U', with cooker and refrigerator facing each other on the arms. It's advisable to place the refrigerator as near as possible to the kitchen doorway, so that family members can get to it without disturbing the cook. If you plan to have a dishwasher, it could either be placed near the sink, or on the same arm as the refrigerator.

With the continuous sweep of worktop found in the U-shaped kitchen, it's often possible to fit in a tall larder and broom cupboard. The usual rule applies here – put them at

each end of the 'U' to avoid breaking up the work surface. Alternatively, if there's a fourth wall in the kitchen, the taller items (including, if you like, a wall oven or refrigerator as well as storage cupboards) can be placed here, linked, perhaps by an appliance centre. Often, that fourth wall is separated from the 'U' by a well-used traffic way. If that's the case, for safety reasons, the walkway should be at least 1.1 m wide, and the wall oven should have an off-loading counter beside it.

In a U-shaped kitchen it is often possible to fit in a spot for eating, even if it's only a bar along one leg of the 'U'. If this is separated by a tall unit from the working area, it could be at a lower level to suit children.

The U-shaped kitchen is not necessarily self-contained; often there is no fourth wall, and instead, the kitchen interconnects with another room. Another common situation is that units and appliances run along two walls, and the third arm makes up a room divider. The area above the divider can be left completely open; the divider then becomes a serving surface, or perhaps even a breakfast bar.

Alternatively, open shelving or a high divider can partly screen the work zone from the living or dining area. This way, the cook can still see what's going on, but any mess can be hidden.

It's a good idea if the units which make up the divider have doors opening into both areas; for instance, if there's a dining table on one side, store all crockery on that side, while cooking utensils would be better kept in the part which opens to the kitchen.

As in many types of kitchen, corners are a problem in the U-shape. Most manufacturers include corner units in their ranges; carousels for wall or base units, and units with bifold doors. Especially in a small kitchen, it's important to squeeze in as much storage as possible; efficient use of tricky corners can give valuable extra space. If a corner unit backs onto a dining area, doors that open on the dining side will allow full access to it.

It's also important to make sure that doors don't open into each other, and that appliances such as refrigerators are placed at least 30 cm in from the corners so that doors can be opened completely, without banging into the walls.

Left: The true U-shaped kitchen can be varied to accommodate doorways and appliances while still offering a large expanse of workspace
Below: Four different U-shaped configurations

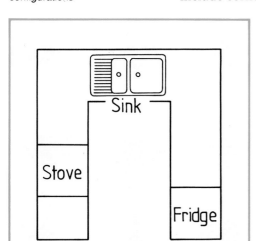

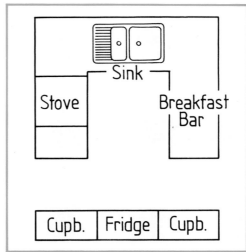

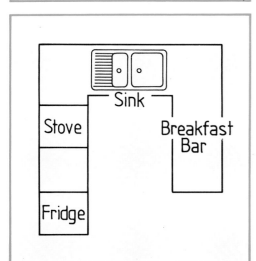

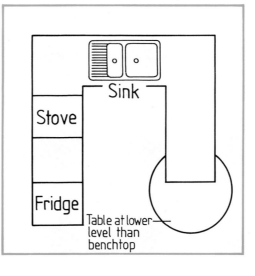

A large U-shape can offer a large expanse of worktop, but, if you're not careful, it can also create an elongated work triangle. It's best to confine the triangle to the base of the 'U', unless you want all the walking you do in the kitchen to contribute to your overall exercise program.

The single-line kitchen

If space is a problem, the single-line layout may be the most practical and efficient arrangement.

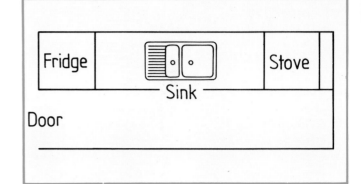

It's a challenge to the designer, but if planned carefully, the single-line kitchen can look neat, and work as well as a beautifully designed machine. In a multi-purpose room, it has the advantage of being able to be contained in one area, leaving most of the floor space free for dining and/or relaxing.

The main thing with a single-line kitchen, especially in a small area, is to allow as much worktop space as possible. To do this, you will need to be flexible in your choice of appliances and in your approach to storage. A built-under refrigerator and a cooktop (hob) with a pull-down cover give extra work space. There are dozens of styles of sinks available with chopping boards and drainer baskets; these are particularly handy when space is at a premium.

The most usual configuration in the single-line kitchen is for the sink to be in the middle of the worktop area with refrigerator and cooker on either side. For convenience, the refrigerator door, and the oven door (if it's a side-opening one), should open away from the sink. Most refrigerators offer the option of doors that open from either the left- or right-hand-side. If you have a dishwasher, place it next to the sink for easy access and to minimise plumbing costs. With a dishwasher, you may be able to manage with a sink without draining board.

Use every inch of wall space for storage; hang cupboards where possible, making sure that they are at least 60 cm above the work surface. To create a finished look, and to maximise storage, take all wall cupboards up to the ceiling. If the kitchen is in a corridor-type room, use the opposite wall for narrow shelving, fitted from floor to ceiling. Incorporate a fold-down shelf or table which can be used at breakfast time, for light snacks, or for handy extra workspace.

Above: Single-line kitchens require imaginative use of storage space
Below: A single-line kitchen is the best solution when space is at a premium

The galley kitchen

The galley kitchen, generally a narrow room with cabinets on the two long walls, is one of the most difficult types of kitchen to make work satisfactorily.

The most awkward arrangement is when the room is essentially a passageway between the back door and the main living areas. Much less troublesome is the corridor with one completely enclosed end wall, in which the only traffic is that coming into, and not through, the room.

In either case, there should be at least 1.2 m between the facing units, to allow two people to work together comfortably in the room and also, when it is a thoroughfare to the back door, to enable the family to walk through without getting too much in the cook's way. Any narrower than 1.2 m means that bending down to get something from a base unit would become a contortionist's feat, and it would also be impossible to simultane-ously open doors on opposite sides of the room. If you have the space, a walkway of between 1.5 and 1.8 m is ideal. Much more than that and the working spaces are too far apart.

The most usual, and usable, arrangement for the galley kitchen is for the sink and cooker to be on one side with the refrigerator and storage on the opposite wall.

Alternatively, the refrigerator and sink can be on one side, with cooker on the other. If possible, place the refrig-erator at the end of the kitchen most accessible to other rooms, so that everyone can use it with-out disturbing the cook. Work areas and appliances should be grouped together in such a way that you are not continually crossing the room. For instance, the dishwasher should, if possible, be near the sink and crockery storage cupboards.

One great advantage of the galley kitchen is the potential for expanses of workspace. As is the rule with all styles of kitchen, locate tall items such as the refrigerator and broom cupboard at the ends of the walls to allow for uninterrupted sweeps of worktop.

Elizabeth Whiting and Associates

The most usual, and usable, arrangement for the galley kitchen is for the sink and stove to be on one side with the refrigerator and storage on the opposite wall.

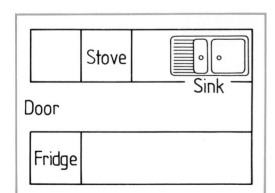

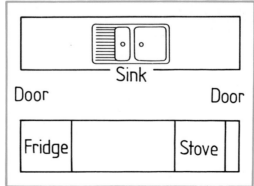

Above: A galley kitchen is like a narrow corridor, and utilises wall space with cupboards extending to the ceiling
Left: The galley kitchen's main advantage is the expanse of workspace it offers

Fold-down table

A small kitchen may not have enough room for a permanent table at which a couple of people can eat breakfast or quick kitchen meals, but it may have a wall to which a fold-down table could be attached.

MATERIALS

60 x 60 mm DAR (PAR) softwood
tabletop as discussed
piano hinge
2 regular hinges of the best quality
caselock, as used for musical instrument cases
spring latch
masonry bolts or screws and plugs
locking stay
paint or lacquer

TOOLS	TIME
spanner	1-2 days
screwdrivers	
handsaw and/or power saw	
drill	
spadebit and masonry bit	

Such a table can also provide extra workspace when needed as well as a place for family and friends to sit and keep the cook company while meals are being prepared. Folding chairs, some kind of cosy lighting arrangement and a spot for a small television on a facing wall could make previously dead space the most popular spot in the house.

Before making any decisions about the size of the table, decide on your chairs and place them in situ, working out whether you actually have enough space and what restrictions the table will place on movement in the kitchen. Bear in mind that a comfortable minimum width must allow two people to sit opposite each other without banging knees.

The distance the table protrudes from the wall depends on its height as it cannot be so long that it won't fold down flush against the wall. About 72 cm plus the mounting block is about right (see fig. 1) but test it with the chairs you intend to use.

The tabletop could be made from a variety of materials, depending on availability and your tools. Possibilities include:
❏ 25-30 mm thick fibreboard (MDF) which you could buy cut to size at a timber yard, or cut it yourself using a circular saw and a clamped straightedge as a guide. Clamp the sheet to a bench or table to stop it shifting when you make your cut. Draw the line along which the cut is to be made then establish where your straightedge needs to be clamped. It will be parallel to the cut line at a distance which is determined by the distance from the blade of your circular saw to the edge of its baseplate, which will be pushed along the straightedge during the cut. Experiment on some scrap sheet to get that distance exactly right. (See fig. 4).

The surface finish could be either high- or low-gloss enamel paint or a laminate, although a laminate could be as easily applied to regular coarse grain particle (chip) board (see box).

❏ Glued and clamped pine lengths (90 or 120 x 40 mm). Sash cramps are needed for this and the amount of surface sanding required depends very much on the straightness of the timber. Sometimes cabinet makers can be persuaded, for a nominal fee, to surface-sand such items in their big belt sanders. The assembly should be glued together first, with PVA adhesive, and cut to size afterwards, using the same technique as for fibreboard. The surface may be finished with either paint or lacquer. Be sure to clean excess adhesive off the surface before it dries as it is very difficult to remove when dry.

As we are proposing only a fairly small table here, one leg should be sufficient, although two may be fitted if desired. One leg has the advantage of allowing easier access for people and chairs.

STEP BY STEP

1 Cut a length of 60 x 60 mm timber to the desired width of the table. This is the block from which the table will be hinged and which will be fastened to the wall. If it is a stud wall use at least two 80 mm coach screws, counterbored 20 mm or so with a spadebit in a drill, secured into separate stud beams. If it is a brick wall use masonry bolts of the same length or greater, also counterbored 20 mm. When using masonry bolts be sure to drill to the exact depth the bolts will be inserted and hammer them in until solid contact is made with the bottom of the hole, or the bolts will not grab properly.

You can use various types of hinge but a piano hinge which runs the length of the block is recommended (see fig. 2). Other types of hinge require rebates to be made in the mounting block.

2 The leg will be too long to fold between the tabletop and the wall so it is cut and hinged. Where you make the cut is up to you but halfway is recommended. Use 60 x 60 mm timber for the leg and chamfer each corner to about 5 mm. When the leg is supporting the table it is fixed into one rigid length with the aid of a caselock on the side opposite to that with the hinge (see fig. 3). A caselock is often used on musical instrument cases and camera cases, available at well-stocked ironmongers. For appearance the caselock and

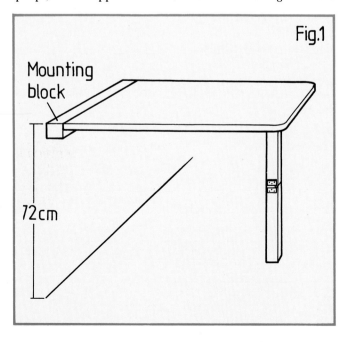

Fig.1

Mounting block

72 cm

the hinge should preferably be made of the same metal. Rebate for both hinges. Where the top hinge connects with the underside of the tabletop a rebate is not strictly necessary although it would improve the firmness of the joint.

3 All that is now required is to clip the folded leg to the underside of the table for when it is folded down against the wall and not in use. Some kind of ball and spring cupboard door latch can be used although your DIY shop will have a variety to choose from. A locking stay is also required to stop the leg from folding under when the table is in use (see fig. 3).

4 Painting should be done very carefully in a dust-free environment with a good quality gloss paint. For toughness, at least three coats with a light sand between each one is required. For extra toughness you can even finish with a couple of coats of lacquer. Remember that time spent sanding all components will be well rewarded with a superior finish.

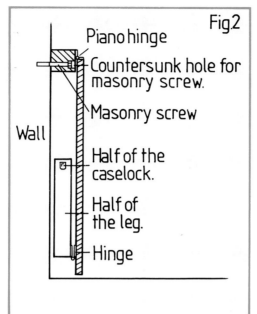

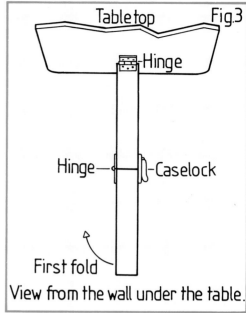

View from the wall under the table.

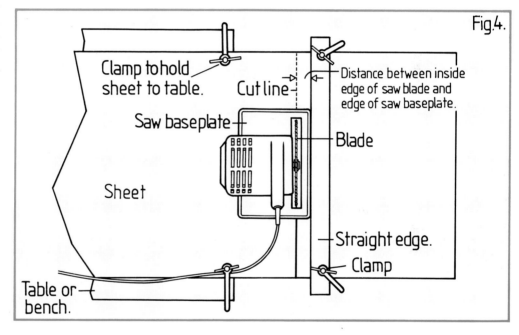

Right: Circular saw with blade guard omitted to show where to place straightedge to make a cut

APPLYING LAMINATE TO PARTICLE (CHIP) BOARD

Draw the pieces you want on the decorative side of your laminate sheet, allowing sufficient extra on the surface piece for the strips that will be glued to the edges.

Use a square and double check your measurements. If unsure of how much extra to allow for the thickness of the laminate on the edges, first cut off a couple of pieces to experiment. The contact adhesive, if applied correctly, will add about 0.5 mm.

Score along your lines with a laminate cutter, a simple and cheap device with a tungsten carbide tip. Once you have achieved a good clean break through the laminate's decorative surface, break the sheet along a straightedge, applying downward pressure over the whole length of the cut. It should snap in two along the score line, after which the backing, which may be jagged on the edge, can be sanded smooth. You may even want to try

sanding it back at an angle with a sanding block for a mitred join.

Cover both surfaces to be joined with a thin and even coat of thixotropic contact adhesive, making sure to avoid lumps, and wait until the adhesive dries to a tacky, almost dry feeling. Line up the laminate carefully and press it onto the particle (chip) board a bit at a time, making full use of the laminate's flexibility, and smoothing it firmly with a cloth.

A drawing pin pushed into the edge will assist in positioning the top surface laminate. Once the two glued surfaces come into contact you are fully committed to your positioning because contact adhesive works like its name: full adhesion is achieved with contact.

Add your edge pieces and clean excess adhesive off the laminate with the manufacturer's recommended solvent as soon as possible.

Gone are the days when the kitchen was a purely utilitarian room. Today we put as much thought into the look of our kitchens as we do to any other part of the house.

KITCHEN STYLES

Once you've finalised the floor plan of your new kitchen, you can concentrate on the style. Are you after a comfortable and cosy look, or something more streamlined? Here we look at the elements found in various types of kitchen – combine them to suit your own style.

Country

As soon as you walk into the country kitchen, it's as if there's a huge welcome mat at the door. You see it in the lovely comfortable clutter, the warm timber, the informality and the deliberately mismatched old tiles in the splashback. Bowls of fruit and vegetables on display – perhaps just one type, such as lemons or pears – indicate a love of nature. Herbs and spices are decanted into pretty jars; farmhouse loaves sit on the breadboard; wire baskets full of eggs add to the mood.

The first impression may be that while it's appealing to look at, it doesn't work very well. That need not be the case at all; as long as the country kitchen is designed carefully, there is no reason why it need not be every bit as efficient as any other type of kitchen.

One of the most vital aspects of the country kitchen is storage. While in many other styles of kitchen, the idea is to hide everything away, it's just the opposite for the country look. A dresser can be used to show off collections of china or glassware; a similar effect can also be achieved with open shelving. A large plate rack built in above the sink gives a definite country feel, but also serves a very useful purpose, doubling as draining rack and storage space. A rack suspended by chains from a crossbeam or joist provides valuable extra storage space. Buy one ready-made, or make your own from lengths of piping or broom handles, and use butchers' hooks or cup hooks to hang anything, from copper pans to dried herbs.

What country kitchen would be complete without a large walk-in pantry, lined with shelves? It's a nostalgic, as well as an entirely practical, option.

Of course, timber is the predominant material in the country kitchen. Tongue-and-groove cupboard doors finished with matt lacquer or, if you're a perfectionist, waxed, give an authentic feel. A butcher's block can be used for a worktop, and it looks especially good to mix light and dark timbers, to give the impression that the kitchen has evolved rather than been built in one go.

You can even use timber on the floor, but terracotta, flagstone, slate or earthy-coloured tiles are just as appropriate and are easier to maintain.

As in any other kitchen, you should also be concerned about getting in as much natural light as possible. A stable door would be the obvious choice here, especially if it leads onto a lovely outside eating area. If that's not suitable, consider installing a skylight, french windows or a glass door, large windows or a bank of smaller ones.

A mesh-front cupboard with small drawers and a plate and mug rack

Leadlight and shelves with wooden rails add character to a country kitchen

As long as the country kitchen is designed carefully, there is no reason why it need not be as efficient as any other type of kitchen.

Rangewood Kitchens

Cabinetcraft Kitchens

Above: Shelves and a drawer are an attractive feature for a kitchen corner
Below: A country kitchen featuring wood cupboards, leadlight and patterned wall tiles

Above: A dresser is a way to include extra storage and display areas

Cabinetcraft Kitchens

Ultra-modern

Is it a space station, is it a laboratory – no, it's a kitchen, an ultra-modern one. Here you'll find the best of everything, the very latest technology. No room here for comfortable clutter – everything's hidden from view, or displayed purely for its functional qualities. Small appliances sit in purpose-built cabinets, always close at hand – the message here is efficiency, speed and streamlining.

Materials for the ultra-modern kitchen are chosen for their practical attributes; worktops of stainless steel are hygienic and easy to look after, as too are the stainless steel splashbacks. For a particularly streamlined effect the whole worktop, including sink and draining board, are moulded out of one piece of stainless steel. Alternatively, use granite for a sleek worktop. Colour can come into its own in the ultra-modern kitchen. If you've got the courage, the sky's the limit – the more vibrant, the better. Be bold, this room can take it.

Take your ideas for storage from the commercial world – use metal shelving, industrial systems, wire grids. Steal inspiration from the chemistry laboratory to give your ultra-modern kitchen the serious look – deep sinks, winged taps, glass beakers and glass-stoppered storage jars. Cupboards should look sleek and unadorned. Choose one of the new iridescent laminates, or MDF with a durable polyurethane finish.

For flooring, tough rubber gives a suitably industrial effect. For over-the-top modern, use it on walls too. For something a little more restrained, and as a foil to the super-efficient laboratory look, choose timber boards, parquet, or plain coloured ceramic tiles.

The ultra-modern look is not for the fainthearted; it's the home of the brave.

Take your ideas for storage from the commercial world – metal shelving, industrial systems, wire grids. Steal inspiration from the chemistry laboratory to give your ultra-modern kitchen the serious look – deep sinks, winged taps, glass beakers and glass stoppered jars.

An ultra-modern kitchen that combines stainless steel with dark surfaces to give a dramatic and unusual effect

Kitchen Architecture

Above: A midway storage shelf
Right: A large butcher's block, with a rack for hanging kitchen implements and shelves above and below

Below: An ultra-modern kitchen is devoid of clutter and features streamlined walls, appliances in purpose-built cabinets, hygienic surfaces and the very latest in kitchen technology

Family

By definition, the family kitchen is expansive; the hub of the house where everyone can get together to eat, to talk, to cook, or just to relax. For the cook who hates to feel isolated, this is the answer. It's a room which should take the whole family into consideration; tough enough to deal with the kids, comfortable enough for everyone.

Planning is vital; clearly defined areas and traffic patterns have to be established to avoid chaos. The cook has to be able to work happily in a carefully-designed food preparation area without fear of children underfoot as they make a beeline for the refrigerator or sink.

Try to incorporate an area for the children to do their homework (perhaps the dining table can double as a desk); a comfortable seating spot for friends and family to relax; a couple of stools near a worktop so that guests can have a drink, and maybe even lend a hand while you're preparing a meal.

If you've got the space, an area in the family kitchen can be set aside for watching television, for bookshelves, for hobbies. A lovely touch, which would add atmosphere to the room, would be to build in a fireplace.

Because this is the most well-used room in the house, orientate it, if you're in at the planning stages, towards the best view, the sunniest outlook. If you can install french windows opening to a balcony, garden or patio, so much the better.

Choose the most hardwearing surfaces you can possibly find – this is certainly not the place for fragile materials. It's a room that will work hard for you, and should answer your every demand.

Planning is vital; establish clearly defined areas and traffic patterns to avoid chaos. The cook has to be able to work happily in a carefully designed food preparation area without fear of children underfoot as they make a beeline for the refrigerator or sink.

The family kitchen – a place where everyone can gather, that features expansive work areas and plenty of room for a busy traffic flow

Professional

The professional kitchen can take on many guises – at first glance it can look like a country kitchen or an ultra-modern kitchen, even a family kitchen, or anything in between. It's only at closer inspection that you realise there are things here which set it apart – you can see that whoever's in control here really is in control. This is the working environment for someone who's not beaten by soufflés, and for whom cooking is far more than just slinging a few chops under the grill at the last minute.

The professional kitchen is an individual room – the design of it depends entirely on the person using it. It'll be the sort of kitchen in which everything has a place, but apart from that, it can vary enormously. The sink will probably need to be larger than average to accommodate large commercial cooking equipment. Many professional (and enthusiastic amateur) cooks find an extra sink indispensable. Perhaps this can be set in a central island away from the main working area; or it could be handy to the vegetable preparation area.

A bank of ovens is also a popular choice – perhaps one regular, the other fan forced; or one gas, the other electric. An alternative would be to have a capacious professional range. A microwave oven will almost certainly find its way into this kitchen too.

If the cook is catering for large numbers of people, extra storage will be needed to house larger-than-average equipment – baking trays, casserole dishes and so on. The normal household refrigerator is far from adequate for the professional cook – two refrigerators standing side by side may be more suitable, or even a commercial glass-fronted refrigerator, the type more commonly found in takeaway and grocery stores.

Everything has to work here – you'll need the best ventilation system possible to clear cooking smells; all equipment will be top quality; and the design of the kitchen has to be functional above all, to keep extra work to a minimum. Materials will be tough and easy to look after – the practical side of things is top of the list.

Kitchen Architecture

The professional kitchen is an individual room – the design of it depends entirely on the person using it. It will be the sort of kitchen in which everything has a place, but apart from that, it can vary enormously.

Right: A midway storage rack for kitchen implements
Below: A professional kitchen varied to include an eating area. It still incorporates modern storage systems and appliances which are hidden from view
Below left: Stainless steel and wood are combined to give a hygienic work area. Like most professional kitchens an extra sink is included to accommodate the amount of cooking equipment

Kitchen Architecture

Kitchen Architecture

Installing a kit kitchen

So you have decided to do it yourself. You have designed it around your lifestyle, your budget and the range that is available. It has finally arrived in cartons and your new kitchen is only hours (or days) away.

First take the time to go through the cartons to check that what you've got is what you ordered. Don't try to adapt something to fit, because manufacturers will not exchange goods once they have been modified or altered from the original specification.

Make sure the kitchen is ready: have the walls been repaired? Do you need to change your plumbing? Should you move your power points or light switches or add more? Has the plumbing and electrical work been organised for the dishwasher, new wall oven or cooktop (hob)?

Finally, consider the height of the person who will be working in the kitchen when deciding on how high the worktops and wall cupboards should be.

STEP BY STEP
Floor units

1 Assemble all the cabinet carcasses following the manufacturer's instructions to the letter. Do not attach cupboard doors until the kitchen has been completely fitted.

2 Check the level of the floor to determine whether the base requires packing or planing.

To do this, run a pencil or chalk line around the wall at the height the cabinets will finish – usually 870-900 mm but it may be higher or lower. Alternatively, use a spirit level (see fig. 1). Also check whether the cabinets are on adjustable legs.

3 Check walls for plumb and straightness using a straight-edge and/or a spirit level (see fig. 2), or a length of string and a weight.

4 Check walls for square, using 3:4:5 method (i.e. from the corner, measure 3 units – metres, yards or an arbitrary unit of measurement – along one wall and 4 units along the other. If the corner is a right angle the distance between the two marked points, the hypotenuse, will be 5 units.) (see fig. 3).

5 Begin with a corner cabinet. Set the cabinet in the corner, pack it with wedges until it is level but do not raise the cabinet above the line. Now take a pencil and scribe a line around your cabinet at the wall and floor. Alternatively, pack the gaps so that when fixed into position the cabinet still sits square and level (see fig. 4).

6 Plane the edges so that they run parallel with the scribed line. Use a no. 4.5 smoothing plane or electric planer, taking care not to break out edges and corners. When fitted, fix back to the wall with the correct fasteners (masonry plugs and screws, or just screws) at two points around the top of the cabinet.

7 Repeat the last process for the next cabinet, ensuring that it joins neatly to the corner unit and that the front edges and top line up flush.

Wall oven and pantry units
End panels are supplied for most wall oven and pantry units separately, and these need to be attached to the assembled pantry/wall oven before the cabinets are installed. Installation procedure for wall oven/pantry units is the same as for floor units.

Worktops
Most prefabricated worktops have joints at the major corners. The usual method of holding the joints together is with toggles (see fig. 5). The toggles fit into recesses precut into the underside of the worktop. Tightening the toggles can present some difficulty for fixing. But to begin, we will start by fitting a length of worktop.

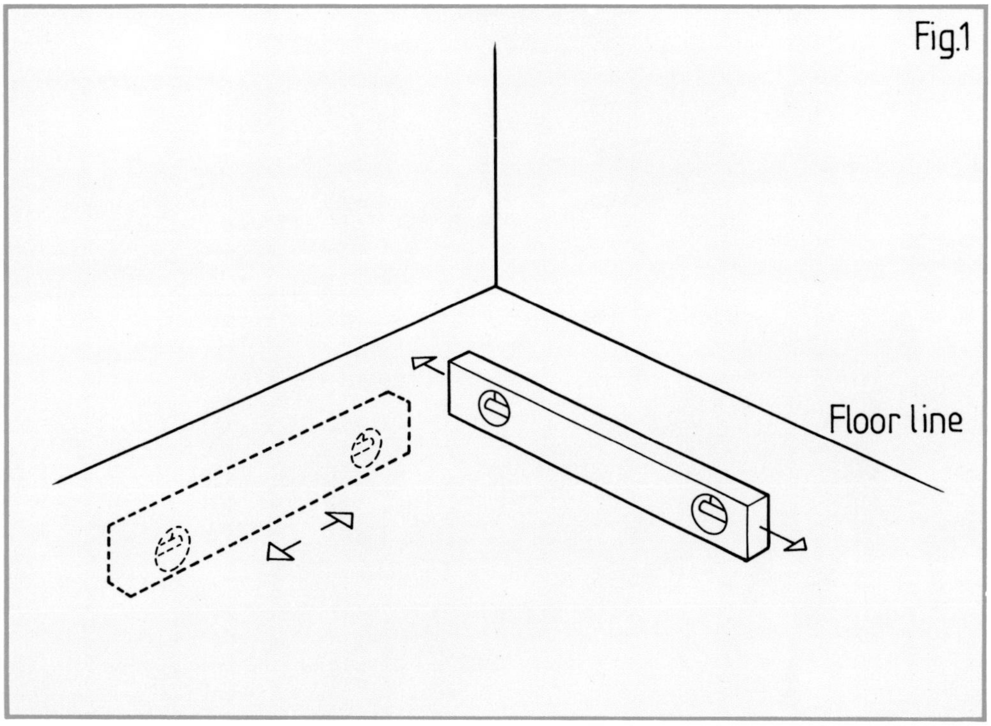

Fig.1

Floor line

Check the floor level with a spirit level

MATERIALS
kit kitchen
silicone sealant

TOOLS
spirit level
screwdriver or power driver
chalk line
square
hammer and mallet
power saw
plane (manual or electric)
clamps
drill and bits

TIME
2-3 days

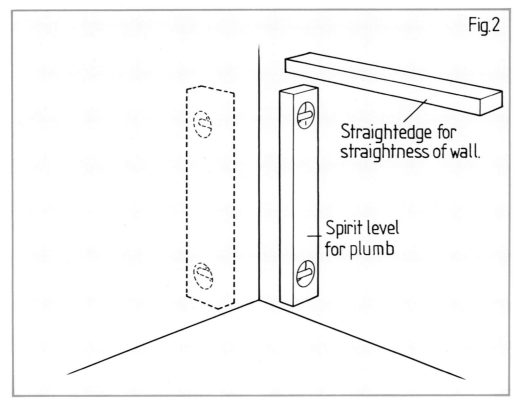

Fig.2

Straightedge for straightness of wall.

Spirit level for plumb

1 Mark the worktop length carefully. Use an electric planer or smoothing plane if only a small amount needs to be trimmed. If a a large section has to be removed, score first with a laminate knife to just below the coloured outer surface of the laminate, then trim with a jigsaw, power saw or handsaw, cutting on the waste side of the line (see fig. 6).

2 Scribe the back edge and plane to fit. Do not touch any pre-machined joints. With the worktop fitted, wedge it into place temporarily. Fit the next piece as above but, as before, do not attempt to alter any premachined joints.

3 After fitting all pieces, raise worktops about 150 mm above the tops of the cabinets. Make sure you support them on bearers of some kind.

4 Coat each joint with silicone sealant before bringing joints together. This prevents water

penetration and stops the laminate from lifting.

5 After tightening all toggle joints, carefully remove all bearers and fix the worktop into place with screws (not too long). Run a line of silicone sealant around the wall/ worktop joints.

Wall units

Fitting wall units is the same as for floor units except that you don't need to scribe anything to the floor. You should run a level line around your walls in the same way as you have done for your base units. Before you start fitting wall units several points must be considered.

❑ Do your wall units have to meet up with a pantry or wall oven? If so, then your level line is best run from the top of these units.
Note: If you are planning to fix wall tiles between your worktop and underside of wall cabinets, the top row of tiles may need to be cut to fit.

❑ If there are no restrictions on the height of your wall cabinets, you would be wise to use your tile size as a guide to the height above the worktop level for fixing wall units. e.g. 4 courses of 100 x 100 mm tiles = 400 mm above. Allow 2 mm for each grouting gap, say total of 410 mm, or with 3 courses of 150 x 150 mm tiles, total would be 450 mm plus 8 mm grouting gap = 458 mm.

❑ As wall units need to be suspended from the wall, extra fixing points may be required. It is recommended that each cabinet is fixed both at the top and bottom of the back. Otherwise two fixings at the top will usually be sufficient.

Kickboards

Your kit kitchen will come with kickboards or baseboards. In most situations these will require scribing to the floor before fixing into position. Use

Above: A straightedge and spirit level are used to check walls for plumb and straightness
Right: The 3:4:5 method for checking walls for square

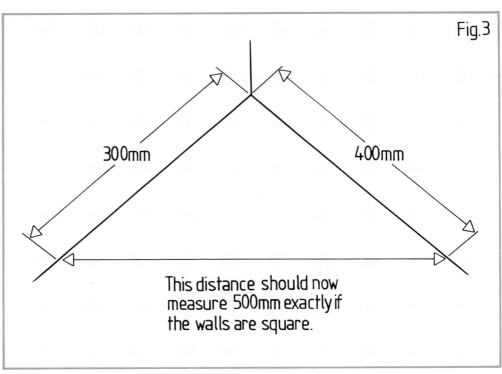

Fig.3

300mm

400mm

This distance should now measure 500mm exactly if the walls are square.

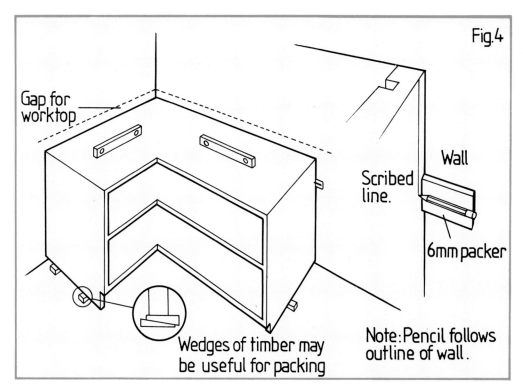

Gap for worktop

Wedges of timber may be useful for packing

Scribed line.

Wall

6mm packer

Note: Pencil follows outline of wall.

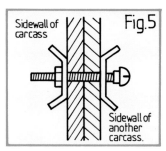

Sidewall of carcass

Sidewall of another carcass.

Fig.5

Left: Pack a corner cabinet with wedges until it is level
Above: A toggle bolt

the same methods as described in scribing floor units on page 172. If the kickboards are to be fitted to the legs, follow the manufacturer's instructions closely. Other types may be nailed on or glued with suitable wall-board adhesives. Mitre joints may also be required for external corners. These must be cut carefully. If mitre joints are not used you will have to finish off one edge.

Cutting and fitting appliances and sinks

Sinks Care should be taken at the planning stage to ensure that it is possible to install the sink you want in your kitchen. Note: You should check that all plumbing will fit into one cabinet. This may include the waste disposal unit or water purifier. Make sure they do not inhibit the opening and closing of doors or drawers.

Marking out: The cut required should be done carefully, allowing enough space for the taps selected, if no provision is made for them in the sink. Allow for overhangs.

Note: Check twice and cut once (exceptionally good advice). Avoid putting the sink over any worktop joints if at all possible, as this will create a weak spot which water can penetrate. Use a straightedge for marking as a

cutting guide. A jigsaw is the best cutting machine for this purpose. A small portable circular saw can be used but it must have fine, sharp teeth.

Fixing down: Use the clips provided by the manufacturer. Do not remove the foam strip that may be provided. After fixing, run a fine bead of silicone sealant around the sink. Allow it to set slightly before removing excess with a razor knife.

Cooktop (hob) and wall oven
Follow the same steps as for the sink except that no silicone sealant is required unless manufacturers specify it.

Note: Ensure that all plumbing and wiring meets the required regulations.

Doors and Drawers

Doors Fix the hinges to all your doors before you hang them. Do not drill any holes for handles until all doors have been hung and adjusted. Follow the manufacturer's instructions as there is a wide variety in use today. Generally all modern hinges are 3-way adjusting: up and down, in and out and across and back.

1 A hinge plate may be required to be screw-fixed to the

inside of cabinets. Care should be taken to ensure that these are located correctly.

2 Hold the door against the cabinet in the open position and mark the position of the mounting plate.

3 Fix the door onto the mounting plates, tighten up and adjust. Now drill for handle holes if necessary.

Drawers These may come assembled or in kit form. Either way the main body of the drawer runner should be attached to the sides of the drawer unit. Assemble the drawer following the manufacturer's instructions. The drawer-fronts should already be attached. If not, this is the procedure:

1 With the bottom drawer in place, hold the bottom drawer-front against the drawer. Line the bottom edge

Score worktop with laminate knife to just below the coloured outer surface of the laminate

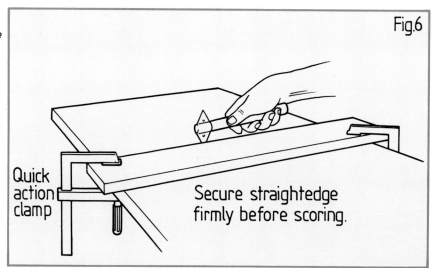

Quick action clamp

Secure straightedge firmly before scoring.

Fig.6

of the drawer-front up with the bottom edge of the adjoining doors and mark along the inside top edge of drawer.

2 Remove both drawer and drawer-front and attach temporarily with suitable nails.

3 Return drawer and adjust fit.

4 Insert next drawer. Place 1.5-2 mm packers on the top edge of bottom drawer-front. Sit the next drawer-front on top of packers and line up side gaps. Mark along the top edge. Repeat steps 2 and 3.

5 When all drawer-fronts have been attached and adjustments made, drill and screw-fix into place with four screws and fit handles if applicable.
Note: For appearance's sake,

all screws should be counter-sunk flush with all surfaces or a decorative cover cap should be used.

6 Any gaps may now be filled using a suitable gap filler (not a timber putty) or use quadrant mould pinned in place.

TIPSTRIP

Build two stands that will sit on the worktop to support the wall units at the correct height (see fig. 7).

Below: The impressive result of a few days work

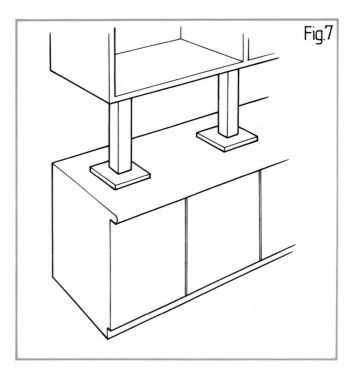

Fig.7

Pro-Pak Kitchen, Mad Barry's

175

Cooking in a good light

Good light in a kitchen is essential from both a safety and a practical point of view. During the day, try to gain maximum benefit from natural light because it is easiest on the eyes.

While it's not always feasible to enlarge a window to make a dark kitchen brighter, there are other possibilities to consider; in a bungalow a skylight will greatly increase the general light level. One that opens or incorporates a vent is sensible for kitchen use. Other options include clear or opaque glass and blinds – the choice will depend on factors such as whether or not the skylight is in full sun or semi-shade. If you can't shed new light from above, look to the walls. Perhaps you can replace some of the masonry with glass bricks; they let light through without exposing you to public scrutiny.

If you can't alter what you have, remember that small windows should be kept clear of overgrowing vines on the outside and fussy curtains on the inside. If you need a covering to reduce glare or give privacy, choose a neat blind that folds or rolls up clear of the window panes. Light colours in the kitchen, and on any walls or fences immediately outside the window, will make the room appear brighter.

Once the sun goes down, of course, window size is irrelevant. You may need to cover it for privacy, to cut heat loss or simply to reduce distracting reflections. Any window covering in a kitchen should be easily cleaned –

cooking generates steam and grease and these trap dirt – so venetian blinds, wipeable roller blinds or washable curtains are ideal. Never have flowing curtains or paper blinds near the oven or cooktop (hob) because of the fire risk.

Light after dark

There are three main types of electric light for use in the kitchen. The first is the familiar tungsten bulb which can be used in hanging lamps, track lighting, semirecessed eyeball lights and underlights for wall cupboards. It gives a warm, yellow light which is pleasant, but its disadvantages are that it casts shadows and that the brighter the light the more heat it emits – a significant factor in a hot and steamy kitchen.

Fluorescent lighting overcomes the problems of shadow and heat and is also economical. But while it gives an excellent overall light level, it can be harsh. Food doesn't look its best under fluorescent lighting and many people find it tiring after a while. If your main source of light is fluorescent, specify that you want a natural, soft or daylight tube. Fluorescent lighting is not suitable for use with a dimmer switch, so it

should be avoided in dining areas. Small fluorescent tubes are ideal for installing under wall units, however.

Becoming more and more popular are halogen lights. These give a very pure light that is pleasant to work by. The

bulbs last longer than ordinary ones and are economical to run; they are available in a range of different angles of spread, making them suitable for both general and spot lighting. Of course, there have to be disadvantages, too. Halogen bulbs

Style Kitchens

Above right: The windows form one end of the kitchen and have been extended to the roof to give maximum light
Right: A stained glass window hides an ugly view while allowing natural light into the kitchen

are more expensive to buy in the first instance and they need careful handling – even traces of grease can affect their performance; because they are low-voltage, they need a transformer to step down the power. Some bulbs have their own built-in transformer, but this makes the bulb bulky. In a kitchen it is better to have one transformer for the entire lighting circuit – not a problem as long as the electrician knows what he's doing.

Light patches

When it comes to electric lighting, plan in advance. Installing wiring is easiest before the kitchen itself is actually built – otherwise be prepared for a lot of disruption. Every kitchen needs good general light, specific task lighting and, if the kitchen is also an eating area, atmospheric lighting.

General light usually comes from an overhead lamp. In a kitchen with a single, central light bulb, it is a simple matter to replace it with a fluorescent strip light or several spot lights on a track.

The spots should not be directed at the work surfaces (you'd forever be in your own shadow) but bounced off the ceilings and walls to give soft but good overall illumination. If you are building new or totally renovating, look at lights (either tungsten or halogen) recessed into the ceiling. Carefully positioned, these give good general and specific light – and they don't collect dust the way pendant light fittings do!

For food preparation and cooking you need light where you are working. The best way to illuminate worktops is with small lights (either fluorescent or tungsten) fastened to the underside of the wall units as close to the front of the cupboard as possible. Small baffles or a pelmet in front of the tubes cut glare. Good light over a stove can be provided by an extractor hood that incorporates a lamp as well.

In a kitchen/dining room, the eating area needs its own lighting with, ideally, its own switch. A rise-and-fall pendant light over the table, operated by a dimmer switch, enables you to control the light level.

Top: A spot light set in brass
Above: A triangular-shaped shade can be suspended from the ceiling

Project 3

Cafe curtains

A scalloped heading is often used on cafe curtains. They look particularly good when hung from wooden curtain rings.

1 To work out the amount of fabric required, measure the width of the window and add 3 cm for seam allowance. Measure the length from the rod or track to the desired length of the curtains. Add 5 cm to the lower edge to allow for the hem and add 1.5 cm to the top edge for the scallop heading.

2 To make the scallop heading, first decide on the width of the scallops and the band between each scallop. As a general guide, scallops can be 8 cm wide with a 1.5 cm band in between, but you can alter this to suit the width of the window. Use a drinking glass and marking pen to draw the scallops onto a piece of cardboard to form a scallop template (fig. 1). Cut out the template and using a water-soluble pen, trace scallops 1.5 cm down from the top edge of the curtain.

3 Cut a fabric lining piece the width of the curtain and 6 cm longer than the base of the scallops. Stitch a narrow hem along the base of the lining piece. Pin and tack the lining to the top edge of the curtain, right sides of fabric facing. Stitch the two pieces together, following the scallop lines (fig. 2). Trim, neaten and clip seam. Turn curtains to right sides and press.

4 Turn in side and base hems and stitch. Stitch curtain rings to the centre of each band piece (fig. 3). Curtains are now ready to hang on a rod or track.

MATERIALS	
fabric	curtain rings
scissors	tape measure
pins	
marking pen	
drinking glass	

TIME
1-2 hours

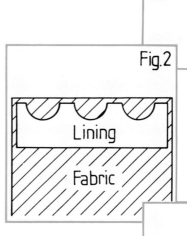

Fig.1

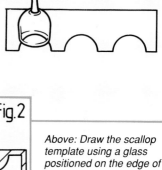

Fig.2

Above: Draw the scallop template using a glass positioned on the edge of the cardboard to form a semi-circle
Left: Stitch fabric and lining together, following scallop lines

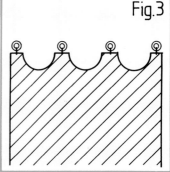

Fig.3

Stitch curtain rings to centre of straight scallop edges

Selecting a suitable flooring from the dazzling array available can be a daunting task. Here we look at some practical considerations to help you make your choice.

THE RIGHT FLOOR

Choosing the flooring may be among the most difficult decisions you have to make in the design of your new kitchen. You'll be looking for something that's tough enough to stand up to spills, grease, damp and everyday wear and tear, that's not too hard underfoot and is non-slip, that will last a long time and not require too much maintenance, that looks attractive and, preferably, doesn't cost the earth. It's a tall order, and not all possibilities meet all those criteria; decide which ones are most important to you, and you'll be able to make an educated choice when you go out shopping for flooring.

One of the most important things you'll have to consider is whether the flooring of your choice is suitable for the construction of your house. You can lay almost any type of flooring on solid concrete, but you can't, for instance, put heavy quarry tiles on the average domestic timber-suspended floor without first seeking expert advice.

Your choice will be further narrowed down by the style of kitchen you want; if you're after a country look, rustic terracotta tiles may be the best choice, whereas if the effect you're aiming for is more sleek and modern, one of the new generation linoleums could be more suitable. Here we offer a general rundown of the most common types of flooring available, looking at their advantages, as well as possible disadvantages.

Vinyl sheeting and tiles

One of the most economical types of flooring, vinyl is also one of the most versatile. It comes in many different grades – from ultra-rigid tiles to the soft cushioned sheet flooring – giving you virtually any effect you desire. You can choose from patterns or plain colours or, for a fraction of the cost of the real thing, go for one of the look-alikes; marble, slate, tile or timber.

The main advantages of vinyl, apart from its price, are that it's hardwearing, easy on the feet, quiet, and resistant to water, grease and most domestic chemical products.

It's extremely important to lay vinyl correctly on an even surface to avoid lifting edges that eventually rip or bend. It can be laid on virtually any level, dry surface, except floorboards. To lay vinyl over timber, first put down an underlay of hardboard, smooth side up.

Vinyl's come a long way since those days when the very mention of it brought visions of hours of tedious waxing and polishing. Most of the new vinyls require very little maintenance; generally a daily sweep to remove grit, and washing once a week is sufficient. It's not strictly necessary to polish them, but their life will be prolonged if they are polished two or three times a year with a special vinyl polish. This is a simple job, easily done with a mop.

Linoleum

Linoleum's making a big comeback around the world, as manufacturers have shifted right away from the drab colours more often associated with school corridors and doctors' waiting rooms. Today, lino comes in a wide range of fabulous colours, from bright reds, blues and yellows to the more subtle greys and beiges, in plain or marbled effect.

It's an ideal flooring choice for the kitchen, being hardwearing, comfortable to walk on, usually forgiving to dropped china and glassware, handsome to look at and reasonably economical, being about the same price as mid to high-quality cushioned vinyl.

A 100 per cent natural product, lino is made of cork, resins, wood flour, mineral colours and with a backing of hessian. It's the cork in the lino that gives it its spring, which not only makes it easy to walk on, but also allows it to be laid on slightly uneven surfaces, without a hardboard underlay. However, a hardboard base is recommended if the lino is being laid on old irregular timber planks. Unlike vinyl, lino should be laid by a flooring expert; it is not a job for the do-it-yourselfer.

Maintenance of lino is simple: regular sweeping and mopping with an emulsion dressing. There is no need to use wax or polish. To get a high gloss finish, you can apply an acrylic sealer; manufacturers do not recommend it, however, if you're after low-maintenance flooring, as the sealer has to be stripped and re-applied every few years.

Unlike vinyl, lino is a homogeneous product,

Floor Country Floors

Above: Mexican tiles are highlighted with a strong coloured border
Right: Small colourful ceramic tiles break the warm effect of these terracotta tiles

Floor and Jug Country Floors

One of the most important things you'll have to consider is whether the flooring of your choice is suitable for the construction of your house. You can lay almost any type of flooring on solid concrete, but seek advice before laying heavy quarry tiles on the average domestic timber floor.

meaning the colour goes right through from the top surface to the hessian base. Scratches and other surface damage, therefore, do not show up as easily. It's a tough product all round – with normal domestic use, it will last as long as you want it to. In fact, there have been instances of it being virtually as good as new after 80 years.

Daytile Cork, Armstrong Nylex

Rubber

Another option that's hardwearing, with excellent insulation and sound absorption qualities is rubber. Available in a number of fashionable colours, rubber tiles generally have either a round or square studded profile. They can be laid on a cement or hardboard base, and could be tackled quite easily by the enthusiastic do-it-yourselfer.

Rubber doesn't take much looking after – just regular vacuuming, and it

may be shined with a water-based polish to give a glossy surface.

Cork

Because of its elastic properties, cork makes an excellent kitchen flooring material. Its soft and springy surface is more likely to cushion the fall of glass than, say, ceramic tiles would. It's a good insulator, is tough, and easy to look after. Maintenance, apart from re-coating when necessary, consists only of washing with warm water and a mild detergent.

Part of the appeal of cork lies in its colourings – warm tones ranging from honey to deep brown, and also, with new liming techniques, soft greys – which complement many types of kitchen decor.

Cork tiles can be glued onto almost any level, dry, clean surface including steel-trowelled concrete,

although over timber floorboards an underlay of hardboard is required. After the tiles have been laid – a job which can be carried out by the amateur – they are sanded and given three or more coats of sealer. You need to wait 24 hours between each coat of sealer; therefore, care must be taken to make sure that dust particles don't get trapped in the cork.

Although cork is easy to maintain, it does have a few disadvantages. It can rot if water is trapped underneath it; strong, direct sunlight can fade it; the edges of the tiles are vulnerable to chipping, and it needs to be re-sealed every few years.

Parquet

Parquet flooring, a handsome choice for kitchens, comes in blocks or tiles, and is available in dozens of patterns and many different types of timbers. It is certainly not a low budget option – but actual price obviously depends on the timber used and

the pattern. It can be laid on any level, clean and dry surface, including concrete or timber. It's easy to look after; requiring only regular sweeping, and then re-sealing every few years.

Vinyl has come a long way since those days when the very mention of it brought visions of hours of tedious waxing and polishing. Most of the new vinyls require very little maintenance; generally a daily sweep to remove grit, and washing once a week is sufficient.

Left: Vinyl tiles can give many different effects – these resemble a cork floor
Below: Parquet flooring allows interesting patterned effects

Ware Collingwood Floors

The Slate People

Slate

An expensive but beautiful flooring option, slate is available in a wide range of colours, from greeny-grey to black. It's very hardwearing and easy to care for, needing only a regular mopping with household detergent or washing soda, but it can be quite noisy, as well as slippery when wet. Slate is not as cold a material as you would expect, warming up to room temperature quite quickly, and retaining heat efficiently. Being non-porous, there is also little risk of it staining.

Slate tiles, which have either sawn edges or are guillotined to give a hand-cut appearance, can be laid on timber, concrete or a cement base, and is a simple DIY project.

Both slate and marble can be slippery, so think carefully about using them if you have small children.

Marble

Although wonderful to look at, marble is not the most practical material for kitchen floors, as it is slightly porous, easily scratched, and stained by things like wine, citrus juice, oils and vegetable dyes. If you are determined to use marble, seek expert advice as some types are more suitable than others.

To clean, wipe over with diluted dishwashing liquid, without allowing the floor to get too wet. Abrasive cleaners must not be used on marble, as they scratch. If the floor does become stained or badly scratched, seek professional advice.

Ceramic tiles

There's an almost unlimited range to choose from here – from large plain tiles in subtle tonings to highly patterned, brightly

coloured ones in modern designs, plus any number in between. They can be slightly cold in the kitchen – you may need under-floor insulation to cope with those chilly winter mornings. Without sound-absorbing furnishings, they can also be noisy, and, of course, are unforgiving to dropped china and glassware. However, they are tough, water-proof, available in non-slip grades and impervious to most household liquids. For cleaning, you only have to mop over them with warm soapy water.

With the country and provincial looks being so fashionable today, terra-cotta tiles, especially quarry tiles, are very popular. Unsealed terracotta is generally unsuitable for kitchens, as it stains, but pre-sealed tiles are available, which are easier to look after.

Left: Slate comes in a wide range of colours
Below: Studded rubber floor tiles form a clean and practical floor surface

Studz, Kenbrock Floors

Project 4

Laying a vinyl tile floor

Vinyl tiles are an excellent surface for kitchen floors, easier to lay than sheet vinyl and easier to repair by replacing individual tiles.

To do the job properly it is essential that the floor underneath is perfectly flat, achievable only with concrete slabs that have been steel-trowelled or finished with self-levelling cement, or with rougher slabs and floorboards that have been covered with underlay sheets. This second option is more accessible to DIY enthusiasts.

Note: Manufacturers supply information sheets that cover all aspects of this kind of job.

STEP BY STEP

1 The underlay

Underlay sheets are most likely to be of either masonite or fibrecement, the latter being easier to lay, immune to water damage and giving a better, more rigid surface.

Floorboards must be flat. If boards are badly warped the whole floor must be roughsanded before the underlay can be fixed. Floor sanders can be hired and are worth the expense. Remove lumps from concrete with a cold chisel.

Start laying the sheets in a corner of the room, keeping sheet edges about 3 mm away from walls. Lay out all the sheets on the floor and cut where necessary before fixing any to the floor. Ensure that nailheads are flush with the surface of the sheets before laying the tiles. It may be necessary to sand the joints between the sheets if the floor beneath is really rough.

2 The tiles

When setting out, try to avoid tile edges falling within 80 mm of underlay joins. Avoid narrow pieces near walls and always use the cut edge against walls or cupboards rather than against other tiles. Use only the adhesive recommended by the tile manufacturer and follow instructions carefully.

3 The centre line

Use tiles laid loose to establish the longest perpendicular line through the room that will give an equal distance to the closest walls on either side. Use a chalk line or a tight string line suspended between two nails.

4 Beginning

Sweep the floor carefully. Loose-lay tiles along and out from the centre line (see fig. 1), establishing what size the border tiles will be. Any one of these centre tiles can be your first laid. Using a notched trowel to spread the adhesive, prepare an area equal to about six tiles along the centre line. Place the tiles as close to their proper position as possible to avoid having to slide them.

As each tile is laid, press it down with the palm of your hand and rub the surface firmly. You must assume that the tiles are cut perfectly square during manufacture so you should not allow any cracks to appear between them as they are laid. Immediately remove any adhesive which has spread on the floor or smeared the tiles.

Note: Boxes of tiles should be well mixed before the first one is laid because you cannot assume that the colour will be constant from box to box. Selecting boxes with the same batch number when purchasing tiles gives some insurance.

5 Cutting tiles

When cutting tiles around the edges, lay the tile to be cut over the adjacent tile, making sure the pattern is the right way up. Then lay another full tile over the top and push it hard against the wall. You will now have a thickness of three tiles. Using the top tile as a gauge, score the second tile with your trimming knife (see fig. 2). Remove the top tile and cut through the second tile and it will fit perfectly into the space. Repeat this process until all edge tiles are in place.

6 Finishing

Walk around for a while on the tiles or hire a roller, making sure that all adhesive is removed and that all tiles are sticking down well. Wait 24 hours before moving heavy items such as the fridge into place on your new floor.

MATERIALS
tiles
adhesive
underlay sheets
nails

TOOLS
knife
hammer
notched trowel
string or chalk line
disposable cloth
steel ruler
tape measure

TIME
1-2 days

Lay the tiles along and out from the centre line

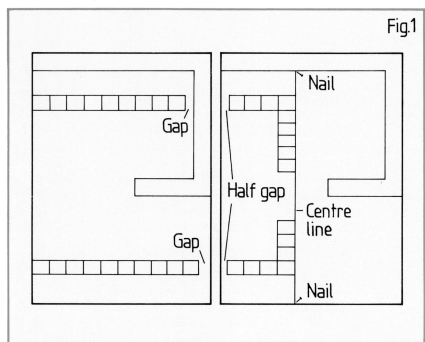

Fig.1

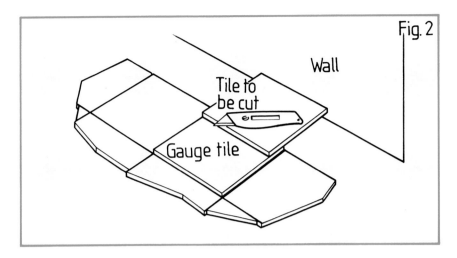

Fig. 2

Wall

Tile to be cut

Gauge tile

Left: A foolproof method of cutting tiles.
Below: Easy-to-lay vinyl tiles make a great surface for kitchen floors

Daytile Flint, Armstrong Nylex

TIPSTRIP

LAYING A CORK FLOOR
Contact adhesive can be used for cork tiles. Place 20 to 30 tiles face down and tightly butted together in a dust-free environment and, using a brush or foam roller, apply the adhesive. Then apply the adhesive to the floor. The adhesive will be ready to stick after a few minutes, when the surface will feel only mildly tacky. The process will be speeded up by blowing air across the adhesive-covered surfaces with a fan. Once tacky, the adhesive will be ready to use for quite some time. Position the tiles very precisely as full bonding occurs the moment the two glued surfaces meet.

After laying, if the surface is slightly uneven, sand lightly with 80 to 100 grit paper. Vacuum thoroughly. Apply a liberal first coat of cork tile sealant with either a wide brush or a lambswool applicator. Allow to dry as per instructions on the can, then sand lightly with 120 grit paper. Vacuum and wipe down with thinners then apply the second coat. Repeat for the final coat. Allow 12 to 24 hours before walking on the floor and 4-5 days, depending on the weather, for curing.

Start with a well-designed kitchen; mix that with a carefully thought-out colour scheme and personal decorating touches, and the result will be an individual and interesting room that will be in keeping with the rest of the house.

COLOUR AND DECOR

While the working parts of the kitchen are vitally important, so too are the decorative aspects – you want to create a room that you feel happy working in. There's no point in having all the latest appliances and high technology if you're miserable every time you set foot in the kitchen. Think just as carefully about colour and the decorating of the room as you do about every other aspect. The beauty of decorating decisions is that few are final – if you get tired of the wall colour, it's a lot easier to change than, say, the oven or worktop. For this reason, you can be a little more adventurous with your decorating scheme, safe in the knowledge that if you discover you've made a terrible mistake it's not irrevocable.

As the actual bones of the kitchen – the cabinetry, flooring and appliances – are expensive, it's probably wise to exercise restraint in these areas. It's safer to be conservative in your choice of colours for these elements, reserving the more exciting tones for the less permanent features such as paintwork.

The first thing to do when you're thinking about colour in the kitchen is to decide whether you want your kitchen to have the same colours as used in adjacent rooms. If you do, your choice will be narrowed down enormously. If not, you will have a virtually open palette.

Then think about the effect you want to achieve. As a rule of thumb, if you want to create an intimate, cosy mood, you should choose warm tones such as reds and oranges, or even blues and greens containing a lot of yellow. If you're after a more sophisticated, cooler look, blues and greens are more suitable, or, again, reds and yellows with a great deal of blue. Even whites, greys, browns and blacks can seem either cool or warm depending on the amount of yellow or blue they contain.

Have a look at the quality of natural light in the room. Do you want to emphasise it, or not? Cool colours can tone down the heat of such light, while warm ones can intensify it.

Colour in the room can come from a variety of sources – paintwork, wallpaper, the splashback, fabric, prints, china – the

The beauty of decorating decisions is that few are final – if you get tired of the wall colour it's a lot easier to change than the oven or worktop.

Bright, adventurous colour can be used to great advantage in the kitchen

Kitchen Architecture

list goes on. The most obvious way to inject life into the room is with paint, and not just on the walls; have a look at the detailing of the room – windows, doors, picture rails and so on – and see if any of these can be picked out. Red might be too much for complete walls, but the odd touch on architraves or window frames may be just right. Similarly, brightly coloured cabinetry might be overwhelming, but drawer handles of that same colour can add a certain amount of pizzazz.

Be careful, if you do decide to emphasise certain features in the room, that you pick out the more attractive ones.

elements to avoid a bitty and confusing effect. Be as bold as you like with these trim colours.

In some kitchens, it is worth featuring certain structural elements. A case in point would be a window with a deep sill. Choose a contrasting colour for the complete recessed area to emphasise this attractive architectural feature. The window frame itself can be painted in another shade. The sill can then be used as a shelf for cookery books, or for displaying treasured objects. If light is not a consideration in the room, extra shelves could be installed into the recess, and these could be used for display or storage.

Tablemats, napkins and teatowels, can create a single, bold colour in an otherwise monochromatic scheme. Have several sets to suit your moods.

scheme of the room – you could select something that coordinates with your colour scheme or provides contrast.

Cups and Saucers The Bay Tree

 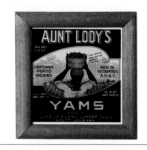

To create a room with appeal and individuality, group together well-loved and carefully chosen objects that share a common theme. These could be anything from plates, boxes and kitchen utensils to baskets and glassware. Decorative plates can look wonderful hung on the wall; basketware sitting on top of the kitchen cabinets is equally appealing. For a completely individual look, start collecting something unusual; how about framed orange wrappers; jelly moulds or old kettles?

Artwork need not be reserved for the living areas of the house; framed posters, children's artwork, botanical prints or lithographs can look terrific on a kitchen wall. Choose the frames and mountings carefully to tie in with the decorating

For instance, the doors, cornices and skirting boards may be worth painting in a contrasting colour, but the pipes and pillars may be decidedly unappealing. When picking out details, it is probably best to err on the side of conservatism; highlight only one or two

Even with an all-white kitchen it's possible to add a little bit of colour – one or two drawers can be fronted with a different coloured laminate, as, too, can the splashback and perhaps a small area of worktop. When you tire of these colours it's not a major job to update them.

Above: China and other kitchen crockery or accessories can be used to coordinate with the colour scheme
Left: Inject colour into the kitchen with pictures or prints
Right: Wallpaper is an unusual but interesting feature which can add colour and pattern to a kitchen

Practicalities

Paint

❏ **Acrylic paint:** You use water to wash your brushes with this type of paint. It's longer lasting than oil-based gloss paint, as it's not as brittle and therefore less likely to flake or peel. Water resistant and tough, it's easy to use and suitable for wall and ceiling areas. Flat finishes are not recommended for hard-working areas in the kitchen; the glossier finishes are a lot more dirt-resistant and easier to clean.

❏ **Oil-based gloss paint:** With this type of paint, you use turps (white spirit) to clean your brushes. It's recommended where a glossy, hardwearing surface is required. Kitchen cupboards, skirting boards and doors are best painted in gloss. Make sure you sand carefully between coats for a long-lasting and smooth finish.

Always use washable paint in the kitchen.

Try some of the fashionable paint techniques like spongeing, rag rolling and stencilling to give your kitchen an individual look. You don't have to use these techniques over the entire walls – a window frame, archway or door may be enough.

Gloss paints can give new life to existing tiles. Wash the tiles down thoroughly with soap and water, and leave for 24 hours. To remove all traces of grease, wipe down with methylated spirits and then paint. One coat will be sufficient, and there is no need to use undercoat. Gloss paint, however, can show up every irregularity in plasterwork – you may opt for a softer sheen.

Before committing yourself to a particular colour in the kitchen, buy sample pots of paint and brush small patches onto different parts of the wall (the lightest and darkest areas). Live with them for a while before making your final decision.

Wall coverings

Always use a wallpaper paste with a built-in fungicide.

Washable wallpapers are inexpensive and are coated with a thin plastic film. They can be wiped over but are not tough enough to be scrubbed. They are not recommended for heavy duty areas; here, the more durable and more expensive ranges in which the design is actually printed onto a layer of vinyl are more suitable.

Interesting objects like these pastry cutters can add a unique decorative touch

Pastry Cutters The Bay Tree

Nairn Decor

Try some of the fashionable paint techniques like rag rolling and stencilling to give your kitchen an individual look.

Left: Kitchen utensils have been chosen to complement the wall colours
Below: A wonderful tile mural can give an artistic and vibrant touch to a kitchen

Tile Mural Jenny Orchard

Timber panelling

Tongue-and-groove softwood panelling is ideal for covering ugly plumbing or uneven walls. It can be stained or varnished or, for a softer look, painted to match the decor.

In a country-style kitchen, a dado of timber panelling can be installed, with the wall above painted or papered. As there is a gap between the wall and timber panelling, it is a good choice for the kitchen which has condensation problems.

Cork tiles

They retain heat and absorb moisture so are a sensible choice for rooms that are either cold, or suffering from condensation problems.

Use presealed tiles, or give unsealed tiles two coats of polyurethane varnish after installation.

Bricks

If you have a wall of exposed brickwork, seal it with a masonry stabiliser to prevent it absorbing grease and stains.

Tiles

Tiles are the toughest form of wallcovering. There is a huge range available, from comercially produced tiles to hand-painted ones which you can buy singly and use as a feature. On areas prone to constant splashing, such as behind the sink, use waterproof and stain-resistant grout.

A drawback of tiles is that they are difficult to remove once in place, so choose carefully.

189

Project 5

Stencilling

A stencilled frieze on your kitchen wall is a lovely and very individual decorative touch.

Dab the paint onto the stencil, making sure you don't overload the paintbrush

Wait until the first stencil is almost dry before you position the next one

You can also stencil a border or motif on your kitchen cupboards, the backs of wooden chairs or on a painted table.

STEP BY STEP

1 Draw your design onto a sheet of acrylic film or a piece of manila cardboard using a felt-tipped pen. If using cardboard first strengthen it by liberally applying a mixture of 50 per cent linseed oil and 50 per cent turpentine (white spirit) to both sides of the board. Allow it to soak in and then rub off excess moisture with a soft cloth.

Carefully cut out the stencil with a sharp craft knife or a surgical scalpel.

2 Using masking tape, fasten the stencil in position. Make sure the edges of the stencil are straight, and the design a uniform distance in from the edges so that you can simply butt the stencil up to the cornice, worktop or door frame when positioning it.

If your frieze is to go around corners, take measurements first to establish where a corner will occur in the pattern. Small positional adjustments at the start may prevent difficult or awkward painting at the corner. Some designs will simply slide around the corner with no visible disruption to their continuity – others are clearly unbalanced as they turn. Sometimes you can stop the stencil just slightly short of the corner and simply take some single design element and place it right in the corner, continuing the stencil again on the other side.

3 Pour a little acrylic or emulsion paint into a saucer. Do not add any water, and be sure your brush is dry. Using a dabbing movement, dip the brush into the paint, dabbing off any excess. It may be necessary to paint a few strokes first, on spare fabric or kitchen towels to make sure the brush holds only a minimum of paint. Too much paint on the brush will seep under the stencil edges and cause indistinct outlines.

Start to fill in the stencil design with paint using a dabbing movement. Do not stroke the brush. Don't try to make the paint coverage entirely even. Part of the charm of stencilling is that paint shades and definition will inevitably differ from motif to motif. Once the paint is almost dry remove stencil carefully. It is important not to allow excess paint to build up on the cut stencil, so either wipe over or wash the stencil between uses. Dry paint build-up can distort the outlines of the stencil and encourage paint to seep in and blur the edges.

4 Once the first motif is finished and the paint is almost dry, you may position the stencil again to continue the border pattern. Acrylic paint dries very quickly (2-3 minutes). This repositioning is easy with acrylic sheeting because it's transparent. If you're using manila cardboard, notch the edges of it and use the notches as a repositioning guide.

If you have blurred the edge of an outline, quick attention will solve the problem. Usually a water-dampened cotton bud can be used to wipe this edge or to fix any other small mistake. Touch-ups with a fine paintbrush can be useful for redefining small areas you have missed or that are indistinct.

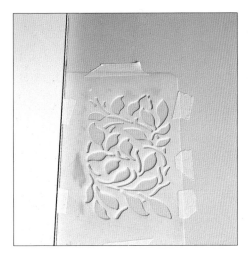

Tape the stencil in position with masking tape. Make sure the edges are straight

MATERIALS

acrylic or emulsion paint
clear acrylic film or manila cardboard
linseed oil and turpentine (white spirit)

TOOLS

flat-topped brush
craft knife or surgical scalpel
cloth

TIME

1 day

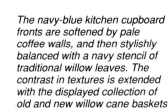

The navy-blue kitchen cupboard fronts are softened by pale coffee walls, and then stylishly balanced with a navy stencil of traditional willow leaves. The contrast in textures is extended with the displayed collection of old and new willow cane baskets

The requirements of a worktop are that it should be tough enough to cope with all sorts of attack, yet sufficiently good-looking to be a design element in the kitchen.

WORK SURFACES

The worktop is probably the most hardworking part of the whole kitchen; over the years it has to stand up to all sorts of abuse from knives, hot saucepans, water, kitchen chemicals and certain foods.

Some materials wear better than others or are relatively easy to repair; think about these things when you're deciding what to use for your worktop. You should also consider what maintenance will be required, and how often; whether splashback edges and corners can be well sealed; if you have a long worktop, how many joints there will be; and then, look at the relative prices of the different materials. These are the practical considerations – after that it's a matter of making your decision purely on aesthetic grounds.

Laminates

The most economical worktop material, laminate is also one of the most practical. It comes in an extraordinary array of colours, designs and textures from subtle and sophisticated to zany and eye-catching; one type or another is certain to be suitable for your kitchen, whether you want a country look or are more into high-tech. Some of the newer designs also offer quite realistic, and much cheaper, alternatives to expensive timber, marble and granite.

There are different types of laminate – the standard variety, which is a thin coloured layer stuck down to a particle (chip) board or plywood base, and, a more recent development, solid laminates which allow for softer curved edges and eliminate the black edging joins seen in the conventional laminates. The solid variety also makes scratches and chips harder to see.

Horizontal-grade laminates are reasonably hardy, and can withstand a reasonable amount of abuse, but it's important to use heatproof mats to avoid buckling and scorching, and chopping boards to avoid scratching. Prolonged exposure to water may cause warping. If looked after carefully, they have a long life, but once damaged, they're very difficult to repair.

Laminates are easy to maintain – they resist grease and stains, and clean up well with mild household detergents and warm water.

Tiles Country Floors

Some worktop materials wear better than others, or are relatively easy to repair.

Corotone, Parbury's

Left: Hand-painted tiles are one of the stunning choices available. Tiles can be used for splashbacks and as a workbench surface
Below: This man-made solid surface, similar to Corian®, extends along the worktop and includes a sink made from the same material

Right: Laminate surfaces now come with softly curved edges in a wide range of colours

Laminex Industries

Corian®

Corian is the registered trade mark for a man-made worktop material which looks like marble but is much tougher than the real thing, being highly resistant to heat and stains. It can be cleaned with abrasive cleaners and scourers, and has the added advantage that if scratches do occur, they are easily sanded or scoured away. Corian can be worked like timber, and such features as rounded edges, non-drip edges and juice grooves are often incorporated into the worktop design. It is certainly not a budget option.

Avonite®

This is another manufactured composite material which has the appearance of granite, can be worked to form almost invisible joins and comes in about a dozen colours. As with Corian, it's virtually maintenance-free, and is resistant to staining and heat. Any scratches that do occur can be removed with light sanding.

Timber

While undoubtedly an attractive material, timber, in solid planks, glue-laminated or recycled forms, is not always the most sensible choice for worktops. It can deteriorate and lose colour after constant wear from hot and cold liquids, eventually exposing the grain. The only thing to do then is to strip the timber back, sand it and reseal it. Hot saucepans and timber worktops do not make a good combination, and neither do chopping knives and timber. If it is washed down too often with detergents, it can lose its natural oils and split.

Having said all that, timber will acquire a rich patina over time and you may feel the scratches, nicks and stains add character rather than look unattractive.

However, if the imperfections would annoy you, and you're determined to have a timber kitchen, your best bet would be to use either one of the plastic laminate timber look-alikes, or restrict the use of timber to shelves and cupboard doors.

Stainless steel

Much more popular for commercial than domestic use, stainless steel is, nevertheless, making inroads into the home kitchen. First seen as sinks and draining boards, it's now often used to form complete worktops. It's hygienic, easy to look after (as long as you don't scratch it with scourers or abrasive powders), doesn't stain and is impervious to heat. On the down side, though, it can be noisy; insulation boards glued to the underside of the worktop can help reduce clatter. It is also expensive, but does look especially good with other industrial-type components such as commercial ovens and wire mesh shelves.

Marble

An expensive choice, marble is not altogether practical as a worktop. It's slightly porous, and therefore stains easily, with the biggest culprits being some reasonably common foodstuffs such as certain vegetable dyes, wine and citrus juices. Being quite a soft material, it also scratches fairly easily.

Some types of marble are less porous than others, so if you are determined to use it in your kitchen, it is worth seeking expert advice before you decide on the variety. For those who enjoy baking, marble provides a naturally cool surface for pastrymaking; however, a marble inset may provide a more practical alternative than surfacing the whole worktop in the material.

Soap and water can be used to clean marble; abrasive cleaners are unsuitable as they scratch. Severe stains can be polished out by professionals, and the use of commercial sealers will prevent some staining.

Granite comes in colours from grey and green to blue, black and red

Kitchen Country Form

Plate, Cups and Saucers The Bay Tree

Above: Wood is an attractive and durable work surface
Left: This man-made work surface resembles granite but is less expensive

Granite

This would have to be the ultimate worktop choice, if budget concerns were not taken into consideration. It's virtually indestructible, impervious to heat and liquids, scratch and chip-resistant, and non-porous. It's available in fabulous colours from greys and greens through reds and blues to black, and comes with square, bevelled or bullnosed edges. One thing you have to be careful about, though, is that granite is a very hard material, and unforgiving to dropped china and glassware. When it's first installed you have to adjust the force with which you put down the china to avoid chips or breaks.

Ceramic tiles

With the increased choice of worktop materials over the years, ceramic tiles are

Laminate is the most economical and practical worktop material.

losing their popularity for this particular job. That's probably just as well, as they are not particularly suitable. The grouting, unless epoxy, can very quickly become discoloured and is difficult to clean; the tiles themselves are noisy, and can crack if hot saucepans are put onto them. They are also quite fragile, and can chip or break if anything heavy is dropped onto them. Highly glossed tiles tend to show wear fairly quickly, too. All in all, it's probably sensible to restrict tiles to floors and splashbacks.

194

Tiling a kitchen wall

Project 6 77

Tiles still make the best wall surface between kitchen worktops and overhead cupboards.

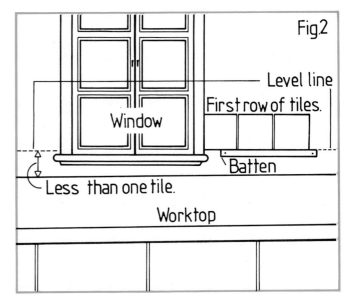

Fig.1

Half tile · Half tile · Full tile · Full tile · Battens · Level line · Worktop

Fig.2

Level line · First row of tiles. · Window · Batten · Less than one tile. · Worktop

They are easy to clean and make a watertight seal between walls and worktops as well as providing an opportunity for colour and decoration.

The most important thing to remember when tiling is to think it all out carefully before beginning. A careful sketch based on laying the tiles out on the worktop is worth the time it takes and will almost certainly reduce the likelihood of mistakes that might not become obvious until towards the end of the job.

STEP BY STEP

1 If you don't have a smooth rendered or plaster wall to start with you'll have to fit 6 mm fibre cement sheeting (e.g. Masterboard) as a flat base to which the tiles will be fixed. Nail or screw the sheets into place with 2-3 mm gaps between them to allow for movement.

2 Using a spirit level establish whether your worktops are level. If not, the first row of tiles

you fit will have to be one tile up from the lowest point of the worktop and the bottom row will have to be cut to fit later.

3 Draw a level line around the walls as the baseline for your first row of complete tiles. A chalk line may be best for this if a window has to be negotiated. Pin a batten along this line. The first row of tiles will rest on it (see fig. 1).

4 Lay your tiles out along the batten using matchsticks or bought plastic tile spacers between them to allow for the grout. Where this is awkward, mark out tiles plus joint widths along a length of batten and use this as a measuring stick. Choose the most inconspicuous spot for the inevitable cut tiles. This is often in a corner. Now decide on where to place your picture or feature tiles (see fig. 2).

5 Remember that it is much easier to cut a tile towards the

middle than to trim off a small piece. Remember also that you must tile along a level line regardless of whether the verticals and horizontals of your worktops, cupboards and windows are true.

6 Now that you have it all worked out, start applying your adhesive with a notched trowel, about one square metre at a time. Use matchsticks or tile spacers and never, under any circumstances, allow the gaps to vary as you place the tiles.

Start at the centre and work outwards, leaving all cut tiles to the end. Bed the tiles into the adhesive firmly, sliding them back and forth a little and tapping them with your fist or a piece of wood. Use a straight-

edge to ensure that they are bedding evenly. Ensure that the adhesive does not come up between the tiles. Wipe it out, and off the face of the tiles with a damp cloth as you go.

Leave the battens and matchsticks, if used, in place for at least 12 hours as the adhesive takes a while to gain full strength.

7 Now for cutting in the odd-shaped tiles. When marking, hold a full tile over the last tile laid in the row. Butt the tile to be cut against the wall and under the tile you are holding while you mark the cut with a fibre-tip pen, allowing for grout.

8 A tile-cutting device, hired cheaply, is the best way to go. In

MATERIALS	TIME
tiles of your choice fibre cement sheeting grout tile adhesive stud adhesive clouts or countersunk screws and plugs	Normally 2-3 days. Don't rush it

TOOLS
notched tiler's trowel tile cutter, wheel and handle type (hired) tungsten-tipped tile cutter tile file cloth, sponges and bucket spirit level drill and high quality masonry bit

the end the number of tiles saved from breakage will almost certainly make for a cheaper, less frustrating job. Place the tile in the machine face up, line up your marks with the scribing wheel, scribe and press down on the handle. The tile should snap cleanly along the scribed line. Do not try to cut off less than 40-50 mm. Lay as you cut them.

9 Fitting around tap holes and power outlets can mean the loss of a few tiles. If possible, avoid having to cut a complete hole in a tile. Instead, lay your tiles out so that you cut sections out of three or four tiles. Cut a bigger hole or bite out of the tile than you need but not so big that the tap or powerpoint cover-plates will not cover it. Use a tungsten car- bide-tipped tile cutter, score the marked line and take it out piece by piece with tile pincers. Alternatively, use a hacksaw with a tile cutting blade. A com- plete hole in a single tile can be achieved by drilling a starting hole with a masonry drill and cutting out with a tile-cutting blade. Smooth the cut edges with a tile file.

10 Grouting should not be- gin for at least 24 hours after your last tile was laid. Mix the grout as per the instructions on the pack. If colouring the grout add a small amount of oxide at a time until you reach the desired colour, or use precoloured grout. Apply the grout by hand (use rubber gloves) or with a rubber-bladed grout applicator. Fill all joints to overflowing and wipe off excess with a damp sponge. Use silicone sealant or a pro- prietary sealing strip on the joint between the wall and the worktop.

11 When the surface is dry remove the excess grout. Dust with a clean polishing cloth.

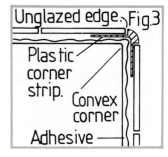

Tiles Country Floors *Kitchen Country Form*

Ceramic tiles are not only the most hardwearing surface for the area between your worktop and cupboards, but also can be your kitchen's focal point

196

Cat door

A cat door not only benefits the cat, it brings peace of mind to the cat owner.

The hole should be cut in the bottom of the door on the lock-side so any framing will not interfere with the normal door operation. The door needs to be approximately 250 x 250 mm or smaller, depending on the size of your cat.

The door shown in the drawings can be locked for security, if required, or to simply stop a draught. Make sure that the cat door is positioned far enough away from the door lock, so that it cannot be reached by long-armed bandits! In any case, don't leave the key in the lock.

STEP BY STEP

1 Remove door, mark out the opening (250 x 250 mm) and cut out. The opening should be approximately 100 mm from the edge of the door. Take care not to damage the facing of the door. Use a fine bladed jigsaw or pad saw.

2 Make up the cat door frame from 60 x 12 mm DAR (PAR) timber to outside dimensions of 250 x 250 mm.

3 Make up the door from 8 mm plywood with a timber trimmer on top. Create an 8 mm slot in the trimmer with saw and chisel or an electric router. Round off the top with a plane and sandpaper. Leave 2 mm clearance around the door and pivot it on 32 mm brass wood screws. Make holes in the frame with clearance to allow the door to swing freely.

4 Insert the frame and door as an assembly into the pre-cut hole in the back door. Secure it to the door with 8 mm quadrant on both sides (see fig. 3). Fit lock if required.

5 Paint with a good oil-based primer then one or two coats of gloss.

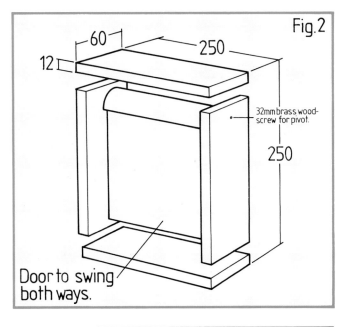

Fig.2

60 — 250 — 12 — 250 — 250

32 mm brass wood-screw for pivot.

Door to swing both ways.

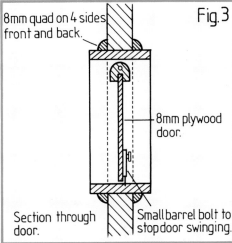

Fig.3

8mm quad on 4 sides front and back.

8mm plywood door.

Section through door.

Small barrel bolt to stop door swinging.

Fig.1

MATERIALS
timber
PVA adhesive
nails
sandpaper
paint
lock, optional

TOOLS
electric drill
jigsaw or pad saw
hammer
chisel or electric router
plane
tape and pencil

TIME
4 hours

Sinks and taps

Not long ago, sinks and taps were the most boring things in the kitchen. Now they are among the most colourful.

Sink Clark

Sink Omega-Smeg

Sinks and taps can add a touch of glamour and good looks to every kitchen. Indeed, the variety of styles and finishes now available calls for careful selection.

Sinks

Finance and space, for most people, are unalterable influences on the choice but, working within those parameters, you should also consider how you will use the sink.

Probably the most important factor is whether or not you have a dishwasher. If you do not, the prime purpose of the sink should be to make the task of washing up as easy as possible. Ideally, you should have twin bowls and double draining boards: this allows a natural work flow of stacking dirty dishes, washing, rinsing and draining. If space limits you to a one-and-a-half bowl style, take into account whether you like to work from left to right or the other way round. The larger bowl should be convenient for washing, and should be a minimum of about 17.5 cm deep and wide enough to take your biggest baking dish, the grill pan, oven shelves or anything else that may need long soaking.

It is best to avoid round sinks – it's surprising how many kitchen items don't fit into them – and any without an integral draining board, as you will inevitably end up with small puddles of water lying on the worktop.

If you do have a dishwasher, or if space is very limited, you can look at the more compact styles, with smaller bowls and one or no draining board. The more sophisticated models make up for their lack in size in ingenuity: accessories that can be brought out as required include chopping boards, cutlery holders and plate racks that fit over the bowl, and separate draining boards. Other space-saving designs are corner sinks, which have the draining boards and bowls at right angles. They make good use of often 'dead' areas without encroaching on precious work surfaces. Well worth considering, whether or not you have limited space, is an allowance for a waste disposer.

A good setting

Virtually all compact designs and some larger sinks are designed to be set into the worktop. This allows flexibility as far as positioning goes: the hole can be cut anywhere along the worktop as long as there is sufficient room underneath for the sink bowls. Sit-on designs, supported by a unit of the same length, have the same depth as the worktop. Check that there is a watertight seal between the edge of the sink and the adjacent worktops.

Material matters

As far as material goes, stainless steel still holds the number one position for durability and ease of cleaning. Enamelled and china sinks give you the opportunity of introducing colour but, although they have improved over the years, they are not a wise choice if you wash up by hand as they can chip. Brass looks charming in a traditional setting; it is durable and fairly easy to clean with a cream cleaner or brass polish.

Over the last decade or so, several manufacturers have developed composites which offer, at a price, considerable advantages. Not only are they extremely tough, resisting scratches, knocks, stains and heat, they are also much quieter, greatly reducing the clatter of pots and pans. They are available in a number of styles and different colours.

Above: A corner sink allows more room for dishes and maximises space
Top: Stainless steel is a popular choice for sinks

TIPSTRIP

❏ Use a sink trap over the plughole to stop solid waste blocking the pipe.
❏ Don't pour melted fat down the sink – it may block the pipes as it congeals.
❏ To clear a blocked sink, bail out any water, sprinkle about a cup of washing soda crystals onto the plughole and pour over a kettleful of boiling water. If this fails try a rubber plunger.
❏ No luck? Put a bowl or bucket under the U-bend, undo the nut or locking ring and push some stiff wire into the pipe to dislodge the blockage. Repeat the washing soda treatment.

Tap lines

Like sinks, taps have danced their way into the nineties. Those immovable spouts fitted with coloured rubber nozzles are, thank goodness, things of the past. So too, are dripping taps. Improved technology – a ceramic disc instead of a washer – has put an end to drips for good. Because the discs are much longer lasting than washers, that tedious task of changing washers is destined to become a distant memory.

And there are other follow-on advantages: it's goodbye to ugly and immovable mineral stains on sinks and, of course, to a colossal waste of water. Quite apart from the environmental considerations, a dripping tap could cost you dear in areas where water use is metered. The new discs mean that a quarter turn of the handle is all that is needed to stop the flow, but tap designers have worked out ways to make water control even easier. Ergonomic single-lever designs mean that even the stickiest hands have no difficulty at all in turning the water on and off, or adjusting the temperature.

The two-handle, single-spout mixer-tap design is still appropriate in a traditional kitchen setting, but the single-lever designs win hands down for ease of use. They are operated by the lightest touch – even the nudge of an elbow if your hands are full or filthy – a fact that is appreciated by the elderly and disabled.

It's not just performance that has changed. Some taps have such sleek lines that they almost enter the art category; others are available in a positive rainbow of colours to complement or brighten any decorative scheme. Finishes available include numerous coloured epoxies, chrome, brass and gold. The last sounds like the ultimate extravagance and, of course, it is very expensive but it is gradually gaining preference over brass because it is less likely to corrode.

At the other end of the price range, it is possible to change the handles on many of the less expensive tap designs: an old-fashioned tap that still functions well can be given a more modern look or a splash of colour with a very simple do-it-yourself project. You don't even have to turn the water off at the mains!

Whatever style you choose, it should be compatible with the sink in terms of finish, colour and function. The spout should swivel easily and be high enough for you fill a tall vase without tilting it. Don't be wooed by an aesthetically beautiful tap if the handles are hard to control. Gimmicks are best avoided but extras that have proved their worth are brush and spray attachments and detergent dispensers. Along with the dozens of styles and colours there is, of course, an equal range of prices. Good taps are not cheap. If you are renovating your kitchen, don't treat taps as an afterthought. Choose the type you want and make allowances when you plan your budget. Buy the best you can afford – you will never regret investing in a good quality tap – but check, especially if it is an imported model, that it complies with your local water board regulations. New taps don't always suit old plumbing systems either. If in doubt, ask the advice of a plumber.

Don't treat taps as an afterthought. Choose the type you want and make allowances when you plan your budget. Buy the best you can afford – you will never regret it.

Above: The gold sink set – a combination of classic styling and modern technology
Below: Chrome and white kitchen mixer. A mixer is the most convenient tap for the kitchen

Above: A streamlined chrome mixer tap, incorporating a watertight ceramic disc cartridge
Below: White kitchen mixer with a single lever which can be operated with the touch of an elbow

The kitchen outlook

Standing at the sink, up to the elbows in dirty dishes, is a lot less painful if you are gazing at a landscaped garden or beautiful view.

No one would pretend that washing up is fun, but, if you really do have to stand up to the elbows in dirty dishes, the whole exercise would be a lot less painful if you were gazing at a beautiful view or landscaped garden. Unfortunately though, while planning can take care of making the interior of your kitchen as attractive and functional as possible, it's impossible to conjure up a fabulous panorama if you don't happen to have one at your back door.

However, in almost every case, you can make your kitchen outlook more pleasant; one that will add appeal to the whole room.

If you happen to look onto a brick wall, don't despair – that's easy to improve upon. To bring more light into the kitchen, and brighten up that dreary brickwork, consider painting it a colour that will coordinate with your interior decorating scheme. Use weatherproof paint for a long-lasting finish. If you really want to fantasise as you're slaving

over the dishes, and you're artistically inclined, you could paint a trompe l'oeil mural outside the window. For starters – a fabulous beach scene, complete with crashing waves and sunbathers; or how about an alpine scene with snow-capped peaks; or a panorama across the Tuscan hills to a superb palazzo? There's no harm in dreaming!

For something a little more down to earth, look for metal pot rings, which you should be able to find in your local nursery. These are installed into the wall, and terracotta pots sit in them. An alternative would be wall-mounted terracotta plant holders. Grow herbs or, for a splash of colour, geraniums or annuals such as pansies. Likewise, a window box installed under the kitchen window can add a lively touch to an otherwise drab scene, or even a practical touch – keeping herbs literally close at hand. If you decide to grow flowers,

find varieties that will give year-round colour.

Lattice or trelliswork attached to fences can give privacy as well as improve your outlook. Paint or stain it to suit, and then either leave it as is, or grow a climbing plant over it. Check with your local nursery to find the best plant for the position; choose from a flowering one, such as jasmine or one of the climbing roses, or a non-flowering variety, such as an ornamental grape, creeping fig or a variety of ivy.

If none of the above solutions is suitable for your particular problem view, you can always solve it from the inside. Consider venetian blinds – they can be tilted to get rid of offensive sights without blocking out the light completely, or you could invest in a translucent scenic roller blind.

Full-length windows take advantage of a fabulous panorama

Kitchen Country Form/Egg basket and Teatowel/The Bay Tree

Window box

A simple wooden window box on your kitchen windowsill, filled with flowers or herbs, is the easiest way to improve your kitchen outlook.

You can fill the window box with soil or use it to hold plastic pots or a plastic trough. The size you make it should be determined by the size and type of window for which it is built. For a brick window it should fit snugly between the brickwork of the window opening, and for a timber house it should be the width of the window plus the exterior architraves.

STEP BY STEP

1 Choose your material. Pine is cheapest but tends to warp with the weather. Maple is better but cedar is the best. It is also the most expensive. Depth of the box should be determined as a pleasing proportion of the overall window size. About 200 mm is typical. Buy enough timber (200 x 25 mm DAR/PAR) for two sides, front, back and a bottom but check the timber as you buy it, rejecting any pieces that are not straight and true.

2 Measure and cut the pieces as in fig. 1, remembering that the nominal size of the timber is greater than what you will actually have in your hand. Note: If you are using only one size of timber, say 200 x 25 mm, then the front-to-back dimension of the box will be equal to the width of the timber plus two thicknesses for the front and back. The bottom, nailed on all sides, will sit snugly within the frame.

3 The rebate joint. The front piece needs to have a step chiselled out of each end for both strength and appearance. In this way no endgrain is visible from the outside. Across each end of the front piece, scribe a line at a distance from the end equal to the thickness of the timber, and another one about one-third of the way in on the endgrain (see fig. 2).

Using a mitre box or similar, cut across the grain about two-thirds of the way through the timber, making sure that both ends are cut to the same depth. Cut the side pieces last, as they will determine the overall width of the box, regardless of what depth you make the rebate. Carefully cut for the rebate with a saw and chisel at the step, using a 25 mm chisel.

4 The back needs only to be butt-jointed so the length of it will be the same as the front. The bottom should be the width of the timber to avoid a long cut, and as long as the overall length of the box, less two thicknesses for the sides. The sides should be cut last to ensure a good fit against the front and back.

5 Now the box is ready to assemble, but first the timber should be sealed with a synthetic preservative. Nail through the sides into the front at the rebate joints and then to the bottom, using rustproof nails. Also nail the front and the back to the bottom. Waterproof adhesive should be used on all joints for strength. Drill a number of holes in the bottom, towards the front, and seal the exposed timber with synthetic preservative.

6 If the sill is not wide enough to support the box, braces may be needed. Galvanised metal L-shaped braces may be used or simple timber ones can be easily made (see fig. 3).

7 To install, drill through the sides into the edge of the brickwork on both sides of the window opening with a masonry drill. Hammer the plastic wall-plugs into the brickwork, then screw through the sides into the plug. Repeat the technique to fix the braces. If installing in a timber-framed house, fixing is done by screwing the sides of the box into the edge of the window frame. Braces in this case must line up with the studs in the wall.

Finish with a coat of paint or stain.

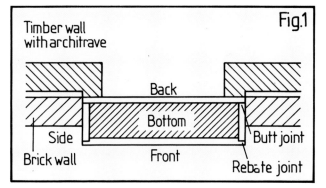

Fig.1

Timber wall with architrave · Back · Bottom · Side · Front · Butt joint · Brick wall · Rebate joint

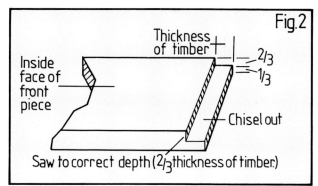

Fig.2

Thickness of timber · 2/3 · 1/3 · Inside face of front piece · Chisel out · Saw to correct depth (2/3 thickness of timber.)

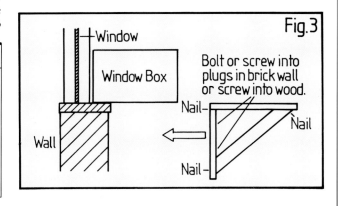

Fig.3

Window · Window Box · Bolt or screw into plugs in brick wall or screw into wood. · Nail · Nail · Wall · Nail

MATERIALS		TOOLS	
timber	wall-plugs	hammer	chisels
nails	braces	handsaw	level
screws		square	hand plane
waterproof adhesive		nail punch	paintbrush
timber preservative or		screwdriver	
waterproofer		tape measure	
		hammer drill and bit	

TIME
4 hours

Bringing the outdoors in

Eating outside is one of the great pleasures of life. A simple lunch achieves cordon bleu status if served in the fresh air, and there is no more enjoyable way of passing a summer evening than a leisurely dinner outdoors.

Even in a small garden it is worth setting aside an area for a table and chairs. Ideally your spot should be sheltered from the wind; it should catch the winter sun, but offer shade in the hot months. No, you can't change the course of the sun, but you can grow deciduous plants that let warm rays through in winter and cast dappled shadows in summer.

If you plan your patio area so that it can be seen from the kitchen window, you will gain an immediate impression of extra space – an effect that can be further enhanced if it is possible to use the same flooring, such as terracotta or slate, or similarly coloured materials. Wide french windows or a glazed door will reduce the visual barrier between outside and inside and you can strengthen the garden link with botanical prints on the kitchen walls, a pretty floral blind, even a flowery apron.

Conservatories

An alternative – or an addition – to a patio, that will beat the most spiteful vagaries of the weather, is a conservatory. Long associated with gracious mansions, it is now finding itself at home even in modest gardens.

In order to reap year-round benefit, a conservatory should be sited to catch as much winter sun as possible. All windows and doors need to be thoroughly draughtproofed, and in cooler climates, double glazing or some sort of heating is almost essential. Don't, however, underestimate how hot a conservatory can be at the height of summer. There should be at least two large opening windows in the roof to allow the heat to escape.

Off-the-peg conservatories can be bought, or you can have one tailor-made to your own requirements. Make sure the design you choose doesn't have any inaccessible valleys that may get clogged with leaves. Toughened glass should be used for doors and windows; on the roof panels it should be laminated

Kettle The Bay Tree

to reduce the risk of breakage should a tile or slate slip from the roof of the house. Ideally, double glass doors should link the kitchen and the garden room. If the room will be used regularly as an eating area, remember that swing doors are easiest to operate when you are carrying a laden tray. Conservatories are not just for daytime: the design should also incorporate subtle lighting for night-time use.

Most conservatories need some sort of shading to screen out the fiercest summer sun. The choice ranges from simple roller blinds to sophisticated automatic devices. If you need blinds for privacy as well as shade, make sure they do the job and remain opaque when you have the lights on at night.

A small patio leading off the kitchen provides a pleasant setting for a meal or entertaining guests

Fitting furniture

The type of furniture you choose will depend very much on the size of your patio or conservatory. If space is no object, you may prefer a table and chairs that are left permanently in place. For a patio, they should be heavy enough not to blow around and, even in a well-sheltered spot, they must be fully weatherproof. This rules out wicker and cane although, if you like the romantic associations of wicker, you can look for traditional all-weather woven furniture, which is available at a price. Other options include cast iron, coated aluminium and the more sophisticated plastic furniture.

Even if the furniture can be left outside, it's advisable to bring the cushions in at the end of the day. Modern materials have improved greatly and the problems of mildew and rot are less likely to occur, but no technology, alas, can protect fabric from atmospheric dirt, bird droppings and non-colourfast leaves.

The classic choice for a conservatory is casual and comfortable: wicker and cane fit the bill perfectly here, but they tend to be bulky. If you want to use the room as a second dining room you need to choose compact pieces. Look at chairs and tables that are slightly lower than standard dining room furniture and take into account the amount of space needed to move a chair up to and away from the table – a minimum of one metre.

If space is limited, outdoors or indoors, look at lightweight folding furniture that can be brought out and put away easily as required.

In order to reap year-round benefit, a conservatory should be sited to catch as much winter sun as possible.

Conservatories often become the most well-used room in the house

Alexander Bartholomew Conservatories Ltd

For both patios and conservatories, an old fashioned trolley can be a boon when it comes to serving and clearing away; the trolley may also be useful for storing condiments, place mats and the like.

For safety's sake, especially when children are around, it is worth investing in non-breakable plates and acrylic glasses for outdoor eating. There is a wonderful range of bright and sophisticated designs available.

A place for plants

Plants, of course, play a vital role in establishing a relaxed and pleasant atmosphere. Start with some evergreens, such as conifers and ivy outside, or ferns and palms in a conservatory. Ring seasonal changes with bulbs and colourful bedding plants. Make the most of the kitchen connection and grow your own decorative

foods: herbs, tomatoes, chillies and peppers, even a grape vine, all will flourish in sheltered, sunny conditions. Citrus trees in tubs will also thrive as long as they are protected from frost; their flowers smell heavenly and you may even have a fruitful harvest.

203

Making a kitchen garden

Your kitchen garden can be as simple as a few herbs in pots outside your back door, or a proper vegetable and herb garden.

COMPANION PLANTING CHART	
Plant	**Compatible with**
beans	cauliflower, rosemary, sage
cabbages	beetroot, celery, onions, tomatoes, dill, mint, oregano, thyme, nasturtium
carrots	peas, lettuce, radish, chives
lettuce	carrots, strawberries, radishes, cabbage, beetroot
onions	beetroot, carrots, lettuce, cabbage
peas	radishes, carrots, cucumber, beans
tomatoes	basil, parsley, cabbage, marigolds, chives, carrots, borage, garlic, lemon balm, parsley
Avoid planting strawberries near the cabbage family and peas and beans with the onion family.	

The type of garden you choose will depend upon the space you have available, the amount of sun it gets, the time you have to spend in the garden, and to a certain extent, your own taste in food. A small-scale kitchen garden could perhaps consist of a few herbs and some tomatoes, lettuce and carrots.

Siting the garden

You'll need a spot close to the kitchen which gets plenty of sun (at least two-thirds of the day) and is protected from strong winds. Border your site with bricks, stones or logs and dig in a good quality organic material such as compost or well-rotted manure. Special attention to soil condition at this stage will repay you handsomely later on.

The compost heap

Starting a compost heap is easy. Heap your lawn clippings, stray leaves and vegetable waste from the kitchen into a pile, keep it moist and regularly turned and when it has broken down scatter it over your garden to provide organic material which will replenish the soil.

Succession planting

The key to providing enough vegetables for your family over the whole growing season is succession planting. If you sow too many seeds at the one time you'll have a glut of vegetables and then nothing. Plant only six vegetables every fortnight, selecting varieties with different maturing dates. Seed packets and labels will often indicate 'early', 'mid-season' or 'late'. This way you will have new plants coming on as the older ones mature.

Intercropping

This is particularly useful when space is a problem. The idea is to plant two vegetables close together – tall slender growers such as onions or leeks can be interspersed with compact growers such as lettuce and radish. Or lettuce and spinach can be grown with tomatoes – the leaf vegetables will mature before the tomatoes overshadow them. If you plant radishes close to carrots, the radishes will mature first and help to loosen the soil.

Crop rotation

The principle is that a crop of light feeding plants should follow a crop of heavy feeders.

A kitchen garden can be as simple as a few herbs in pots

This maintains soil texture and fertility and controls pests and diseases at the same time. Leaf crops such as lettuce and spinach, which use plenty of nitrogen, should be followed by root crops such as carrots and radishes, which do not. Peas and beans return nitrogen to the soil and raise trace elements from lower layers which can be used by surface rooting vegetables. Do not plant members of the same family in the same spot in successive years .

Companion planting

This is planting one particular vegetable or herb with another for their mutual benefit. For example, basil planted close to tomatoes deters the white fly which transmits fungal diseases. Garlic keeps aphids and red spider mites away from tomatoes but should not be planted close to peas, beans, cabbages and strawberries. Marigolds prevent root-rotting bacteria and nasturtiums are a useful general insect repellent.

This kind of organic gardening gives many benefits:

❏ It prevents the soil degradation that comes from too-frequent use of chemical fertilisers.

❏ Beneficial soil organisms, such as worms and bacteria will thrive, aerating the soil and preventing diseases.

❏ Natural predators such as birds will rid the garden of pests. At the same time as helping the environment, you get fresh, healthy vegetables and herbs.

TIPSTRIP

Safe garden pesticides include those based on soaps and garlic. Or make your own by boiling rhubarb leaves in water for 20 minutes. Strain, cool and pour over your vegetables.

Denise Greig

Heating and cooling

The perfect kitchen is toasty and warm in winter, cool and airy in summer but, alas, the situation is often reversed.

The floor

However magnificent they may look in an old farmhouse, cold, grey flagstone floors don't conjure up a sense of winter comfort. The fact is, if your feet are cold, so is the rest of you. Ironically, in the right location, solid floors are an important factor in maintaining a good ambient temperature.

The 'right location' is a room that enjoys sunshine for most of the day. Stone and other solid materials, like concrete and brick, absorb heat while the air temperature is high; this has the effect of cooling the room. When the air temperature drops, the laws of nature dictate that the heat is released again, and the room will be warmed. In summer and winter alike, the temperature should remain pleasant and constant.

Even in a not-so-sunny situation, you can capitalise on a solid floor's ability to store heat. Underfloor heating elements set into the concrete slab, can be installed at the time of building or renovating. Once the floor has warmed up, it gives out a constant, even temperature and it is quite economical to keep the heat 'topped up'. Because it is slow to respond, however, this type of heating is not suitable for, say, a weekend cottage. By the time it had warmed up you would be packing your bags and heading back to town.

Aga-Rayburn

Stone or ceramic tiles are good flooring choices unless you have a solid floor that does not get any sunshine and doesn't have heating beneath. Then some sort of insulation between the floor and your feet is essential. A rug is fine in the dining area but not advisable in the kitchen, where it may slip, or trip people up. Instead, think about laying cork tiles or cushioned vinyl sheeting. Most carpets are not suitable for kitchen use but there are tight-looped synthetic carpets which are very resistant to staining (but which will melt), and heavy duty carpet tiles which can be lifted for cleaning and, if necessary, be replaced.

Heating well

In a centrally heated house, it seems obvious to incorporate a radiator or hot air outlet in the kitchen – but in this era of fitted units it can be hard to find an appropriate spot. Radiators, fortunately, are available in a huge variety of shapes and sizes, from tall and thin to long and low. Hot air outlets should be kept as low as possible (hot air rises) and can sometimes be incorporated into the plinths of the units. In the interests of efficiency and economy, don't position a source of heat next to the fridge or freezer.

If you're using a plug-in appliance, make sure that the flex doesn't trail across the traffic area.

A gas-fired Aga cooker can add character and warmth to a kitchen as well as deal with the practical aspects of cooking

Kitchen comfort

The thought of a big, cosy stove is very comforting in inclement weather and the appeal of the Aga stove and similar models remains strong. Solid fuel models are still available, or you can opt for the convenience of gas or oil. Many people love cooking on these stoves and enjoy the other benefits: hot water and heating for the house. Disadvantages are that they generate heat in summer too, and the kitchen must be well ventilated to allow the excess warmth to disperse.

Keeping cool

The simplest form of ventilation is, of course, an open window but in summer it can let in more than fresh air. Simple mesh screens will keep flies, mosquitoes and moths at bay while letting cooking fumes escape and cooling breezes in to soothe the harassed cook.

Windows alone, however, can rarely cope with the heat and smells created by frying and grilling. If you do not have a rangehood (cooker hood), think about installing an extractor fan (see page 209). Because the fan will cut out light if installed in a window, it is preferable to mount it in an outside wall. The supplier should advise you on the best location – it should be close to the source of fumes but should not be positioned so that it creates a draught that 'drags' flames towards it.

The model you buy must be powerful enough for the size of your room and, ideally, should have several speeds. Other features to look for are timer switches, efficient draught proofing when the fan is not in use, air intake as well as expulsion and a strong outer grille.

Shelves and storage

Project 10

MATERIALS	TIME
6 mm plywood PVA adhesive nails	2 hours

TOOLS	
saw	tape measure
ruler	
hammer	

In any kitchen, but especially a small kitchen, where space is at a premium, it is important to make use of all available space for storage.

These DIY projects will enable you to keep kitchen essentials within easy reach. While they are simple to make, they look smart and help keep your kitchen neat.

All these projects are suitable for novice carpenters.

Saucepan lid drawer

Saucepan lids are awkward to store but if you make this practical rack to fit a deep drawer, you will always be able to find the right lid to fit every saucepan when you need it.

STEP BY STEP

1 Cut spacers to a height of 15 mm less than the depth of the drawer (measuring from the inside).

2 Cut spacers to length (see detail A).

3 Glue and nail these spacers to the inside of your drawer sides allowing 7 mm between them (make sure the nails do not protrude through the drawer sides).

4 Cut dividers to width and length and slip into place.

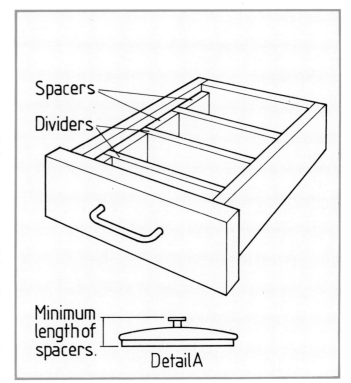

Spacers

Dividers

Minimum length of spacers.

Detail A

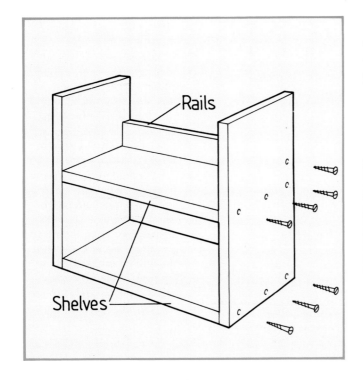

Rails

Shelves

Bookshelves

The size of these shelves will vary depending upon the space available and the number of books you want to display.

STEP BY STEP

1 Cut shelves and rail to the same length.

2 Cut ends to size and drill holes for screws.

3 Screw and glue the unit together. Drill for the screws and countersink the holes with a countersinking bit in your drill.

4 Sand and paint or lacquer in your choice of colour.

MATERIALS	
Suggested timber sizes: **ends and shelves** 200 x 25 mm **rail** 50 x 25 mm (these are nominal sizes; planed sizes are slightly smaller) screws 50 mm x 8 gauge PVA adhesive	

TOOLS	TIME
mitre box or similar saw screwdriver or power driver sanding block and paper	3 hours

Plate rack

This simple folding plate rack is elegant and convenient as well as relatively easy to make. The material is all stock size so it is readily available at your timber yard

STEP BY STEP

1 Cut 27 legs from 25 x 25 mm DAR (PAR) softwood to 350 mm long.

2 Drill a 4 mm diameter hole for the bolt 125 mm from one end of each leg. A vertical drill stand is best but it can be done carefully by hand with an electric drill.

3 Insert the bolt into the holes and fit the nuts and washers but do not tighten.

4 Insert cardboard spacers (approximately 1 mm thick) between legs and finger-tighten the bolt (see fig. 1).

5 Lay the assembly flat on a bench and screw and glue the top rail on at 100 mm below the top of the legs. Make sure you only screw to alternate legs (see fig. 2).

6 Repeat step 5 for bottom rail, 97 mm from bottom.

7 Turn the assembly over and repeat steps 5 and 6 but ensure that you are screwing the rails to the opposite legs (i.e. legs without screws on the other side).

8 Cut rails to length where they overhang and sand flush.

9 Remove cardboard spacers and sand and paint in your choice of colour.

The wooden plate rack can be positioned on the sink or just next to it for handy access when washing dishes

MATERIALS	TOOLS
legs 27 lengths of 25 x 25 mm DAR (PAR) softwood at 350 mm long	tape measure
rails 4 lengths of 25 x 25 mm DAR (PAR) softwood, approx 500 mm long	drill
screws 54 of 32 mm x 8 gauge, countersunk	saw
bolt 4 x 520 mm, brass, chrome or galvanised steel threaded full length with 2 nuts and washers to suit	screwdriver
waterproof adhesive	sanding block
lacquer or paint	countersinking bit

TIME
3¹/₂ hours

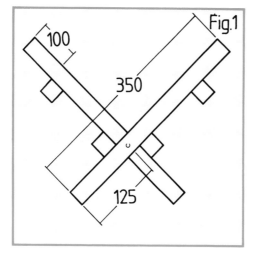

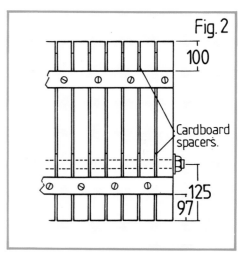

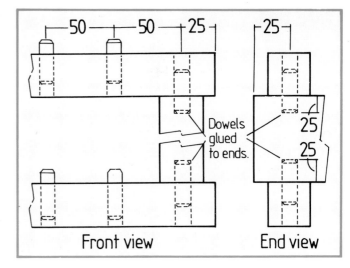

Front view   End view

Left: The wooden wine rack is simple to make and will hold a large number of bottles

Wine rack

Here is a simple wine rack that you should be able to make in 4 hours.

All the timber is stock size so it will be readily available from your local timber supplier.

STEP BY STEP

1 Cut the ends to 270 mm long and drill 8 mm holes in both edges at both ends, four holes in all. The holes are in the centre of the edges, 25 mm deep and 25 mm from ends.

2 Cut the rails to length (700 mm) and drill 8 mm holes 50 mm apart, starting 25 mm from the ends. Drill all holes right through the rails.

3 Glue the dowels into the rails in all holes with the exception of the end holes. Make sure that the dowels finish flush on the bottom.

4 Glue four dowels into the ends and make sure that they are hammered right down.

5 Sand and paint or varnish as required and assemble.

MATERIALS	
6 lengths of 100 x 38 mm DAR (PAR) softwood at 270 mm	
8 lengths of 38 x 38 mm DAR (PAR) softwood at 700 mm	
120 38 x 8 mm furniture dowels	
PVA adhesive	
paint or varnish	
sandpaper	

TOOLS	TIME
saw	4 hours
8 mm drill bit	
drill	
hammer	

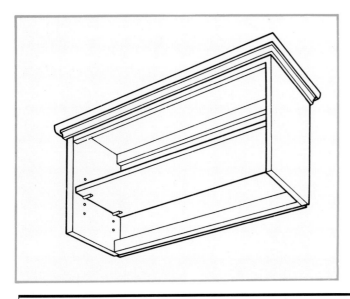

Dresser shelves

This simple dresser can be made to any size, although if it is to be wider than a metre the shelves may begin to sag if a lot of heavy china is placed on it.

It is designed to sit on top of a worktop or sideboard. Screw the unit to the wall to stop it falling forward.

STEP BY STEP

1 Cut the wood for the ends to length and drill for adjustable shelf supports.

2 Cut front and back rails to length (three in all, one at the front top and two at the back).

3 Screw and glue rails between ends and glue and nail plywood to the back to hold it square.

4 Cut top 40 mm wider and 80 mm longer than size of unit and round ends and front with a plane and sandpaper or an electric router.

5 Cut and fit scotia moulding under top glue and nail. Use a mitre box to achieve 45° cuts.

6 Cut shelves to length (1 mm clearance each end).

7 Glue and nail a thin strip of wood as a plate stop to front edge of shelves if required. Paint or lacquer in the colour of your choice. If painting be sure to undercoat properly first.

8 Insert shelf supports and install shelves. Shelf supports may be proprietary metal rods, cut lengths of aluminium rod (3-4 mm) or dowel.

MATERIALS		TOOLS	
top 200 x 25 mm DAR (PAR) softwood		saw	mitre box
ends and shelves 150 x 25 mm DAR (PAR) softwood		ruier	hammer
rails 38 x 25 mm softwood		square	drill
back 6 mm ply		screwdriver	
moulding 25 mm scotia		TIME	
paint or varnish		4-6 hours	

Rubbish and fume disposal

Every day in every kitchen, an enormous amount of waste is generated.

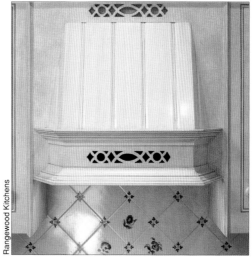

This extractor fan is cleverly hidden in an interesting wooden hood with carved details

Rangewood Kitchens

Waste comes in all shapes and forms – paper, cardboard, plastic, food scraps, liquids, oils, even airborne waste – the list goes on, and we all create literally mountains of the stuff.

A lot of our rubbish is a product of modern packaging methods, particularly in the case of cardboard wrapping, plastic bags and containers and metal cans. We can all do our bit by refusing to buy over-packaged products. It's easy enough to cut down on plastic carrier bags by recycling them or by using canvas or string bags.

However, that still leaves a lot of waste to deal with, and there are alternatives to just throwing it in the bin.

If you have a spare corner of the garden that's dry and well drained, think about making a compost heap. This is an ideal way of getting rid of all sorts of organic waste – food scraps, egg shells, coffee grounds and tea leaves, as well as wood shavings, newspaper, grass clippings, leaves and natural fibre clothes. Add fresh waste regularly, rather than occasional large deposits. Every 30 cm or so, add a layer of soil or manure, and, to prevent the top layer drying out, cover with an old damp sack.

For other types of rubbish, find out if there are council pick-ups for recyclable material such as paper, glass, plastic or aluminium; or alternatively there may be a deposit centre in your area.

Even if you do manage to get rid of most of your rubbish in an ecologically sound way,

A canopy rangehood fits neatly over a kitchen island and is positioned above the cooktop (hob)

Omega-Smeg

you'll never be able to completely do away with a rubbish bin somewhere in your kitchen. You can choose from the traditional freestanding bin, or, especially if you are designing a new kitchen, plan to have a concealed one, usually in a cupboard under the sink.

Another possibility for getting rid of kitchen waste is to have a waste disposer fitted to the sink. Electrically operated, it is attached under the sink waste outlet and grinds rubbish into fine particles. These are then washed down the drain and become part of the already overburdened sewerage system. In a high-rise flat, a waste disposer may be acceptable, but for anyone with a garden, the food scraps that are eaten up by the unit would be put to far better use on the compost heap.

Airborne smells in kitchens – the dreaded boiled cabbage or grilled chops – can permeate the whole house if they are not dealt with close to the source when they're produced. Water vapour from cooking can cause condensation problems in the room, leading to mould spots and rotting window frames. Opening a window or the back door is the obvious answer, but that's not always possible or practical.

The most effective way of getting rid of smells and water vapour is to install a rangehood (cooker hood). These come in various shapes and sizes, either off-the-shelf or custom-made. They can be completely inconspicuous; either installed behind a hinged door which, when opened, activates the mechanism, or the telescopic variety, a slimline unit which, when not in use, can be pushed back in to sit flush with adjacent cupboards. Otherwise, a feature can be made of the hood; in beaten copper for the country kitchen, or stainless steel for a more modern look.

You can also find extractors fitted into the worktop as part of the cooking hob itself. Installed below the worktop, the only part you see is a metal grille. This type of extractor is much more expensive than the more conventional type.

One word of advice before buying an extractor – try it out in the showroom first by holding a piece of paper to it. If the paper attaches itself, the extractor will probably be powerful enough for your needs. If it doesn't, keep looking, or open a window.

Refrigerators and freezers

Fridges and freezers are no longer huge white shapes looming in the corner. While they may be less bulky on the outside, their internal capacity is what counts for most people.

Despite all the streamlining, size, more than any other factor, determines which model of fridge or freezer we buy. A tall larder fridge and a matching freezer give ample easily accessible storage space but many kitchens are simply not big enough to accommodate them. Alternatives include a freezer kept separately – in the utility room, garage or wherever – or a combined fridge/freezer unit. Whatever you buy, choose a model on which the door is hinged correctly – it should not open into the central space of the kitchen.

Cold comforts

If the outer dimensions of the refrigerator are limited, the interior space should be as flexible as possible. Make sure all features really will be useful. Adjustable shelves and a facility for storing tall opened bottles are essential; egg racks are not and take up valuable space. If you use a lot of fresh vegetables, look for a good-sized crisper drawer; a butter compartment is handy – but not if you are on a cholesterol-free diet! Gadgets like drink dispensers and ice makers come into their own during hot weather – and kids love them all year round. A freezer compartment is not necessary if there is also a freezer in the room; if not, it

is useful for storing ice cubes and soon-to-be-eaten foods.

Icy conditions

Freezers come in chest or cupboard (upright) types. The former tends to hold more, but if you are not very organised, food at the bottom can be forgotten. The cupboard type has accessible drawers which conveniently divide the food into, say, meat, vegetables, desserts, bread and pastries.

Winning combinations

The advantage of a combined fridge/freezer is that it uses only as much floor space as one unit. Most people find a 50:50 or 60:40 fridge/freezer ratio the best, with the freezer section at the bottom. Combined appliances usually have only one compressor. This makes them quieter but, if there is a problem with the compressor, both sections are out of use.

Getting the best from your freezer

❏ A full freezer is more economical to run than a half-full one. If food stocks are low, fill the drawers with loaves of bread or even newspaper.
❏ Put the freezer in a cool, dry place, not in a sunny spot or next to any other source of heat.
❏ Before freezing food, set the thermostat to its lowest.
❏ Wrap foods thoroughly to exclude all air and moisture.

❏ Don't put hot food into the freezer – it will cause condensation. Cool foods as quickly as possible by standing dishes in a bowl of cold water.
❏ Label foods clearly – lamb stew and chocolate mousse look alike when frozen.

Power failure

❏ Food will remain in good condition for at least 8 hours – provided you do not open the door to check it out.
❏ Stick the telephone number of the service engineer to the side of the freezer.
❏ Take out insurance against loss of freezer contents.
❏ If the freezer is not in the kitchen, invest in a freezer alarm to alert you to an excessive increase in temperature.

Defrosting the freezer

❏ Try to do this when stocks are low.
❏ Switch off the freezer and take out all the food. Wrap the food in thick newspaper and put it in the fridge if there is room, in a picnic cool box or even wrap it in a quilt.
❏ Let the ice melt naturally – scraping it off with sharp tools may damage the lining.
❏ Wipe the inside with warm

water and bicarbonate of soda.
❏ Switch the freezer to its lowest setting and wait at least an hour before replacing the food.

Getting the best from your fridge

❏ Don't overfill the fridge.
❏ Don't open the door more often than you have to, or leave it open for more than a few seconds.
❏ Cover all food to stop strong flavours from tainting other foods.
❏ The door is the weakest part of most fridges: don't overload it or force large items into narrow shelves.
❏ Cool hot food before putting it in the fridge.

Phillips Whirlpool

Omega-Smeg

Stoves and cooktops

With such an enormous variety of stoves, ovens and cooktops (hobs) on the market it is essential to do a little homework before you buy.

Start by making a list of basic requirements. How much can you spend – and does that amount include installation? What fuel do you prefer – gas, electricity, solid fuel, oil? How much space do you have? Do you cook mainly for just one or two, with occasional dinner parties? Regularly entertain on a grand scale? Produce non-stop meals for the family and assorted friends? What sort of cooking do you do – baking, frying, grilling and barbecuing, steaming and stir-frying?

Armed with this information you can identify the appliances that best suit you. If you do a lot of baking, look at a double oven; if you cook mainly 'on top', put the emphasis on a good-sized cooktop.

Omega-Smeg

Which fuel?

Most cooks have a decided preference for one sort of fuel over another. Electricity is clean, convenient, readily available and much has been done by manufacturers to improve its performance. Electric ovens give an even heat throughout, so the food on the bottom rack cooks at the same rate as food at the top – ideal for batch baking.

Gas is highly controllable, quick to respond and, generally, cheaper than electricity. Gas ovens give 'zoned' temperatures, which is good if you are baking different foods at the same time. If you are a gas-lover living far from the nearest supply, consider an appliance that runs on LPG (keep a spare cylinder to hand).

Kitchen ranges that run on gas, solid fuel or oil are wonderful in a traditional farmhouse kitchen and can perform various other functions too, such as heating the water or, indeed, the whole house. You don't have to stick to one fuel: many cooks find perfection with a quick responding gas cooktop and a clean electric oven.

Which type?

The appliances themselves fall into three main categories: free standing, built-in and slip-in.

While the traditional free-standing stove doesn't generally compete in the glamour stakes, it has its advantages. It is economical to buy and install; a drawer for storage or plate warming is very useful; there is usually a good-sized separate grill. To minimise cleaning problems, butt adjacent units right up to the stove and seal the gaps. If this is not possible, buy a model that has wheels or runners so that you can pull it out easily for cleaning.

Slip-in stoves are designed to fit flush with the units, giving a built-in appearance, but unlike built-ins they can be taken with you when you move house. The advantage of a built-in oven is that it can be installed at any convenient height and, because it is away from the cooktop, heat from the oven doesn't add to the discomfort of the cook. When buying a new oven check that the open door doesn't obstruct access to the dishes inside – particularly important in a wall oven. Controls should be positioned where they cannot be accidentally knocked. A glass door and an internal light show the progress of the food inside. In gas ovens, look for automatic ignition and a safety device that shuts off the gas should the flame extinguish.

Cooktops

Cooktops are available for electricity, gas and bottled gas. The most popular format remains the four rings arranged in a square, but variations include elongated elements for fish kettles and deep fryers. On gas cooktops, pan supports have always tended, for some reason, to be dirt-traps. The problem hasn't been totally overcome, but some designs are more streamlined than others. Totally flush ceramic and glass cooktops, on the other hand, come clean with a wipe, if you are diligent about clearing up spills as they occur. If allowed to burn on you may need to scrape them off gently with a sharp razor blade: no abrasive cleaners should be used on these cooktops.

Responsiveness has also improved. While the solid hotplate still has its fans, the new breed of cooktops uses halogen heat and magnetic induction, both of which offer precise control. Halogen cooktops glow when warm and magnetic induction tops don't get hot; on other cooktops a warning light that comes on when an element is in use and remains on until it has cooled is an invaluable safety device. On any electric cooktop it is important to use flat-bottomed pans for maximum contact with the heat source. Make sure that pan bases and cooktop are dry before use or the steam created will make the pans dance.

Above left: A stainless steel hob and oven
Below: Halogen and fast-start ceramic hobs are electrically powered and allow infinite heating adjustment

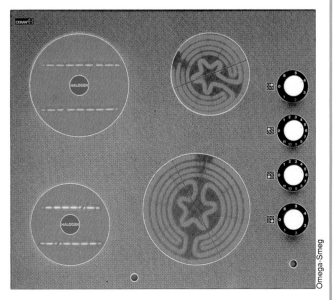

Omega-Smeg

Microwave ovens

The new generation of microwave ovens sports an impressive array of sophisticated options, but think carefully before you spend money on features you may not use.

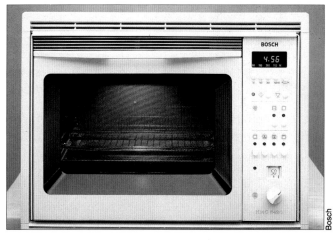

Bosch

Owners of microwave ovens seem to fall into two categories: those who genuinely use them as an alternative means of cooking, and those who use them for defrosting and reheating – and until you have tried one, it is hard to know whether a basic model will suit you or whether you would get real benefit from the extra features offered by the more expensive models.

Making waves

All microwave ovens work on the same principle. Microwaves – very short high frequency radio waves – pass through the food and make the moisture molecules vibrate rapidly; this creates the heat that cooks the food. The microwaves bounce around randomly in the oven and, to ensure even cooking, some sort of distribution device is required: wave stirrers (fans), a turntable or both. Debate continues as to which is the more efficient.

A turntable limits the shape of dish you use (large square ones are likely to catch on the walls of the oven) and makes it impractical to include a shelf.

Every oven includes a timer and power settings ranging from about 90W to 650W or 700W. Simpler models may have several preset levels, while top-of-the-range ovens offer fully variable settings and additional features. Whether or not you buy an oven sporting all these aids is down to personal preference; the size, however, is an essential factor. If you prepare a lot of meals for one person, a small-capacity oven will suit your needs. If you cook for a crowd you must have a larger one – even if only to defrost a family-size pizza!

If your oven is not built in, be prepared to lose a lot of bench space or install a special shelf at a convenient height.

Combined forces

A single oven which can be used for both conventional and microwave cooking is an attractive prospect. It reduces the amount of space taken up by your cooking equipment, and it overcomes the chief disadvantage of microwave cooking: that foods do not brown. You can use either method on its own or alternate bursts of both.

Project 11

Microwave shelf

This shelf can be made to any length to suit your requirements.

Your microwave will have vents on the end or top which require at least 50 mm of clear space opposite them.

STEP BY STEP

1 Securely fix the steel brackets to the wall. The brackets should be buttressed, of galvanised or plastic-coated steel and large enough to support the microwave without actually using a shelf. Use good quality masonry bolts if your wall is brick, or screw directly into the studs if it is a timber-frame wall. Do not hang brackets on cavity fixings such as toggle bolts.

2 Cut shelf to length. Use two or three widths of softwood as required; they will be held together by the screws from the L-bracket. Sand and/or chamfer the ends.

3 Cut end to size and screw and glue it to the shelf once it is installed.

4 Paint or lacquer the shelf as required.

MATERIALS		
softwood, 20 x 20 mm thick, width as required		
shelf brackets minimum size 300 x 300 x 18 x 6 mm		
PVA adhesive	heavy-duty wall plugs	
screws	paint or lacquer	

TOOLS		TIME
hammer	handsaw	2 hours
hammer drill	sanding block	
screwdriver	paintbrush	

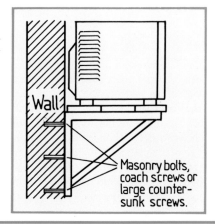

Wall

Masonry bolts, coach screws or large countersunk screws.

Dishwashers

Dishwashers are no longer considered luxury appliances. They are near-necessities in the modern kitchen.

If you still feel traces of guilt about using a dishwasher, take heart: it is a much more hygienic method of washing up – tea towels and dish cloths are perfect breeding grounds for germs – and, if you choose the model with care, it uses no more power and water than washing up by hand.

A few checks will make sure you are happy with the model you buy. First, find out the length of the shortest and the longest cycles, and the amount of water used – the lower the numbers, the kinder it is to your pocket and the environment. Does the machine have to be plumbed to the cold water supply? If you have abundant gas-heated hot water, it seems silly to pay for the machine to heat water from cold electrically. Some machines can be plumbed into the hot water

system, a few models are both hot and cold fill. If you have a kitchen that is too small for a plumbed-in machine, there are worktop models and machines which can be stored elsewhere and then connected to the kitchen tap.

Capacity

Dishwashers with no central column are the most spacious. Most standard 600 mm models will hold 12 or 14 international place settings – that is, soup, dinner and dessert plate, glass, cup and saucer, soup spoon, knife, fork, dessertspoon and teaspoon – plus serving dishes.

If your service has oval plates or unusually large dishes, or you have very long-stemmed glasses, there may be problems fitting them in. Look for adjustable baskets and racks – on some models the upper rack

Omega-Smeg

For many, a dishwasher is the most treasured appliance in the kitchen

can be lowered to accommodate tall glasses. Sliding racks facilitate loading and unloading; a removable bottom rack makes it easier to reach and remove the filter for cleaning.

Taking control

Washing programs are selected by dials, push buttons or touch controls. Some machines indicate what stage of the cycle has been reached; others have helpful warnings when water softeners or rinse aids are running low. Some sort of childproofing is a worthwhile feature if there are likely to be toddlers about.

The number of programs varies. While the idea of having several options is appealing, in practice most people end up using only one or two on a regular basis. Short economy cycles are invaluable for lightly soiled crockery or if you need dishes quickly – at a dinner party, entree dishes can be washed during the main course and re-emerge as dessert plates.

Another feature worth looking out for is a drying cycle that can be turned off: most dishes will dry in residual heat, albeit more slowly.

A noise annoys

A dishwasher that sounds like a jumbo jet taking off and can only be used when the family's gone to bed or left the house is hardly a modern convenience. Unfortunately, the noise level is one of the hardest aspects to check – although manufacturers of quiet machines are very keen to tell you about it – and all machines will grow noisier as they get old and worn. Machines that are built into a run of units, with insulation around them, tend to be quieter than free-standing models.

Tips for top performance

❑ Follow the manufacturers' instructions regarding the type of detergent to use. Preferably, use the same brand of detergent and rinse aid.

❑ Don't use too much detergent – excess suds will stop the machine from operating efficiently and can leave a chalky film on china and glass.

❑ If a film still starts to appear, check the level of the rinse aid and try a different brand of detergent.

❑ Follow instructions about loading: dishes should face the spray and large items shouldn't shield smaller ones.

❑ Glass, plastic and wooden handled cutlery should be washed at a low temperature.

❑ Cups, bowls and glasses should have their rims tilted downwards so that they don't fill with water.

❑ Don't wash stainless steel and silver together – the silver can be stained and pitted. All cutlery should be removed as soon as possible when the cycle is complete.

❑ Don't put plastic items near the heating element as they may distort or melt.

❑ Secure plastic and lightweight items (like lids) with other dishes so they don't fall and block the filter or jam the runners.

❑ Make sure large items like baking trays don't hamper the action of the jets – the arms should be able to rotate freely.

❑ Do not wash thin plastic, valuable glassware or china, antique or hand-painted china, china decorated with silver or gold (it will gradually wear off), crystal (it will turn opaque), lacquered metal, pewter, iron, or wooden dishes.

Kids in the kitchen

Not for nothing is the kitchen called the heart of the home.

The family tends to gravitate towards the kitchen at all times of the day and, while it must serve primarily as a food preparation area, it's good if it also has a comfortable, companionable and welcoming atmosphere.

If there are children in the house, try to incorporate a space in the kitchen where they can play, paint and draw and, when they're older, do their homework. It will allow you to keep an eye on them while you get on with your own tasks and, at the same time, provide them with occupation, education and company.

From the earliest age, children are intrigued by the kitchen. It is, after all, the place where parents spend a lot of time, it's the source of food and, above all, it's filled with grown-ups' toys. These 'toys' can spell danger to un-supervised youngsters (see Safety below) but it is possible to organise the kitchen so that it gives pleasure to both parent and child.

At the crawling stage, a playpen keeps the baby out of harm's way and reduces the chances of your tripping over scattered toys. Make sure you can see each other and, so that he doesn't feel left out, give the child some safe kitchen utensils to play with. A spoon and a plastic jelly mould or, if you can stand the noise, a saucepan will do nicely as musical instruments. A child who can stand and walk is going to want a more active involvement – washing up and cooking are still fun at this age. Invest in sturdy steps so that she can reach the sink and worktop; a pinafore-type apron that offers maximum protection to clothes is also a good idea. A sinkful of sudsy water and some plastic beakers, or a bowl of flour and water 'dough' will keep pre-schoolers entertained for some time. Try to set up the play area away from where you are working so that you can get on with things unhindered and without having to watch for in-quisitive fingers near the food processor. Resign yourself to the fact that the trade-off for this lack of interruption is that you will have to clear up pud-dles of water and spills of flour.

Older children will get pleasure, not just from playing with dough, but from making something, too. Simple biscuit recipes or jam tarts are good starting points, even if dolly, teddy and the dog eat most of the end products. As the child grows older, get him more in-volved with meal preparation. A simple explanation of why you are serving certain foods together will help lay the basis of good dietary knowledge.

Take advantage of a will-ingness to wash lettuce leaves and lay the table while it lasts. For some time this 'help' will undoubtedly slow things down rather than speed them up, so for the sake of your nerves, make allowances for this. After all, it's probably better to take an hour and have a happy child than half an hour and have a child who feels neglected.

Introducing children to the kitchen and aspects of safety and diet at an early age will help them understand the intrigue of the many 'toys' it contains

From the earliest age, children are intrigued by the kitchen. It is, after all, the place where parents spend a lot of time, it's the source of food and it's filled with grown-ups' toys. These 'toys' can spell danger to unsupervised youngsters.

Gradually introduce the child to the supervised use of kitchen tools and appliances. Moving blades, control knobs, glowing elements, flames and steam are all fascinating to a child and there is less risk of accidents if she understands how to use them. You may reap the benefits in other ways – with tea and toast brought to you in bed on Sunday morning.

SAFETY WITH CHILDREN IN MIND

❑ Keep appliance cords as short as possible (look for models that have cord storage): toddlers may well be tempted to yank on trailing cords.

❑ Cover all electric out-lets that are not in use to stop inquisitive young fin-gers. Use purchased socket covers.

❑ Store knives and other sharp implements out of reach of children. Wall-mounted magnetic racks can be positioned safely; wooden knife blocks can be kept at the back of the work surface. Use plastic guards with food processor blades and electric knife blades.

❑ Be aware of possible risk items: serrated edges for cut-ting foil and film can cut young skin too; plastic film can cause suffocation.

❑ Whenever possible, cook on the back burners of the stove. Keep handles turned towards the back so that they cannot be knocked by passers-by or grabbed by children.

❑ Buy a stove guard to stop pans being pulled off the top of the stove.

❑ Make sure children are out of the way when you serve up hot food.

❑ Keep all household deter-gents, cleaners, bleaches, scourers and anything else that may possibly be poisonous on the highest shelf possible. Do not transfer the contents to soft drink bottles.

❑ Don't add dishwasher de-tergent until you are ready to switch on the machine.

❑ Fit childproof catches to all drawers and cupboards that contain anything that is potentially harmful. Remove those catches before dis-posing of cupboards, fridges and freezers – children, find-ing a new 'play house' have been known to get trapped.

❑ Keep all rubbish out of reach of children.

❑ Never leave an iron on when you leave the room, and don't let young children anywhere near the board while you are ironing.

PART 5

Bathroom
Improvements

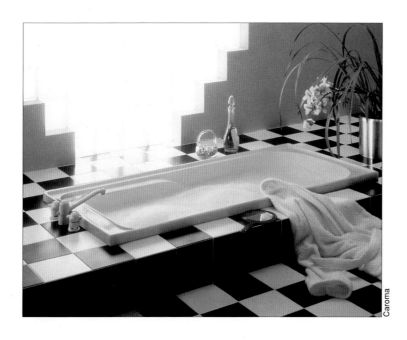

A bathroom means different things to different people, and this is reflected in bathroom design. Whether a bathroom is very simple and modern (above), or loaded with character (right), maximum comfort is everything

Materials

Any materials used in the bathroom must be smooth, moisture resistant and easy to keep clean. Flooring materials must also be antislip for safety.

It's important to choose materials that will provide long service and help to create a bathroom which looks and feels good to use.

Walls

When it comes to finishing basic materials, there is a number of options to choose from other than the more traditional methods of painting and wallpapering.

Basic lining materials

Plasterboard – common as lining on timber frames; available in water-resistant grade; normally painted or wallpapered

Fibre-cement sheet – cellulose fibre-reinforced cement building sheets; recognised as the most reliable lining for wet areas on timber frames; excellent as a base for ceramic tiles; can be painted, wallpapered or tiled

Render – a sand-cement finish for brickwork; can be plastered, painted, wallpapered or tiled

Prefinished materials

Prefinished fibre-cement sheets – installed as panelling (with adhesives and mechanical fixings)

Plastic laminate boards – double-sided waterproof sheets; stuck or screw-fixed to wall frame (see wall panelling section)

Glass block and brick – allows light through but obstructs clear vision; may be used for internal or external walls

Mirrors – can be used as complete walls fixed to basic wall lining materials or, more commonly, screw-fixed in sections; makes small areas appear larger

Glazed ceramic tiles – the most popular finish in wet areas; fixed to suitable lining materials with joints grouted to shed water

Marble and granite – high quality and normally more expensive finishing materials; normally as tiles, but slabs are also available

Slate – a popular natural stone which needs periodic sealing to look its best; stuck to lining materials

Timber – several species suitable in non-wet areas, e.g. Western red cedar (WRC) or dressed/planed treated pine; must be well sealed with polyurethane

Ceilings

Basic lining materials are most commonly used for ceilings, although a timber-panelled ceiling can look fantastic and provides extra warmth.

Fibre-cement sheet – particularly in wet areas; smooth or textured surfaces

Plasterboard – fixed to ceiling joists and skimmed with plaster with joints set; commonly painted

Timber – as for walls

Floors

Floors are covered in all but the most basic bathrooms and the range of materials used is vast. Choose the best quality and most water-resistant material you can afford for your bathroom. Antislip qualities are important.

Basic flooring materials

Concrete – formed and poured in place, and finished to take a range of floor finishes

Compressed fibre-cement thick sheet – can be used as a floor when timber-framed; will accept ceramic tiles or paving paint

Water-resistant particle (chip) board – suitable for wet areas but you must apply an underlay before tiling (e.g. fibre-cement sheet); choose a grade impregnated with fungicides

Water-resistant plywood – must be waterproof grade; apply an underlay before finishing (e.g. fibre-cement sheet)

Underlays – quite a number available; only special fibre-cement sheet and impervious liquid and coating give the hard and resilient finishes suitable for wet areas

Floor finishing materials

Glazed ceramic tiles – a hard flooring stuck to concrete or fibre-cement sheet underlay over timber; must be non-slip

Marble and granite – hard tiles for high quality bathrooms; fixing as for ceramic tiles

Slate – hard tile that needs to be sealed to look its best; fixing requirements as for other hard tiles

Vinyl – a resilient flooring available in sheet form or as tiles; tiles do not provide high water resistance at joints; fixing by loose-lay or full-stick method to fibre-cement or hardboard underlay over timber floors, or direct to concrete

Rubber – resilient tiles normally studded or embossed; fixing similar to vinyl

Cork – resilient tiles; tiles are fixed to an underlay and sealed with polyurethane to provide a waterproof floor; tiles will need occasional recoating

Carpet – should be nylon with a waterproof backing to prevent premature decay or rotting of the floor

Sanitaryware

Toilet suites, basins, baths, bidets and so on must have a completely hygienic surface, be sturdy enough for heavy use and easy to clean.

Vitreous china – the most common material used for toilets and basins; very durable

Porcelain-enamelled steel – baths and handbasins

Enamelled cast iron – a popular choice for baths; very durable (also more expensive)

Fibreglass-reinforced plastic – gaining popularity for baths, shower bases and integrated vanity tops

Acrylic – popular as baths and shower bases

Synthetic marble – similar in use to fibreglass-reinforced plastic (e.g. Corian®, Avonite®)

Plastics – not commonly used except for some of the cheaper ranges of cisterns

Shower screens

Shower screens must be tough yet light.

Glass – must be safety glass, either toughened, laminated or wired; glass doors are available as two-and-three panel sliding and as framed and unframed hinged or pivoting doors

Fibreglass – not common any more, but still available, often with designs in the resin

Tapware

Although plastics are making some inroads into the tap and mixing valve area, most quality taps are still made of brass or, sometimes, stainless steel, and coated or plated. The coatings are normally epoxy or similar powder coats. Plating may be chrome, satin chrome, black chrome, pewter or gold; brass may even be polished and clear finished. It is important that the finish matches the expected use – soft gold plating is not of much use in a busy family bathroom. Plastics are used mainly for handles and, in some cases, spindles.

Furniture

Bathroom furniture is often cheaply made from materials that are not particularly water resistant. For the best results, choose designs made from good quality water-resistant materials (or materials with a water-resistant finish), and ensure that they are properly installed.

Particle (chip) board – used for making vanity units; normally melamine-coated and laminated on wearing surfaces; must be water resistant (or the board will swell and delaminate when water penetrates)

Timber – not used as a base material; all-timber, clear- or stain-finished cabinets are available

Plastic laminate – provides a hard-wearing surface; normally adhered to particle (chip) board; the joints are the weak point (water may penetrate into the board and cause swelling to occur)

Polyurethane – hardwearing, high-gloss, coloured polyurethane is available as a finish to vanity units

Plastics – found mainly in shaving and accessories cabinets

There is no reason why your bathroom can't be practical, beautiful and affordable! Let's face it, the bathroom is a very important part of your life – if you've just been 'making do', now is the time to consider how it can be improved.

GETTING STARTED

The bathroom is not a simple room to renovate, restore or redecorate. It can also be pricey, as any undertaking can turn into a major task if plumbing is involved. However, as the home projects in this section will show, DIY in the bathroom can provide easy and satisfying solutions to give your bathroom a new look. You can completely transform your bathroom by adding accessories, tiling a wall, putting up a fancy blind or installing a large mirror.

Once upon a time the bathroom was a room which contained a bath and very little else. Today the bathroom has many more fittings, is often larger and is a real centre of activity. It is also no longer a purely functional room – some people think of their bathroom as a place to relax in the spa.

A bathroom must work efficiently and safely and be pleasant to use. It can be leisurely and luxurious or simply streamlined.

Because the bathroom is one of the most frequently used rooms in the house, and often used by more than one person at once, it makes sense to choose the design, materials, fittings and appliances that you like. Your bathroom is also part of a whole and should fit in with the rest of your home as well as your lifestyle – if your house is Victorian or Art Deco in style, your bathroom should retain the same character.

Pointers

❏ Budget wisely – spend most on the things that will improve your bathroom's efficiency and comfort.
❏ Get the basics right: style, surfaces, fixtures and fittings, lighting and storage. Pay attention to essential details. Choose simple decoration and colour schemes to provide the right setting.

Where to start

It's essential to work out what you want and how best to achieve it. There are two important factors to bear in mind: the amount of work that has to be done and how much it will cost, and how the space you have can best be utilised and enhanced.

The design of a bathroom will depend on what you are starting with. In a new house the bathroom can be made to suit the size of the fixtures. In an existing house, bathroom renovations usually fall into two categories: the first involves total renovation, including stripping of the room, refurbishing and often adding extra space; the second involves upgrading the room by retaining some features or fixtures and fittings and renovating around them.

Don't try to import a complete bathroom layout and finish into your bathroom – this rarely works

Planning Your bathroom should be functional yet attractive, safe for the whole family to use and easy to look after. Plan the space carefully because bathrooms are expensive to fit out and the fixtures are relatively permanent once installed.

If you are renovating, there may be fixtures that you can't afford to, or don't want to, replace. Try to incorporate these without letting them spoil the new look. The size of the room will dictate the amount of equipment you can have and where you put it – everything needs to be conveniently located for comfort.

Ask yourself: Is there a problem with dampness? Do you need better ventilation? Is the bathroom warm and dry in winter, cool and dry in summer? Does it need better insulation? Is there sufficient lighting? Do you need more storage capacity?

Your bathroom may need to be redesigned to accommodate young children, the elderly, or a person with a disability; or to allow for more privacy when several people are using the bathroom at the same time. Remember, special facilities will require specialist advice and it's best to consult the professionals before you undertake a major project. Check with your local authority (or Building Centre) before redesigning the layout of your bathroom.

Budget Hold your budget in one hand and your priority list in the other! A restricted budget doesn't mean that the result will be shoddy or inferior – good design and basic improvements don't have to be expensive. Take time to really think about where the money should go and allow 10 per cent of the total budget for contingencies.

Style is sometimes very hard to define – an informed eye is a real asset when it comes to appreciating what does and doesn't work in a particular room. Look around you, especially at other people's bathrooms, and visit a few bathroom showrooms. Do you like the decor? Would it suit your lifestyle? How could it be adapted to suit your situation?

Books and magazines are a good source of inspiration but beware the fickle fashion statement. New fashions come and go, but the basic lessons, especially where bathrooms are concerned, don't change. From a purely functional point of view, a bathroom must be efficient, warm and dry, well-ventilated, safe and easy to maintain. Ultimately, the test is whether or not you feel happy and comfortable with the end result.

DIY projects Make sure you have all the tools and materials you need for a project before you start. Make an allowance in your budget for essential tools and materials. Remember, more expensive specialist equipment can be hired. If you are lucky enough, you may have a generous friend or relative who has already made the investment!

Checklist

❑ It may seem like an obvious question, but what do you actually use the bathroom for? Work out where things are

1 A small and dingy bathroom before renovation

2, 3 and 4 The bathroom after renovation – the colour scheme and the whole look have been transformed by clever tile design

Amber Holdings

going wrong, especially at peak times when everyone needs to use the bathroom. How can things be improved?
❑ Is your existing bathroom well located? It should be easily accessible from the bedrooms; ideally with a separate toilet near the living area.
❑ Do you need a second bathroom, toilet or shower? It could be connected to a bedroom. Even the smallest most awkward space can be partitioned off and fitted with a corner bath, sit-down tub or compact shower. If you have a large, busy household, it may be a

worthwhile investment.
❑ Will plumbing work be required?
❑ How much hot water do you need? Is your present hot water system adequate?
❑ Do you need new bathroom fixtures?
❑ Do you prefer showers to baths, or does your family need both?
❑ What type of taps do you want?
❑ What type of storage do you need?
❑ Does anyone in the family have special needs? For example, an elderly relative or person with a disability.
❑ How safe is your bathroom? Do you need to make any

special safety provisions for old people or young children?
❑ Are the wall and floor surfaces suitable for the hot, steamy atmosphere in the bathroom?
❑ Is the bathroom well ventilated? Do you need to install an extractor fan?
❑ Is the bathroom centrally heated, or does it need a separate wall heater? Do you need a heated towel rail?
❑ Do you need new light fittings?
❑ Is there good natural light, or do you need to consider a skylight installation?
❑ What accessories do you need?

From first thoughts to final details, you'll be confronted with an awesome array of bathroom products and styles. Here's how to establish what you have, what you want and how to get it.

THE GRAND PLAN

It's taken a long time, but the smallest room in the house has at last grown up. Gone are the days when comfort was a dirty word in a place of austere cleanliness: today's bathrooms are designed to be enjoyed, whether your fancy is for fragrant foamy baths, a work-out with the weights and a muscle-pummelling shower or a re-enactment of the Armada with a fleet of plastic boats.

For everyone planning an all-new bathroom, or giving a facelift to a functional but old-fashioned room, there's a dazzling array of bathroom fixtures and accessories. Such a proliferation of colours and styles has one serious drawback: there's homework to be done! Start collecting brochures, look at magazines for inspiration, carry a notebook with you and jot down ideas, brand names, prices, measurements. You'll soon be agog with all the options, so before

The Before and After pictures of this once drab, compact bathroom show the striking effect and feeling of spaciousness that can be achieved with new tiles and fittings

Amber Holdings

you draw up any plans, conduct a filtering-out process: a tiny bathroom will never have room for a keep-fit centre; a traditional Victorian-style bathroom would not be right in a modern house; marble tiles and gold-plated fittings are not in the running if your budget is limited.

And, while it's fun to fantasise about unlimited luxury, don't lose sight of the practicalities. Above all, a bathroom has to be functional. The most glamorous decor in the world will give you no pleasure if you bang your funny bone every time you brush your teeth. You may be lucky enough to achieve an efficient bathroom by accident, or the limitations of the room may mean you have no

choice in where you position the fittings but, generally speaking, thorough planning at the very earliest stage pays rewarding dividends.

Dream time

Not sure where to start? That's easy: start with what you already have. Sit down with a pencil and paper divided into two columns headed 'Bad Points' and 'Good Points' and think what it is that you dislike, and like, about your current bathroom. Hate the colour? Is the whole family queuing to brush their teeth while dad shaves or big sister fixes her make-up? Write it all down . . . You might even pin the paper up in the bathroom for family members to jot things down as they think of them.

Imagine what your ideal bathroom would have – movie star mirrors with sidelights? a spa bath? a really good shower? two washbasins? Perhaps you won't be able to include such luxuries, but dreaming is free and who knows, some of them might just prove possible.

As things stand

The next stage is to draw up a scale plan of the bathroom as it stands,

Collect brochures, look at magazines for inspiration, carry a notebook with you and jot down ideas, brand names, prices, measurements

Talk about texture! Practically all the non-tiled surfaces in this dusky-pink bathroom have a sponged paint finish which complements, rather than matches, the pattern in the tiles

showing the position of all fixtures and features. Start with a rough sketch of the room on which you note all measurements – total wall length, distance from corner of room to edge of bath, dimensions of all fixtures and so on. It's a good idea to draw side-view plans of each wall, as well, marking the position of windows, the height of cisterns and washbasins, the location of light switches and power points. Otherwise it is easy to overlook space for a fixture underneath a window or, worse, imagine there is more room than there really is.

Once you have completed the sketch, draw the plan and elevations to scale on graph paper. Mark solid walls with a thick line, partition walls

with a thinner one. If you know them, show the route of supply and waste pipes with dotted lines. Using compasses for accuracy, indicate the area taken up by the doors (including cabinet doors) when they swing open. This exercise alone can sometimes pinpoint problem areas. You may find, for instance, that all the doors open into the same space – a recipe for obstructed access, potential injury and irritation. Simply replacing hinged doors with sliding doors may overcome the problem, and a hopelessly small bathroom may suddenly have adequate room.

Finding the ideal

Keep your scale drawings as the master plans and use scale cut-outs of fixtures and tracing paper overlays to experiment with different bathroom layouts.

Obviously, the fewer major changes you make, the cheaper your improvements will be. You don't want to spoil the grand plan but if you can leave just one existing fitting in place, you will save yourself money. While it's

sometimes hard to determine what constitutes a major change, when you're an amateur playing with plans, remember that if you have timber floors which give easy access to the pipes beneath, alterations to plumbing are much cheaper than with, say, a concrete slab, when even a small change may require the floor to be broken up. Removing a load-bearing wall or relocating a window is also a major upheaval; installing or

Where space is limited in the bathroom, fixtures and fittings need to be kept as streamlined as possible. In this one-wall bathroom, the shower forms the short leg of an L-shape. Warm, grey tiling has been used to create a sense of space

shifting a partition wall is comparatively simple.

There is no one 'correct' layout, but there are certain desirable elements. First of all, you need to get in and out of the room easily – no squeezing round doors, or bumping into wash basins. Because they are the most used items, washbasins should be placed out of the main traffic flow or anyone using the basin will block access to the rest of the room.

Once in, you need to be able to reach and use all the fixtures, cabinets and shelves and have plenty of space in which to move. Try towelling yourself down in a cramped bathroom! You'll be banging your elbows and knocking things over – and if there's someone else in the room you might as well resign yourself to dripping dry. As a rough guide, you need a clear space of about 1000 x 700 mm in front of a shower or washbasin; about 800 x 600 mm in front of a toilet or bidet.

The most economic use of space is to put fixtures side by side; if they are opposite each other you need a good 750 mm clearance. Baths and basins, of course, come in a large range of sizes; start by working with standard sizes. If the layout looks too cramped, investigate the slimline and compact models available; if you have room to spare, look at the more generously proportioned lines.

There is also the aesthetic consideration of what can be seen from the door, especially if the bathroom is off a hallway. Most people prefer to look on to the window or vanity unit rather than the toilet or bidet.

Keep referring to your list of desirable features and decide which should take priority in view of your lifestyle. Lack of privacy in a family bathroom can be a real problem, so consider how this can be improved – an extension, a bathroom partition or a second toilet may be the solution. If your family suffers from a morning rush hour, a second washbasin will prove a godsend. If you have a young family, try to find space for a change table and baby bath – and remember that toddlers prefer baths to showers so try to find space for a bath even in a tiny bathroom. Elderly and invalid family members should also be taken into account; allow for grab rails and, if necessary, space for a walking frame or wheelchair. If the bathroom is being designed primarily for a disabled person, seek professional advice from the start – there is a wealth of specialist equipment to make life easier.

If you're designing an en suite, don't make the mistake of skimping on space and facilities, believing that any private bathroom is better than none. If you don't plan it properly, you won't use it properly. For example, if you like to check your weight regularly, make sure there's a convenient spot for the scales – you are fooling yourself if you say 'Oh, I'll use the ones in the family bathroom'. Spend some time working out how this bathroom can really make your life easier. In a working couple's en suite, you might consider an extra-large shower recess with two showerheads (set at his and her heights and with separate taps, of course!) so that both can be ready to catch that morning train.

The planning stage is also the time to tackle problems like inadequate lighting and poor ventilation. If you would like a larger window or a new extractor fan, make provision for it on the plan. What about heating? The position of a wall heater should be marked, as should vents or radiators connected to a central heating system. Towel rails should be positioned in such a way that towels can actually dry!

Keep moving the pieces round until you find a layout that suits as many of the criteria as possible – it can then be fine-tuned to suit your budget without having to make too many sacrifices.

Tackle problems like inadequate lighting and poor ventilation at the planning stage

Take the floor

To get you started, here are some common layouts to suit different rooms, together with their pros and cons. Remember, though, that flexibility is the key. If your bathroom is simply too small to include a shower recess, think whether there is somewhere else in the house that it could be located. A teenager's bedroom may not be big enough for a full en suite, but a washbasin and vanity unit might easily fit in one corner. Wasted space under the stairs may prove big enough for a toilet and handbasin. Check the Building Regulations before you get too carried away!

The one-wall bathroom
Having all the fixtures in a line is economical on space and also on plumbing. All water-supply connections can be hidden away behind a single false wall and drainage under the floor along one wall. Good for a narrow room – but not very convenient if it is to be used by more than one person at a time.

The L-shaped bathroom
Again, all the plumbing can be arranged along one wall, with the bath taking up one leg of the L. This plan leaves plenty of uncluttered space, giving good access to all the fixtures.

The corridor bathroom
Positioning the fixtures down two opposite walls gives good access as long as the corridor between them is wide enough – at least 750 mm is desirable. Two walls require plumbing.

The U-shaped bathroom
This is practical in a square room, although with fixtures on three walls, it is more expensive to plumb in. It is easy to use and gives good access.

Plumbing may not be a consideration if it can be shared with an adjacent room, such as the kitchen.

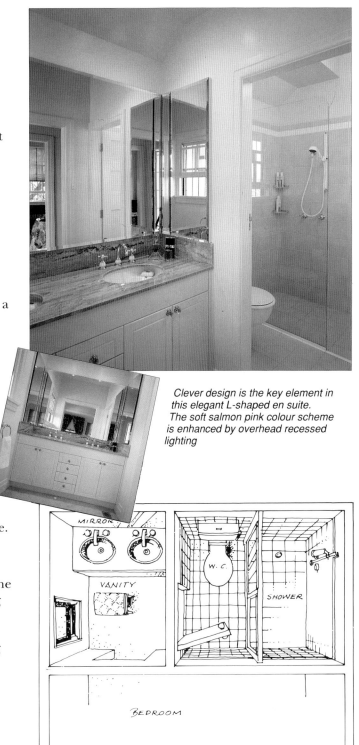

Clever design is the key element in this elegant L-shaped en suite. The soft salmon pink colour scheme is enhanced by overhead recessed lighting

Put on the style

Once you have the plan in mind, you can turn your attention to the colour and style of your bathroom.

Your choices are almost unlimited and while your final selection boils down to personal taste, there are a few general guidelines.

To some extent, the bathroom is a place where you can indulge your decorative whims, but try to ensure that its decor – and the budget allocated – is in keeping with the rest of the house.

Colour codes

Light and space are assets in any bathroom and they can be enhanced by light colours – dark colours or a mix of strongly contrasting colours tend to close the walls in. The idea of a boldly coloured bathroom may appeal to you but it

may not be to the taste of future buyers. There's a fine but distinct line between a dramatic colour scheme and one that is garish. From the resale point of view, white and neutral colours are the most popular if only because they offend no-one and keep the room light and bright! They weather the whims of fashion well and also happen to be the easiest to keep clean: water splashes and soap scum are very conspicuous on dark colours.

Texture and touch

An all-white bathroom may be inoffensive, but it can also end up looking

Terrace & Cottage

clinical. With any mono-chromatic scheme, how-ever, it is possible to introduce interest and variation with texture. Indeed, contrasting textures are part of the visual appeal of any bathroom – just think how inviting soft fluffy towels look against shiny tiles, sudsy water against the gleaming bath.

Introduce variations in texture with patterned tiles or by using different-sized tiles on the floor and walls

Variations in texture can be introduced with pat-terned tiles or by using different-sized tiles on the floor and walls. Don't

overdo it: tiny mosaic floor tiles and massive 300 mm wall tiles are too different, and too much variety looks disastrously busy. Often the subtlest contrasts are all that are required.

Mood points

It's not just the choice of colours that has ex-ploded of late: there's an impressive variety of bathroom designs to complement every archi-tectural style. This gives you an opportunity to make a strong decorative statement without the drawbacks of experiment-ing with bold colour. You should avoid choosing a bathroom style that has nothing in common with the rest of the house, but that, and your budget, are

IKEA

1 Modular bathroom furniture, as shown here, is purpose-built to accommodate plumbing, lights, mirrors and all your special storage needs

2 An elegant Victorian-style bathroom with hand-crafted red cedar and kauri pine cabinets

3 This spectacular bathroom features highly decorative ceramic tiles laid in geometric patterns, and very distinctive light fittings which are in keeping with the unusual style of the room

the only constraints.

The designer ranges are considerably more expensive than standard fittings, but don't be downhearted if they are beyond your price range. Focus instead on the accessories – wisely chosen, they can convey the same mood. Here are just some of the effects you can achieve:

Traditional Suitable for Victorian and Edwardian houses, this style has become very popular with renovators in the past few years. Washbasins and toilets with decorative pedestals look authentic (you can even install an old-fashioned high-level cistern), but the secret is attention to detail. Tessellated floor tiles, decorated

Light and space are assets in any bathroom and can be enhanced by bright and airy neutral colours

border tiles for the walls, brass accessories, etched glass and polished wooden cabinets all help create a period mood. Old-fashioned creams, pinks and beige are appropriate colours to work with.

High-tech Some of the fittings in an ultramodern bathroom look more like pieces of sculpture. Characteristically streamlined – using materials like stainless steel – high-tech bathrooms have an added plus over good looks: they're wonderfully easy to keep clean. A wall-hung toilet, for example, makes washing the floor a breeze! Again, the accessories can tell the tale. Look for strong, clean lines – even the choice of toothbrush holder can add to the effect. Colours should be clear and strong but not overpowering. Black and the primary colours work well as accents.

Don't choose a bathroom style that has nothing in common with the rest of your house

Country The emphasis here is on the soft surfaces without, of course, losing the practicality of moisture-resistant tiles and vanity unit surfaces. Choose a floral fabric for the window covering and the shower curtain (back this with an ordinary shower curtain); pretty china dishes are perfect for

Villeroy & Boch by Argent Australia

holding soaps, cotton wool, bath oils. Not everything has to be practical – botanical prints, plants and flowers all add to the fresh country feeling. Soft pastels are the best colours.

Hollywood glamour
Unadulterated luxury is the key here. Only the best materials will do . . . marble tiles; gold-plated taps; the fluffiest towels, mats and bathrobes; mirrors, lights and action – in the form of bubbling spas! If your budget is limited you may have to forgo the marble and gold – look for more economi-

cally priced ceramic tiles that still add a touch of glitz and glamour.

Bathroom surfaces, like those in a kitchen, have to work hard – choose the right materials when you decorate your bathroom and it will emerge unscathed from the steamiest affair.

SURFACE VALUES

Inevitably, bathroom surfaces are subjected to the arch enemy of all decorative finishes – water. Spills and splashes cause puddles or worse, while steam insidiously works its way into every crack and crevice. The surfaces also receive their fair share of knocks – slippery fingers easily drop bottles of shampoo or hair colour, and junior can pack quite a punch with a plastic bath toy. Despite all the punishment, the surfaces must not attract dirt and harbour germs.

Moisture and stain resistant, durable and easy to keep clean – with such stringent requirements, the wonder is that there are so many suitable bathroom surfaces available.

When it comes to choosing the best for your bathroom, budget – as always – is probably the most limiting factor. Remember that affordability depends on more than just the price of the materials. The cost of installation should be taken into account and this, in turn, will be influenced by the size and shape of your bathroom. In a small bathroom, for instance, or one with lots of angles and alcoves, you should choose small tiles rather than larger ones

which need a lot of cutting to size as this is expensive in terms of both labour and wastage.

You should also bear in mind the use that your bathroom will get. While all bathroom materials are easy to clean, some are more easy than others. In a family bathroom it is probably wisest to steer clear of dark colours (they show every splash mark), marble (it's not sufficiently stain resistant) and carpet (children always seem to manage to get as much water out of the bath as there is in). Here's a guide to the qualities of the most common bathroom surfaces.

Paint It's not as glamorous as many of the other surface materials, but paint is economical, relatively durable and comes in an unrivalled range of colours. Traditionally, gloss or semi-gloss (satin) finishes were used because they offered greatest resistance to moisture and were washable. Paint technology has improved, however, and you can now buy matt (flat) and low sheen finishes that have the same washable qualities – good if you are painting a less-than-perfect wall or ceiling as irregularities will not be

BEFORE

A bathroom before and after resurfacing

AFTER

THERMOGLAZE

so conspicuous. If mildew is a problem in your bathroom, you can buy paint with a mould inhibitor – but this, of course, is not a permanent solution to the problem; the ventilation needs improving, too.

Wallcoverings Like paint, wallcoverings are an economical and quick means of introducing colour and pattern into the bathroom. For maximum durability, choose a vinyl covering with a paste containing fungicide to prevent mould growth behind the covering.

Vitreous china This continues to be the most popular material for washbasins, toilets and bidets. It's very easy to keep clean; colours do not fade or change with age; and it can be moulded into virtually any form. It is also durable, although it will break if a heavy object is dropped on to it.

Enamelled steel or cast iron Steel has largely taken the place of cast iron in the manufacture of bathtubs, and offers advantages in terms of strength and reduced weight. The enamelling

1

2

Renditions Tiles

1 Bathrooms can look fabulous with several types of surfaces – this bathroom features ceramic tiles, timber furniture, marble vanity top and brass fixtures

2 The ceiling and walls above the tiled area have been painted to give the appearance of marble

3 Selection of laminated plastic panels (formica)

4 This bathroom, again, has several types of surfaces: acrylic paint, formica, ceramic wall tiles and vinyl floor tiles

5 A classic bathroom renovation – traditional but very stylish

3

CSR Wood Panels

4

Dulux

5

Villeroy & Boch by Argent Australia

process gives colours that stay true and a surface that is easy to clean and durable – although it can be chipped by heavy objects.

Synthetic materials The advantages of acrylic baths, basins and shower trays over vitreous china and metal are: cost (they are less expensive); their light weight, which makes the installation of baths, in particular, easy; and their thermal quality. Unlike metal baths, acrylic fittings always feel warm to the touch. This means that very little of the warmth of the water you put in is absorbed by the material, leaving more heat for you to enjoy. The disadvantages of acrylic are that it flexes and so must be adequately supported and that it can be difficult to keep clean in hard-water areas because you can't use scouring cleansers.

There are also some newer synthetic compounds (such as Corian® and Avonite®). These are more usually seen as kitchen worktops, but are becoming more popular for integral basin/vanity tops. They are expensive, strong and extremely durable and can be moulded into virtually any shape. The choice of colours continues to increase.

Ceramic tiles If ever a product has stood the test of time, it is the ceramic tile. Popular since the days of the Romans, ceramic tiles are still the most versatile of the bathroom surfaces. They can be used for both floors and walls and are available in a huge variety of colours, shapes and prices.

When choosing tiles, select ones that are in scale with your bathroom. If you choose a fancy shape, such as the ogee or Moorish designs, keep the colours simple: too much variety looks over-fussy.

High-gloss tiles are not suitable for floors as they are slippery, especially when wet. Choose unglazed or mosaic tiles for maximum non-slip qualities. Small tiles also provide good 'grip' – so the small tessellated tiles, which are unglazed and of varied shape are excellent from a safety point of view. Floor tiles should always be washed with a mild detergent solution and never polished as this would make them slippery. Dark floor tiles will show talcum powder dust.

Bathroom surfaces need to be moisture and stain resistant, durable and easy to keep clean

Marble and granite
These materials carry the luxury price tag but, as people are becoming more prepared to invest money in their bathrooms, marble and granite are increasing in popularity. Their advantages are that they can be durable, water-

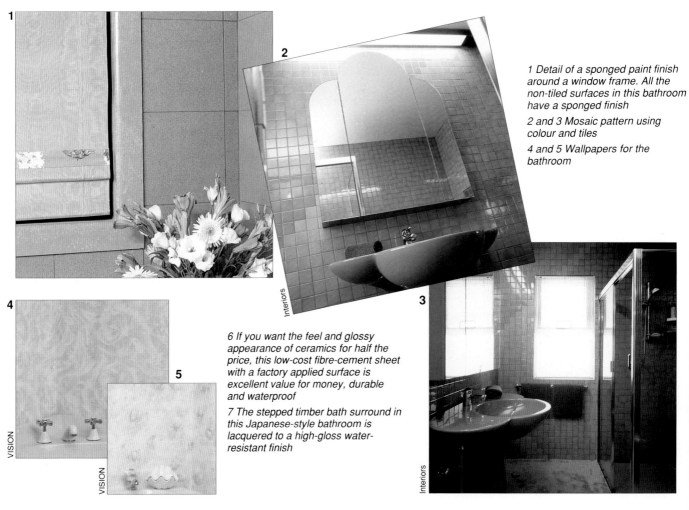

1 Detail of a sponged paint finish around a window frame. All the non-tiled surfaces in this bathroom have a sponged finish

2 and 3 Mosaic pattern using colour and tiles

4 and 5 Wallpapers for the bathroom

6 If you want the feel and glossy appearance of ceramics for half the price, this low-cost fibre-cement sheet with a factory applied surface is excellent value for money, durable and waterproof

7 The stepped timber bath surround in this Japanese-style bathroom is lacquered to a high-gloss water-resistant finish

Interiors

VISION

VISION

Interiors

proof and very good-looking. The disadvantage is that they can be slippery unless finished with a matt surface – and the matt surface on marble tends to be slightly porous, which can pose problems with spilt oils, nail polish remover, hair colours, make-up and the like. Good installation is essential: poorly finished marble and granite can have dangerously sharp edges and with such an expensive material you don't want shoddy workmanship.

Slate The qualities that make slate good for roofing, make it good for bathrooms, too. It's durable and impervious to water. It also has a slightly

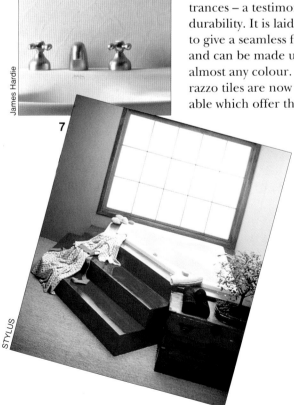

6

7

TIPSTRIP

With a little imagination the cheapest square tiles can be used to give a bathroom a unique look. Try working diagonally across a wall instead of horizontally, or create a shaded effect by using several different shades of the same colour – deep blue through to very pale blue, for example.

irregular surface which gives it a natural non-slip property. Its main disadvantages are to do with installation. It's heavy, irregular in thickness and, as with other stones, its good looks depend on good workmanship. Slate needs to be sealed to protect it from staining and to bring out its beautiful colouring. This sealing needs to be repeated every few years, so there is an ongoing cost to consider.

Terrazzo This composite of marble chips set in concrete has long been popular in public entrances – a testimony to its durability. It is laid in situ to give a seamless finish and can be made up in almost any colour. Terrazzo tiles are now available which offer the same

lifespan, although not the same continuous look.

Vinyl This product has greatly improved over the years in terms of looks, durability and comfort. It is available in sheet or tile form and both are suitable for bathroom use if properly laid. Sheet vinyl should be cut oversize and left for a while to allow for shrinkage. The edges must then be firmly sealed, as any dampness will weaken the adhesive. In a small bathroom, tiles are often easier to fit and lay. If laid over timber flooring, vinyl tiles must have a reliable underlay, such as fibre-cement sheet.

Wood and cork Warm to the touch and mellow to the eye, wood and cork can be very successfully used in a traditional or country-style bathroom. But their suitability depends entirely on their being properly sealed – otherwise moisture will play havoc with the finish, causing, at best, discoloration and, at worst, warping and rotting. Two or three coats of a clear polyurethane finish will give good protection but you should be prepared to reseal exposed timber every few years.

Carpet It's very cosy underfoot in chilly weather, but carpet is not really a practical floorcovering in the bathroom. If comfort comes first, choose a rubber or synthetic foam-backed carpet (it's less likely to rot than a natural jute-backed one) and make sure it can be lifted for drying should the worst (burst pipes or

an overflowing bath) occur. Much more practical and almost as cosy are thick fluffy bathmats. Any loose mats or carpet should always have a non-slip backing.

Beneath the surface

Whether you are dealing with floors, ceilings or walls, the materials you choose for your bathroom will only be as good as the base on which they are laid. Flimsy partitions, damp walls and springy floorboards spell disaster for rigid materials. Before you invest your hard-earned money in expensive tiles, make sure the subsurface is absolutely sound and is itself unaffected by moisture. Tiles laid on an ordinary partition wall will look fine at first, but as soon as moisture gets behind them (as it inevitably will – steam can sneak through the tiniest gaps in grouting) the partition material may begin to swell and distort. It won't be long before the tiles crack or fall off and paint finishes are spoiled. The only cure will be to start again, working with water-resistant materials, such as fibre-cement sheets, which are immune to water damage.

TIPSTRIP

If you plan to have a ceramic-tiled floor, think about installing underfloor heating at the same time. It is a pleasant and safe way to warm the bathroom during cool weather. This is only practical with a concrete floor, and then only if the whole house is done.

On the tiles

**DIY tiling needn't be a tale of woe –
it can be fun, cost-saving and easy when
approached in the right way.**

Tiles can be a lot easier to fix than you think. Good preparation and planning is the true secret of success – if you get this right, your tiling will be something to be proud of.

How many tiles?

Before you buy or order tiles for the floor or walls, work out approximately how many you need. This is especially important if you are tiling large areas or using a pattern. Most tiles are sold by the square metre. Suppliers have tile charts which will tell you approximately how many tiles are needed per square metre. Coverage is also stated on boxes. Remember that the smaller the tile the more work will be involved.

To roughly calculate the number of tiles you need, simply multiply the length by the breadth of the area to be tiled, making allowances for any sections which don't require tiles. Remember to add on 5 per cent for cutting and wastage.

Adhesives

There are two types of adhesive: one that is buttered onto the corners of the tile and in the centre, and a thin-bed adhesive that is 'screeded' onto the wall with a notched trowel. The first is not recommended for use in wet areas. Cement-based adhesives can be used on cement-rendered walls, while rubber latex, polyvinyl acetate (PVA) or epoxy resin adhesives can be used on most surfaces. Flat-backed tiles are best for use with thin-bed adhesives where the bed is up to 3 mm thick. Thick-bed cement-based adhesives are best for ribbed or studded tiles and for floors.

When using adhesives never wet the tiles prior to laying. Always apply the adhesive horizontally on a wall, using a notched trowel. If the adhesive is notched vertically, any water penetrating the grout joints of the finished tiling will then run down the wall and collect at the bottom (rather than being held at the level of penetration where it is more likely to evaporate).

Ceramic tiles set the underlying mood in your bathroom and will fit any budget

Project 1

𝍫𝍫𝍫

Tiling a floor

With good planning and organisation, tiling a floor is not at all difficult. Modern materials make tiling easy for the amateur.

There are several types of floor tile to choose from. In the past, soft biscuit tiles – where a hard glaze was fired onto a softer biscuit – were commonly used. These are still available. More popular now, and more practical, are the so-called monocottura, or single-fired, tiles. These are fully vitrified, and therefore very hard, with the glaze being fired on at the same time as the body of the tile.

Unglazed vitrified tiles are also popular. As monocottura tiles have little suction due to their vitreous nature, it is important to choose a suitable adhesive. Consult your tile merchant when you buy the tiles.

A bathroom floor tile must be non-slip. While there are treatments that can make tiles less slippery, there is a large range of tiles available that fulfil the function by design. When testing a tile, try wetting it and rubbing a track shoe over the surface to see how slippery it is.

As most bathrooms have a slight fall to a waste, the floor area is actually a very broad conical shape, and the smaller

1 Sponge 2 Notched adhesive spreader 3 Tile file 4 Pencils 5 Rubber squeegee 6 Tile cutter (heavy duty) 7 Tile cutter (scriber) 8 Tile pincers 9 Straightedge and spirit level in one

MATERIALS

tiles
adhesive
waterproof, compressible grout
tile spacers if necessary
piece of round dowel (optional)

TOOLS

straightedge/spirit level
pencil
measuring tape
tile scriber or tile cutters (hire)
tile (rod) saw and/or pincers
tile file
10 mm notched trowel
rubber squeegee
sponge
buckets and rags

TIME
One weekend

the tile the easier it will be to adjust the grout joints to accommodate any variation. Joints will be narrower near the waste, and wider near the perimeter of the room.

Calculate approximately how many square metres of tiles

Once you've selected the right tiles, it's time to consider the other materials needed for the job: adhesive, grout and tiling tools

you need, making allowances for any alcoves or areas where tiles are not required. Over-order slightly to allow for difficult cutting, the odd mistake, and for future breakages or chipping.

Now it's time to consider what else you need, such as tiling tools, adhesive and grout. Tiling tools are quite cheap and are worth buying, especially if you also intend to tile the walls.

We recommend tiling the floor before the walls. Professional tilers often choose to apply wall tiles first because they can stand on the floor while fixing the wall tiles and then lay the floor all in one day. However, this runs into the problem of floor tiles butting up against wall tiles and providing a potential vertical joint for

water to leak down. It makes more sense to lay the floor tiles first, then the wall tiles can fit over the floor tiles, giving a more water-resistant joint.

STEP BY STEP
Don't try to do too much in one day and make sure you arrange alternative washing and toilet facilities with a neighbour if necessary.

1 **Preparing the floor** The most suitable surface for laying ceramic tiles is concrete. However this must be wood-float finished (rough textured) – if it is a mirror-smooth or steel-trowel finish, it will first need to be scratched, roughened with a chisel or acid-etched.

Ceramic tiles are rigid and should therefore not be laid directly over a 'moving' surface. Because timber expands and contracts, one layer of fibre-cement underlay sheets should be laid over the timber floor at right angles to the joints between the planks. The underlay should be fastened with annular nails at the points

marked on the sheets by the manufacturer. Fibre-cement sheets may have some construction dust on them and require a coating of ceramic tiling primer to bind the dust and allow good adhesion of the tiles.

2 **Marking out** Tiled floors look best if they are evenly spaced between walls, with equal tile cuts to both sides. This allows you to cut edge tiles to walls not quite running true. Remember, it is much easier to cut a tile into halves than to remove a thin sliver off the side, so adjust any starting point to allow cuts as close to a half tile at the edges as possible.

Accurate working lines are the key to a successful tiling project. Locate the centre point on each of two opposite walls, and snap a chalk line between

A chalk line is a length of bricklayer's line which is well rubbed with chalk, held tight and plucked against a wall, floor or other surface to mark a straight line on it.

The key to laying straight rows of tiles is to first establish accurate working lines

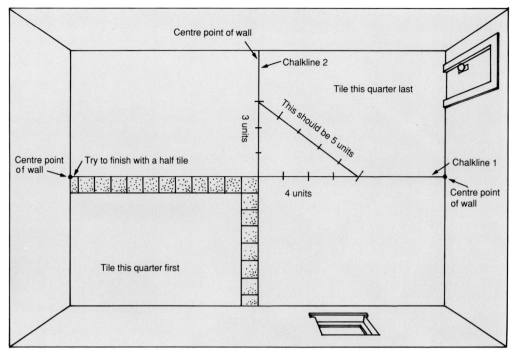

the two points; then find the centres of the other two walls and stretch your chalk line between these points.

To make sure that the two intersecting lines between the walls are truly at right angles, either use a carpenter's square or apply the 3:4:5 rule. If the lines are not at right angles, adjust as necessary and recheck your measurements.

3 Laying the tiles Make a dry run first: loosely lay out the tiles to decide whether to start with a tile joint or the middle of a

3:4:5 RULE
Measure three units from the centre along the shorter line, 900 mm (3 x 300 mm), and four units along the longer line, 1200 mm (4 x 300 mm). The diagonal between the marks should measure exactly 1500 mm (5 x 300 mm) for the two lines to be at right angles.

tile at the centre of the room. Full tiles may start at the walls if the two walls are exactly square. Tiles are laid in the quarters that have been marked out, but ensure that you don't work yourself into the room with no means of escape.

If you are using an adhesive that doesn't require mixing, it can be applied directly from the container. Cement-based adhesives will need to be mixed as recommended by the adhesive manufacturers to a thick creamy consistency, and then left to stand for around 15 minutes before use. Mixing is easiest in a separate bucket but only mix enough to do about two square metres at a time. If there are two people working, one can be mixing to have adhesive ready when the previous batch runs out.

Apply the adhesive near the crossed line in the first quarter and spread it with a trowel to a maximum area of one square metre. Use the 10 mm notched trowel to spread the adhesive to an even thickness, ready to accept the tiles.

This ultra-luxurious bathroom is a showcase for marble floor and wall tiles

Ceramic wall tiles are not only decorative – they resist water, heat, steam, stains and require virtually no maintenance

Fix the first tile at the centre for untrue walls, or against a square wall if square. Position it, then bed it into the adhesive with a gentle rocking motion. Just to make sure that you have the technique right, prise this tile off and check that the back of it is completely covered with adhesive. If not, practise with using a little more adhesive, or by applying more pressure when bedding the tile. It is a good idea to do this from time to time just to monitor how you are going. If you use too much adhesive it will squeeze up between the tiles and prevent grout being properly inserted in the joint.

Make sure you have the technique right by prising off the first tile and checking that the back of it is completely covered with adhesive. Continue to do this from time to time as you tile, just to monitor how you are going

The next tile is laid along the marked-out line, allowing for the appropriate grouting joint between tiles. In most cases a joint of 3 mm is adequate, but some tiles may need up to 12 mm for grouting. It will depend largely on the uniformity of tile sizes – extruded tiles such as glazed quarry tiles may have quite a size variation. This judging of gaps is normally done by eye, but if you don't trust yourself, mark lines every two to three tiles to make sure that the gaps average out over the project.

Wipe away any excess adhesive as you tile as it will set hard and could affect the grouting colour later. The adhesive should not finish at the same level as the surface of the tile. Keep laying tiles until only the edge tiles remain to be fitted.

At this stage, you'll need to cut the remaining tiles to the right size. If you need to walk on tiles that have been laid, carefully put down a 12 mm, or thicker, sheet of plywood to spread the load.

4   Cutting tiles Mark out and cut tiles to fit (see Skill class on marking and cutting tiles). The cut tiles can then be laid individually around the perimeter as needed.

5   Grouting Once all the tiles have been laid, allow the adhesive to set for 24 hours before grouting. The recommended grout is a cement-based material with additives to ensure a certain water resistance and ease of use. Grout is designed to fail should tiles expand with age; the idea behind this is that grout is easier and cheaper to replace than tiles. On floors, it is common to use the adhesive as the grouting medium as well because it is normally grey and won't show dirt as easily as white or coloured grout.

Mix the grout in a clean bucket to a creamy consistency and let stand for about 15 minutes. Apply grout diagonally across the tile joints using a rubber squeegee. Working diagonally stops the grout being pulled out again by the back of the squeegee rubber. With practice, you will be able to fill the joints well, yet leave the surface of the tile with only minor grout stains. Stains can be gently wiped away with a moist sponge, washing frequently, until only the thinnest film is left. This will polish off after a further 24 hours.

If you prefer a uniform joint, run along the grout joints with the end of a thin piece of rounded dowel and then again wipe down the surface. This will give a slightly recessed joint rather than the flush joint achieved using just the squeegee.

The newly tiled floor can be used 24 hours after grouting.

In this tiling project, the floor, bath surround and splashback have been tiled with white ceramic tiles to make the most of good natural light and to contrast with the timber-panelled walls

Cutting edge tiles using a tile cutter

Grouting tiles using a rubber squeegee

Skill class
Marking and cutting tiles to fit

For soft biscuit tiles, it is easy to use a hand scriber to mark the tile and then to snap it over a nail. However, if using hard, fully vitrified mono-cottura or quarry tiles, you will need heavy-duty tile cutters (these can be hired).

To correctly mark out a tile for cutting, place a full tile (B) over the last full tile laid (A), then place another tile (C) against the adjacent wall so that it overlaps tile B. Use the over-lapping edge of tile C to mark the cutting line on tile B, leaving a gap of at least 5 mm to the wall to allow for expansion and contraction.

Place the tile in the tile cutter with the marked-out line along the central spine. When the cutting line is aligned with the wheel, scribe (the tungsten wheel marks out the line to be cut), and then press the handle down to snap the tile along the scribed line.

Alternatively, for softer tiles: place the tile on a firm base and, using another tile or a straightedge, scribe the glazed surface of the tile with a tile cutter. Place a small nail under one end or a pencil along and under the scribed line, and firmly press the tile down. The tile will snap along the line. For thin tiles, use matchsticks and press the edges on both sides, or use a heavy-duty tile cutter to hold the tile firmly during breaking.

Fitting the tiles around obstacles need not cause problems. To cut a shape – for example a curved section for tiles that are to be fitted around tap holes – either make a template out of stiff card to suit the cutout (allow at least 5 mm clearance to the metalwork if fitting around tap holes), or use a profile gauge (a tool consisting of a row of sliding metal or plastic pins which, when pushed

against an object, takes up its shape). In some cases it may be possible to move the obstacle, such as a basin, away from the wall in order to slide the tile behind it before marking out the profile.

If using a template, place the template on the tile and score with the scribing tile cutter. Cut the waste section away with a pair of tile pincers, removing small pieces at a time. Be sure to protect your eyes

from any sharp fragments that may fly up. Also available are rod saws which consist of a wire charged with tungsten-carbide chips which can be used as a saw.

Smooth the cut edge of the tile with a tile file, or by rubbing the edge on some concrete or an abrasive stone. Once you have smoothed the edge of the cut tile, lay it in the correct position to avoid any mix-ups later.

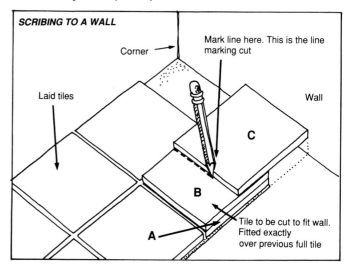

SCRIBING TO A WALL

Corner

Laid tiles

Mark line here. This is the line marking cut

Wall

C

B

A

Tile to be cut to fit wall. Fitted exactly over previous full tile

Polished porcelain tiles have been used on the walls and floors of this elegant bathroom

Tiling a wall

Few wall coverings have the decorative impact and durability of ceramic tile – it's the natural choice for any wall that might be sprayed or splashed with water.

Wall tiles are glazed and generally lighter than floor tiles – the glazing process makes the surface of the tile water-resistant. These tiles come in a great variety of colours and designs, so visit a few showrooms before you make your choice.

Calculate approximately how many square metres of tiles you need, making allowances for any area where tiles are not required. Over-order slightly to allow for difficult cutting, the odd mistake, and for future repairs.

If you plan to use contrasting coloured or patterned tiles with plain ones, sketch your design on graph paper first, using colours to mark where the different tiles go and then counting up the total needed for each pattern.

On a wall with one window, treat the window as the focal point, mark a centre line through it, and tile the two halves identically.

On a wall with two windows, find the centre point between them and arrange the tiles symmetrically from that point.

You should be able to plan the tiles so that there will be a cut tile of the same size, close to half a tile, at either end. Lay the tiles, complete with any spacers, along the floor by the wall, to avoid narrow tile cutting. Mark the position of the first whole tile on the wall – a batten marked out with the width of tiles plus any spacers will help to get the positions right.

STEP BY STEP

1 **Preparing the wall** The surface to be tiled must be sound, dry (and water-resistant), flat, and free from dirt, grease or flaking material. Any damp will need to be treated before starting. Uneven, chipped or cracked surfaces should be filled and levelled with cement or a patching compound.

Cement render is the ideal surface to tile to. A firm, dry plaster surface on a solid brick wall is satisfactory for tiling but crumbling plaster must be cut away and renewed. A skim coat of plaster may be needed to remove any bumps and hollows. New plaster needs a month to dry out before a plaster primer and tiling are applied.

> Two-part epoxy resin is mainly used by professionals instead of grout in commercial hygiene areas

As an alternative to plastering you could fix fibre-cement sheets to the wall and tile over those. This system is only recommended if timber battens are fixed to the wall first at correct spacings and with the

MATERIALS
tiles
tiling adhesive
grout
. timber battens
piece of round dowel (optional)
tile spacers

TOOLS
spirit level
plumb bob
straightedge
tiling gauge or batten
handsaw or circular saw
hammer and nails
pencil
steel measuring tape
tile cutters
tile (rod) saw and/or pincers
tile file
notched adhesive spreader or 4.5 mm trowel
grout applicator, rubber squeegee, spatula or straight-edged float
sponges and clean cloths
bucket
Note: You may also need tools for repairing holes and cracks prior to tiling, such as a paint scraper and filling knife.

TIME
Over two weekends

face plumb and even throughout. If using plasterboard (not in showers), make sure it is a water-resistant variety and fixed firmly to the wall (no less than 10 mm thick).

If the wall is painted, scrape any loose paint away then roughen the surface with a coarse sandpaper so that the tile adhesive will stick to the wall. Never apply tiles over any type of wallcovering as the adhesive holding the covering will not be strong enough to hold the tiles. Strip the covering off completely.

Villeroy & Boch by Argent Australia

For inspiration – this luxurious and spacious bathroom is distinguished by a blue and white tile design scheme which is fresh, clean and vibrant

Tiles can be stuck directly onto brickwork as long as a thick-bed adhesive is used. The job will be easier if the brickwork is rendered first – this is a difficult job best left to an expert and you'll need to allow time for the render to cure thoroughly.

2 Marking out Accurately marking out your tiling lines is the first step – don't use the floor or skirting boards as a true horizontal or the corners as your vertical guide. Start by marking the wall one tile high (also allowing for a spacer) from the lowest point on the floor or skirting board depending on where the tiling is to end. Next fix a 75 x 25 mm

straight batten across the full width of the wall so that the top edge of the batten is on a line with your mark. Use a spirit level to make sure it is absolutely horizontal. Don't drive the nails fully in as the batten will be removed later.

If more than one wall is to be tiled, establish the lowest point of the whole floor (the point at which the floor or skirting board deviates most from a horizontal spirit level) and start fixing battens around the room from that point, one tile high, using the spirit level to check the horizontal. The battens will also support the tiles until the adhesive dries.

If you wish to have a whole row of tiles immediately under-

neath the window opening, then measure down from the opening to determine where the first row of tiles, and therefore the batten, will be.

The simplest way to accurately mark out your tile widths is on a batten the length of the wall. This will ensure that you have equal-sized cut tiles at each end. Start marking in the centre and then mark the tile widths on both sides of the centre point, allowing for grouting gaps. This will allow you to make any necessary adjustments in layout and to avoid awkward cuts.

Finally, to establish a true vertical line hang a plumb bob or spirit level down the wall so that the vertical line passes through the point where you want to position the first tile, and mark it.

3 Laying the tiles Starting at the point where the vertical line meets the horizontal batten, smooth on a layer of adhesive using a spatula or a straight-edged float. Spread on only enough to lay one square metre of tiles at a time to prevent the adhesive drying out or 'skinning over' before you reach the end. When the area is covered, 'comb' the adhesive across in horizontal lines using a notched adhesive spreader.

Position the first tile on the

batten, lining it up against the vertical. Press the tile firmly into the adhesive with a slight twisting motion. If your tiles have built-in spacing lugs on the edges for grouting, butt the tiles up so the lugs just touch. If not, plastic tile spacers or matchsticks can be inserted between tiles for uniform grouting gaps.

The whole of the back of the tile must be in contact with the adhesive. To check this, occasionally remove a tile that has just been positioned to ensure that complete coverage is being achieved. Remove any excess adhesive from the face of the tiles with a damp cloth as you go. If you intend using a coloured grout, remove the adhesive to below the face level of the tiles (otherwise the white adhesive may show through in patches). Remove any spacers, such as matchsticks, once the adhesive is holding the tiles firmly in place. Nylon spacers are normally left in place.

After you've completed the first square metre of tiling, check that the tiles are perfectly straight by holding a spirit level to the edges and adjusting where necessary. Also check against any marked-out lines which you have drawn on the wall. Then go on to the next square metre area as before. Check your progress with the

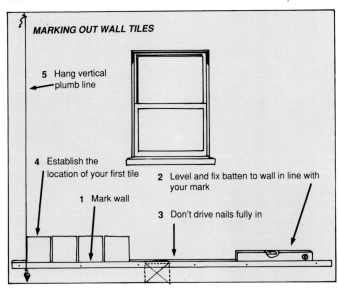

MARKING OUT WALL TILES

5 Hang vertical plumb line

4 Establish the location of your first tile

1 Mark wall

2 Level and fix batten to wall in line with your mark

3 Don't drive nails fully in

3

4

spirit level frequently. Leave the supporting battens in place until you have finished the main tiling (it's best to leave the bottom battens in place for at least 4 hours, preferably overnight).

4 Cutting and fitting tiles
Once the battens are removed, the remaining tiles can be cut to fit the spaces left (see Skill class on marking and cutting tiles). This usually includes bottom and side tiles, tiles around the bath and tap fittings and special-purpose tiles

such as soap-holder or towel-rail bracket tiles.

When installing bracket tiles, make sure you install the rod in the brackets before the second bracket is set in place. Cover these fittings well with adhesive and hold in place with masking tape for 24 hours.

Once the tiles have been cut and the edges smoothed, fix them in the correct position to avoid mix-ups later.

5 Grouting Allow the tiling to cure for 24 hours before

grouting the joints. Grout must be the compressible or flexible type used to fill the horizontal and vertical gaps between the tiles. It can be white or coloured to blend in with the tiles. Mix the grout (as necessary) following the manufacturer's instructions then let it stand for a few minutes. Apply the grout diagonally in both directions across the tiles using a grout applicator, a small sponge or a rubber squeegee. The grout should be pressed firmly into the joints with all the gaps filled to the same level.

Do small areas at a time, wiping off excess grout from the surface with a clean, damp sponge before it hardens (washing the sponge out frequently). Make sure you clean the area before the grout sets. It is best to grout and clean about a square metre at a time.

When the grout is in place, run the end of a thin piece of rounded dowel along the joint. This will ensure a rounded, smooth joint.

Leave the grout to dry for the manufacturer's recommended time, then polish the tiling with a clean, lint-free cloth. This should remove any remaining grout stains.

The wall tiles will be properly set after 24 hours, and the grout cured 24 hours after that.

1 Starting point: Fix a straight batten to the wall, with its top edge one tile height above the skirting board or floor. Use a spirit level to make sure that it is horizontal

2 Bedding tile: Spread the adhesive evenly on the wall with a notched spreader which will create ridges to help the tiles stick. Beginning at the mark you made, bed a tile into the adhesive with a slight twisting motion

3 Marking/cutting the tile: Mark the tile where it's to be cut. Using a tile scriber, align the mark with the wheel, scribe and then press the handle down to snap the tile along the scribed line

4 Cut tiles in place: To fit tiles around obstacles, such as vanities, mark the tile where it's to be cut. Cut waste section away using a pair of tile pincers

TILING NOTES

☐ You can avoid the difficult and time-consuming hammer-and-chisel job of removing old tiles by sticking new tiles on top of the old ones. The old tiles must be clean, dry, and firmly stuck on the wall – there's no need to roughen them. Lay the new tiles so that the joints do not coincide with the old ones. All setting and curing times should be doubled.

☐ If you can, buy tiles which come in boxes with the same batch number.

☐ Remember to allow for grouting joints when working out the area to be tiled.

☐ Always read the manufacturer's instructions to make sure that the tiling adhesive and grout are suitable for your tiles and the area you

intend to tile.

☐ Where basins, baths, laminates and shower enclosures meet tiles, seal the join with a silicone sealant to keep out water.

☐ Remember to keep glazed-edge tiles for exposed edges of corners and sills.

☐ Plastic edging strips are available for putting under the edge of tiles forming an edge to sills or for sealing the gap between the bath or basin and wall.

☐ Never mark the back of tiles with a felt-tip pen – the colour may bleed through to under the glaze; use pencil.

☐ Plan distances between countertops and shelves or cupboards so that you can use whole tiles without any cutting.

TIPSTRIP

DESIGNING WITH TILES
☐ A busy tile pattern or a mix of several colours makes an area look smaller; using a simple pattern or colour has the opposite effect.
☐ Dark colours tend to shrink a given area while light or bright colours make it seem airy and more spacious.
☐ A repeated tile pattern running lengthwise adds depth to the room; running across, it gives a shorter, wider look.

The good news is that you don't have to scrap the entire bathroom and replace all the fittings to create a new look.

Very often there is not a lot wrong with the basic layout and positioning of fixtures and fittings, but the colours may be dated and unattractive or the bathtub showing signs of wear and tear. Surprisingly, impurities in hot water can be quite corrosive and together with normal use over time do considerable damage to the enamel surface of your bath. Rust and discoloration marks appear in baths and wash-basins and are impossible to remove by ordinary methods.

In recent years there have been considerable advances made in the resurfacing of these enamel finishes and a corresponding growth in the number of companies working in the area. This growth is a two-edged sword. Although the service is now very widely available, it is quite hard to separate the reputable firms, who stand behind their work past the payment date, and the 'take the money and run' operators. It is always wise to consult your local Building Centre before proceeding. Ask to see examples of the company's work; perhaps speak to satisfied former clients and visit the factory if you can.

BATHTUB RESURFACING

In the original manufacturing process, the enamel surface is fired onto the metal base of the bathtub using powdered porcelain and great heat – impossible to do in your home bathroom. Resurfacing companies at-

tempt to reproduce this process by using chemical means to bond a synthetic porcelain to the bath surface. The strength of this bond is crucial. Plastic-based spray paint may look great the day it is applied but will not bond effectively with the existing porcelain surface; it is also likely to turn yellow as it becomes affected by hot water and may blister and peel a short time after, leaving you to face the renovation of a shabby bath all over again.

Most companies offer an enormous colour range so you will have no difficulty finding one to match existing floor surfaces or wallpaper. Resurfacing your bath at home will only take two or three hours and the bath should be usable again in only a day or so.

The finished product should look good and be rea-

sonably chip and scratch resistant for a number of years. Some companies even claim a life of ten to fifteen years for the new surface. An added benefit of the process is that it also leaves your bath with a less slippery surface than before. All resurfacing companies will offer a guarantee, usually three to five years, that covers the materials used and the workmanship. It is very important to be quite clear about what is covered by the guarantee and for how long.

A WHOLE NEW LOOK

Not only is it possible to resurface a bath but the same treatments are available as a 'stop-gap' that will give your bathroom a whole new look in a fraction of the time it would take to create a new bathroom in the usual way. If the wall tiles and fixtures are basically sound but stained or the wrong colour, then it is quite simple to resurface the wall tiles as has been done in the bathroom pictured below. It is a good idea to compare the cost of resurfacing tiles with that of tiling over the top of existing

tiles. You may find that the retiling, which will last 'forever', is cheaper than resurfacing in the long run. Before deciding, take into account the condition of the rest of the bathroom and whether or not you are planning to pull it all out before long.

TOUCH-UP TIPS

❏ If your bath has a couple of chips but is otherwise OK, it is much cheaper to repair the chips yourself rather than having it completely resurfaced. There are epoxy touch-up paints which are ideal for the job.

❏ Even cheaper than resurfacing your bath is painting it with a special epoxy paint made specifically for the purpose. It requires very little preparation (just a good clean and sanding of the surface) and lasts about five years. Any rust marks should be well sanded and then treated with an epoxy filler before painting. The bath will be ready for use after seven days.

BEFORE

This bathroom has had a radical facelift – the results speak for themselves!

New Pride Bathrooms

Although resurfacing is a job for professionals, you can do many of the other jobs involved in a new-look project – install a new vanity and shower screen, paint and wallpaper and fit a new mirror

AFTER

Let's face it, because the bathroom is such a wet area, water poses a potential problem for every material used.

Most activities in the bathroom generate water, either as liquid or vapour or both. In some cases, water can even affect finishes at the other end of the home – hence the importance of damp-proofing.

Ease of cleaning and moisture control should be given priority from the planning stage onwards. Select sanitaryware that is easy to keep clean, and aim to streamline surfaces as much as possible. Do your best to eliminate any seams where moisture and the resultant mould will accumulate.

Moisture can be generated from any number of sources: a poorly sealed shower screen, a faulty or missing shower tray, exuberant water use in splashback areas, leaking gaskets and washers in plumbing and overflows, condensation from hot water usage, and others. Most moisture sources can be cured or repaired.

Damp can also exude from the ground under the house, the moist vapours causing the timber floor above to remain moist for long periods, possibly rotting the floor and the underlay sheets if they are not waterproof. This is a serious problem but can usually be overcome by creating adequate flow-through ventilation under the floor structure, and using fibre-cement underlay sheets.

James Hardie

RISING DAMP

Rising damp is a specific problem associated mainly with old homes that either have no damp-proof course (DPC) installed in the masonry, or where the existing DPC has failed due to deterioration or physical damage. When the

When you choose to retile your bathroom walls and floors, it's important to choose the right materials, such as a waterproof underlay for ceramic floor tiles and fibre-cement sheet as a base for wallpaper, paint and tiles

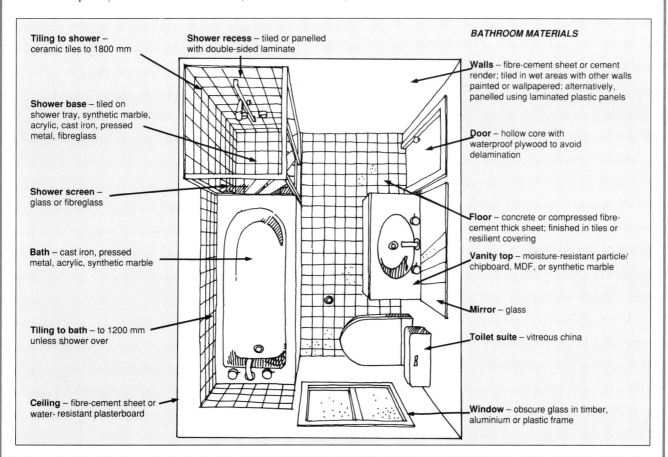

BATHROOM MATERIALS

Tiling to shower – ceramic tiles to 1800 mm

Shower recess – tiled or panelled with double-sided laminate

Shower base – tiled on shower tray, synthetic marble, acrylic, cast iron, pressed metal, fibreglass

Shower screen – glass or fibreglass

Bath – cast iron, pressed metal, acrylic, synthetic marble

Tiling to bath – to 1200 mm unless shower over

Ceiling – fibre-cement sheet or water- resistant plasterboard

Walls – fibre-cement sheet or cement render; tiled in wet areas with other walls painted or wallpapered; alternatively, panelled using laminated plastic panels

Door – hollow core with waterproof plywood to avoid delamination

Floor – concrete or compressed fibre-cement thick sheet; finished in tiles or resilient covering

Vanity top – moisture-resistant particle/chipboard, MDF, or synthetic marble

Mirror – glass

Toilet suite – vitreous china

Window – obscure glass in timber, aluminium or plastic frame

A & K Tiling Products

DPC is ineffective, moisture will rise up the porous masonry by capillary action, to a level where the evaporation from the wall equals the amount of moisture available. This level rarely goes much higher than one metre of the wall. The level of the rising damp is often marked by an ugly tidemark with associated salts.

Rising damp must be treated if it is causing a problem. Normally this damp will bring with it soluble salts from the earth which can cause damage to the fabric of the building over time. Soft bricks, stone, plaster, and paint and wallpaper finishes are all susceptible to salt attack. It would be foolish to undertake a major bathroom renovation without first treating the damp.

Damp can be treated by

the installation of a new DPC, either below or just above floor level. It may be a physical barrier of polyethylene or polypropylene, or a chemical injection or flooding of the wall. Generally these are not DIY jobs and you should consult an expert for advice.

SEALING AND DAMP-PROOFING

Water tends to settle where horizontal and vertical surfaces meet, and if this joint is not sealed adequately, moisture penetration of the framing or structure behind may occur.

Angled flashings installed behind wall linings and adhered to the floor surface will, in effect, 'tank' the room. There is then little need to use sealants at the joint. However, where this has not been done, a flexible silicone or caulking compound is needed.

It may also be possible to use coving tiles or plastic coving strips where vertical joints meet horizontal surfaces. They make cleaning easier and shed water well.

Use silicone to seal between glass and metal and between metal frames and tiled walls, such as shower screens.

In the average bathroom it is probably not worthwhile waterproofing the tiling any further. Instead, make sure that all grouting is in good order and flush with the surface of the tile, so that water is easily shed. If regrouting, special additives can be added to cement-based grout to make it more water-resistant (available from ceramic tile adhesive manufacturers).

Shower recesses

Repairs to shower trays must be finished before you start decorating. Shower recesses

have their own peculiar problems. Where a shower is a preformed and finished unit, installed with wall tiles lapping over raised sides and properly plumbed to the waste, there are few problems.

However, where a shower is built on site, with a fibre-cement thick sheet or concrete floor, a bedding of mortar to form a fall to the waste, and tiled, there are many potential problems. As a general rule, wall and floor surfaces can be expected to move independently of each other, and this causes the joint between the wall and floor tiling to open up. This allows water in, which can then penetrate through the floor or into adjacent rooms. A frequent and expensive problem is water flooding from an upstairs shower into a downstairs lounge or living area.

The correct method of building a shower involves the installation of an under-tile shower tray, and the provision of corner flashings which direct water into the tray. The shower trays are made of copper, fibreglass or plastic; or can be applied acrylic or epoxy materials – all of which act as a waterproof barrier. These

Above: In this bathroom the ceramic tiles are finished around the edges with a hard-wearing aluminium strip for a straight, safe and even finish to the tiles. Tile trim is available in a wide range of colours to contrast or tone with sanitary fittings, tiles and overall decor

BEFORE

THERMOGLAZE

Tiled shower before and after resurfacing

AFTER

should be taken at least 150 mm up the wall and over the hob or rim to prevent any water escaping the shower, and sealed to the waste. A bedding is then installed in the tray and the recess can be tiled as desired. This installation is best undertaken by a professional. The alternative is to use a prefinished shower base of enamelled steel, acrylic or fibre-glass-reinforced plastic.

Sealing around fittings

It is not normal to seal around plumbing fittings that penetrate the walls unless the wall lining is plasterboard in which case it is essential that you seal all cut edges and fill the gap around the plumbing with silicone sealant. Even in showers these fittings are normally not a major source of damp problems – but, if in doubt, seal! If there is a known problem, a very thin bead of silicone around the edge of the cover plate may be effective, but make sure there is a gap at the bottom to allow any water caught behind this to escape.

Sealing around baths and showers

Baths and preformed showers themselves do not leak, but there is a potential for leaks where tiles or splashbacks fit

against them. Wall linings and tiles should lap over the preformed lip on baths, and the joint can be sealed if necessary with a flexible silicone sealant.

Vents

Make sure that walls enclosing a bath are vented and removable so that access is readily available if a leak or water damage occurs.

Moisture below timber floors (ground level)

If the subfloor area is damp, you should either remove the source of moisture (usually very difficult), or improve ventilation of the subfloor area by installing more vents or introducing a forced-air extraction system. Failure to remove moisture-laden air can lead to early rotting of timbers and non-waterproof underlay sheets and, as the vapour permeates through the house, extensive mould growth can result.

Cutting down condensation

Condensation is the phenomenon of water being deposited on cold surfaces in the form of dew when near-saturated humid air cools or comes into contact with cold surfaces. As the temperature of the air drops, so does its ability to hold moisture as vapour. Favoured deposition areas are themselves cold surfaces, such as glass, tiles and metal. In areas where the average minimum winter temperature is 4° C or less, condensation should be considered a building hazard.

In bathrooms, most walls are fairly impervious to condensation; however, wherever walls are susceptible water vapour can penetrate into other areas and, if these are cold, condensation may occur.

There are several ways to cope with condensation: cut down on water vapour generation; keep the room and surfaces warmer, thus raising the threshold where dew will form;

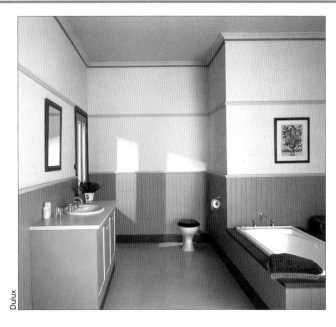

Dulux

Acrylic paint is recommended for the bathroom – it is easy to clean, water-resistant and will keep its good looks for years

or encourage moisture-laden air from the room by means of ventilation. Ventilation is the most sensible option, although ceiling insulation in an uninsulated house can help a great deal.

Where ventilation relies on passive air vents in the home, the positioning of the vents is all-important – if incorrectly placed they won't achieve a good flow-through of air. It should also be noted that in a built-up urban environment, there may be too little wind movement at vent level for them to be effective.

If the bathroom has no vent, a mechanical extractor fan will be needed. This should be ducted to the outside of the building to avoid transfer of the problem to another area. Extractor fans can be wired to the light switch in the bathroom to come on whenever the room is in use and to turn off automatically with a built-in delay. They can also be controlled by a humidistat, which turns the fan on whenever a predetermined humidity level is detected (say 60 per cent).

A ceiling fan (unless ducted) may simply transfer the problem to the ceiling or roof cavity, leading to a stained ceiling.

Mould

Cutting down on condensation is the most effective method of controlling mould. Where there is no moisture, there will be nothing for the mould spores to flourish on. If you have mould, it can be cleaned off using a small amount of strong chlorinated bleach solution in water. The chlorine will temporarily kill the mould. Make sure you wear gloves and open the window to allow a flow-through of fresh air. Don't use too much bleach as it is not environmentally friendly. A warm solution of washing-up liquid is also effective.

Use silica bronze or galvanised steel nails in wet areas – steel, copper or brass nails will corrode over time and stain your timber panelling

Moisture-resistant materials

As the bathroom is a wet area, any material used should be water-resistant. Waterproof materials are only needed where components are constantly submerged, or where a total moisture barrier is needed, such as around showers.

Some common materials used in bathrooms are not very suitable, and will give limited life. These include particle (chip) board, ordinary plasterboard and hardboard (often used as carcass materials in vanity units), and certain timbers such as pine unless it is properly treated.

Most 'normal' wall materials can be used in all but direct shower or splash-back areas, where fibre-cement wall lining is recognised as the most reliable. There are special water-resistant grades of particle (chip) board and plasterboard available; however, if you cut water-resistant plasterboard you must seal the edges of the exposed plaster core. This is important around holes for plumbing fittings.

If timber is used as a finishing material, it must be smooth and finished with three good coats of paint or polyurethane. It is important to sand between coats to ensure a smooth surface.

AROUND THE BATH

Probably the worst area in the bathroom for mould and build-up of soap is the area around the bath. The reason is simple: there are so many nooks and crannies where moisture is held, even after a quick wipe-out. So for the renovator, it is a challenge to make this area as easy to clean as possible. The real story begins below the bath.

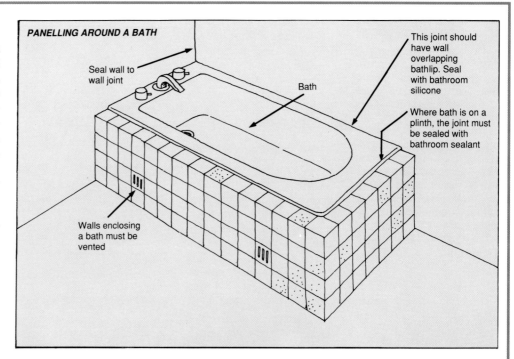

PANELLING AROUND A BATH

Seal wall to wall joint

Bath

This joint should have wall overlapping bathlip. Seal with bathroom silicone

Where bath is on a plinth, the joint must be sealed with bathroom sealant

Walls enclosing a bath must be vented

Wall enclosing bath

A bath is often supported at least in part by a small wall frame just inside the rim of the bath. This may be panelled with fibre-cement sheets and finished in tiles or laminated sheet to suit the rest of the bathroom. This area must be well ventilated. It is possible that a small leak may occur here from time to time, from the plumbing or drainage, or that water may penetrate some joints between the bath and the wall, or that moisture condenses under the bath. Without good ventilation this will create problems. Normally two vents are installed, one at each end of the bath.

Bath to wall seal

When buying a new bath it is often necessary to slightly notch into the wall framing or into the render, to allow the installation of tiles over the rim. If the bath is also used as a shower, water will then run down the walls and straight into the bath (instead of entering behind the bath – assuming the grout is in good order). As the tiles do not overlap by much, a silicone sealant suitable for wet areas can be used.

Bath to laminated panel seal

Where laminated wall panels are used instead of tiles, it is easy to install the panel over the rim of the bath. The bottom edge should be sanded or planed smooth; it may not be necessary to seal the joint but this will depend on use. If sealing is necessary, it is best to use a silicone designed for wet areas. It should be white or coloured to avoid the appearance of small mould growths behind the silicone.

Laminated panel edge moulding

Laminated panels at the edge of the bath look much neater if they are fitted with a plastic edge moulding before being fixed in place. Put a small bead of silicone in the opening of the edge moulding then press the bottom edge of the panel in place before fixing the lot to the framework.

Bath in-plinth seal

The greatest potential problems arise where baths are installed into plinths and also have a shower over. Here the edge of the bath sits on top of a tiled rim, and relies on waterproofing around the perimeter of the bath to stop water running between the bath and tiles all the way around. There would be few problems with this installation if there were no shower present, and indeed it is becoming more popular as a spa installation. However, there must be a good seal between the bath and the tiles around the entire rim. This can be done with a silicone designed for wet areas. Put the silicone in place as the bath is being fitted, then trim off and neatly round off when the bath installation is complete.

The area around the bath is probably the worst area in the bathroom for mould and build-up of soap

Stale air and odours can be a problem in any bathroom, particularly if it is small. Baths and showers create an additional problem because the water vapour they produce can result in the moisture-laden air causing condensation and damp. With most rooms, it's easy enough to open the window for ventilation but, in a bathroom, this often results in unwanted draughts and a lack of privacy. Although a simple window vent can provide a partial solution, its effectiveness is limited and hard to control. The simple answer to all these problems is to install an electric extractor fan which will produce an easily controlled airflow. An extractor fan can be mounted on your window, wall or ceiling

Good ventilation and a controlled temperature are essential for bathroom comfort. When you remodel, consider adding an extractor fan to freshen the air and draw out moisture, and a heater to warm you on cold mornings

With a little planning and a few decorator's tricks your bathroom can be practical, warm, comfortable and attractive.

These goals are readily achievable, even if you are saddled with an inherited colour scheme that you detest and old fittings you cannot afford to replace.

PAINT

The walls are the largest single surface in your bathroom so whatever wall treatment you choose will have a great influence on the total 'look'. The cheapest and easiest wall treatment is a painted finish but make sure you choose the right paint for the job. The bathroom is subject to very high humidity and demands a paint which is moisture and mildew resistant.

Acrylic paint is an excellent choice for the bathroom – it is easy to clean and will keep its good looks for years. Although acrylic paint is generally more susceptible to mould, this can be dealt with by choosing either a semi-gloss (satin) or gloss acrylic with a mould inhibitor.

Low-sheen, semi-gloss and gloss vinyl paints are also suitable for use in the bathroom (they are also cheaper than acrylics). There are some paints which have been developed for use in wet areas, for example, rust- and heat-resistant oil-based (enamel) paints for metal pipes, radiators and plumbing fittings.

> Because acrylic paint is water-based it is easy to clean up after painting. You'll need to use turps (white spirit) and a good brush-cleaning solution if you use oil-based paints.

This cottage-style bathroom features coordinated decorative elements such as the wall frieze and matching curtain; the green, red and white colour scheme

Laura Ashley

This rustic bathroom with its painted, plastered walls, ceramic tiles and collector's items has its own charm

Laura Ashley

Preparation of the walls is important if your paint job is to last without cracking or peeling. Surfaces should be clean (wash off all dirt and grease) and all holes and cracks filled with a good quality filler then sanded smooth. Surfaces previously painted with high-gloss paint should be roughened with abrasive paper to provide a key for the new paint. All this rubbing and sanding will make a lot of dust, so vacuum before you begin painting.

The existing finish will normally determine whether you use a water- or oil-based system. If you are repainting over oil-based paint, it is advisable to stick with oil-based paint – different paint systems don't mix. Acrylic or vinyl paint is the best choice if you are painting a new bathroom for the first time.

> ### TIPSTRIP
> If you don't know what type of paint is on a surface, rub it with methylated spirits. If it starts coming off, chances are it is water-based; if not, it is probably oil-based.

Oil-based systems for woodwork require that you use a primer, undercoat and topcoat for the best result. All unsealed surfaces will need to be sealed before painting.

Bathrooms in older houses can often be dark and poky. Painting the walls in a light, bright colour will add new zest. New bathrooms can suffer from a different problem. With all the shiny, hard surfaces they can look very clinical and bare. Add interest to your painted walls with a little decorative trick such as a stencilled border, a wallpaper frieze, an unusual colour scheme or a dado rail.

Stencils

You can buy ready-cut stencils at paint supply stores or cut your own design out of firm plastic (try using old X-ray film). Stencilled patterns generally look good just under the cornice, around the top of the tiles or as a special feature around a

This quaint bathroom features a lemon yellow, white and blue colour scheme. The wall has been sponged and stippled using blue on white; yellow has been used as an accent colour

In this high-tech bathroom paint and ceramic tiles have been used to create broad, clean planes, emphasising the room's spare, uncluttered character

mirror or a wall. (See Project 3, Bathroom frills.)

Wallpaper friezes (borders)

These are an inexpensive and stylish way of giving your bathroom a decorator's touch. They can be applied at any height to decorate a plain wall or to divide one pattern or texture from another.

Dado rails

These are another attractive way of dividing a bare wall so that you can paint below and wallpaper above for added interest. A dado can also be fixed above the existing wall tiles and painted in a colour to match or contrast with the tiles.

Colour

Be courageous when it comes to choosing your paint colour. Dramatic colours, such as glossy black or dark green, can make a great statement in an otherwise dreary bathroom. Remember, however, that gloss paint also highlights imperfections, and is more difficult to repaint. Add accent colour with bright towels, pots of ferns and framed pictures.

WALLPAPER

Vinyl or vinyl-coated wallpapers are ideal for your bathroom where you need a surface which can withstand a high degree of humidity and condensation.

Proper preparation of the wall before hanging the paper is not difficult but is vital if the paper is to stay on the walls. The paste must contain a fungicide. You should aim for a clean, non-porous surface. If water sponged on the wall is quickly absorbed, the surface is porous and should be treated with a coat of size before you hang the wallpaper. If the wall has been previously painted with gloss paint, it should be sanded with a coarse-grade paper before applying the size.

Flaking and powdery painted walls should be thoroughly rubbed down, washed, sealed with a binder and then sized. Newly plastered walls must be completely dry before wallpapering. The walls may also have 'hot spots' caused by lime in the plaster mix – these will need to be neutralised with a solution of 1 kg zinc sulphate in 4.5 litres of water before being sanded, sealed and sized.

TROUBLE WITH TILES

If you can't stand the colour or pattern of your tiles, and only want a quick cosmetic solution, painting the tiles is an easy stopgap. Alternatively, use an alkali sealer.

Before you start painting, wash the tiled area down with a good quality cleanser and degreaser to remove all traces of soap, grease and grime. When the tiles are completely dry, sand down with a heavy-duty abrasive paper (aluminium oxide paper is very effective) to provide a key for the paint. Clean the tiles then coat with an oil-based sealer binder. Allow to dry then sand again with an extra-fine paper.

Once the tiled surface has been properly prepared, you can use either an acrylic or an oil-based paint for the finishing coats. A low-sheen or semi-gloss (satin) acrylic paint with a mould inhibitor will do the job. Paint on as many coats as it takes to cover the original colour. You may want to finish with a high-gloss topcoat.

Remember, this is a short-term solution only – paint manufacturers don't recommend it – and the tiles will need to be repainted every couple of years to stay looking good. Good ventilation and the installation of an extractor fan will help this quick-fix last a little longer.

There are so many simple ways to brighten up your bathroom – add a splash of colour, pattern and texture with a simple craft project or two!

1 Shower cap, toiletry bag and toilet roll holder make pretty bathroom accessories

2 Beautifully appliquéd towels

3 White towelling bath mitt with decorative trim

4 Pine bath mat using plastic tubing to link the boards

Project 3

Bathroom frills

Transform your bathroom with a whole new look – a candy-striped blind and matching stencilled border, basin skirting and a stencilled mirror frame.

FESTOON BLIND

For a soft, romantic look, nothing beats festoon blinds. The fabric you choose will set the style for your blind, from the soft and feminine look of sheer lace to the charm of this crisp cotton.

Planning

To calculate how much fabric you need, measure the width and length of the window and multiply each measurement by two. If you need to join two pieces of fabric to achieve the right width, do so with small, flat seams.

If you are going to trim your blind with a frill, you will need twice the distance to be covered by the frill, a length of purchased piping (or make your own) equal to that distance and bias binding as long as the frill.

STEP BY STEP

1 To make the frill, bind one long edge of the frill fabric with bias binding. Gather the other edge to the length required to fit around the sides and lower edge of the blind.

2 Baste the piping around the side and lower edges of the right side of the fabric piece (or joined pieces) with raw edges matching. Pin the frill to the edge, over the top of the piping, with raw edges matching and right sides together.

Stitch through all thicknesses. Press the seam allowances onto the blind. Stitch again in the gutter of the piping, securing the seam allowance. Turn in 2.5 cm on the top of fabric piece and frill. Press.

3 Unravel the draw cords of the first 5 cm of the pencil pleating tape. Pin the upper edge of the tape to the top of your blind fabric, 1.5 cm from the edge. Stitch down all edges of the tape, stitching the top hem as you go. Do not draw up the cords.

4 Stitch the ring tape down the sides of the blind, just inside the frill, and at two equally spaced points across the blind from top to bottom hems. Leave an extra 6 cm of tape at the

Threading arrangement of cords for festoon blind

bottom of each length. See the cord-threading diagram for the location of the cords.

5 Loop this tape back on itself so that the end is just above the hem. Stitch. These loops are to hold the bottom rod.

6 Gather the pencil pleating cord, until the blind gathers to the width of the track.

7 Attach the eyelets to the window frame, just below track, to correspond with the top of each strip of ring tape and another, just below one curtain track bracket, through which you will thread blind cords.

8 Cut a cord for each strip of tape, long enough to reach

from the bottom rod, up the blind, through the eyelets, across the top and down to the side where the extra eyelet is, leaving sufficient length for knotting them together below the eyelet.

9 Thread the cords up from the bottom, tying the three bottom rings together as you go to form a permanent blousing effect. Attach the blind to the curtain track with the hooks. Insert the rod through the tape loops at the lower edge of the blind.

BASIN SKIRTING

These simple-to-make panels of fabric can hide unsightly plumbing and even create new storage space, as the space they

conceal can contain shelving. As there are countless shapes and sizes for bathroom basins/units there is no precise pattern – rather a method for making the frill, with several variations for fixing it in place.

First measure the depth and width of the frill. If you plan to gather the fabric, allow double the width needed. If you take advantage of a pattern in the fabric, such as these stripes, to form pleats, work out the width of pleated fabric required. The striped panel holds the pleats in place.

Establish how you are going to secure the frill, as this will have a bearing on the style. Rounded basins on a pedestal can have a frill with a casing,

MATERIALS

For each blind:

fabric, bias binding and piping (see Planning)
pencil pleating tape, twice the width of your window
ring tape, four times your blind length plus 24 cm
one cleat for fastening blind cords
metal rod or dowelling for holding lower edge, 1 cm in diameter to measure 2.5 cm shorter than the width of the window
eyelet screws – one for each length of ring tape plus one
curtain track of your choice
sufficient hooks for fastening blind to track

allowing strong elastic to be threaded through it. The ends of the elastic are hooked over two cup hooks fixed to the wall on either side of the basin at the height of the casing. The frill will naturally gather onto the elastic.

Pleats work well with basin units, where there are angles like this one. Screw cup hooks into the wall at the height of the striped panel, and again in the concave angle. Add more hooks elsewhere if it seems appropriate. Pleat the fabric to fit exactly. Attach small rings by hand at the back of the stitched panel to coin-

cide with the hooks.

Don't forget to make a split in a suitable place for access to the storage space behind. You can achieve this by making your frill in two sections so that each can be drawn back as needed.

Consider using the same fabric to make shower curtains and frilled blinds. A truly coordinated look can work wonders in an otherwise basic bathroom!

Note: Simply enlarge or reduce these stencil designs (below and opposite) to your preferred size. Trace the design onto Manila card prepared as instructed in step 2 of Stencilling a border, and cut out the areas to be painted, using a cutting board and a sharp craft knife

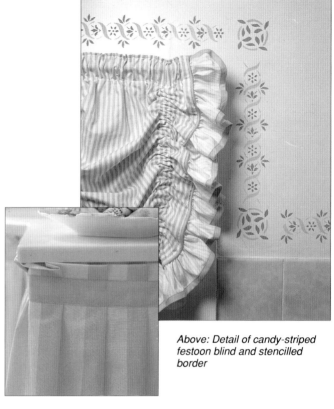

Above: Detail of candy-striped festoon blind and stencilled border

Detail of basin skirting

STENCILLING

Stencilling is one of the oldest decorative effects and can be as simple or ornate as you wish. Traditionally, stencils were cut from oiled cardboard or even brass sheets. Today inexpensive plastic stencils are now also readily available in an enormous variety of contemporary and traditional designs. Alternatively, you can design and cut your own stencil using a plastic sheet and tracing the chosen design with a chinagraph pencil or a fine, indelible, felt-tipped pen.

It is important to use the correct brush for stencilling. Stencil brushes are flat-topped and are used by dabbing the brush down onto the area to be coloured, rather than stroking. This prevents paint being pushed under the stencil edges and smearing the design. You can use small natural sponges.

As for your paints, it is best to use acrylic or special fast-drying stencil paint. If mixing colours to achieve a desired tint, mix enough for the whole area to be stencilled, as it is difficult to duplicate a particular colour mix. The paint

should be mixed to a creamy consistency – not so thick that it clogs the brush or sponge, and not so thin that it runs under the edges of the stencil.

If your stencil design involves using several colours, it is a good idea to mask off the second-colour areas with masking tape as you go. Wait for the first colour to dry before stencilling with the second one, and so on – this will stop one colour from bleeding into the other. Stencil paint can be dried quickly with a hairdryer on low force and medium heat to prevent the colours running into each other.

Inexpensive plastic stencils are readily available in a variety of contemporary and traditional designs

MATERIALS

suitable paint
stencil brushes
Manila cards
linseed oil
mineral turpentine (white spirit)
sharp craft knife
cutting board
pencils
plumb line
spirit level
chalk
masking tape

STENCILLING A BORDER

Add a designer touch to your bathroom walls with this border.

STEP BY STEP

Making the stencil

1 Decide on your stencil design. You can use the one given here or trace your own out of any pattern or shape that you like.

2 Coat both sides of the Manila card with a 50:50 mixture of linseed oil and mineral

Apply the paint in circular movements from the centre of each cut-out area to the edges

turpentine (white spirit) and allow to dry. Remove any excess oiliness by wiping with a soft cloth.

3 Trace the design onto the Manila card and cut out the areas to be painted, using the cutting board and the sharp craft knife.

The border

4 Paint the wall in the normal way. Then, using a plumb line and spirit level, mark the position of your border, marking both horizontal and vertical base lines.

5 Place the stencil on the wall, aligning its edges with the drawn lines and marking each corner of the stencil with easily removed blackboard chalk. Continue placing the stencil along the guidelines, marking the corners along the entire length of the border.

6 Attach the stencil to the wall with masking tape. If you are using more than one colour, cover over any areas to be painted in another colour with masking tape to avoid paint overlapping.

7 Be sure to remove any excess paint from your brush or

sponge before applying it to the wall. You will find surprisingly little paint is needed. Work in circular movements from the centre of each cut-out area to the edges. Part of the charm of a stencilled decoration is the variation that occurs in paint application, so don't feel compelled to paint until a solid block of colour appears, or to match one motif exactly to the next.

8 When the paint is dry, unmask the stencil and clean it if necessary. Then move the stencil to the next set of chalk marks and paint as before. Continue in this way until the border is completed.

Detail of mirror stencil pattern

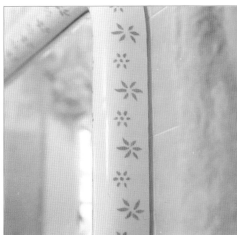

STENCILLING A MIRROR FRAME

Turn an inexpensive plastic-framed mirror into a unique decorator item with a pretty stencilled outline. If the frame surface is in good condition, you will not need to basecoat it before you begin stencilling. Make your stencil or buy a ready-made one and work in exactly the same way as for the wall border; although, of course, you won't need plumb lines and chalk marks.

When choosing these essential components for your bathroom, be as generous as you can with both time and money. Don't rush into buying fixtures and fittings – after all, you'll be living with them for many years.

FITTINGS

Buying the best you can afford makes good sense as far as bathroom fittings go. Installation costs are the same regardless of the product, and top quality fittings will have a much longer life. The more expensive ranges usually have the edge on style and colour choice, as well as using the most durable materials. Whatever you spend on the fittings will be reflected in the tone of your bathroom.

Baths

The enamelled cast iron bath is still the yardstick against which all others are measured and, as proof, there is a hot trade in renovated antique baths. Their style and durability is exemplary, but their weight and size rules them out for many modern bathrooms. Enamelled pressed steel is the modern equivalent of the cast iron bath, but even more common now are the acrylic or fibreglass baths. The latter are light and easy to handle but, because they flex, must be supported in a frame.

Baths are available in a huge range of sizes from extra small ones for tiny rooms to generous two-person baths. The most popular shape is still the rectangle, but non-standard shapes, such as oval and corner baths, are easily found.

Safety features to look for, especially if you have young children or elderly family members, are grab rails and non-slip bottoms.

If there really is not a size and shape manufactured to suit your bathroom, you could consider having a custom-made tiled bath – after all, that's what the Romans did! However, great care must be taken to adequately waterproof this type of bath.

The pleasures of a hot

Sampford

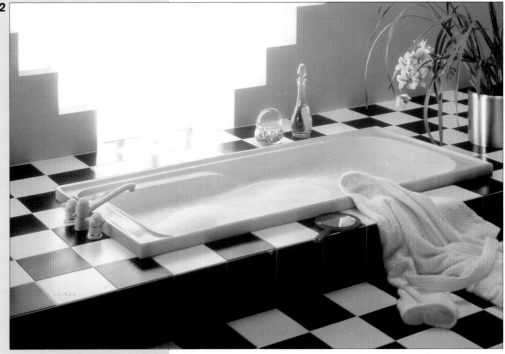

Caroma

3

Fowler Bathroom Products

1 *Who said
a shower had to be
boring?*

2 *This bath features contoured lumbar
support and arm rests for maximum comfort*

3 *The bathroom with everything!*

4 *The ultimate in luxury – a marble-tiled bathroom
with top-flight fittings to match*

4

The Marble Galleries

bath have been given a new boost by the advent of spa and whirlpool baths.

In the former, air is forced through small nozzles in the bath to give a gentle massaging effect; in the latter, water is pumped out of the bath, mixed with air and then recirculated through nozzles which can be adjusted to vary the pressure. Both types are considerably more expensive to buy than ordinary baths and must be professionally installed. Room will be needed for the pump, often in an adjacent room.

Showers

A good shower is a quick, refreshing and economical alternative to a bath – but the pleasure it gives is directly related to the pressure of the water. In areas where you can have mains pressure showers, there is no problem. In a gravity-fed system, where the water is supplied via a tank, the pressure depends mainly upon the height of the tank in relation to the shower but may also be affected by the diameter of the pipe to the shower.

In rare instances a pump may be needed to ensure an adequate flow of water. The more sophisticated power showers use a twin-impeller pump (or two single-impeller pumps) and allow the user to control the exact pressure of the shower – anything from a gentle bubbly effect to needle-sharp jets.

By their very nature, showers splash water around more than baths. Waterproofing in and around the shower tray is of paramount importance if you are to avoid damaging the flooring or the ceiling of the room below.

If you are creating an en suite shower in a bedroom, it is worth checking out the self-contained moulded shower cubicles as they minimise the problems with leaks. Don't forget that whatever you buy will have to be carried through the doors of your house – make sure they are wide enough! The alternative to the cubicle, which can feel slightly claustrophobic, is an enamelled steel or acrylic shower base with tiled surrounds.

Don't forget that whatever you buy will have to be carried through the doors of your house – make sure the doors are wide enough first!

Bases should have a non-slip surface and are available with square and rectangular bases or as corner units. For maximum comfort, and if space permits, the shower base should be at least 900 mm square.

If there is no space in your bathroom for a separate cubicle, the shower can be fitted over the bath. The shower can have separate controls or can be linked to the bath taps using a diverter.

1

2

3

Fowler Bathroom Products

Fowler Bathroom Products

Terrace & Cottage Co

Check that your water authority allows bath/ shower mixers.

A shower curtain is the simplest, cheapest but least effective means of keeping the water inside the shower unit. Hinged, pivoted or sliding doors are more costly but much more efficient. For obvious safety reasons, toughened, laminated or reinforced glass or acrylic should always be used.

Basins

Vitreous china is still the preferred material for basins although high-tech materials like stainless steel are being used for ultramodern designs, and

Always buy the basin and taps at the same time to ensure that they are compatible

the luxury synthetic compounds are gaining in popularity, especially for vanity unit tops. Enam- elled steel is also very popular. Acrylic has a clear price advantage and is worth considering if your budget is limited. Shapes, colours and sizes are as varied as your imagination, ranging from compact corner basins for a guests' cloakroom, to large hand- painted shell shapes. To make cleaning easier, look for a basin on which the

surrounds and soap holders are angled to be self-draining.

Pedestal types have a plinth that supports the basin and hides the plumbing; with a wall- hung basin the pipes are often hidden behind a false wall. The latter type is easier to clean around. Basins for vanity units fall into two categories: those designed to sit under the vanity top and self-rim- ming basins that sit on top.

Check the type of plug (free, chain or plunger) and whether or not you need an overflow (it is advisable).

Always buy the basin and taps at the same time to ensure that they are

compatible. Basins are available with no holes for taps, one hole for a single lever mixer tap, two holes for conventional hot and cold taps, three holes for a mixer spout and two handles. You also need to make sure that the spout gives sufficient clearance for rinsing your hands.

Vanity units

The usefulness of a vanity unit is obvious: pipes and drains are hidden away and cupboards and drawers take care of much of the clutter that accumu- lates in a bathroom. But it offers far more than just these very practical quali- ties – it can set the whole style of the bathroom.

4

1 This bathroom collection captures all the style of the past, complete with decorative scrollwork, to recreate the spirit and quality of the Victorian era

2 Semirecessed vanity basin

3 Timber vanity with matching mirror

4 This bathroom collection offers the smooth, clean lines of modern design

5 A luxurious double vanity basin in a marble-tiled bathroom

6 Toilet suite and accessories

5

Interiors

6

Caroma

Baths, basins and toilets are, at the end of the day, bathroom fittings: the vanity unit is a piece of furniture and it can be as unique as you care to make it.

The range of ready-made units is now extensive. Straight and corner units with single and double basins are available in solid timber, laminated and high-gloss polyester finishes; the more expensive the brand, the more sophisticated the styling of the cabinet. When buying, look for flexibility (doors that open to the left or right; adjustable shelving); strong hinges; drawers that open and close smoothly. Some models have optional organiser trays for storing cosmetics.

When it comes to the tops, the choice is even greater. Luxury materials like marble and granite never lose their appeal and laminates always offer excellent value for money – and the choice of colours and finishes continues to grow. If you are having a top custom-made, ask for a post-formed or D-edge finish – square edges are painful if you knock against them. Accuracy is essential when it comes to cutting the holes for taps and basins, and care must be taken to seal all joints. Colour-matched silicone sealants are available to make joins as unobtrusive as possible.

Problems with sealing are greatly reduced by the new integral vanity unit tops. Top, splashback and basin(s) are moulded as one unit, with holes only for the taps required. As well as being easy to clean, they look smart and streamlined and, like laminates, are available in a dazzling array of colours and finishes.

When it comes to installing the vanity unit, check and double-check that the top is horizontal or angled down fractionally towards the front; if there is the slightest backward slope, water and soap scum will collect along the base of the splashback.

Toilets

Vitreous china, because it is easy to clean and durable, is used for toilets, although cisterns can be plastic. Traditionally designed toilets with high-level cisterns are available for Victorian-style bathrooms but generally the trend is towards more compact models.

The ultimate is a wall-hung pan with a concealed cistern. (If you are renovating, bear in mind that changing from a floor-mounted style to a wall-mounted one causes considerable upheaval.)

Close-coupled suites, where the cistern sits directly on the back of the pan also look very neat. Both these styles are more expensive to buy and install than the type with a waist-height cistern and separate pan.

Siphon-flush systems are the quietest and most efficient, while cisterns which offer half and full flush help water conservation – an average household can save up to 90 litres per day.

Bidets

In their original capacity, bidets are an invaluable

The born-again bidet! Did you know that bidets can also be used as foot baths and are excellent for soaking laundry and washing toddlers?

aid for personal hygiene, but they are also useful as foot baths, for soaking laundry and for washing toddlers! Models are available with flexible hose sprays, central vertical sprays, or ordinary mixer taps. Some models have rim jets which help keep the bowl clean. Like toilets, they are made of

vitreous china and are available in wall- and floor-mounted designs. There are strict plumbing regulations for bidets to prevent contamination of the water supply.

Tapware

Taps are often neglected by the bathroom renovator until the last minute – a bad mistake because good taps are expensive (but well worth budgeting for) and also add the finishing sparkle to your bathroom. Chrome, coloured enamel, ceramic or acrylic finishes are the most popular but gold-plate certainly introduces a touch of luxury. (Brass-coated taps are available and are very popular with renovators.)

Separate hot and cold taps, mixer taps with separate controls and single-action mixers are all available but must be compatible with the basin you choose. Some look more like modern

sculpture than household necessities, but don't let yourself be totally carried away by their beauty.

Ease of use should be a prime consideration, especially for elderly people who may have trouble gripping a smooth, moulded acrylic handle. Cross-head taps are easily turned even by soapy hands, but levers – which can be nudged by an elbow if need be – are easiest of all. Taps with ceramic discs rather than washers are also effortlessly controlled – a quarter turn is all that is required to regulate the flow of water – and they guarantee an end to drips.

Thermostatically controlled taps for baths and showers prevent scalding and are a worthwhile safety feature, particularly if the hot water temperature is set high. Childproof tapheads are also available.

For technology buffs, the touchless tap is on its way: just put your hands in front of the spout and an electronic sensor automatically turns the water on and off!

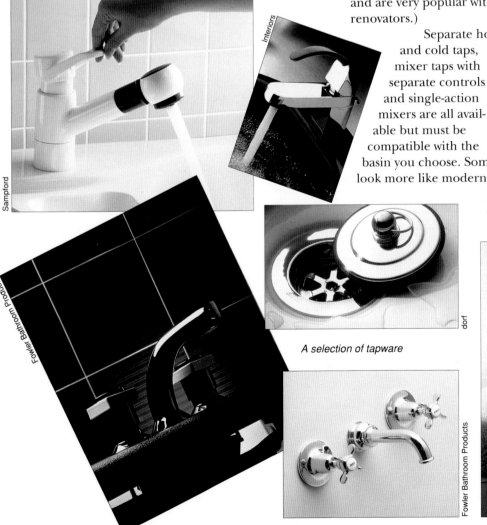

A selection of tapware

If you can't afford that sparkling new bathroom, make the most of what you've got with a few simple but well-chosen accessories.

Just look at the choice of accessories – hooks, towel rails, toothbrush holders; they are useful and a great way to add a touch of luxury or colour to your bathroom.

Change door knobs and cupboard handles to match. Give your taps a quick facelift by changing their handles – you don't even need to turn off the water supply.

A larger mirror will make the room look more spacious. Buy a lightweight acrylic mirror instead of a heavier, more expensive glass one if you're worried about your budget.

Light fittings are often overlooked – you won't even need to rewire to change a single bulb fitting into a more versatile track lighting system, providing that this is out of reach of anyone using the bath or shower. An electrician should make the changeover. How about installing lights each side of the mirror or a track above it to help at make-up time?

Argent Australia

IKEA

Give your bathroom a lift and pamper yourself at the same time!

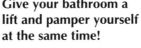

Argent Australia

Caroma

A selection of bathroom accessories

IKEA

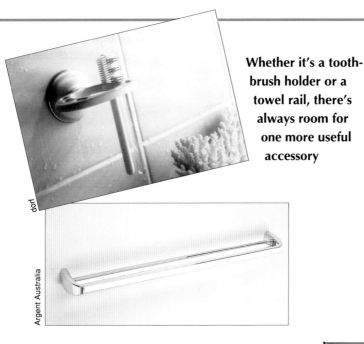

dorf

Argent Australia

Fowler Bathroom Products

Whether it's a tooth-brush holder or a towel rail, there's always room for one more useful accessory

Skill class
Wall-mounting accessories

GOING UP THE WALL

From soap dishes to towel rails – there are loads of essential and not-so-essential accessories for bathroom walls. The three main types are surface-mounted (installed over the wallcovering using adhesive, screws and mounting clips); flush-set (mounted on the wall like tiles or panelling and installed at the same time as the wallcovering); and recessed accessories (fitted into holes in the wall at the same stage as wall finishing).

The way you fasten the accessory to the wall will depend on whether it is ceramic or metal.

When fixing a wall accessory with screw holes to a tiled wall, locate it as near to the centre of the tile as possible. Use masking tape to stick a thin piece of card over where the accessory will go. Hold the mounting clip for the accessory against the card and mark the screw holes with a pencil. Drill with a masonry bit and a variable-speed drill at low speed, applying light pressure only. Peel the card from the wall after the holes are drilled.

Ensure that fixing screws and wall plugs are long enough for at least 25 mm to be in the brickwork of masonry walls. On timber-framed walls, try and screw directly into the studs. Alternatively use hollow-wall fixings.

Other systems are also available.

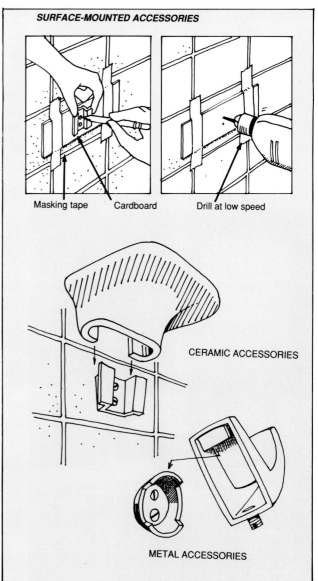

SURFACE-MOUNTED ACCESSORIES

Masking tape   Cardboard   Drill at low speed

CERAMIC ACCESSORIES

METAL ACCESSORIES

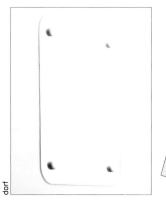

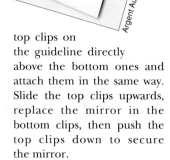

Hanging a mirror

Mirror, mirror on the wall . . . If your bathroom is the smallest room in the house as well as the most private, why not create the illusion of extra space with a large wall mirror?

STEP BY STEP

Don't attempt to drill holes in the mirror yourself – it's a job best left to a glazier.

On solid brick or masonry walls, drill holes and insert wall plugs to hold the fastening screws. On timber-framed walls screw directly into the studs if possible; use hollow-wall fixings if the studs are not in the right places. If the wall is faced with ceramic tiles, use a masonry drill bit to drill through the tiles and into the wall behind.

1 Before hanging the mirror, slide a straight board or a spirit level, longer than the mirror is wide, around the wall to see if it wobbles on a high spot. If the wall has irregularities of more than 3 mm, insert a couple of adhesive-backed felt or rubber pads behind the mirror to keep it from coming into contact with the high spots.

2 If the mirror has predrilled

MATERIALS

MATERIALS
spirit level
electric drill
mirror screws or clips (J-clips/ corner clips)
wall plugs (for masonry or hollow walls)

holes near the corners, it will need to be fixed with mirror screws. Mirrors without holes are attached using either J-clips or corner clips.

Fixing with mirror screws

You'll need a helper to support the mirror against the wall in the correct position. Use a spirit level to check that the mirror is horizontal, then mark the wall with a pencil through each of the predrilled holes. Remove the mirror, drill holes at the marked points and insert wall plugs.

With your helper supporting the mirror again, secure the screws. At each hole in the mirror place a spacer washer or rubber electrical grommet behind the mirror and then insert the mirror screw with its cup washer.

Tighten the screws only until the cup washers press against the mirror (any tighter and you may crack the glass!). Finally, screw the domehead covers into the threaded heads of the mirror screws.

Fixing with clips

Using a spirit level, mark a horizontal guideline as wide as

the mirror for the bottom. J-clips should be positioned about one-third of the width of the mirror in from the edges. Hold the bottom clips on the guideline and mark the positions for holes. Drill the holes, insert wall plugs, then attach the clips with the screws and plastic washers provided.

Support the mirror on the bottom clips and draw a line along the top. Remove the mirror, position the slotted

top clips on the guideline directly above the bottom ones and attach them in the same way. Slide the top clips upwards, replace the mirror in the bottom clips, then push the top clips down to secure the mirror.

If using corner clips, position and fix the clips to the wall in much the same way as for J-clips. Secure the bottom clips first, then insert the mirror and attach the top clips.

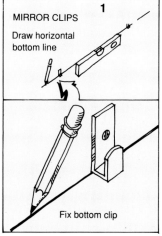

MIRROR CLIPS
1
Draw horizontal bottom line

Fix bottom clip

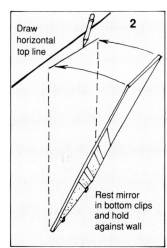

2
Draw horizontal top line

Rest mirror in bottom clips and hold against wall

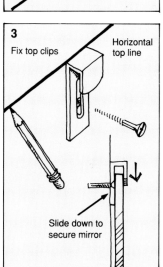

3
Fix top clips

Horizontal top line

Slide down to secure mirror

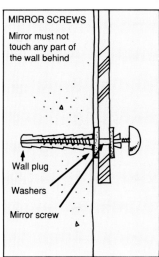

MIRROR SCREWS
Mirror must not touch any part of the wall behind

Wall plug
Washers
Mirror screw

New ideas in modular furniture mean that the modern bathroom can be as stylish and functional as any room in the house.

Modular bathroom furniture first took off in Scandinavia but has quickly caught on around the world. It's a basically simple idea, employing the same kind of design and constructional techniques which have been used in fitted kitchens for years. Modular shelves and cupboards can be linked together in different ways to suit the available space and provide tailor-made storage. And the units are purpose-built to accommodate plumbing, lights, mirrors and special storage for everything you would want to keep in the bathroom.

As with kitchen units, it's the doors and worktops which give the bathroom system a particular look but, as you'd expect, these come in a range of designs and materials which suit the bathroom environment. And while kitchens are based on a standard arrangement of deep-base cupboards, worktops and shallow-top cupboards, the arrangement of bathroom units is more flexible, including shallow-base cupboards and several different widths.

Most systems are designed to stop well short of the floor, allowing plenty of space underneath so that accidental spillages are easily mopped up and easy to clean. Some cupboards are simply hung from wall supports, while heavier units are normally designed to have a pair of stilt legs near the front. Solid plinths are an option with some base units.

BASIN UNITS
These are the largest module – normally around 480-500 mm deep and 600 or 800 mm wide with double doors. They can be used with a one-piece basin top which incorporates the surround, made either from enamelled steel or a synthetic material such as Corian® (much more costly). Alternatively, they can be fitted with a worktop with a separate inset basin made of enamelled steel or porcelain, which makes it simple to match the basin with the rest of a bathroom suite. All the plumbing for the waste and taps is concealed inside the cupboard, which also incorporates some shelf-storage space.

Modular units are purpose-built to accommodate plumbing, lights, mirrors and special storage for everything

PLAIN BASE UNITS
Available in the same sizes as basin units, base units can be fitted either with drawers or cupboard doors and shelves to provide versatile storage. They can be used with a separate top or installed under a continuous worktop run.

WALL UNITS
These are shallower units, usually either around 150 mm or 300 mm deep. Widths are commonly either 400 or 600 mm, although some systems include extra-narrow units. All sizes normally come in two heights, as full-height units and top cupboards. The base section of a full-height unit is the same height as a base unit and the top section matches a top cupboard.

Internal storage options vary, including open shelving and enclosed cupboards. Narrow cupboard units have single doors, while wide units may have single or double doors. Mirror doors are an option with some designs.

FINISH
Choose a finish to suit your decor. The most common options include pine (either solid or louvred panels), white lacquer or white laminate, but a range of colours (mostly pastels) is available in some ranges. Mirror doors may also be included.

All good quality bathroom furniture should be designed to cope with splashes and a damp atmosphere, usually with a thick laminate or lacquer coating on all exposed surfaces. Drawers, which can suffer from accidental spills, are commonly plastic mouldings, while some systems come with the option of pull-out wire or plastic storage baskets instead. These are immune to splashes and will keep towels aired. Glass shelves are available to fit some cupboards. Handles are optional on some ranges so that you can tone neutral cupboards with the colour of your choice.

CUSTOM FITTINGS
Available to suit most ranges, fittings include mirrors, towel rails, toothbrush holders, soap dishes and toilet roll holders. Most are designed to be fitted independently of the units but come in a finish to match. Other extras may include matching bathroom stools. Many of these items can be fitted to any bathroom, whether or not you are installing the rest of a system.

Start by choosing a style of bathroom system that you like and check exactly what sizes of units are available

IKEA

LIGHTING AND PLUMBING

These are often not included in the system, although you may find matching mirror lights are available. Taps are normally completely separate, allowing you to choose ones that match the rest of your suite.

PLANNING

To make the most of a fitted bathroom, it should be installed as part of a complete refit, but there's no reason why you shouldn't leave an existing bath, shower or toilet and fit the units in around them – they should certainly prove flexible enough. It's better, however, to dispense with an old pedestal or wall-hung basin and include a new basin unit if you can.

Start by choosing a style of bathroom system that you like and check exactly what sizes of units are available. Then make a plan of your bathroom using graph paper, indicating the positions of any fittings you intend to leave in place. Ink these in. Then sketch in the possible positions for the units using a pencil. If you are installing a new basin unit, bear in mind the need to connect up the supply and waste pipes. They can easily be moved a short distance, but in the case of long runs or awkward corners, it's as well to check in advance that these won't cause problems. When you have decided on a layout that you like, double-check the measurements in the bathroom itself to ensure that everything will fit properly.

Although the units are simple to put together and easy to fit, it may take some time to prepare the rest of the bathroom, if this means stripping out old cupboards, removing fittings and making good the decorations. Before you start, think about how you are going to make the changeover, to ensure that the bathroom is out of commission for as short a time as possible.

> To help you plan, cut out the shapes of the units, to scale, from Post-It stickers to allow easy repositioning.

IKEA

A very contemporary looking bathroom combined with the charm and warmth of natural wood

---

Project 5

IKEA kit cabinet

Kits make it easy for the home decorator – even in the bathroom! These days you can mix and match furniture and accessories in the same way that you mix and match your clothes.

Self-assembly is not only a breeze, it's also a great way to save money – simply decide what you want, take it home and 'create' your own design! Kits are flat-packed to fit snugly and safely into your car. Clear instructions are included in every package, as well as most of the tools you need. Care and cleaning instructions are also included with your furniture.

It's important to remember to tighten all the screws, nuts and bolts after a few months usage as this will reduce wear and tear.

A typical IKEA kit for a basic bathroom storage cabinet is made up of the following parts:

Frame

Made of particle (chip) board finished with white textured lacquer specially treated for bathrooms; frames have fibreboard backs.

Drawers

Drawer bottoms of white lacquered fibreboard. Drawer sides and guide rails of plastic; drawers can be bought singly or in packs of four.

Doors and drawer fronts

White high-pressure laminated particle (chip) board with a textured surface.

Supporting legs

ABS plastic tubes.

Countertop

High-pressure laminated particle (chip) board with plastic edging strip.

CHECKLIST

❑ Before you begin, read the assembly instructions for the kit carefully.

❑ Check the package to make sure that the set of fittings is complete.

❑ Retighten the screws and nuts about two weeks after assembly and then again after a few months usage to reduce wear and tear.

No matter what the size of your bathroom, there are kit storage cabinets and accessories to efficiently make the most of the space you have

STEP BY STEP

Select the basic cabinet frames, doors, drawers and countertops that best fit your tastes and needs. Add extra shelves, baskets and legs where needed. Suspension fittings are enclosed and hinges are included with doors.

The following photographs show the four steps involved in assembling a basic storage cabinet.

Check exactly what sizes of units are available and, once you've decided on the layout, double check the measurements in the bathroom itself to ensure everything will fit properly

1 Fix the top panel into the side board of the cabinet.

2 Attach the hinges to the cabinet door before screwing into the cabinet.

3 Fit the sides of the drawer together.

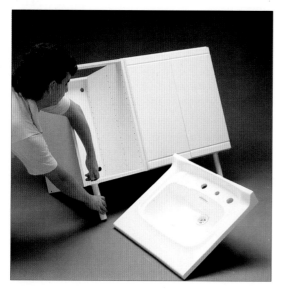

4 Screw the cabinet leg to the base of the unit.

Make sure that any cupboard you want to use for medicines or cleaning materials has a lock or secure safety catch. If the range you like doesn't include one, you can fit doors and drawers with a child-resistant catch like those sold for kitchen cupboards

Installing a safety catch

A child-resistant safety catch on the door of your medicine cabinet is an inexpensive and very effective way to be in two places at once!

It's often the small things in life that help to give us peace of mind

Safety catch on a cupboard

MATERIALS
proprietary safety catch
electric or hand drill

TIME
About half an hour

It's often the small things in life that help to give us peace of mind. When you have curious young toddlers to supervise, a child-resistant safety catch on the door of your medicine cabinet will help.

This project is for the installation of a proprietary safety catch which works in a very simple way. The plastic shaft part of the catch is screwed to the inside of the cabinet door or drawer. This then clips into a slotted catch inside the cabinet when the door or drawer is closed. When the cabinet is opened there is enough available room for an adult's finger to push the shaft down to disengage the catch from the slotted part. This action is easy for an adult but virtually impossible for a small child. Any type of bathroom cabinet can be fitted with this type of safety catch, which only takes about 20 minutes to install. The only special tool required for installation is an electric or hand drill.

Proprietary safety catches are available through DIY stores; although the recommended installation method will be very similar for all, make sure you read the manufacturer's instructions carefully before installation.

STEP BY STEP

1 Mark the position of the slotted catch and shaft on the cabinet with a pencil before drilling the holes (10-15 mm in from the door edge should be sufficient). Be careful not to drill straight through the door!

2 Screw-fix the slotted catch inside the cabinet in the position recommended by the manufacturer.

3 Screw-fix the shaft to the inside edge of the door. Some units have slotted holes for fine adjustment in a vertical position.

4 Adjust the shaft so that it falls easily into the slotted catch when the door closes.

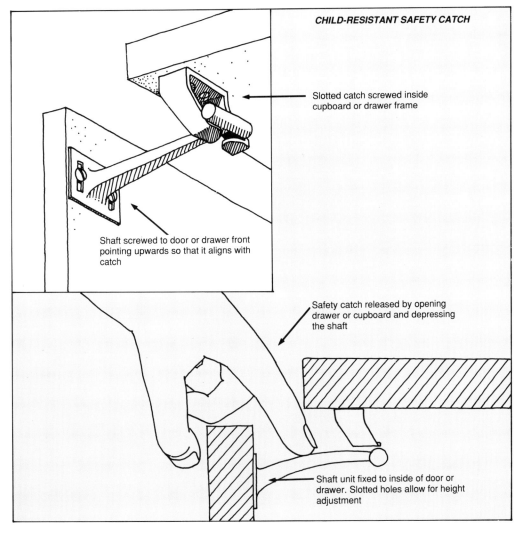

CHILD-RESISTANT SAFETY CATCH

Slotted catch screwed inside cupboard or drawer frame

Shaft screwed to door or drawer front pointing upwards so that it aligns with catch

Safety catch released by opening drawer or cupboard and depressing the shaft

Shaft unit fixed to inside of door or drawer. Slotted holes allow for height adjustment

Without good lighting, the best bathroom will look uninviting – and may even be decidedly dangerous. It's essential – and even illuminating – to choose the right lights! And if your bathroom gets good natural light, try to make the most of it.

KNOW YOUR LIGHTS

Good lighting in the bathroom is essential not just because you look foolish if you apply your make-up like a clown but, more seriously, because you run the risk of misreading the directions on a bottle of medication.

Good lighting does not have to be harsh and bright. In these days when bathrooms are for relaxation as much as for cleansing, there is a greater appreciation of the different types of illumination: ambient, task and accent.

Ambient light can be quite soft; while you don't want deep shadows in the room, you should avoid the type of glaring light that makes sleepy eyes wince.

Task lighting in the bathroom is for making up, shaving, putting in contact lenses, taking medication – activities that generally take place near the vanity unit. If you're fond of a leisurely soak in the bath with a novel, you'll also need to install task lighting for reading.

Accent lighting can be used to show off something special – a classic architectural detail or a handsome print can lift your bathroom out of the ordinary.

What comes naturally

The best light of all is natural light, but even this needs to be planned and controlled. As a rough guide, the window area should equal 10 per cent of the floor area. If you have a choice, bathroom windows should face away from the midday and evening sun. When planning the layout of the bathroom, position vanity units and mirrors beneath or at right angles to the window so that the light falls on your face. If the mirror is opposite the window, your face will be in shadow but your eyes will still have to contend with the reflected glare.

Expanses of clear glass are not always appropriate if your house is overlooked by a close neighbour. Heavily textured glass guarantees privacy but can

Remember water and electricity don't mix, so choose glass or plastic fittings that are sealed and moisture resistant

be difficult to keep clean – if algae builds up in the crevices too much light is blocked. Alternatives include lace curtains, lightly frosted glass and etched glass. Even if privacy doesn't require frosted windows, slightly opaque glass will diffuse strong sunlight and give a more even ambient light. In a high-tech home you can have the best of both worlds by installing windows that change from clear to opaque at the touch of a switch – molecules in a liquid crystal

'sandwich' align to let light through when an electric charge is passed through them; without the charge they disperse randomly and diffuse the light.

Any large expanse of glass in the house is a potential danger but in the bathroom, where wet surfaces increase the chance of slipping, the risk is greater. If the bottom of the bathroom window is below shoulder height, consider using safety glass.

Where wall space is too limited to allow for windows,

there are other options for introducing natural light. Glass bricks are enjoying renewed architectural popularity. They can be used where windows would not be feasible – on a boundary wall, for example – and offer greater insulation against heat loss and sound than ordinary panes of glass. They also offer greater security than ordinary windows because they cannot be opened – but, for the same reason, the bathroom needs a separate ventilation system.

A skylight is another possible option for many bathrooms. There are several different styles available and many different prices.

This large and rather palatial bathroom combines good natural light with ambient and task lighting

Concord Lighting

James Hardie

Features worth paying for are opening devices to allow steamy air to escape, and solar deflectors or blinds to enable you to shut out the overhead sun in warm weather – a bathroom that is too hot is as unpleasant as one that is too cold.

Fitting lights

Daylight alone, of course, is not enough. It must be supplemented by some sort of artificial lighting and this, too, needs careful planning. Bear in mind at all times the fact that water and electricity do not mix. For safety's sake choose glass or plastic fittings that are sealed and moisture resistant. Avoid ones that have metal brackets or exposed bulbs – a hard task, perhaps, when you are aiming for a Victorian mood, but some compromises are worthwhile. Keep hunting:

there are plastic fittings available that have a very creditable appearance of etched glass.

Pull switches are safest in the bathroom; wall switches could be positioned outside the bathroom but must be out of reach of anyone using the bath or shower. If you have a wall-mounted light switch, think about installing a dimmer switch. This will enable you to leave the bathroom light on, at a low level, all night – a great comfort to youngsters and house guests. (Note, however, that ordinary dimmer switches cannot be used with fluorescent lighting.)

Task lighting should be properly planned from a very early stage. Never compromise by using portable lights: they are dangerous in a bathroom. When positioning lights around a mirror, aim to have the light fall on to

Soft and kind – ambient lighting in a bathroom

your face from above and from the sides. A row of incandescent lights up either side of the mirror is very effective – not for nothing was this system chosen for the stars of stage and screen! A small fluorescent strip above the mirror also ensures you can see what you are doing, but the light is less flattering. Special tubes are available.

Even natural light – the best light of all – needs to be planned and controlled

PART 6

Outdoor
Improvements

*Above: A blossoming container garden
brightens up an entrance
Right: Stylish, elegant and private, this
balcony is designed for home entertainment
and enjoyment*

Whether you have a house with a garden, or live in an apartment with a small courtyard or balcony, there are many easy ways to make outdoor improvements that will enhance your lifestyle and add value to your property. The first priority is to work out what you want, how much it will cost and how you can achieve it.

GETTING STARTED

As houses and blocks of land shrink with rising building costs, most families want to stretch living space by making maximum use of the garden. It makes sense to turn a mediocre, unappealing garden area into a well-landscaped one which will provide for a variety of family needs – and encourage the family out-of-doors where house-keeping is minimal.

Begin by identifying the goals you and the family want from garden remodelling, and then, with some hard work and practical advice (which is what this section is all about), you can set out to imaginatively develop your outdoor space. With do-it-yourself projects you really do save money and the work can even be fun.

Outdoor living

Most families want a place where they can relax, cook alfresco meals, and entertain guests. Logically this has to be placed near the house, with sheltered sunny and shady patio or deck areas spacious enough for comfortable furniture. If the patio flows straight from the living room and

colours are coordinated throughout, both areas will seem larger.

Barbecue area
Site this close to patio seating but also near the kitchen. Summer prevailing winds should blow the smoke away from the patio.

Safe play area
This could include lawn, or an area surfaced with bark chips, with climbing frame and swing. Consider a paved path around the lawn for tricycle and wheeled toys; a sandpit and/or paddling pool; and a seating area for adults. When children are older, a sunken sandpit could become a pond and other areas could be paved or planted.

Privacy and security
Privacy from neighbours ranks high in family priorities, particularly in areas where houses adjoin or are built close to land boundaries. It is best achieved with fences, walls, screens, and perimeter planting of dense shrubs and trees. You may want the added privacy, security and safety of having lockable gates, grilles, possibly a swimming pool fence. Well-designed lighting also adds to

security and safety and is essential beside steps, doors, garage and entry points. Some lighting will need indoor switches.

Trafficways
Basic to successful landscaping are evenly laid, fast-draining paths which allow easy, logical circulation through the garden and around the house. These can be decorative as well as practical. Consider them among the first elements of your landscape, to link entries and exits, clothes-line, garage and toolshed. Choose materials which blend well with the house

structure and avoid using too many different kinds of materials, which could appear garish.

Garden structures
A summerhouse or gazebo provides a quiet corner for reading or meditation, or a cool shelter for alfresco dining.

Pergolas or arbours serve a dual purpose: they support climbing plants and vines and also act as effective solar screens – screening out the worst of the sun from spring through to summer, and allowing maximum sun penetration in winter. A greenhouse means you

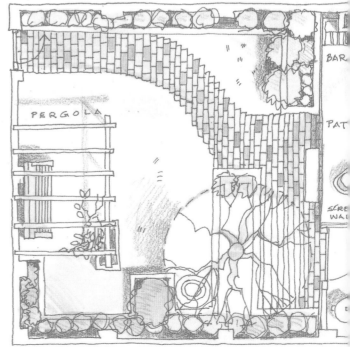

A detailed drawn-up plan results in a better garden

can enjoy gardening all year round. An easy-to-install kit greenhouse could be just what you need.

Conservatories offer a perfect compromise between outdoors and indoors. There is comfortable living space for the family and a reasonably controlled environment for plants. If you want to add an extra room, think of building one or installing a kit conservatory.

Swimming pool
This might be a focal point for entertaining but it does take some time and money for upkeep. It needs an area with full sun, free of overhanging shrubs or trees. Check local authority regulations on building a pool.

Other possibilities
Raised beds for easy gardening by the elderly or disabled; a vegetable plot, which needs a sunny sheltered position, and/or a small orchard; a garden pond, waterfall or

This renovated inner-city terrace house has an uninterrupted flow of space between interior and exterior. A large deciduous tree offers shade to the house and courtyard during the summer months, and allows winter sun to shine through

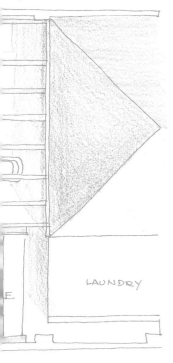

LAUNDRY

bridge; an automatic watering system; low-voltage lighting for night drama; a large lawn – or no lawn; a dog kennel or fenced dog run.

Separate areas
Think of the garden as a series of separate areas, such as the front garden and entrance; drive and car-parking areas; patio and barbecue areas; shrub and tree background plantings for privacy; garden beds; a shrub and flower-lined path leading to a focal point such as pergola, gazebo, pond, or garden seat. You will need a windy, sunny place for the clothesline, a screened area for the rubbish bin, outdoor tool and furniture storage, potting bench, and compost heap.

You may start with an existing garden which already has structures, paths, garden beds and trees. Some can be worked into a new landscaping plan, but don't retain in

your long-term plan any features or plants which you dislike or which seriously impede your landscaping goals. Look at the garden from various viewpoints, and from house windows, and ask yourself 'Do I like what I see?'. A little ruthlessness now will ensure that you are happy and comfortable in the remodelled garden, enjoying all its features and plants.

Some garden structures are expensive but improvements can be made gradually if your budget is tight. You can do one area at a time providing you are working to an overall plan, either your own or a landscape designer's.

Workload
How much time or inclination have you for active gardening? Some people garden for the fun of it, others because the neighbours might complain. Do you want a

garden that demands the least work? All gardens should be planned for ease of maintenance but some gardens cater for particular interests which demand more work, such as vegetable gardening or conservatory plants.

Plan ahead
While planning current needs for garden use, don't forget to also consider future needs, when you might want a garden that is easy to look after as you get older. Or you might want to install a swimming pool as toddlers grow to teenagers. Or incorporate more car-parking space as teenagers become drivers.

There are various puzzles to solve when landscaping or remodelling the garden, but a clear list of preferences and some preliminary planning will help to make your outdoor improvements work.

A framework will begin to emerge as you decide what features you want the garden to have and where they can be placed.

GARDEN PLANNING

Plan areas to suit your needs – for example, the patio has to go near the living areas of the house. The clothesline should be easily accessible from the laundry area. Service pathways (as opposed to winding garden paths) should go direct to their destination. Play areas must be near the house and easily reached. A vegetable garden needs a sunny aspect. The positions of screen plantings are dictated by neighbours' houses, and could include a secluded seating area. Any beautiful view beyond the garden could be framed by plants and used as part of the garden backdrop, this being a technique the Japanese call 'borrowed scenery'.

The site also influences garden style. A sloping garden rising from the house may encourage a feeling of an amphitheatre of shrubs and trees linked by paths; whereas a flat, featureless garden benefits from being given some changes in level with possibly a sunken garden or path. Or it could have a formal symmetrical design with herb garden and espaliered fruit trees. In another garden, drainage problems might be solved by making a bog garden

and pond, or building a dry-stone stream bed.

Keep each area generous in scale and as uncluttered as possible. Outdoors, everything from the size of the patio to the width of paths, benefits from a far more spacious scale than indoors. If you can't afford a lot of paving for a large patio, make it look larger by adding inset flower beds or a low-level rock garden, or hand-laid pebble mosaic insets. A wide path looks better than a narrow concrete strip even if it is initially only laid out with stepping stones in pine chips or grass.

You can do your own landscape design or ask a landscape architect or designer to do one for you. Detailed drawings by a professional show structural work, drainage, irrigation, lighting and planting, but be careful to check the qualifications and experience of any landscaper you use – and ask for a quotation before any work is undertaken.

If you are building, don't strip or bulldoze the entire land – topsoil gets buried by subsoil and the compaction caused by heavy machinery makes gardening difficult later. Make sure builders stockpile topsoil removed for

building so that you can use it later. Getting landscape advice before you build can save money by coordinating work such as drainage or soil shifting, and preplanning the access needed. A crane may be the only way to lift in large rocks or building materials for landscaping if the new house does not enable free access to the back garden.

If you have just bought a house, leave garden remodelling until you have experienced a round of the seasons, which will show you what is planted and which plants are worth keeping. Very often, care and pruning will improve existing straggling plants.

Preserve natural features and mature plants on the land where possible – it gives the garden character and often a look of maturity. Local native plants, trees and natural rocks also help to sustain local wildlife.

If the ground slopes severely, consider clearing only one area at a time for designing and planting, or you will lose too much topsoil and have drainage problems and erosion while plants are too small to bind and hold the soil. Some terracing and retaining

walls may be needed if the land slopes too abruptly from the house, but cut-and-fill methods are more expensive than making a garden on a natural slope. A cheaper method may be to build a timber deck or verandah, and walkways from the house to the slope.

Start with a rough plan

Draw a map of the garden on graph paper using a scale of about 6 mm to 30 cm ($^1/4$ in to 1 ft), showing in detail what already exists in the garden which you want or have to keep, such as mature trees, buildings, walls, fences, slopes, good and bad views, position of taps, water pipes, gas pipe and electricity supply cables. Show the house outline and its doors. Use tracing paper over this to mark out the rough position of the areas and pathways you want to incorporate. It helps to indicate north/south aspects, areas of shade, the path of the sun throughout the year, and prevailing wind directions.

Keep each area generous in scale and as uncluttered as possible

This beautifully landscaped garden has been planted to make the most of spring colours

This is a good time to consolidate your general ideas of what is your ideal garden. Don't start planning with budget costs dictating the design. Do a rough design of exactly what you want. Later you can look for ways to adapt it economically if you have to. Before doing a detailed plan, now is the time to explore all the possibilities.

For some structures such as walls or pool fences, or for lopping and removing trees, it may be necessary to check local authority regulations.

Whatever the size of the garden, the landscaping techniques are the same. You are still shaping land, designing improvements and choosing plants for specific purposes. Before you pursue your personal vision of the ideal garden, list the tools you will need and decide on the order of work and the budgeting. It is useful to complete the hard landscaping and planting of one area at a time, so that plants can progressively become established. Try to choose and use materials which are sympathetic to the house design and which will enhance its value, creating harmony between architecture and plants.

Leave garden remodelling until you have experienced a round of the seasons – this will show you what is planted and which plants are worth keeping

Style and atmosphere

A successful landscape needs a garden style which appeals to you, and this is often linked to the house design. It can also be influenced by the kind of plants you like, or by your garden site and its climate.

Formal garden

Cottage garden

Oriental garden

Garden styles

There is a variety of garden styles, from formal to cottage garden, each with its own atmosphere and character. A predominantly natural or wild garden might look best in the country, or, alternatively, it could turn a town garden into a green oasis and bird sanctuary. A Mediterranean courtyard style would suit a small garden or echo Spanish-style architecture. You may like a formal garden for its symmetry, or an oriental garden for its serenity.

There is no need to follow a style slavishly but it provides a good starting point. Keep its essential flavour and use your own site, climate and way of life to give it individuality. Following are some style examples.

Natural garden

This will have relaxed informal shapes; local trees, shrubs and wildflowers; mulch, gravel or stone paths; natural textures such as old brick, stone and timber; log edgings; naturalised bulbs and perennials growing in longer grass; woodland corners; rough boulders and informal watercourses and pond. Plantings are wayward, with interlacing shrub and tree branches, and tumbling ground covers. Plants to choose are irises, day lilies, native plants, old-fashioned roses, fragrant plants such as evergreen magnolia, berried shrubs, violets, liquidambar, eucalyptus and larch.

Oriental garden

A tranquil, orderly design contrasts open space, such as raked sand or moss, against the shape and position of plants and rocks, asymmetrically placed in threes, fives or sevens, and used against real or simulated ponds and watercourses. Use stone lanterns; water basin and bamboo flume; bridges; stepping-stone rocks across water; pavilion; teahouse; hand-washing basin; pebble, rock or moss paths; pebble-covered beds. Plants, often carefully pruned or clipped to shape, include azaleas, camellias, rhododendrons, black and other pines, cycads, nandina, bamboo, podocarpus, Japanese maples, flowering cherries and other prunus, mondo grass and Korean grass, chrysanthemums, wisteria and bonsai.

Cottage garden

A profusion of drifts and clumps of flowers, herbs and vegetables epitomises the cottage garden, with perhaps stone-paved patio, crazy-paving paths, or paths of gravel or basket-weave brick, and rustic seats, arbour and pergola. Plants include old-fashioned shrub roses, violets, lavender, nasturtiums, marigolds, foxgloves, delphiniums, lupins, stock, wallflowers, forget-me-nots, lilies, mixed hedges, rough-cut grass with spring bulbs planted through, lilac, clematis, honeysuckle, and fruit trees.

Mediterranean garden

This ranges from the more formal tiled-and-walled fountain court to the dry-landscape garden which is simple, drought-proof, antique-looking, with wrought iron gates and grilles, and tiled paving. It could have painted rough-cast brick, or tile-topped brick walls; terracotta or wrought iron accessories; stone fountain; statues; and shuttered windows. Plants include acacia, jacaranda, crepe myrtle, olive, hibiscus, oleander, lavender, rosemary, geraniums, marigolds, gazanias, verbena and marguerites. This style adapts well to gardens in dry areas and could include plants such as succulents and cacti, yucca, strelitzia, palms, and pepper tree. Crushed rock, raked sand and gravel surfaces can be used.

Tropical garden

Plenty of scope here for shady tunnels of green tree ferns overhanging trickling water, with mossy logs and rocks along the banks and leaf mulch underfoot. Plants could include philodendrons, palms, *Dizygotheca elegantissima*, gardenias, strelitzia, cycads, ornamental bananas, monstera, agapanthus, ginger, Eucharist lilies. In non-tropical climates use large-leafed foliage plants for a tropical feel, such as acanthus, ferns, palms, *Fatsia japonica*, New Zealand flax, calla lilies, cordyline, hostas and yucca. The tropical garden style is easily adapted to an irrigated shady garden, or in cooler climates to a greenhouse or conservatory.

Formal garden

This style relies heavily on symmetrical design, clipped hedges and topiary; clipped balls and spirals of box or myrtle; rose or herb garden with geometrical layout; fountain court or patio paved with terrazzo, slate or stone; flanking pairs of urns or conifers; rows of trees or other plants; statuary and stylised plantings as in a knot garden or parterre; or low, clipped, box-edged beds. Plants include magnolia, lilies, standard roses and gardenias, agapanthus in pots, irises, tall grasses, conifers, and citrus.

Contemporary garden

The contemporary look has clean lines based on rectangular modules or curves, with harmony in shapes, scale and textures. Features such as curved lawn area and flower beds, patio, pond or pool, and barbecue are fitted into the suburban rectangle. Some gardens have strong architectural features such as pergola, raised beds, retaining walls, latticed screens and paved areas.

Keep a style's essential flavour and use your own site, climate and way of life to give it individuality

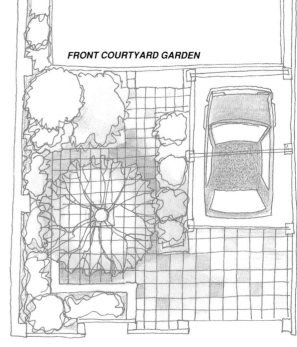

FRONT COURTYARD GARDEN

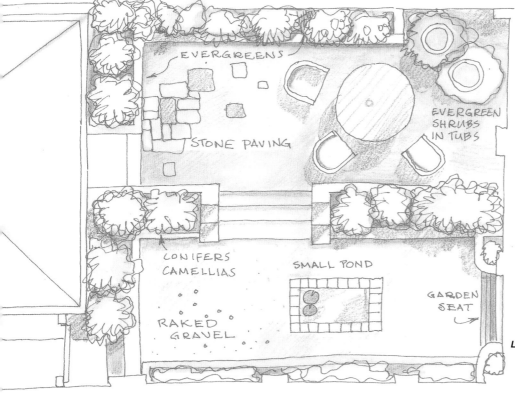

LOW-MAINTENANCE FORMAL GARDEN

273

Landscaping

There's always a solution even when blocks are difficult, so test your landscape planning as you go.

When you have decided on the general design, go outside and check it three-dimensionally in the garden. Outline areas with stakes, or a curved hose-line, and check that the entire family likes the proposed features. Measure the width of car doors opening in the parking areas; try out furniture placement.

Now from a rough area layout, begin to fill in detail on tracing paper laid over the basic layout of the garden which is drawn to scale. Dovetail traffic routes, areas of privacy, views, and sun and shade patterns. Keep in mind any noise or wind problems. Add in shapes for paved areas and other surfacing materials, decks, screens, walls, pergola, garden beds. Decide on the type of plants needed, marking in the heights and widths wanted and the purposes the plants are to serve. For example, deciduous trees planted along a hot, sunny aspect provide summer shade but are bare in winter when the sun is needed.

Consider devices which add interest, such as continuous space from indoors to outdoors; changing levels; using a focal point of particularly striking plants or a large tree; adding an intriguing element by screening part of the garden from full view. Although you are working on a flat plan, don't forget the element of height supplied by structures such as a pergola, trellis or arch clothed with climbers.

Keep in mind aesthetic considerations of scale, proportion, balance and colour – all being fairly crucial to a beautiful garden. Experience and a good eye can help; so do visits to other gardens which are known successes. Restraint in the number of building materials and textures used, simplicity of line without fussy details, and the use of plants in groups and masses rather than singly, will help to create unity.

As the essential elements of what you want are built up in detail on your plan, the advantages and disadvantages of your

Skill class
Setting levels

Landscaping will almost certainly involve some levelling of the land, and some changes in levels. You will need to plot the slope of the land by marking out levels to work from. Paths cut or contoured into a slope, for example, have to be quite level from one side to the other for comfortable walking. The path can gently rise or fall in length, and steps or a ramp can be installed on steeper grades. Retaining walls may be needed alongside the path.

Ramps are quite simple to build and take a wheelbarrow or provide wheelchair access. They are comparatively safe if evenly surfaced. To find the length of ramp needed for a comfortable walking slope, multiply the height of the rise by 5. You can use a longer ramp than this for even less slope. The width of steps and ramps should allow about 1.2 m per person in width, and 1.5 m for two people walking abreast. Generally speaking, steps should be wide when the riser is shallow and, if you want, slightly sloping paths can be turned into wide, shallow steps.

To cut into a slope to make a level area, place a long, straight timber board on edge across a fixed point where you want to cut. Hold the board steady against a short timber board and use a spirit level to adjust the level of the long board. Measure the distance from the top of the board to the ground and drive a peg in level with the original fixed point. Repeat the process until you have a series of pegs across the area you want to level.

Patio or terrace areas also have to be levelled. And if you want ponds and cascading waterfall, levels between one pond and the next might have to be worked out, or you may need to take levels to dig a perfectly even excavation for a pool.

Terracing land by using a cut-and-fill method can be expensive and is often more formal in style, but very effective if the retaining walls or banks are well planted. If the terracing is shallow, the retaining walls can be built quite easily by a home handyperson, but will need provision for drainage.

Sculpturing the land into mounds and hollows, which partly follow the lie of the land, is a particularly useful way to deal with hill-side gardens and natural-style garden slopes. It discreetly organises garden levels and gives the illusion of space. Many plants, including natives, enjoy the well-drained conditions of mounded beds, while the moisture for plant roots is trapped in the hollows, which act as drainage channels.

> If you are redistributing soil next to the house, make sure it doesn't bridge the damp-proof course (DPC) in the house wall – usually about two bricks up from the ground level.

An example of a beautifully landscaped garden

particular garden shape and site will become clear. And these will also help to dictate your design. The more you change a site's physical character, the more it usually costs.

Check any plan against any possible house additions later, or access if you want to build a swimming pool or summerhouse in the future. Make sure the plan meets local authority building requirements. Finally, work out the cost and substitute some economical materials for expensive ones if you have to. Concrete could be used instead of brick or stone, or most plants could be bought very small, or sections of the plan could be constructed later. Working with the essential contours of the land is more economical than a lot of building and relevelling.

Once a master plan is developed on paper, planning how to implement it can follow. List the order of work, and what you can do yourself to keep the costs down.

Garden shapes

Long and narrow
Common in city gardens, this shape can be divided across its width, but some glimpses of its entire length will make it seem larger. It could be a series of 'rooms' for entertaining, then through an arch to a children's play area, with perhaps a secluded sitting area beyond, or a vegetable garden. Plan key areas, then screening elements and linking pathways.

Rectangular
This may encourage a symmetrical formal garden, or one with changes of level. It may suggest perimeter planting, leaving the central space open for lawn or patio, but curves and circular shapes will soften the rectangular outline.

Square
Again, oval or curved lawn or paving in the central area and asymmetrical groupings of shrubs or trees will modify the square look, or it may be emphasised by a series of geometrical shapes leading to a balanced, formal look as in the courtyard garden.

Odd shape
This could be a tapering or triangular-shaped piece of land, or it may be that the house is placed aslant the site, creating an odd-shaped garden. This might be turned to advantage by using the apex of the triangle for a private area such as a small summerhouse or glasshouse, and using plantings to screen boundaries and focus attention on the wider sections of the land. Small pieces of land might suit specific purposes, such as vegetable garden, play area or utility area. It may be possible to frame views beyond the garden, minimising its shortcomings.

Plan key areas, then screening elements and linking pathways

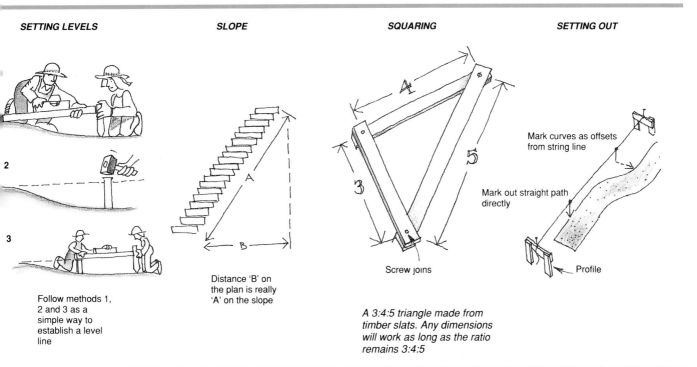

SETTING LEVELS

2

3

Follow methods 1, 2 and 3 as a simple way to establish a level line

SLOPE

A

B

Distance 'B' on the plan is really 'A' on the slope

SQUARING

4

5

3

Screw joins

A 3:4:5 triangle made from timber slats. Any dimensions will work as long as the ratio remains 3:4:5

SETTING OUT

Mark curves as offsets from string line

Mark out straight path directly

Profile

Garden steps and ramps

Changes in levels in a garden can be treated in a number of ways. However, the most popular are steps and ramps.

1

GARDEN STEPS

Any set of steps must be comfortable to use – the general rule of two times the height (riser) plus length (going or tread) equals 610 mm, plus or minus 20 mm (for example, [2 x 150] + 300 = 600) will ensure comfortable steps. Most people like to use steps that have a riser of 150 mm to 175 mm with a tread of 250 mm to 300 mm. As the tread width increases, the rise lessens. Each step in a flight must be the same as the others otherwise they may be dangerous to use. In some situations other dimensions may be appropriate.

Garden steps can be made in many ways. Following are some common methods:
❏ concrete poured in formwork
❏ brick with concrete slabs
❏ solid bonded brick
❏ preformed concrete steps and risers
❏ sleepers and fill
❏ timber riser and fill
❏ brick riser and fill

2

❏ stone block
❏ timber stringers and treads

Among the most popular steps for gardens are preformed concrete steps or brickwork. The building of formwork and the subsequent pouring of concrete is not a job to be lightly undertaken. The formwork must be strong enough to withstand the forces of wet concrete being vibrated, and it is necessary to have the right skills and materials for the task.

However, precast concrete steps can be managed by most avid landscapers, and they are available in a number of widths. The step length is usu-

ally about 275 mm and the step height around 180 mm. These are comfortable step sizes for most people. Precast steps can be bedded in mortar or sand-cement mix, and you can work at the speed that suits you.

Steps can also be made of brickwork. The bricks should be dry-pressed, that is, without extrusion holes, if laid on flat (as opposed to on edge). If the soil is a stable, well-draining soil, the rough shape of the steps can be cut out of the soil as a foundation. If in any doubt, or the soil is clayey or unstable, the steps should be built on a concrete base, or a bed of compacted hardcore.

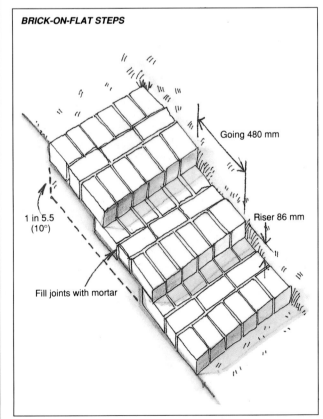

BRICK-ON-FLAT STEPS

Going 480 mm

Riser 86 mm

1 in 5.5 (10°)

Fill joints with mortar

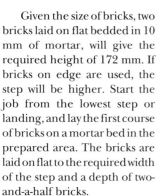

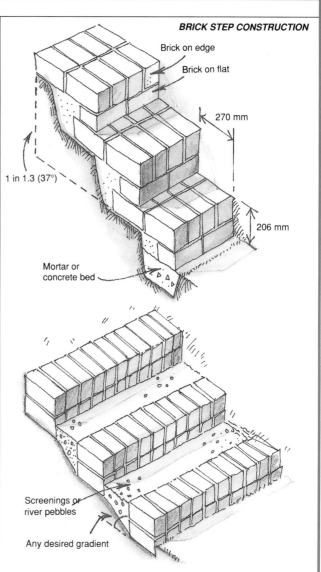

BRICK STEP CONSTRUCTION

Brick on edge

Brick on flat

270 mm

1 in 1.3 (37°)

206 mm

Mortar or
concrete bed

Screenings or
river pebbles

Any desired gradient

Amber Holdings

Given the size of bricks, two bricks laid on flat bedded in 10 mm of mortar, will give the required height of 172 mm. If bricks on edge are used, the step will be higher. Start the job from the lowest step or landing, and lay the first course of bricks on a mortar bed in the prepared area. The bricks are laid on flat to the required width of the step and a depth of two-and-a-half bricks.

The rise of the second step will need to start 300 mm from the nose of the bottom step, and likewise is built back two-and-a-half bricks. The top course of the first step is laid directly on this, set forward

1 Attractive brick paver steps provide a stylish and non-slip surface

2 Stone slab steps in a natural-style garden

3 Elegant stone steps link an entertainment area to the garden beyond

4 These brick paver steps have a unique texture and colour and are an integral part of a larger paving design

35 mm. This gives the steps a more attractive appearance.

The steps are continued on in this fashion to the height of flight required.

RAMPS

Older people, or those with physical disabilities, are unable to cope well with stairs or changes in level unless very well-designed paths are made for them. The beauty of ramps is that they can be attractively landscaped to snake around the garden, incorporating considerable height changes – without a steep gradient.

When designing ramps for access to different levels of the garden, remember that people in wheelchairs need enough room to manoeuvre comfortably. Find out the recommended dimensions and other standards for wheelchair facilities from your local authority.

Gradient

The maximum gradient that an independent wheelchair user can cope with (except in short lengths) is one in 12 (1:12). If the wheelchair is being pushed by an attendant, this could be increased to one in 8 (1:8), but this is not recommended for around the home. Level rest areas should be provided every 9 m or less, and these rest areas should be 1200 mm to 1800 mm in length. The transition from landing to ramp should be smooth. Landings or rest areas are also recommended at any change of direction of the ramp. If the ramp is steeper

than one in 12 (1:12), rest areas need to be provided every 5 m.

It is suggested that where gradients are between one in 20 (1:20) and one in 12 (1:12), the ramp should be kerbed and handrails provided. At gradients lower than one in 20 (1:20), kerbs should not be necessary and the surrounding ground can be graded to the sides of the ramp.

The ramp should also be able to shed water to the sides. It may have a domed top or a slope to one side. The recommended maximum for this camber is one in 100 (1:100).

Widths

Wheelchairs need a minimum width of 800 mm to go anywhere, and 950 mm is preferred. If you want to pass a wheelchair on a path, you need at least 1200 mm. If a wheelchair is to turn around through a right angle, it will need at least 950 mm square. These sizes can be taken as the minimum width of ramps. It would make sense to have a minimum width of around 1 m wherever possible. If kerbs are provided as well, these should be outside the required width. Therefore, if a kerb 50 mm high by 100 mm wide is to be provided both sides of a 1 m wide ramp, the total width needed would be 1200 mm.

Handrails

Most authorities recommend that handrails be provided on ramps for wheelchair users, to enable them to pull themselves up or brake on the way down. The recommended height for a handrail is around 750 mm, somewhat lower than for walking adults.

Sub-base

The sub-base for a concrete or paved ramp is very similar to

Concrete wheelchair ramps are durable and easy to maintain

that described in the Skill class on page 309).

Concrete ramp

A ramp is formed-up the same way as any other concreting job. However, if the sides need to be built up, a retaining wall of double brick or concrete block can be used to retain the sub-base.

The concrete should be 75 mm or 100 mm thick, and be reinforced with a light steel mesh, held off the sub-base with bar chairs or spacers. Extra formwork for the kerb needs to be built. The kerb should be about 50 mm high and 100 mm wide, and separately reinforced with small-diameter steel bars. The kerb can be poured at the same time as the concrete: build formwork to the height of the top of the kerb on the outside with a separate board fixed in place from the top to the inside to form-up the inside edge of the kerb, 50 mm lower. A small gutter can be formed at the base of the kerb to deal with runoff.

A standard-duty concrete mix (see Concreting Skill class) is suitable. It should be poured, well compacted and screeded, and the ramp and top of kerb finished as required. Recom-

mended finishes for wheelchair ramps are a broomed finish, a sponge finish, or wooden-float finish (page 295). A decorative alternative is exposed aggregate, as long as it is not too rough.

Paving

Paving is a reasonable alternative to concrete, as long as a suitable sub-base is prepared. It may even be best to provide a concrete base over which pavers are laid. The reason is that if there is any subsidence in the pavers, the ramp may become difficult to use.

Pavers are best installed on a bed of sand and cement, e.g. try six parts sand to one of cement (6:1), to ensure that the pavers do not slip down the ramp. They must be installed flush and the joints, if any, should be recessed only to a maximum of 5 mm.

Timber

Timber is suitable for ramps for people without disabilities, and a ramp of timber beams and decking is quick and easy to build. But timber ramps can be a different matter for the disabled person, especially in the wet when timber can be quite slippery and traction for wheelchairs difficult.

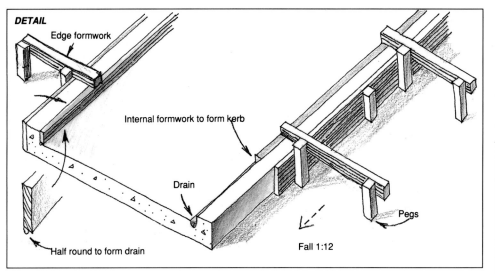

DETAIL
Edge formwork
Internal formwork to form kerb
Drain
Half round to form drain
Fall 1:12
Pegs

Garden walls

Garden walls give a pleasant sense of enclosure, trapping sun, excluding wind and guaranteeing privacy. They look best when in harmony with the house materials and style.

Walls are perfect backgrounds for plants that like shelter, or which drape easily or climb. Painted white walls provide backdrops for dramatic plant silhouettes such as those of agapanthus or palms. The majority of walls are quite solid and are made of brick, stone or concrete block.

Low dry-stone retaining wall

Retaining wall built from preservative-treated timber logs

Mortared stone-slab retaining wall coupled with a clipped hedge above

---

 ## Skill class
Bricklaying

Successful bricklaying requires a careful, methodical approach and the confidence gained from experience. If you are laying bricks for the first time, it's wise to start on a small project.

Bricklaying seems to be the one trade held in awe by the inexperienced and many will not even attempt bricklaying. Granted, it's not easy, but if you are willing to start slowly and take time to check that individual bricks are properly aligned and, most importantly, select the best mortar for the job, there is no reason why you shouldn't have a go!

BRICKS
The first thing to firmly understand is that bricks, and the resulting brickwork, are quite heavy. Bricks weigh on average around 4 kg each and, if wet, can be more. Because of this, it's important that the bricks are placed on a properly designed footing (see Footings, page 281).

Bricks are made to a standard metric size. Most bricks should be within one or two millimetres of the standard size. In every square metre of single-thickness brickwork, there are around 50 bricks. This takes into account a standard mortar joint of 10 mm. If ordering bricks, it may be wise to order about 5 per cent more than is needed, in case of wastage or the odd faulty brick.

Dry-pressed bricks are solid, and usually have an indentation, called a 'frog', on the top of the brick. Extruded bricks have a number of holes through the brick due to the extrusion process. Concrete and sand-lime, or calcium silicate bricks are also available depending on the look you want.

All the bricks needed for a particular job should be bought at the same time. This allows bricks to be taken randomly from each stack as work progresses, to ensure that a good colour mix results.

MORTAR
Mortar is used not only to 'stick' bricks together, but also to keep bricks apart. There is a slight variation in size between bricks, which would make laying very difficult if there was no way to adjust for the different sizes.

Also, bricks are one of the few building materials that 'grow' slightly with age, and if there was no separating medium, the brickwork would fail.

Mortar is essentially composed of two main materials. Cement and lime are the bonding materials. The other material is sand.

Cement is a totally dehydrated powder, which when water is added causes a chemical reaction to occur, where the cement particles 'grow' and envelop the surrounding particles. For this to work properly, it is important that the cement is fresh.

Lime is recommended in most mixes. Hydrated lime aids in the bonding of the mortar and adds to the 'fattiness' of the mix. This is important because a non-fatty mix is very difficult to work.

The sand should be specially blended bricklaying sand. Blends from 50:50 to 70:30 of clean, sharp sand and clayey sand are available.

There is only one rule with water – if you can't drink it, don't use it in your mortar.

There are a number of additives on the market but these should be used with caution. Air-entraining agents or mortar plasticisers add air to the mix, resulting in mortar that is easier to work. Air entrainers are not a lime substitute, as is often claimed, and do not aid in the bonding of the bricks.

Mortar mixes depend on the application and the level of economy sought. The commonly used mixes often include all three major ingredients: cement, lime and sand.

If any oxides or other colouring agents are to be added to the mix, they should be added in precise amounts as stated on the packet. Oxides are generally added to dry cement and will not show their true colour until the mix is wet.

Mortar is normally mixed on a mixing board on the ground with a square-nosed shovel, in a wheelbarrow using a larry (a tool similar to a hoe with holes in it), or in a cement mixer. Water is added to form a thick, creamy mortar. There is no reason for not using bagged premixed mortar, which is available from builders' merchants, especially if you are short of time.

The quantities of mortar needed can be worked out on the basis that one cubic metre of sand will make one cubic metre of mortar. This is enough, allowing for wastage, to lay 1000 to 1500 bricks.

There is only one rule with water – if you can't drink it, don't use it in your mortar!

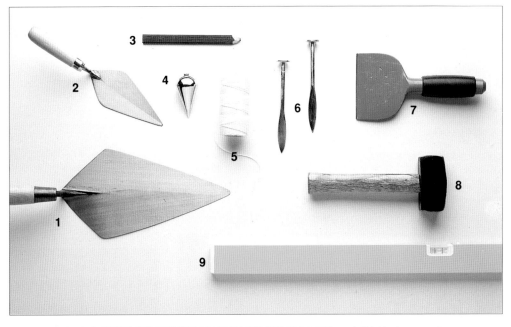

CEMENT	LIME	SAND	
1	1	6	Quite durable, for general brickwork, in and above ground
1	2	9	Brickwork above ground level
1	0	4-6	Mix commonly used by professional bricklayers together with additives

1 Bricklaying trowel
2 Pointing trowel
3 Carpenter's pencil
4 Plumb bob
5 String line
6 Pegs
7 Brick bolster
8 Club hammer
9 Combination straightedge and spirit level

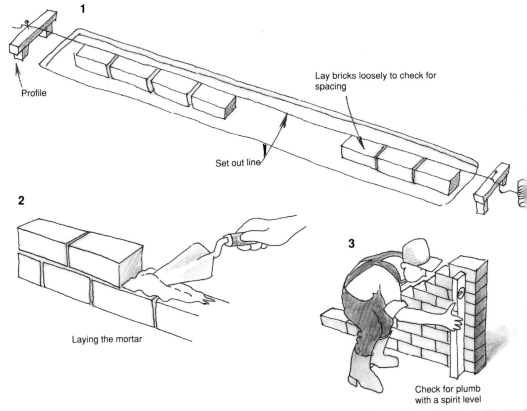

1

Profile

Set out line

Lay bricks loosely to check for spacing

2

Laying the mortar

3

Check for plumb with a spirit level

BUILDING A SIMPLE BRICK WALL

1 Lay out the first row of bricks dry to work out the exact spacing, and see if there is any need to slightly expand or compress the joints to save on brick cutting. When you are completely happy with the way the bricks work out, you can begin to lay them.

Porous bricks must be wetted before they are laid, or adhesion problems may occur. Set the line to the marking on the profiles (see Footings). The string should not actually touch the brickwork but be about 4 mm away.

2 Place the mortar down and furrow, a process whereby the point of the trowel is passed through the mortar to spread it evenly to both sides. Place the brick in this bed, aligned into its correct position in relation to the string line, and tap into place.

The second brick will need to be buttered on the end face (header) to form the vertical joint (perpend), and this is done by striking mortar directly onto the brick.

Align the brick and adjust the vertical gap to the correct thickness, then bed the brick. If a brick seems to be too low compared to the previous brick, lift it and relay it. Lay the rest of the first course.

3 Once you have laid the first row of bricks, it is usually wise to build up the ends of the brickwork to about five to seven courses high. This is because it is difficult to achieve truly vertical ends when approaching them from a long run of brickwork. Make sure the two ends are the same height and plumb, by using a gauge rod and spirit level.

4 Once the ends are accurate, string lines can be stretched between them, and the bricks infilled. Then go up the next five or seven courses, always keeping an eye on the wall to make sure it is plumb.

Bricklaying is slow initially, but satisfying – just don't expect miracles. The normal speed for beginners is 15 to 20 bricks an hour, which will gradually increase along with your proficiency. Your eye will begin to recognise what is and is not actually straight, so that you rely less on the spirit level.

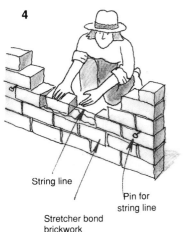

4

String line

Pin for string line

Stretcher bond brickwork

TOOLS AND EQUIPMENT
- ❑ bricklayer's trowel – medium to small size
- ❑ bolster and club hammer – for cutting bricks
- ❑ spirit level – 900 mm long, horizontal measuring (bubble visible from the top)
- ❑ string lines
- ❑ line pins and blocks or spare bricks – to hold string
- ❑ pointing trowel – for filling joints
- ❑ raking tools or jointers – for making neat joints
- ❑ gauge rod – home-made, a timber strip which is marked with brick course heights on one side, and header and stretcher bond spacings on the other
- ❑ assortment of buckets, shovels, mixing boards, sponges, etc.

Footings

Footings can be thought of in terms of a human foot. They are the bottommost part of a structure, and support the whole structure. Footings are typically placed in the ground, where they will be stable in fluctuations of topsoil moisture.

Footings are normally made of concrete – and in many countries the concrete has to be reinforced. However, in some instances, brick footings or cut stone may be used.

The standard sizes of footings vary with the soil types present. In general, sandy and gravel soils pose few problems. As you move into clay soils that are still considered stable, the depth of the footing should be increased. This adds to the stiffness of the footing and prevents it from bending when subjected to soil movement. As a rule of thumb, a footing in stable soil should be about 100 mm wider both sides than the wall to be built on it.

Before constructing a footing in unstable soils, get advice about the best size of footing to use from a structural engineer.

SETTING OUT
The footing is marked out using profiles. Profile boards are pegs which are driven into the ground with a crossbar to which string lines are tied. Adjust the string lines until they are in the correct position. If you have to remove the string lines temporarily, nails can be driven into the crossbars to mark their position. Mark the edge of the footing, the edge of the brickwork, the thickness of the brickwork, and so on.

Mark the edge of the footing on the ground with chalk dust then excavate to the required depth. This will depend on the size of the wall and footing, but aim to have the top of the footing about 50 mm below finished ground level. You can excavate by hand or use a machine like a backhoe (on a contract basis) for a larger project – it will make life much easier.

Footings are best constructed of reinforced concrete with a minimum strength of 20 MPa, or, if you are mixing your own concrete, a mixture of one part cement, two parts sand and four parts gravel (1:2:4). Trench mesh is commonly used for reinforcing and is available in a range of widths to suit various footing widths. Place the mesh clear of the bottom of the excavation, and surround it by at least 40 mm of concrete to prevent corrosion.

Mix and pour concrete (see Concreting Skill class). It need not be finished to a high level, just well compacted and screeded. The concrete should be cured damp or covered for about a week.

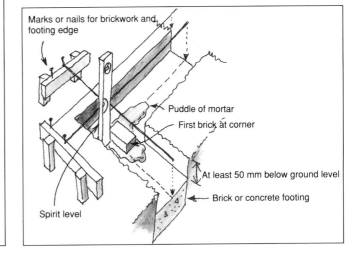

Marks or nails for brickwork and footing edge

Puddle of mortar

First brick at corner

At least 50 mm below ground level

Brick or concrete footing

Spirit level

Retaining walls

Low retaining walls are well within the skills of a home handyperson.

They are used to support banks and create level spaces in terracing, or to make raised beds in gardens where changes of level are needed or drainage is poor. Raised beds involve less stooping and can be gardened from a wheelchair. The walls make strong patterns in the landscape and are virtually earth containers which you can fill with the right soil whatever the quality of the ground soil beneath. Vegetables and flowers in raised beds are more easily protected from children and animals.

The building material for retaining walls should match house materials if the walls are near the house. There are many choices: brick, precast concrete block, stone or timber. Informal walls can be built of tiered railway sleepers, natural logs, or treated pine poles standing upright or laid horizontally.

Walls from 30-60 cm are fairly easy to build but they still have to retain large amounts of earth and must be stable and properly drained. Stability means solid anchorage against the weight of water-saturated earth. Drainage is provided by rows of weep holes, or drainage pipes through, or behind, the wall which will prevent water pressure building up behind the wall and undermining it, possibly causing its collapse. It is best to backfill the area behind a retaining wall with up to 30 cm of coarse drainage material, such as rubble

and gravel, between the wall and the earth bank. Where possible, direct water around the wall.

Concrete blocks are easy to handle and can be painted or stuccoed, but need a concrete footing, as do bricks, and some stone walls. This could be at least 300 mm deep and 150 mm wider than the wall base. For higher walls, reinforcing rods could be set vertically into the concrete footing to anchor the lower courses of hollow concrete blocks. Don't forget to leave weep holes or insert drainage pipes at intervals.

Crib block walling, where the slabs interlock without mortar, provides a strong wall with planting pockets. It should have a backward lean. It is not suitable for irregular, curved shapes, but walls can be dismantled and blocks re-used.

Low retaining walls of stone will hold earth banks, and can be dry stone or mortared. Provide stability by making the outer face slope well back towards the bank, by about 45° (in some cases 15° may be more realistic). Stones should overlap the course below for at least half their width – following the old adage to always place one stone on two. The inner face can be perpendicular or slope backwards into the earth bank or drainage fill. The higher the wall the more angle is needed on the outer face, but high stone walls need professional know-how. With even small walls, don't stand below stones on sloping land; drop stones from about 10-15 cm onto the stones beneath – the stones bed better.

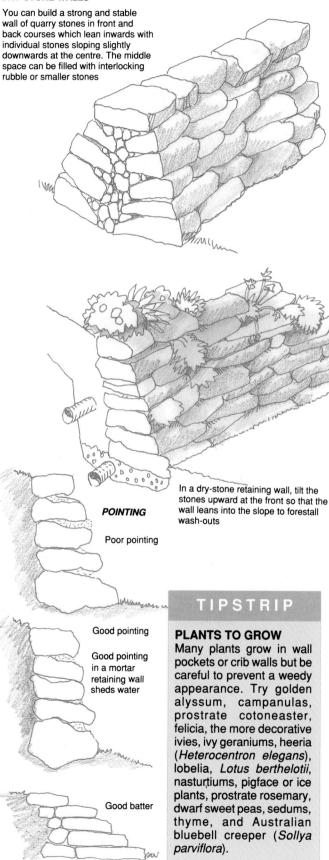

DRY-STONE WALLS

You can build a strong and stable wall of quarry stones in front and back courses which lean inwards with individual stones sloping slightly downwards at the centre. The middle space can be filled with interlocking rubble or smaller stones

In a dry-stone retaining wall, tilt the stones upward at the front so that the wall leans into the slope to forestall wash-outs

POINTING

Poor pointing

Good pointing

Good pointing in a mortar retaining wall sheds water

Good batter

Staggered brick wall

There are many options for building a masonry dividing wall in the garden. Materials range from basic brick to cut stone, staggered brick to screen block, concrete block to rubble, and many in between.

The bonding styles in brickwork give rise to many attractive alternatives including Flemish, stretcher, English and Colonial bonds.

Consideration should be given to the stability of any wall, especially in windy conditions. In general, it would be unwise to build a single-brick wall greater than 1200 mm in height with no other support – yet with double brickwork the wall could be increased to 1800 mm with few problems. As walls get stabilised by adding engaged piers, or by staggering the walls or saw-toothing them, the strength increases remarkably.

Our project idea involves building a garden wall of conventional bricks, 1500 mm high, laid in stretcher bond. At this height, in an area where the exposure to winds will not be greater than 27 m per second, a single-brick wall can be used, as long as it is staggered by 480 mm at 3000 mm intervals. This gives a total depth of wall of 590 mm, and the alcoves created by staggering the wall can be used for planting.

Set out on the ground or use string lines to mark where the wall is to be built. Check all dimensions, and erect profile boards as described on page 281 to locate the edge of the wall.

Mark accurately on the ground where excavations are needed. Then excavate.

The garden wall will require a footing: in this case, a reinforced concrete strip footing 300 mm wide by 250 mm deep is sufficient. Excavate the ground to a firm foundation, at least 50 mm deeper than the footing thickness. Lay steel reinforcing rods or trench mesh and tie in place, then pour the concrete, ensuring that it finishes level. A series of pegs driven in to mark the correct final levels at the edge of the

excavation may help with this. Allow the concrete to cure until the next weekend.

Set out the location of the wall in unbonded brickwork. If previously removed, set up string lines to precisely mark where the brickwork is to be laid. Mix the mortar, and lay the first course of bricks. Make sure this first course is truly level, as the rest of the job will depend on this first base.

Lay down a length of brick reinforcing on the first course, making sure it is centred over the bricks. Build up a corner four bricks high using a gauge rod (see Bricklaying Skill class), and repeat on the next corner. Check each corner not only with the gauge rod, but also with the spirit level to ensure plumbness. The two end corners need to have buttresses built to stabilise them: in this instance a 230 x 350 mm buttress will be sufficient – using a half-brick, this can be bonded into the wall design (vertical DPC if abutting the house wall).

Using string lines held with line pins in the wet mortar, or

by wrapping around brick batts, fill in between the built-up corners.

Repeat the previous steps along and up the entire wall. After each four courses, install another layer of brick reinforcing mesh into the mortar.

The last course at the top will perhaps look best if the bricks are laid on edge. Do this carefully, also to a string line. Even better in this case is to use slightly wider slabs that will allow rainwater to drip away from the wall.

At the end of each half-day's work, carefully rub off any excess mortar, and tool the joints if necessary. Messy mortar over bricks can be cleaned using hydrochloric acid mixed one part with 20 parts clean water (1:20) or brickwork cleaner. Wear protective clothing for this job. Prior to cleaning, dampen the wall thoroughly to ensure that the acid solution stays on the surface where the mortar stains are.

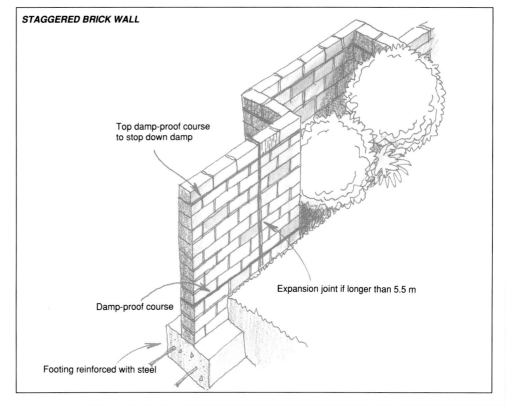

STAGGERED BRICK WALL

Top damp-proof course to stop down damp

Damp-proof course

Expansion joint if longer than 5.5 m

Footing reinforced with steel

Three big basics

A garden has to be functional if you want to fully enjoy it, and this means considering practical points such as drainage, watering, and lighting.

It is no good having flower beds that are swept away in the first storms of autumn, banks that erode, or patios and paths which flood. In a hot, dry summer, hand-watering is tiring and time-wasting when a watering system can do it all. Nor does it make sense to only enjoy the garden until the sun goes down. Lighting the garden means that you can go outdoors to enjoy scented summer nights and softly lit plants.

Drainage

A drainage plan that works prevents erosion, flooding, and swampy conditions in which few plants survive. Take a look during heavy rain to see where and how fast rainwater flows through the garden and where it pools. Drainage is basically an interception process – to stop or slow water down. It is very hard to control water once it gathers speed and volume, particularly in built-up areas where there is little undeveloped land to absorb a deluge.

If you alter land levels, you alter natural drainage patterns and must give rainwater a safe path to follow. There are various methods. In one large garden, a shallow, wide grassy dip forms a small lake in heavy rain, protecting the rest of the garden from flooding – and for a few days water insects and birds visit. A more usual method is to direct water to main stormwater drains through open-dish or channel drains of concrete or terracotta. Don't direct any flow onto your neighbours' land, it may have legal consequences. If you have big drainage problems, consult an expert.

Runoff down a slope is slowed by wide, shallow drainage ditches dug across the slope, which can be used as seasonal streams or decorative 'dry stream' beds as in Japanese landscaping. Even in a shower they help to trap some water for plants on their banks. Water can be directed to a drain running down the side of the site and then to main stormwater drains. Ditches work well if your garden collects water from neighbours' land above you – intercept the water as high on the slope as possible, before it gathers speed. Narrow, deep ditches can be used where space is limited, either open or pebble-filled.

To deal with subsoil water, lay perforated plastic or terracotta land drains over gravel in a trench. The water percolates through the slots. Lay shadecloth or fibre netting over the pipe to keep slots clean, then add a top layer of gravel, then earth. The drain must have a gradual, slight fall towards the outlet, which preferably is a main stormwater drain or, failing that, a soakaway. The pit is 1-1.2 m deep filled with drainage rubble – but it will only handle limited water. Drainage strips rather than pipes are also available and easily laid.

Drains around the house, alongside the drive and patio and at the base of slopes and retaining walls, will direct water away from paths and outdoor living areas. These can be open drains as described, drainage strips, or ready-made drainage channels which come with their own grating.

On steep slopes, never leave earth bare but bind it with ground covers, trees,

1 To avoid flooding, this rock causeway is built to collect runoff from the garden and does not detract from the charm of the garden courtyard

2 Soft, low-level lighting near a path

3 A simple system for watering the garden: rest the garden hose in a hose holder which can be turned to water different areas of the garden

DUANE NORRIS

shrubs and grass. Rocks also hold earth in place, but mulch is washed away.

Watering systems

Installing a watering system minimises water lost through runoff and thus saves on water costs. It delivers water direct to the plants and needs only the time to turn on a tap. Even that can be done automatically if you want. The piping goes underground or beneath a mulch. You can start with a simple system and then progress to more elaborate layouts by adding the numerous components available, and you can rearrange layouts.

Most irrigation works with a main supply line from the tap, to which feeder lines are attached in a pattern to suit the garden layout. These then attach to either sprinklers or drippers – the two can't be mixed on the same line. Feeder lines are narrower for drippers.

Plan your layout to scale on graph paper to work out the amount of tubing and emitters wanted. Manufacturers of equipment or kits give you directions about spray patterns, distance needed between sprinklers and so on. You need to know the flow rate of your water supply to know how many emitters you can operate at the one time. This is done by checking how many seconds it takes to fill a 9-litre bucket with water. You will also need an on-line filter to prevent any clogging (it should be regularly cleaned) and possibly an anti-siphoning valve such as a double-seal

Three types of microirrigation:
❏ *Microsprays provide a gentle spray for watering flower beds, shrubs and trees. The full, half or quarter circle spray heads prevent water being wasted.*
❏ *Drip or trickle irrigation delivers water selectively and slowly to a series of individual plants, pots, or hanging baskets, or a vegetable patch. It waters directly to the root zone without drift and with minimum runoff on a bank. Place drippers outwards from plant stems to encourage root spread.*
❏ *The third type of irrigation is unobtrusive pop-up sprinklers for lawns which are set below ground level – the sprinkler heads pop up when water flows through. There are sprinklers for high or low water pressure.*

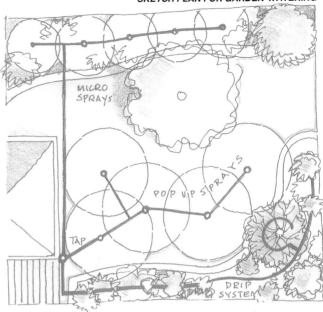

check to stop backwash into the house water supply, and possibly an in-line draincock to allow the supply pipework to be drained in heavy frost areas. Also available are automatic timers, pressure regulators, in-line taps to close off feeder lines, sensors for moisture reading and water gauges.

Lighting

Lighting is both practical and ornamental, whether it is a simple downlight for steps, or a floodlit pool. There are many possible ways to go but while some installations are best left to a skilled tradesperson, low-voltage lighting can be installed by anyone. It is a system whereby a transformer reduces the mains voltage to 12 volts, and properly used there is little chance of any dangerous shock. A transformer plugs into a 240 volt powerpoint which is switched on from the house.

Low-voltage cable can be run along walls or fences, up trees, or along trenches. Make sure the cable is placed

where it will not be damaged by a garden spade when digging. The lighting uses less electricity because of the lower candlepower which contributes to subtle outdoor effects. White light shows the natural colour of flowers and low-wattage halogen globes are long-lasting. The system is virtually maintenance free and can easily be disconnected and moved to another place if wanted.

Lights are easy to install around existing plantings and can be flush with the ground. You can spotlight or silhouette a particular plant, a pool or waterfall, or floodlight the garden in front of a court, patio or deck. Lights can

come on in sequence or all at once, or areas not always used can be on a different switch. Some plants look better top-lit or back-lit, others are better lit from below. Place lights to throw dramatic shadows on walls or shine through translucent leaves. Use soft low-level lighting near steps, drives and paths.

Make a plan of your lighting layout and keep a copy of it for reference for yourself or subsequent owners of the house.

An alternative to low-voltage lighting is solar-powered lights, which can supply several hours of light from one sunny day. Some have a rechargeable battery back-up.

This lawn light is flush with the ground and is designed to light a garden feature

Good earth

Fertile earth is essential to well-grown plants, so keep it in good health by adding home-made compost.

Durable plastic compost bins provide a quick and easy solution for garden and household waste disposal

Composting is really imitating nature, making an organic soil mix from the decay of plant debris, and using it to both feed and condition the soil. It's a thrifty way to recycle kitchen and garden waste. Compost keeps soil texture dark, crumbly and water-absorbent, and encourages earthworms, which also aerate and enrich the soil. It's valuable in potting mixes or used as a mulch.

A well-made compost heap provides moist, aerated conditions in which decay-causing bacteria flourish. You can buy ready-made compost bins, particularly good for small gardens; use a pit; or make your own chicken-wire, brick, concrete-block or slatted-timber bins to take a heap. A bin needs three sides, a removable front and no base – the heap is built on the ground. Put bins in half shade where it is not too dank in winter or dry in summer, and near a water

supply. Ideally you need two or three bins, one ready for use and the others in varying stages of decay. A heap should be about 1.2 to 2 m high and wide. It will take all food waste, straw, hay, ash, seaweed, grass clippings, fallen leaves, pine needles, prunings, green legumes, unprinted paper or card-board, and spent flowers and annuals – but not rampant perennial or seeding weeds or any diseased material which may be a problem if the heap doesn't generate enough heat to destroy them.

On the bottom layer put twiggy rubbish to allow air in and water out. Then add about 20 cm of organic waste. Break up hard material to some extent or put it through a mulcher. Mix in some succulent green material, which adds nitrogen and a scatter of blood and bone manure – if there is too little nitrogen, composting is slow. Then add a 5 cm layer of soil or old

compost, and manure. Build up the heap in these layers. Add a small amount of hydrated or garden lime or dolomite to the heap at intervals but add it separately from manure. Turn the contents every 1-3 weeks to air the heap. Keep it moist, not wet. Cover the heap with a layer of soil and with plastic in heavy rain areas to stop nutrients being washed out. In dry areas a cover will conserve moisture. The compost is ready when it is dark, rich and contents are not really identifiable – usually in two or three months.

For a quick compost method, use a compost shredder or mulcher and mulch garden waste finely. Add to the heap without layering. Turn the pile every few days and keep moist. Fewer nutrients are lost in quick composting.

Improving soil types

Garden soil is seldom perfect. Sandy soil can get dry and hot, and rainwater drains through quickly leaching out nutrients, but it has good aeration and

warmth early in the season. Clay soil compacts, is difficult to work and causes runoff during rain. It holds water and nutrients well but lacks air.

Both soil types are greatly improved by adding large quantities of organic matter and conditioners such as compost, leafmould, well-rotted manure, peat, seaweed, or composted sawdust. Mix into the topsoil and add generous amounts each year. Mulch soil surfaces well.

Garden lime or dolomite (if the soil is acid) can make clay soil more porous, and you can also improve subsoil drainage.

TIPSTRIP

MAKING LEAFMOULD
Never burn autumn leaves – leafmould provides long-lasting humus, is much more water-retentive than topsoil, and is ideal for summer mulching. Fungi break down leaves but take much longer than composting organisms. Add manure to speed decay. Make a wire-enclosed heap in shade, pile leaves high and tamp down. Moisten if they dry out.

HOME-MADE COMPOST BIN

1200 mm (1.2 m)

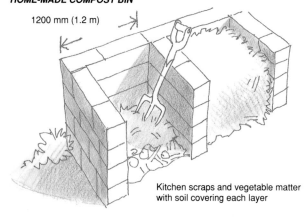

Kitchen scraps and vegetable matter with soil covering each layer

The planting framework

Planting is one of the most important aspects of a remodelled garden but it comes almost last in the landscaping schedule, just before you add finishing touches and furnishings.

Planting for privacy – this hedge archway leads through to a private courtyard

Once the hard landscaping of grading, drainage, paving, fencing, irrigation, lighting and soil preparation are finished, planting can begin.

Choice of plants is influenced of course by your landscape plan – whether, for example, you want an ecological garden of native trees and flowers to attract wildlife, or large sweeps of lawn or ground cover. You may want flowering hedges or a fast-growing concealing vine.

Plants have functions besides being beautiful: they are needed for screening and concealing; shading from hot sun and blocking wind; or covering ground areas, fences, pergola and walls. First of all decide what job the plant is supposed to do, then the eventual size of plant you want and its effect. Do you want an evergreen, or a deciduous plant that lets through winter sun? Then check the conditions the plant will face, whether it's sun or shade, moist or dry soil, windy or hot.

Most plants are suited to particular conditions, although some plants tolerate a wider range of conditions than others. Rainfall, soil (clay or sandy, acid or alkaline), humidity, light, heat and

frost are the variables to check out.

Now go looking for the right plant – armed with your shopping list. When you buy a plant, find out about its eventual height, spread and density, and its growth habit and flower and leaf colour. It's good insurance to buy unfamiliar plants in flower. Don't be impatient and buy too many fast-growing plants – most of these also grow large. Not all your choices will be right but it's possible to retrieve a mistake. Gardens change as they grow and you will want to regroup plantings from time to time.

Buy basic plants first, that is, the larger framework plants such as screening shrubs, two or three trees, boundary shrubs, then smaller fill-in shrubs. Add all the little plants when conditions are sheltered and fertile. The basic plants should be reliable, fairly tough and tolerant. These are likely to be plants that are familiar in local gardens and nurseries – they are commonly about because they survive well.

Low-level hedges and shrubs can be used very effectively to define different areas of the garden

This high garden boundary hedge provides a green backdrop to flower beds planted for their colour display

A profusion of perennials, annuals and ground-cover plants spill out over the pathway, creating a cottage garden look. Fragrant lavender bushes border the pathway

Garden style

Garden style means different things to different people. It can take more than masses of flowers and neat lawns to make your garden distinctive.

Deciding on the style of your garden – for example, whether it is cottage, formal, Mediterranean or contemporary in character – is a good starting point. There's no need to follow a style slavishly – keep its essential flavour, but use your own site, climate and lifestyle to give it individuality, adding special touches with a range of garden accessories and 'found' treasures.

An aesthetically pleasing garden may focus on a few very simple elements, or rely on many different elements to create a broad range of interest. For a small space or courtyard, it could be an oversized terracotta pot full of springtime ranunculus, a set of wind chimes, a classical fountain, or a cottage-style basket over-

flowing with pot plants; for a larger garden – a sundial, a bird bath, a garden statue or two, brass tap fittings or an ornate hose holder.

Whether it's large or small, every garden needs at least one special feature to make it stand out

288

8

9

10

11

12

13

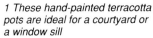

1 These hand-painted terracotta pots are ideal for a courtyard or a window sill

2 This trug makes a quaint pot-plant holder

3 These small terracotta birds are charming pathway ornaments

4 This classical-style fountain and pond enhance an already elegant balcony

5 Garden plaque for a cottage garden

6 This ornate cast iron hose holder adds a touch of class to a common garden hose

7 Water for the birds – a bird

bath is ideal for a larger garden

8 Curved metal hoops serve to define this garden edge

9 Beautifully detailed brass tap fittings

10 For a smaller garden project, why not hand-paint your old watering can?

11 Brass frog

12 Sundial for a formal garden

13 Music to the ears – wind chimes

14 Garden statues can be an integral part of your garden design

15 Pathway planting – flowers in a terracotta pot

14

15

An attractive, welcoming entrance can make all the difference to your home, and not just the front entrance; the focus may be on a single feature or on several.

UPFRONT IDEAS

Your special focus may be steps decorated with flowering plants leading to a front door, a rustic garden path, a framed view through to another area of the garden, a gate or even a boundary fence – it may be quite spectacular, elegantly understated or delightfully simple in character.

Paths

First, paths should be easy to walk along, and secondly, they should take you where you are going without the sort of unnatural curves that give you an irrepressible urge to take short cuts across the lawn or garden beds.

The paving used for fast-drying service paths around the house area is usually determined by the house and garden style. The material can be stone, bricks laid in various ways, brick pavers, tiles, cobbles, an aggregate finish, concrete in situ, or paving slabs. The path should be wide enough for two people to walk abreast. If there is danger of too many paths intersecting in the overall garden plan, then use wide-paved areas interlocking with planted areas – it will look much better than separate paths. Concrete needn't be dull.

By using different-shaped forms you can give it fluid or rough stone shapes – it can be surfaced with aggregate or pebbles, or used with hand-set stones if you lay them yourself to keep cost down, or finished to look like slate.

Stepping stones are charming in more casual areas of the garden, or as side paths, but need to be large and well placed for easy stepping. They can be of stone, precast concrete slabs or timber rounds or sleepers. Plants to use around paving stones and along path edges include alyssum and *Limnanthes* (poached egg flower) which self-sow, gazanias, *Erigeron karvinskianus*, violets, violas, *Festuca ovina* 'Glauca', small ferns, Mondo grass, ajuga, lobelia, forget-me-nots, campanula, baby's tears, thyme and other small herbs.

Timber is more versatile than you may think for path-making. You can build raised boardwalks, or use timber planks or sleepers laid in rough slabs over coarse sand or gravel.

Bark chips, shredded bark, crushed rock, scoria or crushed lava, gravel, mulch, sand or raked earth are suitable ways to surface paths in more distant garden corners

where hard surfacing is not worth the cost. These informal paths can be wide, and even have a tree or shrub growing in them, or they can be narrow, curving mysteriously out of sight. They are easy to install but are best with a border of brick, stone or timber to hold the loose

materials in place. Loose-laid paths need to be stepped down slopes to prevent materials being washed away. The soft materials like bark or mulch will need regular replacement. If you use gravel, make sure the grade is too coarse to stick to shoes.

3

4

6

1 *Springtime makes the front entrance of this home even more welcoming*

2 *A blossoming container garden is the main feature of this rather formal front entrance*

3 *This hedge-lined pathway frames up the view seen in another part of the garden, making an attractive vista`*

4 *The back door – a back entrance made charming by stone paving and pretty ground covers*

5 *A flower-lined country garden path leading to a rustic timber gate*

6 *A wrought-iron gate bounded by a tall perimeter hedge*

7 *This view to the bay is magnificently realised through the framework of this simple pergola*

5

7

Concrete path

A good first concrete project to undertake is a concrete path – it can easily be divided into a number of bays over several weekends if necessary.

This flower-lined concrete path is hard wearing, economical and makes an attractive entrance

The average width for a concrete path is about 900 mm, but there are no hard-and-fast rules. On a flat block of land, there will be few complications. However, on sloping sites, the path may need to take a more indirect route and gradients should be kept lower – a path that winds through a landscaped garden can be most pleasant.

Such a path may require one or several steps at various locations to make up height (see Project idea, Garden steps and ramps). In this situation the path can butt against the top of a lower flight of steps and act as the footing for the next set.

Once the location and route are decided, building the path is simple. Let's say that the path to be built is 900 mm wide, runs for a distance of 12 m and will be 100 mm thick.

PREPARING THE SITE
❑ Mark out where the path is to go; clear the site of vegetation, digging up any roots still visible, then compact the soil.
❑ If the path is to sit above the level of the surrounding terrain, fill sóft spots with hardcore (crushed rock) or gravel or a mixture of aggregate and sand. This material needs to be well compacted.
❑ If the path is to lie flush with the surrounding terrain, dig out the complete area to the intended thickness of the concrete plus sub-base. The

base material, e.g. hardcore, plus the thickness of the concrete will give the finished level of the concrete.

If the path is to butt up against the house wall, the finished level must be at least 150 mm below the damp-proof course (DPC) and vents.

SETTING OUT
Accurately set out the formwork for the path. Old floorboards work well if the path is straight; if it is curved, a double thickness of hardboard supported by pegs can be used. Securely peg the formwork in place.

Cut and fit light steel reinforcing in place, 50 mm inside the formwork, and on 65 mm bar chairs or spacers, so that the reinforcing is 25 mm below the top surface.

EXPANSION JOINTS
Provide for expansion joints in the path. An expansion joint consists of a 10 mm gap between adjacent slabs of concrete. In concreting, one of these should be placed every 5 to 6 m, and also where concrete butts against another surface, such as a brick wall or other concrete slabs. The joint

is normally filled with bituminised, low-density fibreboard, which is available in strips. Foamed plastic expansion joints are also available.

Expansion joints are an ideal point to break off for the day, as the work can be formed to that point. When you start work again, this can be replaced with a similar length of expansion jointing material.

CONCRETE
Calculate how much concrete you need and either order it or mix it yourself. The quantity is easy to calculate. Multiply width by length by thickness: 0.9 x 12 x 0.1 m = 1.1 cubic m of concrete. If only doing one bay at a time, you will probably need half this amount twice over. Pour the concrete, rake it into position, and work it to the correct height.

When surface water has evaporated, finish as required. Tool the edges to make them neat, and also tool in dummy joints at 2 m intervals along the path (these act as planes of weakness should the path begin cracking due to shrinkage).

The concrete should be cured moist for at least a week by covering with polythene sheet or by hosing morning and night. If in a cold area, cover with sacking. The last job is to strip the formwork away and do any necessary backfilling.

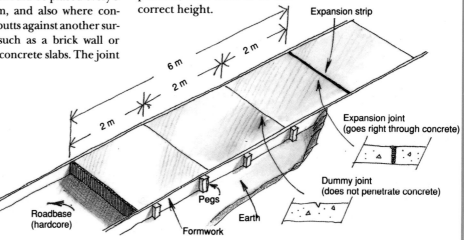

6 m
2 m
2 m
2 m
Roadbase (hardcore)
Pegs
Formwork
Earth
Expansion strip
Expansion joint (goes right through concrete)
Dummy joint (does not penetrate concrete)

Skill class
Concreting

A concrete path, drive or base will last a lifetime, provided that it is properly mixed and laid on a firm foundation.

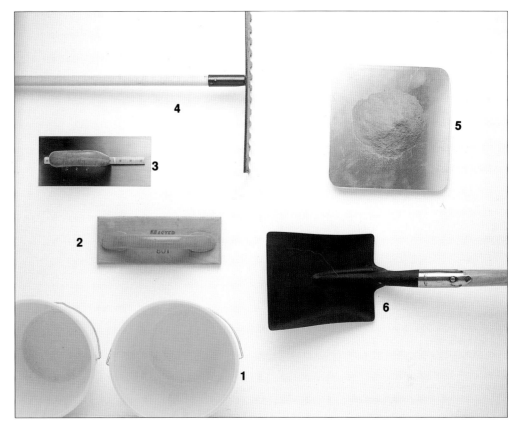

1 Buckets
2 Wood float
3 Steel float
4 Rake
5 Metal hawk (plastering)
6 Shovel

MATERIALS AND MIXES

Concrete is essentially made up of three separate ingredients – cement, sand and aggregate (ballast). A chemical reaction with water causes the concrete components to set into a hard, artificial rock.

Cement is a completely dehydrated powder which is made at extremely high temperatures and ground into a very fine powder before being packaged for sale. When water is added, cement undergoes hydration, which causes it to bond to other components. Cement that isn't fresh will not bond well and results in weak concrete.

The sand used in concrete must be clean and relatively 'sharp' as this provides better bonding than rounded grains.

The coarse aggregate for concrete can be ordered between 7 mm and 20 mm. The aggregate should be a durable material such as basalt, dolerite or cracked river gravel. The preferred shape is cubic but rounded pebbles are common.

The basic rule for the water used in concreting is 'if you wouldn't drink it, don't use it'! Water should be kept to a workable minimum as high water volumes both weaken the mix and increase the amount of shrinkage cracks.

The mixes of concrete vary with the type of project. A popular standard-duty concrete mix is one part cement, three parts sand and six parts aggregate (1:3:6). This is suitable for patios, paths and drives. Others include one part cement to 2.5 parts sand and four parts gravel (1:2.5:4), which is a slightly stronger mix. There are obviously other mixes designed for special purposes.

If ordering ready-mixed concrete, it can be specified by its compressive strength, for instance 20 megapascals (MPa). A typical path on a stable soil would use 20 MPa concrete.

> The strength of concrete may be quoted in megapascals (MPa) or in newtons per square millimetre (N/mm²). The units are the same.

Mixing by hand on site is only warranted if the amount of concrete is small, say up to a quarter of a cubic metre. For on-site mixing, a mechanical cement mixer can be used to mix up to half a cubic metre at a time. Make sure you measure the components accurately, using a bucket or similar.

If a larger quantity is required, order ready-mixed concrete. All you have to do is specify a time and a mix, and any other special instructions. The truck should have easy access to the pouring site. A con-crete pumping contractor can be hired for difficult-access sites. This might seem expensive, but will save muscles, patience and time. An average load of concrete will remain workable for up to 2-3 hours.

All tools should be to hand. For any but the smallest jobs, it is preferable to have at least two people on the job.

HOW MUCH CONCRETE?

It's important to accurately calculate the quantity of concrete needed. To find the volume of concrete required in cubic metres, multiply the length (in metres), the width (in metres) and the thickness (in metres). A concrete area 10 m long by 1 m wide and 100 mm thick will require 1 cubic metre of concrete (10 m x 1 m x 0.1 m = 1 cubic metre).

TOOLS AND EQUIPMENT

❏ buckets – two same-size buckets (one for cement; one for aggregate and the water)
❏ shovels – two (one for ce-ment; one for other material)
❏ screed rail or board – a heavy straightedge used when forming up
❏ a sturdy wheelbarrow – for mixing concrete and transporting loads of mixed cement
❏ steel float – for smooth-finishing concrete
❏ wood float – for a textured finish
❏ tamping beam – for compacting concrete (hire)
❏ garden roller or punner – for compacting base material
❏ rake – for spreading concrete inside formwork

For setting out and formwork: saw, hammer, tape measure, spirit level, straightedge, builder's square, string lines and pegs

PREPARATION

Mixing and pouring concrete is quite demanding physically, and the whole operation must be performed fairly quickly. Remember, concrete is heavy and if placed in the wrong spot is difficult to remove!

The first thing to do is to mark out exactly where the concrete is to go. Setting out can be done using basic geometry (the Pythagoras formula 3:4:5), remembering that the diagonals of a rectangle or square are equal. Use a builder's square, which is in the proportion 3:4:5 – the most convenient size is 900 x 1200 x 1500 mm. The angle between the shortest sides will be 90°. Mark the area to be excavated with a string line, or with lines of lime on the ground if you anticipate using a mechanical excavator.

All organic matter in the area must be removed (this includes the roots of larger plants that have already been removed). Decide whether any large trees are to remain in the vicinity of the concrete – some trees are quite capable of lifting and cracking a concrete path.

The usual thickness of a concrete path is 75 mm to 100 mm which, in turn, should be laid on a prepared bed. Concrete can be laid on most surfaces, but provide a 50 mm layer of base material (hardcore, broken bricks, stone, clean rubble) for a good strong base. The total thickness of the excavation will be about 125 mm to 150 mm minimum, if the concrete is to be at the same level as the surrounding areas.

Formwork must be built to provide a neat, clean edge to the concrete. When concrete is being poured and worked, considerable pressure is brought to bear on the formwork, so it must be sturdy and well fixed. Handy materials such as old 25 mm-thick floorboards are ideal. The formwork must be securely pegged to the ground and well fixed to the pegs to prevent any chance of movement. Using a spirit level (900 mm long) and a length of timber, spend time adjusting the formwork to the exact level of the finished concrete. If wanted, allow for a slope or a slight dome in the centre of the path for drainage. Also allow for expansion joints. Drive the pegs holding the formwork to the same or a lower level than the top edge of the formwork.

In paths, it is of little concern whether moisture can rise up through the concrete, so a waterproof membrane is not necessary under the slab. The concrete will need to be reinforced with steel mesh and/or bars to control shrinkage cracking. A light, welded steel mesh is suitable. Because steel embedded in concrete doesn't corrode, make sure all reinforcement steel is placed 25 mm below the top of the surface. Bar chairs or spacers hold the mesh off the ground while the concrete is poured. They come in a number of heights to suit most slab thicknesses.

POURING CONCRETE

It is best to moisten the ground before you pour the concrete – this stops the water being sucked out of the mix, resulting in incomplete hydration of the concrete at ground level.

Pour the concrete directly into the formwork from the truck or, if you are mixing by hand, from the barrows or buckets. If the mix is poured from a height of greater than 1 m, provide baffle boards to ensure that the heavy portion of the mix does not separate from the lighter sand and cement. The baffle can simply be horizontal slats of timber nailed to a temporary frame.

The wet concrete is poured into the formwork and raked out to about 10 mm above the level of the formwork, allowing for compaction. Air trapped in

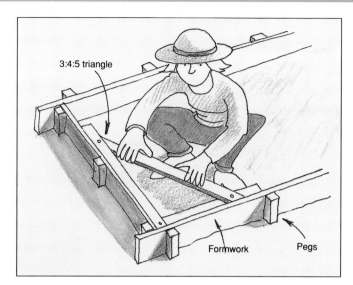

Formwork

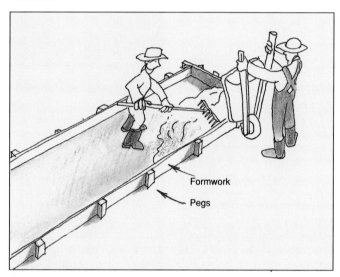

Pouring and raking

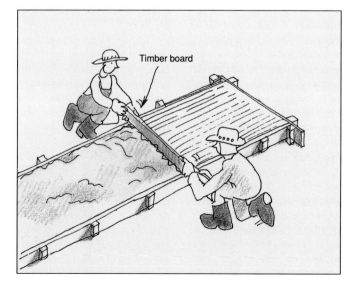

Using timber to level concrete

the mix is eliminated by compacting or vibrating the concrete. This is easiest with two people – one on each end of a 100 x 50 mm timber board, or larger. By using a downward and sideways chopping action, and pushing excess concrete away from the finished area, good compaction can be assured. If there are any tight corners, or if you want to pay special attention to the edges, a smaller piece of timber used as a ramming rod will ensure a perfect job – as will the heel of a boot!

The working of the concrete will cause a considerable amount of water and fine particles to rise to the surface. This will allow easy finishing once the initial surface water has evaporated.

Concrete setting is a chemical reaction of hydration. If the concrete is encouraged to dry too quickly, it will be weak and dusty. Curing involves keeping the concrete moist after the initial setting has taken place. In its crudest form, a light spray with a hose, morning and night, will achieve this. Other methods include covering the concrete with a plastic sheet or wet hessian to control water evaporation. If there is a danger of frost, cover with an insulating material to prevent freezing.

The various finishes that can be applied to concrete will depend largely on the function of the area

Repairing cracked concrete

Cracking in concrete is quite common; however, not every crack is a disaster. Concrete typically forms small 'shrinkage' cracks, which can be ignored. Such cracks are not structural and are usually quite shallow. If you to try to clean this kind of crack out to fill, you will probably make it worse, both structurally and visually.

Concrete that has major cracking with associated displacement, such as when the side of a path subsides, is not possible to patch, and that section should be totally relaid. Straight joints can be achieved by cutting out the section using a concrete saw. The new concrete should be joined to the existing concrete using an expansion jointing material.

Many cracks and holes are annoying, but may show no real displacement. The common material used to fill these cracks and holes is a mixture of one part cement to three parts sand (1:3) – or a bag of sand-cement mix could be used. It is mixed using water with a PVA-based bonding agent mixed 50:50 with the water. It is important the filler is not too wet as it will tend to shrink away from the sides of the crack. An alternative is to use a quick-setting chemical cement.

The crack or hole should be at least 15 mm deep, and it's a good idea (if possible) to undercut the hole to ensure a positive key. This is done with a cold chisel and club hammer. Wear eye protection when doing this as the chips can be quite dangerous.

Paint the cleaned area with the PVA bonding agent, mixed one to three with water (1:3). When tacky, fill the hole or crack with the sand-cement mix. Force it well into the hole and use a float to level it to path or drive level. A smoother finish can be obtained using a steel trowel.

The repaired area should be cured wet for about a week. This can be done by covering the spot with a plastic sheet or gently spraying it morning and night with a watering can or hose set on fine spray.

Where the hole is on an edge, the edge should first be formed up with an old 25 mm floorboard or similar and pegs to hold it securely. Then follow the same procedure as above. An edging tool can be used to match any existing finish.

Some cracks which are only up to 3 mm thick and where there is little displacement, can be effectively repaired with epoxy resins. The adhesion of epoxy to concrete is better than is generally achieved using sand-cement mixes.

The best way to repair the crack is to clean the crevice as thoroughly as possible. If available, use an air compressor and air blower to clear out the crack. Quick-setting epoxy resin can then be mixed and applied using an applicator gun. If the crack is horizontal, let the epoxy run into the crack by gravity.

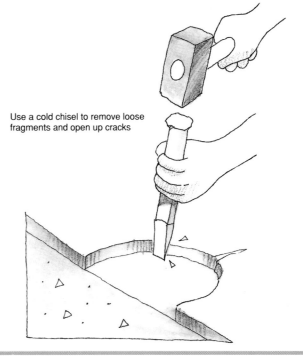

Use a cold chisel to remove loose fragments and open up cracks

Timber picket gate

Gates come in many shapes, sizes and materials. They all have one thing in common, however – they deteriorate over time and occasionally need to be maintained, repaired, or completely rebuilt.

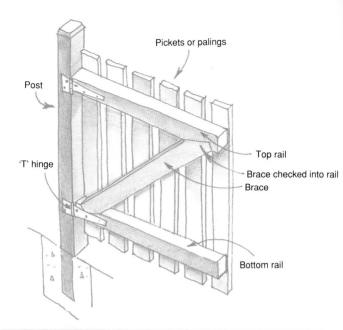

Building a solid timber picket gate is not difficult, and may be a better alternative to repairing old faithful yet again! If the gate posts need replacing, use treated timber 100 x 100 mm, set 450 mm into concrete both sides of the gate.

MATERIALS
top and bottom rails (the width of the opening), 38 mm or 50 mm by 100 mm treated pine
brace, same as rails but 1.5 times as long
palings or pickets to suit, 25 x 100 mm
two 100 mm or 150 mm 'T' hinges
a gate latch and keeper
nails and screws to suit
paint or other selected finish e.g. timber preservative or stain

TIME
One day

STEP BY STEP

1 Mark and cut the two rails to length. Allow for a clearance of 10 mm at the gate posts.

2 Lay the two rails on a flat surface, and place on them two pickets, one at each end. Adjust the distance between the rails so that the bottom rail is about 100 mm up from the bottom of the picket, and the top rail down

75-100 mm from the top of the picket. Nail the two pickets to the rails.

3 Turn the frame over and, measuring the diagonals, square up the frames. Then hold the brace diagonally across the rails, and mark off where it is to be cut. The brace runs from the bottom hinge side to the top latch side. It preferably should be slightly recessed into the top and bottom rails.

4 Dismantle the gate, cut the brace to length, and rebate the rails. Prime and undercoat or stain all the timber components. Then reassemble the rails and brace, driving a screw about 50 mm from the end of the brace into each rail.

5 Turn the frame over and nail into place all the pickets, making sure they are well-and-truly aligned.

6 Block up the gate on offcuts of wood to screw the gate to the posts. Screw the long flap of the 'T' hinge to the gate, and the stub side to the post. Initially only fix one screw for each hinge to the post; then check the operation to ensure it works and is square. Once right, fit the rest of the screws.

7 Apply final coats of paint or stain, and fix on the latch.

Rustic timber gate in a natural-style garden

This tall white timber gate with a hedge surround opens into a private court

DUANE NORRIS

All about fences

Fences come in many different sizes, shapes and materials – they have an important function and are an important part of your outdoor design scheme.

Fences have a number of functions: they are used for decorative purposes, to define a boundary, to act as a screen (for privacy, as a windbreak, and to keep noise levels down), or for safety and security (to keep intruders out and children or animals in!).

Not all fence types will perform all of these functions. For instance, a solid fence is not a suitable swimming pool surround as it would make pool supervision of children difficult. Similarly, a picket fence is not an effective sound barrier.

Fences may be made of a number of different materials including timber and panel, metal, and masonry.

Plastic picket fences are also available. The ranch style is especially popular. This type of fence has hollow posts and cellular UPVC 'boards'.

Timber fences

The options in style and decoration for timber fences are limitless. They include:
❑ post and rail (ranch) – a simple arrangement of uprights and normally two horizontal rails
❑ paling – a post and rail fence with palings fixed to one side
❑ sloped paling fence – a paling fence where palings are installed at an angle
❑ overlapped paling – similar to a paling fence, but the palings are overlapped to provide complete screening
❑ board and batten – similar to a paling fence, but the gap between palings is covered by a batten
❑ lap and cap – an overlapped paling fence, with an additional cap fixed to the top
❑ trellis – a post and rail fence covered with timber or composite trellis panels
❑ picket – a post and rail fence, clad with spaced decorative pickets or slats
❑ panel – a series of posts, sometimes with rails, typically clad with prefabricated panels of timber
❑ log – heavy-looking fence; can be post and rail style, or horizontal screen style

Metal fences

Metal fences are normally galvanised steel, but for some years have been available in factory-applied colours including plastic coating (in the case of chainlink fences). The variations in metal fences include the following:
❑ post and wire – posts of timber, metal or concrete, supporting wire (more suitable for country properties)
❑ chainlink – posts with interlinked wire mesh
❑ post and welded mesh – posts with panels of welded mesh, normally sold as a system. Certain grades available as swimming pool fences
❑ Ornamental 'iron' railings – which today are steel or aluminium – make a strong and durable open fence. Many companies now specialise in Victorian-style railings with ornate railing heads to cap the vertical bars

Masonry fences

Masonry fences/walls grade into garden walls, but are the most suitable for noise abatement. Normally they are of brick, but can also be made of stone, cement block or screen blocks. They may incorporate decorative aluminium lace panels, or even timber panel sections. Masonry fences are the most expensive to erect. They are also the heaviest and need proper footings to avoid early cracking.

This picket fence extends the stone wall, providing a backdrop for climbing and flowering plants

Boundary fences

High front boundary fences in built-up areas should be approved by your local authority. Many front fences are of masonry construction, and you are legally required to meet stringent building standards – to avoid physical damage, and the likelihood of the fence falling onto land outside your property.

Fences as noise barriers

Virtually anything placed between the noise source and the receiver, will have some effect in lessening noise – but to be really effective, the barrier must be continuous, weigh at least 15 kg per sq m and have no gaps, cracks or openings.

Fence types that comply with the weight requirement are masonry, such as brick, with filled mortar joints, a double layer of 15 mm thick timber planks or 7 mm thick fibre-cement sheets overlapped to eliminate any gaps.

The gates have to be designed to the same criteria as the fence and must seal properly within rebates to eliminate cracks.

The fence should be high and preferably continue along the neighbours' front gardens, or up the side boundary without a reduction in height. This would normally require local authority approval as in most cases the fence will not be a standard structure.

The height should be estimated on the basis that the more sound has to bend, the greater the reduction in noise. If sound has to bend through 7° over a fence to reach the hearer, you can expect a halving of the noise. If it has to bend through 20°, the noise will be reduced to about one-third. If you are on the high side of the street, the fence will have to be considerably higher than if you were on the lower side. It may be worth drawing some scale diagrams to work out how high the fence will need to be.

Soundproofing your home is important if you live in a high-traffic area

This rendered concrete wall is an attractive part of the front entrance and also acts as an effective noise barrier. The wall has been designed to complement the house's colour scheme and the timber gates set off the garage roof behind them

Skill class
Replacing a fence post

Paling fences, being timber and in contact with the ground, are prone to lean and rot over the years. Once rot has set in, the post will have to be replaced. Once posts start rotting, chances are that more than one needs replacing, and it may become more economical to replace the whole fence.

To replace a whole post is quite difficult as the posts are mortised to accept the fence rails, and normally the rails are fitted through the post, or two rails join in the mortise on the splay. For this reason, and because the rot is normally confined to the base of the post, it makes sense to only replace the bottom of the post.

To replace the bottom of the post, temporarily support the fence from both sides, either side of the post, with timber braces propped under the top rails, leaving enough room to work. Cut off the bottom of the fence post about 200 mm above the rotted area.

Excavate a hole about 600 to 900 mm deep below the post, pull out the remains of the rotted post, and insert a new galvanised steel post bottom to within about 50 mm of the bottom. When placing the steel pole, align it with the fence post, and hold it in place with clamps. Drill through the post and the fence, insert two or three steel bolts and tighten with washers on the timber side. Then pour the concrete – a premixed bag of concrete is handy for this kind of job. Pack the concrete in well, and cure it wet for three or four days. The props can then be removed and the fence will be supported.

The alternative is to use treated pine, and if the new post is 100 x 100 mm, the post bottom can be notched to sit under the cut-off end of the post as extra support. In some areas, concrete spurs or galvanised steel post supports are available, and their use is essentially the same.

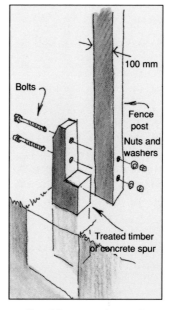

Should you need to replace a whole post, you will need to support the fence as already described. Dig around the base of the post to enable it to be removed. Then remove a paling on one side of the post, and cut through the top and bottom rails, hard against the post. Move the paling fence panel with rails back from the post. If possible, cut through or remove the rail-fixing nails holding the other rails to the post. If this proves too difficult, you will have to cut through these rails as well.

Remove the old post. This is often harder than it looks, as the rot forms an hour-glass shape on the post, with the bottom actually being quite sound, and makes it difficult to remove. You can also lever a post out by lashing a rail to the post and levering it up.

The new post should be of durable timber or treated. If the rails have slipped out of the post on one side, two mortises will have to be cut to take the rails. Otherwise a plain post can be used. Slip the rails (if applicable) into the mortises and stand the posts up. Using a spirit level and temporary braces, prop the post in its correct position. The hole can be refilled with well-compacted hardcore, gravel or concrete, sloped away from the post. This will allow moisture to seep away without the post standing in water. Fit the rails using preformed galvanised arris-rail brackets to secure.

Timber paling fence

This basic timber paling fence is a simple example of composite design, combining timber with galvanised steel poles or angle-iron metal posts.

To start with you will need to adapt our basic project to suit your situation. From this you can work out the quantities of timber required. The timber selected should be a durable timber, such as hardwood or treated pine. Angle-iron metal posts can be used instead of galvanised steel poles.

MATERIALS
timber rails
timber palings
galvanised steel poles or angle-iron metal posts
cold galvanising paint
premixed concrete
bolts
galvanised twisted shank nails
oil stain or fence finish of your choice
string lines
post-hole borer
electric drill

TIME
Two to three days

STEP BY STEP

1 Set out the line of fence with a string line, and mark the post holes. Excavate the holes with a post-hole borer to a depth of approximately 600-750 mm if possible.

2 Sit the galvanised steel poles into the ground, and measure the desired height of each pole. Cut the poles to length (if necessary). Spot-prime the cuts with cold galvanising paint.

3 Using premixed concrete, fill the holes around the poles with concrete and brace the poles so that they are truly plumb. Do the two end poles first and use a string line to ensure that all the others are in a perfectly straight line.

4 Mark the position of the timber rails on the poles. Cut the rails to length and bolt them to the steel poles. If you counterbore into the rail, you will avoid bolts sticking out of the face of the timber.

5 Run a taut string line across the tops of the poles, and start fixing the timber palings to the rails using galvanised twisted shank nails. Fit them about 3 mm under the string line. The palings should not be in contact with the ground.

6 Coat the fence with whatever finish is required. Oil stains or fence finishes are readily available.

White timber fence with matching gate

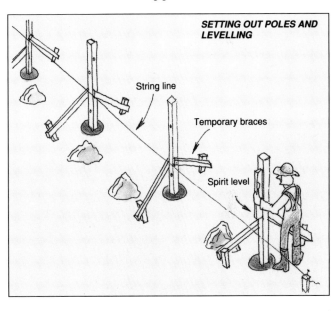

SETTING OUT POLES AND LEVELLING

String line

Temporary braces

Spirit level

PROJECT ALTERNATIVE
Wooden posts can be used in place of metal poles, although you need to adapt the design slightly. There are two methods. Either dig/bore holes for each post and set them in concrete, or use metal post spikes. The latter method avoids having to dig the holes and, although slightly more expensive at first sight, may work out as cheaply since you do not have to buy such long posts and do not need concrete or a post-hole borer.

If using concrete, the method is virtually the same as for steel posts. Treat the ends of the timber that will be buried by giving them a thorough soaking in timber preservative. Fill the bottom of the hole with rubble to assist drainage and stand the post on this before packing with concrete. Slope the top surface of the concrete so water drains away from the post.

For metal post spikes, position these at the centre of the spot you mark for the post. Insert the 'dolly' or driving tool which protects the socket and carefully hold the spike vertical. Drive it firmly into the ground using a sledge hammer, checking from time to time that it is still true. When the flange is flush with the ground, insert the post into the socket. With some types of spike the post is gripped by teeth inside the socket, with others you tighten a bolt until the post is firm.

If you only have a small space to garden – a city pad, courtyard, rooftop or balcony – you have to be well organised in handling it. Once you decide on the style you want, it's easy to create just the right atmosphere and look.

SMALL GARDENS

There are often problems in small gardens – such as wind, shade from neighbouring buildings, reflected heat from masonry, or barren soil. Poor soil can be replaced, or possibly a windbreak installed, but generally you must be careful to choose plants able to take the conditions you can't change. On the good side you will have a close-up familiarity with every plant and more time to meticulously groom plants than the large garden owner.

Don't try to do too much in a limited space. Keep the design simple, have most plants small and in scale, and garden accessories few, concentrating on perhaps one dramatic idea, such as a sundial or fountain. Or think of the sculptural qualities of small Japanese gardens created from a few rocks, a lantern and a grouping of native plants fitted into a few metres of space.

Small-scale plants and lightly framed or built-in furniture tend to make spaces look larger. On the other hand, you may want an oasis of lush greenery against a cityscape. Container plants, flowery window boxes, espaliered or pruned wall shrubs or trees, climbers, creepers and hanging baskets are ways to green a small garden without taking up too much ground space. Plants that espalier well are cotoneaster, pyracantha, flowering quince, citrus, *Camellia sasanqua*, *Photinia x fraseri*, and deciduous fruit trees.

In paved areas, make use of low-growing ground covers and plants that grow happily in small pockets of earth, such as heeria (*Heterocentron elegans*), alyssum or lobelia. Some small gardens and courts are shady and damp in winter and hot and sunny in summer. They need tough, tolerant plants able to take the switch. If you pave large areas in places inhospitable to plants, it will unify the space and save you some difficult gardening. Where courtyard walls and paving predominate, soften them with container plants, espaliers, and vines. Decorate walls with a fountain, grilles, arches, trelliswork with trompe l'oeil effects, or ceramic wall decoration.

Fill containers with annual flowers and bulbs. For these, use smaller containers that you can easily group, move around and replant. They will relieve expanses of paving with leafiness and colour.

1 A formal herb garden

2 Stylish wall decoration in a courtyard

3 A window-box garden

4 A private courtyard

5 A classical wall fountain in a shady court

6 Latticework planter

7 An ornate fountain and pond in a small court

8 Brightly coloured ranunculus in a terracotta pot

3

Keep the design simple, most plants small and in scale and only a few garden accessories

6

5

4

7

8

Left: A small formal garden set in the middle of a lawn

Right: An Italian theme was decided on for this balcony: with terracotta tiles, green wrought iron table and chairs, tiered fountain and lots of pots

Or you can pot up a collection of herbs and vegetables, orchids, or bonsai. Larger pots should also have a feeling of unity with each other and will hold plants for backgrounds and wall cover, such as agapanthus, bamboo, sweet bay, clipped box, palms, lavender, camellias, cycads, or pines.

Don't use garden soil in containers – use a home-made or packaged special potting mix. Turn the containers regularly to produce even growth. Container gardening does take more work in feeding and watering but in small areas it gives you a chance to ring the changes, and if you move house you can take your garden with you.

Balconies

Flowers can transform a balcony from bare masonry into a mini oasis for all to behold. Stalwarts like geraniums, fuchsias, begonias and petunias are all excellent balcony flowers. The more tender varieties prefer the sheltered warmth of semi-enclosed spaces.

Driving rain, strong wind, hotspots and drainage problems are some of the limitations of balcony planting. So start with reasonably sized pots which allow plants to grow and can't be easily blown over. All containers should have a drip tray or saucer underneath.

You may have to consider the weight of built-in planters and pots as they are heavy when filled with earth. Window boxes can be fitted to the outside of rails (if allowed) to increase planting space – just make sure the fixing is strong and designed for safety.

Shady gardens

A big improvement in many gardens is to plant up shady areas with bold foliage plants and beautiful flowers. You may want a shady summer garden, or find that you have little choice about its overshadowing by neighbouring buildings or trees. Nevertheless, some lovely plants appreciate shade, including rhododendrons, azaleas, daphne, fuchsias, hydrangeas, hostas, pieris, gardenia, winter hazel, cymbidium orchids and clivia.

Before you plant, analyse the kind of shady conditions which prevail. A place might receive slanting morning or afternoon sun, or be in quite deep shade at one part of the day when the sun is behind a building, and in bright, hot sun at another time. Sometimes a tree canopy can be thinned to increase filtered sun, which many plants enjoy. Other plants enjoy open, airy conditions and good light without direct sun. Automatic irrigation can turn a dry, shady place into a mini-rainforest with ferns and foliage plants. Good soil and water are conditions you can supply, and if tree roots are greedy, give your shade plants some liquid foliar feeds.

Ferns are ideal for moist, shady places and can be grown with Japanese anemones, hellebores, foxgloves, astilbes, lilies, primulas, cinerarias, cyclamens, boronias, violets, begonias, bergenia, *Dodecatheon* (shooting star) and impatiens. The real geraniums or cranesbills grow well in half shade. Then there are foliage plants such as *x Fatshedera lizei*, *Fatsia japonica*, palms, ivy, aucuba and, for warm climates, tree ferns and ornamental bananas. Two plants with beautiful winter and spring flowers are evergreen camellias and deciduous flowering quince. Barberries, firethorn and skimmia are berry shrubs for light shade.

Latticework provides shade for both people and plants

James Hardie

A cold frame is a simple but effective enclosed structure with a lift-up or lift-off roof which is designed to lengthen the growing season at both ends of summer. This enables you to grow and over-winter certain plants more successfully – it is essentially a mini-glasshouse and can be especially useful for raising seeds and cuttings.

A cold frame is often used in the same way as a cold greenhouse, although, because the plants will be closer to the glass, there may be a tendency for frost damage in very cold weather. To avoid this, you can insulate the frame with bubble polythene, covering the plants temporarily with newspaper – the whole frame can even be covered with carefully weighted old carpet at night.

If you already have a greenhouse, a cold frame can be used in conjunction with it, as an 'overflow' area in spring when you are short of space, or for hardening off bedding plants before planting them out.

Cold frames can be bought from garden centres and greenhouse suppliers. They are usually made of aluminium, glazed with horticultural glass or acrylic. There are cheaper versions made of plastic, covered with polythene or semi-rigid clear PVC – but these only have a short life so try to buy the best model you can afford. Most ready-made cold frames come in easy-to-assemble kit form and are completely portable. A cold frame can be placed to advantage on a patio, balcony or in the garden.

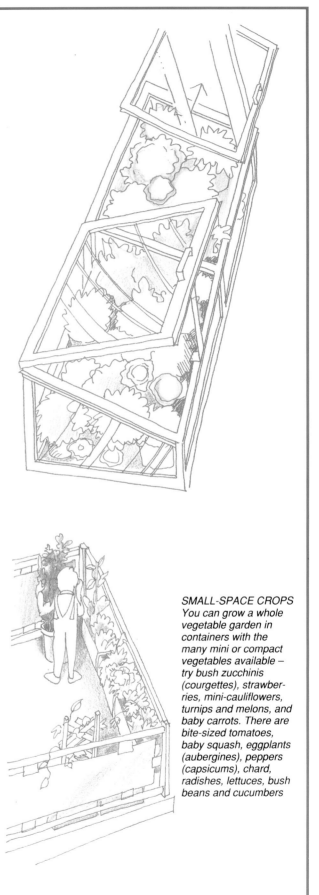

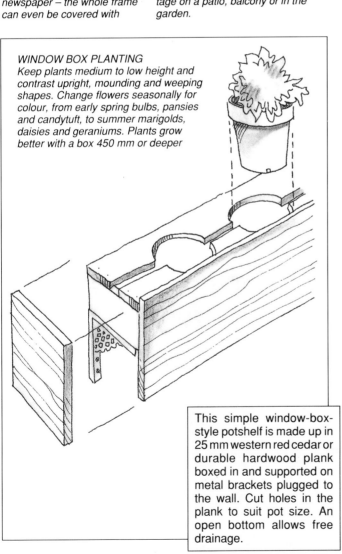

WINDOW BOX PLANTING
Keep plants medium to low height and contrast upright, mounding and weeping shapes. Change flowers seasonally for colour, from early spring bulbs, pansies and candytuft, to summer marigolds, daisies and geraniums. Plants grow better with a box 450 mm or deeper

This simple window-box-style potshelf is made up in 25 mm western red cedar or durable hardwood plank boxed in and supported on metal brackets plugged to the wall. Cut holes in the plank to suit pot size. An open bottom allows free drainage.

SMALL-SPACE CROPS
You can grow a whole vegetable garden in containers with the many mini or compact vegetables available – try bush zucchinis (courgettes), strawberries, mini-cauliflowers, turnips and melons, and baby carrots. There are bite-sized tomatoes, baby squash, eggplants (aubergines), peppers (capsicums), chard, radishes, lettuces, bush beans and cucumbers

Project 3

Planter trellis

Planters are an attractive, practical way to grow and display plants – the plants can be rotated in their own plastic containers as the mood takes you, without having to repot.

Planters can be made of durable timber, stone or bricks. Timber planters are designed to be portable, and allow for good drainage through open slats above the floor level. Pots are stood on top of these slats. Stone and brick planters are usually built-in fixtures and require a liner inside to contain the soil.

This portable planter and trellis is simple to make using a basic tool kit. To be suitable for exterior use it should be constructed of Western red cedar (WRC) or preservative-treated pine.

MATERIALS		
ITEM	DIMENSIONS (mm)	QUANTITY
back uprights, WRC	50 x 50	2/1800 mm
front uprights, WRC	50 x 50	1/900 mm
bottom slats, WRC	75 x 38	4/450 mm
rails, WRC	50 x 25	4/900 mm
trellis bars, WRC	50 x 25	5/600 mm
cladding strips	75 x 19	26/350 mm
50 mm galvanised wood screws	10 gauge	
25 mm galvanised bullet-head nails		
TIME One day		

Throughout the following step-by-step instructions, wherever timbers are fixed together, it is recommended that the timber be primed or stained at the joining surfaces first to give the best possible weather protection.

STEP BY STEP

1 Cut the 50 x 50 mm uprights to length. The rear ones should be 1800 mm and the front ones 425 mm. Mark on the short ones 75 mm from the bottom, and on the long ones 75 mm and 425 mm from the bottom. The remaining area on the long uprights is divided for the trellis bars. Carry each of the measurements around to an adjacent side of the timber.

2 Cut to length the cladding strips – they should be cut 350 mm long.

3 Lay together six of the cladding strips and measure the combined width. This should be around 396 mm. Measure and cut four of the 50 x 25 rails to this size. On the back of the rails mark in 19 mm at both ends, the thickness of a rail. Screw top and bottom rails to a long and a short upright with the markings on the rails corresponding to the marks on both of the uprights.

4 Lay together seven of the cladding strips and measure their combined width. This should be around 462 mm. From this, subtract the thickness of rails and the thickness of the cladding both ends. This will leave a total length of 400 mm. Cut the front and back rails to this length, and screw them in place.

5 Nail the cladding to the sides of the planter first – it should fit exactly. Then centre the cladding on the front and nail, working to either side. The end pieces can be finished off with a sharp plane for a neat, clean edge. Repeat this step for the back.

6 Cut to length the bottom slats to take the pots. These should be around 438 mm to fit, and can be lightly pinned in place on top of the rails, leaving space between the slats for drainage.

7 Cut the trellis bars to 500 mm or 600 mm in length (optional), and screw them at desired locations on the uprights – they look best when equally spaced.

8 Stain or paint the planter to whatever finish is desired. If painting, a primer, undercoat and two topcoats are recommended. Use oil-based finishes if the planter is to go outside.

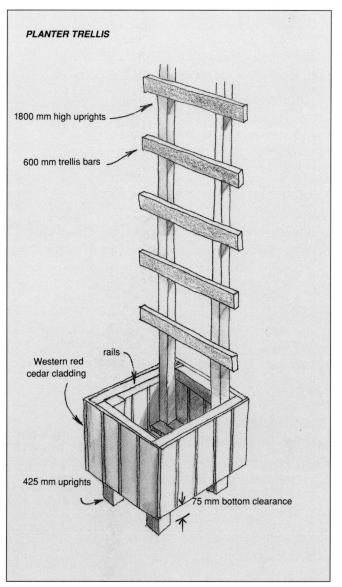

PLANTER TRELLIS

1800 mm high uprights

600 mm trellis bars

rails

Western red cedar cladding

425 mm uprights

75 mm bottom clearance

304

Garden furniture

Having a beautiful garden, courtyard or balcony is one thing, but to enjoy your alfresco setting to the fullest, you need a simple, comfortable set of garden furniture. Why not sit back and enjoy yourself in great outdoor style?

DUANE NORRIS

Most furniture designed for outdoor use is made from wood, plastic, fibreglass or reinforced plastic (or a combination of the two), or cast or tubular metal.

❑ **Wood** is ideal for the more traditional-style tables, chairs and seats. Hardwoods are the most weather-resistant, just make sure you select purpose-grown/plantation timber, not rainforest timber.

❑ **Synthetic resin or plastic** is used for contemporary-style tables, chairs, recliners and loungers. It is usually white, though some colours are available, and is tough and weather-and-scratch-resistant.

❑ Much of the new **cast metal** furniture is polyester-coated aluminium. This is virtually corrosion-proof and very low in maintenance. It is made in decorative reproduction designs for tables, chairs and seats. Heavy, traditional cast-iron furniture can be very charming but needs regular repainting to stay looking good.

❑ **Tubular metal** is used for tables, chairs, loungers, sun-beds, and swing hammocks. Because it has to be brought inside, it is designed to be easily folded up and stored away.

❑ **Cane or rattan** furniture is a popular choice for patios and conservatories but must be stored inside every night and in wet weather.

1 Timber garden furniture
2 Rustic-style timber table and chairs
3 Wrought iron and timber seat
4 Ornate wrought iron garden furniture
5 A charming, classical-style stone slab seat
6 Simple stone slab garden seat

Paving an outdoor area is a great way to extend your living area without over-extending your budget.

PERFECT PATIOS

A well-designed patio can become a room without a roof, giving you extra space for entertaining and a host of family activities. But to ensure a perfect result you should do your homework before the first paver touches base.

Expect to spend as much time planning the project as actually doing it, bearing in mind that it may take longer than you expect to achieve the balance between aesthetic and practical. Then, depending on the size of the job – and the state of your fitness if you intend to do it yourself – you may need as much as two weekends to prepare the area to be paved and one weekend to complete it.

Even if you're employing a tradesperson to do the paving, you should still investigate the various aspects of the trade to make sure the work is proceeding correctly. Before starting your paving, check any local legal requirements and ensure you have space to store building materials and pavers. Don't forget to include rubbish removal as an integral part of the project.

The site

Consider the aspect of the site to be paved. Ideally, a patio should be positioned to trap the winter sun and to be protected from the summer sun, so in the northern hemisphere it should face south and in the southern hemisphere, north. However, in icy climes where the summer sun is a treat rather than a pest, a patio facing either morning or after-noon sun could be a preferred option.

Protection from wind is another important consid-eration if your patio is to be a comfortable living area. A wall of the house could provide the neces-sary windbreak or you may have to erect a screen or grow a hedge, so make sure there's room for this.

If you intend to build a patio in a well-established garden, take stock of any large trees in the area. While they may look wonderful and provide shade in summer, tree roots unfortunately can be a menace to most paving, which will start lifting as the roots grow and spread. Should this happen, the pavers need to be re-moved, the roots cut down and the paving replaced – until the next time.

Remember, too, that patios should be easy to maintain. Who wants the dreary task of constantly raking up falling leaves? The alternative to large trees is planting small trees and shrubs, and shading the area with a pergola.

Design

Before choosing pavers work out the type of design you want for the area, making sure it will comple-ment the house and surroundings. Sketch the house and the proposed patio area or, alternatively, take some snapshots and work from these before deciding on the actual shape of the patio and the design and type of pavers.

Be bold and creative. Patios don't have to be square or rectangular; they can be round or free-form to follow the flow of a garden or the line of the house. You can also be adventurous by mixing different materials such as inexpensive concrete with expensive granite or stone, or bordering concrete slabs with an interesting design of bricks or clay pavers.

Think big and where possible plan to pave a larger area than you think you'll need, remem-bering that some of the living space you expect to be using will also be occupied by various accessories such as decora-tive pots, tubs of flowers and garden ornaments.

Choosing pavers

The range of pavers (paviours) available today is vast, with colours, shapes and textures in man-made or natural materials to suit everyone. Before you make your final choice of pavers you'll need to check price, availability and suitability to climate.

For instance, some paving materials are extremely expensive because of difficulty in handling and hefty trans-portation costs. Others may not be suitable in an extremely cold climate and some may have synthetic colour finishes which will fade in hot sun.

Safety factors are also important when you're paving an outdoor area. Glazed tiles will become extremely slippery when

wet, and dark-coloured pavers will absorb the heat and make your patio feel like a bed of hot coals.

Where do you start? Following is a list of the most practical and attractive paving materials suitable for patios.

❏ **Bricks** have been a popular paving material for many years for a number of reasons. Because of their rough surface they don't get slippery when wet, they're non-glare, tough and solid underfoot and they're easy to maintain.

Generally speaking new house bricks are softer than the ones manufactured more than 15 years ago, which were made of finely crushed materials and fired for longer temperatures than their

This brick-paved courtyard opens up from the family room. A classically inspired fountain, large canvas umbrella and flower-filled terracotta urns all add to its character

modern counterparts. For this reason, old second-hand bricks are often favoured for paving jobs. These bricks also have a pleasing rustic look, but they often require cleaning before laying – a time-consuming job.

House bricks are usually about 75 mm deep, so the site to be paved will have to be excavated deeper than for many other pavers. Bricks are best laid in coarse (sharp) sand.

As bricks are made of natural-coloured clay, the colour won't fade but they're likely to absorb moisture and in extremely

cold climates where there is a degree of frost this moisture may split the bricks. This is particularly applicable to new bricks.

❏ **Clay pavers or paviours** are a modern alternative to bricks and come in a vast number of colours and sizes, usually in either the rectangular shape of a brick or in a square. Most clay pavers are only 50 mm deep, which makes them easier to lay than bricks as the site won't need to be excavated as deeply.

Like bricks, clay pavers should be laid in coarse sand, are easy-maintenance and won't fade in colour. While they're fired at high temperatures to make them harder than new house bricks, they may be affected by severe frosts.

❏ **Concrete pavers or paviours, and concrete blocks and slabs** have been given a new image in the last few years. The pavers come in various sizes in square, rectangular, or decorative shapes which interlock. Blocks and slabs

are usually large rectangles, squares or hexagons.

Concrete paving products come in many different sizes and a variety of textured, non-slip finishes which include those that look like natural stone or slate. Coloured concrete can also be used, although this synthetic colour may fade slightly in time.

Generally, paving materials made from concrete come in thicknesses ranging from 40 mm to 65 mm and are more true to size than other pavers, so they are easy for the home handyperson to lay. They are usually less expensive than most other pavers, but plain concrete tends to hold dirt and to stain. A silicone-based sealer applied after laying may counteract this. Coloured concrete often contains an in-built sealer – check this with your local supplier.

Few surfaces look more attractive around a swimming pool than the rich hues of terracotta tiles

Amber Holdings

A large, private courtyard with crazy paving and reclining chairs

Broken concrete can also be used to make an inexpensive 'crazy paving' patio. Concrete pavers and slabs can be laid in river sand or mortar.

Using new, sophisticated techniques involving cement and reconstituted natural materials, concrete pavers can be moulded to look like the real thing, such as stone and granite. These cast concrete pavers can be coloured or textured and are often hard to tell from the genuine article, and they cost a great deal less.

❏ **Stone paving** can provide a lot of different looks, from sophisticated and elegant to rustic and comfortable. It can be light or dark in colour, new or old, sawn or rough. But whether you like the look of the light-coloured, soft Sydney sandstone of Australia or the dark grey, hard Yorkstone slabs of England, stone is heavy and can be expensive – although if you happen to live in the right area it may be relatively inexpensive as transport is a major part of the cost. With the exception of some stone, such as sandstone, if durable it will also be difficult to cut – an angle-grinder will help and can be hired.

For the best results on a patio, stone should be laid in a sand-cement mix on a concrete slab (preferably reinforced).

❏ **Tiles**, which are made of clay, can look wonderful on a patio, but they should be unglazed as glazed tiles will become slippery when wet. Suitable tiles for patios include unglazed vitrified tiles and terracotta tiles.

Vitrified tiles have been fired at extremely high temperatures to give them a non-porous surface as hard as glass, which means they won't stain. Tessellated tiles, which are cut into different shapes and sizes to form a mosaic, are a good example of unglazed vitrified tiles. If vitrified tiles are laid on a patio it's advisable to use those which have a non-slip slate finish.

Terracotta tiles are non-slip but are more porous so they can be susceptible to staining. They come in a variety of colours from many different countries, they won't fade, and they look particularly attractive on a patio which has a Mediterranean character.

Tiles are thinner than most other paving materials, ranging from 10 mm to 25 mm thickness which makes them more brittle than some pavers. For this reason they should be laid in a sand-cement mix on a rigid surface such as concrete – for best results, lay in a semi-dry screed with very little water to allow compaction. Porous terracotta tiles should be soaked before laying to prevent them from sucking up the sand-cement mixture, which can cause them to become 'drummy' after they've dried. It's not advisable to lay porous terracotta tiles in extremely cold climates where frost may cause them to crack. However, some of the more dense terracotta tiles may be frost-resistant.

Terracotta tiles on a patio can be cleaned with an alkaline detergent and a scrubbing brush. Sealing is not usually recommended outside as the sun can blister the sealant. If it's necessary to seal terracotta tiles – around barbecues for example – a water-viscous silicone is recommended by experts. Terracotta tiles are often handmade and uneven and therefore not always easy to lay.

❏ **Slate** is a natural material and is therefore suited to the outdoors. However, dark slate tends to absorb heat and can become very hot in summer, so it's wise to choose a light-coloured slate for patios.

Slate tiles vary in thickness from around 8 mm to 20 mm in various sizes both in a chipped edge and sawn edge. The ideal laying surface for slate is a rigid concrete slab using either a special slate tile adhesive or a sand-cement mix with a bonding agent.

Sealing slate outdoors is not recommended as grit walked into a sealant can damage it, the sun may blister it and it could become slippery. Because slate has a tough surface with low porosity it won't generally stain outdoors. The best way to clean it is to sweep it regularly and wash it with warm water without detergents.

❏ **Timber** can be used to build your perfect patio if you live in a setting where it is suitable and an area where timber is readily available and not outrageously expensive. It's necessary to use timber decking boards in a reliable and recommended hardwood which come in a variety of lengths and sizes.

Softwood holds water and breaks down quickly, so is not suitable. If untreated, buy a waterproofing compound to overcome this problem – it permeates the timber and forms a film beneath the surface.

A timber patio or deck can be built directly onto the ground or supported by posts in timber, brick, concrete, galvanised steel or aluminium.

Timber has the advantage of being less resilient to heat than masonry pavers so is very well suited to hot climates, although it should be protected from the weather by using a recommended finish. Timber can be cleaned by simply sweeping and hosing down.

For any form of paving to be successful in the long term, careful preparation of the sub-base is essential

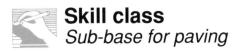

Skill class
Sub-base for paving

For any form of paving to be successful in the long term, careful preparation of the sub-base is essential. If paving is placed on unconsolidated soil, it will subside and move, leading to extensive patching or maybe even complete relaying.

The sub-base chosen depends on the final material to be used as the paving surface. Paving bricks or blocks require a roadbase (hardcore), and concrete is best laid on a well-draining coarse sand.

The area to be paved should be excavated to allow for the depth of the paving, the bedding material and the sub-base. For instance, clay pavers on a clay soil may require an excavation of 180 mm: that is, 50 mm for the paver, 30 mm for the bedding, and 100 mm for the well-compacted sub-base.

In excavating, all vegetable matter should be removed. If there are any roots or other stumps left, these must be grubbed out or treated with a long-term weedkiller, and the resultant hole filled with sub-base material. Any other 'soft' spots should be dug out and filled with sub-base material, compacting it in successive thin layers of 150 mm to build up height.

To achieve the final correct height easily, it may be an idea to drive in a series of pegs to the level of the top of the sub-base, and perhaps another set to the level of the bedding. This allows quick reference to see how the gradients and levels are going.

Other materials can be used as a sub-base but may require grading. Essentially the sub-base should be something that is stable, and not likely to break down over time – crushed well-burnt tiles, clinker bricks and old clay pipes make good sub-base material. Also suitable are cracked, hard gravels such as granite, basalt, dolerite and even hard sandstone. The bottom layers can be 25-50 mm in size, but on top of this gravel 10-25 mm is preferable. If using a material such as sandstone, it can often be rammed into the soft earth and broken up on the site, to achieve a level surface.

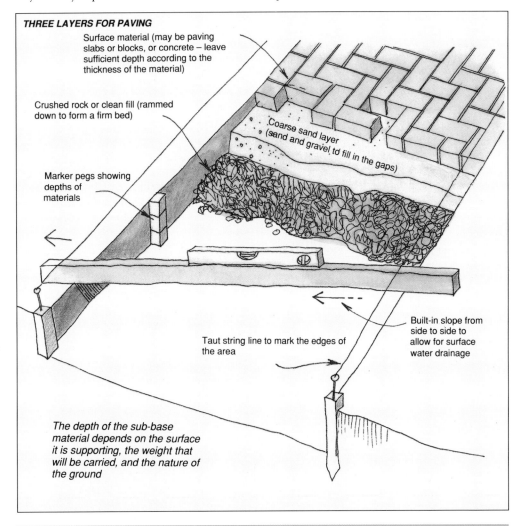

THREE LAYERS FOR PAVING

Surface material (may be paving slabs or blocks, or concrete – leave sufficient depth according to the thickness of the material)

Crushed rock or clean fill (rammed down to form a firm bed)

Marker pegs showing depths of materials

Coarse sand layer (sand and gravel to fill in the gaps)

Taut string line to mark the edges of the area

Built-in slope from side to side to allow for surface water drainage

The depth of the sub-base material depends on the surface it is supporting, the weight that will be carried, and the nature of the ground

Paved area

Whether relaxing in a beautiful courtyard or entertaining on the patio, paving makes an ideal zone for outdoor entertainment.

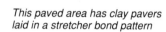

This paved area has clay pavers laid in a stretcher bond pattern

Pavers such as bricks, clay or concrete pavers, which are manageable and can be laid on sand, are by far the easiest for the home handyperson to lay. So, if you're going to tackle a paving job using any of these materials, here are the five major steps.

STEP BY STEP

1 Prepare the site (see page 309). Mark out the area to be paved using pegged string lines.

When you're preparing the site, remember that drainage is extremely important. To ensure your patio doesn't become a swimming pool, paving should be sloped 10-15 mm per metre away from the house or any part of the area which may collect water. Also, if the patio is attached to the walls of the house, it should be built 150 mm below the damp course.

Timber formwork should be fitted around the boundaries to help contain the sand – this also acts as a guide to level paving.

2 Spread the washed (river) sand with a rake evenly over the prepared base to a depth of 25 mm (100 mm for cold, frosty areas) and lightly hose it.

Compact the sand with a hired vibrating bed compactor, or with a home-made compactor. This can be made with a flat piece of 300 x 150 x 50 mm hardwood for the compacting plate with a 1800 x 50 x 75 mm hardwood handle attached. Once the sand is well compacted, level the area by screeding it. The easiest way to do this is to dig two lengths of straight timber, known as screed rails, into the side edges of the compacted sand to the required height of the sand.

When these rails are in place, run a straightedge or screed board between the two screed rails to level the area.

3 To keep the bricks stable, install edge restraints around the area to be paved.

A line of pavers, called a header or soldier course, laid either slightly higher or the same height as the completed paving surface, is a simple and effective edge restraint. This header course will be concreted into place after the paving has been completed.

4 Position and compact the pavers firmly into place.

Set up a grid of string lines by positioning a string line from opposing key pavers, around every eighth paver, and securing string or cord with bricks.

If you have to cut pavers, you should first score the paver all round and use a bolster and club hammer to split it. Alternatively, paving retailers may have a cutting service or you can hire the recommended equipment such as a masonry saw or a hydraulic splitter.

Leaving a gap of 2-3 mm between pavers allows for any unevenness in the pavers, but some pavers can be butted up hard against each other. As you work, tap the pavers into place with a rubber mallet, or a hammer on a length of timber. This is known as tamping. Use a spirit level to check the pavers are even and the fall is adequate for drainage.

When all the pavers are in place, remove the header course and dig a trench below the level of the sand and roadbase. Pour a mix of 4:1 sand and cement mixed with water into the trench and tap the header row back into the wet cement to the height of the other pavers.

A vibrating bed compactor can be used to level the pavers, but the pavers should be protected with a sheet of masonite or a piece of carpet to prevent breakages or cracking of the pavers.

5 Sweep fine, dry sand over the entire surface of the pavers and fill up the gaps with sand.

Tamp the surface again if it's necessary to level any pavers. You may have to repeat this procedure after a couple of weeks as the joints settle.

MATERIALS
washed medium river sand – to be used as a base for pavers
fine river sand (jointing sand) – to sweep over finished pavers
cord for string line to mark paving boundary and for grid string lines; 4 pegs and several bricks to hold grid stringlines
edge restraints (a brick header course or lengths of timber may be used)
4:1 sand-cement mix to cement in the brick header course
2.5 m straight piece of timber – to be used as a screed board

TOOLS
two pieces of timber 40 mm thick by 2.3 m long to be used as screed rails
vibrating bed compactor (optional) – available from equipment hire centres
cutting equipment: brick bolster, hydraulic splitter or masonry saw
rubber mallet or hammer and piece of timber (if not using a plate vibrator)
spirit level
shovel
rake
broom

TIME
Two to three weekends

TIPSTRIP

❑ When laying pavers, work between the string lines and work small areas at a time. Start from one corner so you don't walk on the compacted sand bed.
❑ Stack sand on the side you intend to start working.
❑ Place small stacks of pavers around the laying side before you start working.
❑ Don't tamp or vibrate while the edges are wet.

1 Prepared base with tools, roadbase, sand and screed rails ready

2 Screed sand over screed rail to prepare an even bed

LAYING PATTERNS

Circular bond

Basketweave bond

Tracery bond

Basketweave bond variation

Stretcher bond (or running bond)

Herringbone bond

Stack bond

90° herringbone bond (right-angle herringbone)

Zigzag stretch or running bond (with border)

3 Compact pavers into the sand (make sure you protect them by laying down a sheet of masonite first). When all the pavers have been laid, sweep fine dry sand back and forth over the entire surface, working it into the gaps

SETTING OUT A STRING LINE GRID
Laying out a string line grid makes paving easier, quicker and more accurate

MARKING OUT THE AREA

Level mark

Set string line to finished level of pavers (pavers will come to this level when compacted)

1000

25

25 mm per 1 m drainage slope

Bottom of excavation
Prepare the ground to this line (parallel to string line). Check evenness and depth of base by measuring from string line. Finished surface level of pavers may be at or above ground level

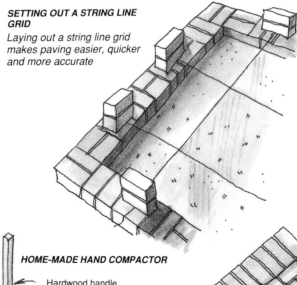

HOME-MADE HAND COMPACTOR

Hardwood handle
1800 x 50 x 75 mm
Head 300 x 150 x 50 mm

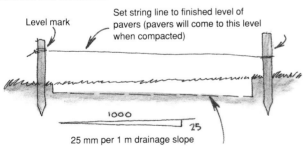

HEADER (SOLDIER) COURSE
A header course of bricks acts as an edge restraint

Conservatories

Bring the garden indoors: a conservatory is a very practical means of adding space, light and interest to your home – creating what is, in fact, a garden room.

An excellent idea if you want to provide a suitable setting for your plant collection, especially exotic foliage and flora. If you also have a greenhouse, plants can be moved from one to the other as they come into season.

Styles

In the 19th century, conservatories were made of wood then iron, and these options are still available. Today you can choose from a range of alternatives: aluminium and Western red cedarwood are very popular materials while plastic (UPVC) conservatories are hardwearing and low in maintenance. There are two basic styles: the modern lean-to conservatory and the more 'traditional' Victorian-style conservatory.

The modern lean-to style may be curved or rectangular and comes in modular alloy frames as well as wood and plastic versions. For the rectangular section style, 'glazing' is often of a plastic cellular construction for

GREEN TIP
Double glazing is a sound investment for a conservatory. It can make substantial energy savings and will also limit noise levels.

heat retention, especially on roofs. There are many optional extras available in a module pack but typically a simple lean-to style might include the main frame, fully lockable patio doors and subframe, fielded (panelled) panels and panels with vent, a double-hinged opening window and integral gutter and downpipe.

Some of the more traditional styles are made from top-grade cedarwood with hardwood sills and modular 'window' style panels, which may be timber or plastic (UPVC). Wooden conservatories are usually pretreated with a protective basecoat, but you should treat all the timber again with a wood preservative within three months of assembly. Traditional-style conservatories are also often made of aluminium and can include cast components which look like cast iron.

A typical module pack would contain the main frame, casement doors and subframe, fielded panels, fielded or fully glazed panels, curved arches and integral gutter and downpipe. Module packs come complete with fittings.

What to buy

Before installing a conservatory it's important to look carefully at what's

involved – do your homework by shopping around and getting the right advice.

Work out a budget and take the structure and its contents into consideration. The cost of preparing the base, delivery, erection, fitting, guttering and tax may not always be included in the price.

Generally planning permission is not needed for a conservatory (except in special cases) – commonly no planning permission is required for extensions of less than 70 cubic metres, provided they are not built onto any wall facing the highway. However, you need approval under the building regulations which the base, foundations and structure must meet. It's best to seek advice from your local planning authority early on. Any reputable conservatory company will also be able to give you expert advice.

Safety is an important consideration so think carefully about what sort of glass you want in your conservatory. Toughened safety glass, which is much harder to break than normal glass, should be used for doors and windows. However, many popular systems use cellular polycarbonate sheeting instead. If you have young children you may need to consider safety glass for the entire conservatory, or choose a style which has wooden panels from the ground halfway up and then glass in the remaining sections.

Good ventilation is necessary in a conservatory and because of the

POINTERS
❑ Location – Convenient access and sunny position are key factors.
❑ Planning – Getting the right advice is essential at the planning stage.
❑ Foundations – The right basework is needed to provide a substantial and secure building.
❑ Condensation – Good ventilation is important. During warm weather, open the windows and doors for 5 minutes daily. On colder days, ensure adequate heating is given via an electric heater or plug-in radiator.
❑ Double-glazing – This is optional but desirable for a year-round garden room.

build-up of both heat and water vapour, fans can be either of the circulating or extractor type. Some fans are solar-powered – a good investment for the energy conscious. Many systems have two large opening windows in the roof to allow heat to escape. Blinds can be added to create shade in summer and these come in a wealth of different styles: roller blinds, plastic reeds, shading netting, wooden laths, woven polythene sheets or shadecloth (netting) and a polyester material.

The conservatory floor is usually made from concrete with a smooth screed – perfect for concrete slabs or ornamental flooring. Tiles are cool in summer and can be chosen to harmonise with indoor flooring or a patio area situated beyond the conservatory. Vinyl flooring can also be used, but if you are planning to have a lot of plants, carpet is not really suitable.

Conservatories do not

heat themselves, and you may need to seek specialist advice when it comes to installing efficient heating. Extending the domestic system is by far the best method, however there are many specialist companies who will put in an independent gas or electric system if this is more practical. The same applies to lighting, which can be both practical and ornamental.

Suitable guttering systems are normally available (or may be included). Link the guttering system into existing drainage (e.g. into a gully) or build a soakaway.

To ensure the long life of your conservatory, treat all the wood with a wood preservative within three months of assembly.

Assembling a module pack is straightforward but careful preparation is essential. Illustrated instructions are supplied with each pack and it is important to read the manufacturer's instructions closely.

A conservatory is a garden room designed to give all-year-round enjoyment

GLOSSARY

Aggregate: The sand and stone mixed with cement and water to make concrete.

Agricultural (land) drain: Rigid or flexible slotted pipe for drainage.

Air brick: A perforated block built into a wall to ventilate a room or the underside of a wooden floor.

Alfresco: In the open (Italian in origin).

Arbour: A leafy bower, shelter or recess (similar to a pergola).

Architrave: The trim around the windows and doors.

Batten/cleat: A sawn strip of wood used to cover joints or to provide support.

Bolster: Short-handled hammer with a heavy square head used for cutting bricks, etc.

Bond: The way bricks are laid in a wall or paving so that they interlock.

'Borrowed scenery': A Japanese technique whereby a beautiful view beyond the garden is framed by plants and used as part of the garden backdrop.

Brick veneer: Building method with a structural timber frame and a veneer of brick tied to the exterior.

Built-in: Made or incorporated as an integral part, e.g. a cupboard built in to an alcove.

Cabinet timber: Fine-quality, dressed (planed) furniture-grade timber.

Camber: A slight upward curve to the centre of a path, ramp or roadway.

Came: Sections of lead used between glass segments in leadlighting.

CCA: Chrome copper arsenic; a chemical treatment used for preserving timber.

Cement: A fine grey powder made of calcined limestone and clay; used as a basis for all bricklaying mortars and in concrete.

Chalk line: A length of bricklayer's line which is well rubbed with chalk, held tight and plucked against a wall, floor or other surface to mark a straight line on it.

Coach screws: Large screws with a hexagonal head, requiring a spanner to turn into place.

Colonial bond: A brick bond very similar to a Flemish bond.

Concrete: A mixture of sand, cement and aggregate mixed in varying proportions according to requirement.

Conservatory: A type of greenhouse for plants, especially exotic ones, most often attached to the house and used as an extended living area.

Container gardening: Growing plants in containers such as window boxes, pots and planters.

Cooktop (hob): A separate flat surface in the kitchen containing hotplates or burners.

Cornice: Plain or ornamental moulding between ceiling and walls.

Course: A row or rise in level of one unit in masonry work.

Cripple: To partly cut through timber to enable it to bed down properly.

Crosshead screwdriver: Also called Phillips head, it is a screwdriver with a cross-shaped point.

Custom-built, custom-made: Made to the specifications of an individual customer.

Dado: The lower part of the wall, often to chair height, which may be defined by a moulding or border.

DAR (PAR): Dressed all round (planed all round). Timber that is smooth, as in planed by a plane or machine tool.

Decoupage: Process of decorating a surface with shapes or illustrations cut from paper, card, etc.

DIY: Do-it-yourself.

Dowel: Round timber.

DPC: Damp-proof course.

DPM: Damp-proof membrane.

Dry stream: A stream bed that does not contain water.

Epoxy resins: Sealants, adhesives and paints used for a variety of purposes; specific formulations for specific tasks.

Ergonomics: The study of the relationship between workers and their work environment; rules for designing to the correct dimensions for effective and comfortable use.

Expansion joint: A joint of flexible material, or a gap left in steel or concrete, to allow expansion and contraction between two elements (thermal expansion).

'Fattiness': Having the properties of fat; greasy or oily.

Faux: False or fake.

Fence: A guide along which timber or a tool is run to reproduce a certain cut or shape.

Fibreboard: A building material made of compressed wood or other plant fibres, especially in the form of a thin semi-rigid sheet.

Fibre-cement sheet: Cellulose fibre-reinforced cement sheet; basic composition is cement, ground sand, cellulose fibre and water; recommended for use in wet areas such as bathrooms.

Fibreglass: Synthetic resins reinforced with alkali-resistant glass fibre; for repairs, as sheets or as finished products.

Fish plate: Lengths of sturdy timber used to

CONVERTING MEASUREMENTS

Although most people have some working knowledge of metrics, many cannot visualise an actual size. In this table approximate metric to imperial measures are given, followed by an everyday example.

LENGTH

1 mm approx $^3/_{64}$ in (a paper clip)
10 mm approx $^3/_8$ in (a mortar joint, thickness of the average little finger)
25 mm approx 1 in (everyone knows what an inch is!)
230 mm approx 9 in (one brick)
820 mm approx 32 in (an average door width)
2400 mm approx 8 ft (10 bonded bricks, or minimum ceiling height)
1 m approx 39 in (a bit higher than a kitchen worktop)
1.8 m approx 6 ft (a tall male)
2.04 m - just under 7 ft (the height of the average door)
3 m approx 10 ft (3 ft higher than the average door)

VOLUME

1 litre approx 1.8 pints (a carton of orange juice)
4.5 litres approx 1 gallon (a large paint tin)

AREA

1 sq m approx 1 sq yd (about 50 bricks laid in a wall)
9.3 sq m approx 1 building square – 100 sq ft (an average bedroom)

reinforce a weakness in a structural timber member.

Fixtures: Refers to lights, switch plates and other permanent items attached to walls.

Flashing: A waterproofing material to prevent water entry at a joint.

Flat-head (roundhead) nail: Large general-purpose nail (20-150 mm).

Flemish bond: A bond used in brickwork that has alternating stretchers and headers in each course, each header being placed centrally over a stretcher.

Flume: A narrow artificial channel or ravine through which water flows.

Footing: The lowest part of a building or structure that rests on the ground; usually constructed of reinforced concrete, or brick in smaller structures.

Formwork: An arrangement of boards, bolts, etc, used to shape reinforced concrete while it is setting.

Freestanding: Not attached to or supported by another object.

'Frog': A recess pressed into a clay brick before firing to reduce its weight, and to assist levelling of brick courses.

English bond: A bond used in brickwork that has a course of headers alternating with a course of stretchers.

Gazebo: A summerhouse or garden pavilion usually sited to command a view; means 'I will gaze' in mock-Latin.

Going: The length, 'tread' or top surface of a step.

Greenhouse: A garden building with transparent walls and roof, usually of glass, for the cultivation and exhibition of plants under controlled conditions.

Grille: A framework, often of metal bars arranged to form an ornamental pattern, used as a screen or partition.

Grommet: A washer or sleeve used to isolate materials, e.g. rubber, hemp, fibre, etc. There are many types of grommet.

Grounds: A frame applied to walls prior to panelling.

Grout: The compressible or flexible filler between tiles.

Grozing pliers: Special pliers for removing thin edges of glass when leadlighting.

Hardboard: A manufactured pulp board; used as an underlay for resilient tiling in dry areas.

Hardwood: Wood from broad-leaved flowering trees such as eucalypt, oak, beech and ash.

Header: The timber member over a small opening.

Header brick or course: A header is a brick that is laid across the line of a wall of brickwork. A brick-on-edge header is a header course laid with bricks on edge rather than on the flat.

Housing: A shallow trench in timber to provide lateral restraint in a joint.

Jack stud: A short stud.

Jamb: The rebated door frame into which a door closes.

Joist: A horizontal framing member to which are fixed floorings or ceilings.

Kit: Pieces of equipment in a set or package ready to be assembled.

Knockdown furniture: Easily dismantled and assembled (kitset).

Laminated plastics: Sheets of paper or textile soaked with a synthetic resin and pressed together under pressure to make a stiff board or glossy-surfaced covering for a wall or board.

Laminated wood: Layers of veneer or wood glued or mechanically fastened together to form a larger section or wide board.

Larry: A long-handled hoe with a hole in the blade; useful for mixing mortar in a wheelbarrow.

Leaf: One half of a cavity wall, generally a half-brick thick wall tied by wall ties to the other half or a frame.

Levelling compound: A fine-grained mortar or similar substance often used to smooth-finish rough concrete; also used to make repairs or fill holes.

Lining: Interior wall covering.

Lintel: A structural support member over a door or window head, usually carrying wall load alone.

Make good: Return to original, or finish off. Masonry anchors: Steel bolts with sides which expand in the wall as the bolts are tightened.

MDF board: Medium-density fibreboard – a high quality manufactured pulp board.

Midway: Usually a shelf for storing knives, food processor blades, or for holding herbs and condiments. It is normally placed midway between the worktop and the wall cupboards, hence the name.

Mineral turpentine (white spirit): A colourless flammable liquid – an essential oil – containing a mixture of terpenes; used as a solvent for paints. Also known as turps.

Mitre joint: A joint made between two pieces of timber that are to be fixed at 90° to each other. Each piece is cut at 45° to its axis so that the line of the joint is seen to cut the corner (endgrain does not show).

Modular system: System made up of standardised units of furniture (each unit is designed to be added to, or used as, part of an arrangement of similar units); easily dismantled and assembled, e.g. IKEA modular systems.

Mortar: Cement, lime and sand mixture for adhering bricks and tiles.

Nogging: Short framing members joining the broad face of studs.

Nosing: Front edge of a step.

Painted finish: Decorative and protective coating system applied to many different surfaces (may be oil-, water- or solvent-based system); special decorative paint techniques include stencilling, dragging, rag rolling, sponging and stippling.

Particle (chip) board: A manufactured wood sheet made of wood chips and adhesive.

Pergola: A horizontal framework or trellis supported on posts; designed to provide a base for climbing plants; may form a covered walkway.

Pier: Masonry column supporting structure above.

Plasterboard: Building board made of a core of gypsum plaster, enclosed between two sheets of heavy paper (water-resistant grade only must be used in wet areas).

Plate: The topmost and bottommost members of a frame, to which studs are joined.

Plinth: The rectangular slab or block that forms the lowest part of the base of a column, pedestal or pier; a flat block on either side of a door frame, where the architrave meets the skirting; a flat base on which a structure or piece of equipment is placed.

Plumb line: Weight attached to a length of string to stretch it in a vertical direction; used to obtain the perpendicular for accurate cupboard or tile fixing.

Polyurethane: A hard yet resilient coating commonly used for wear areas.

Post-hole borer or digger: Similar to a spade but with two plates at the end to lift soil out of holes.

PVA adhesive: Polyvinyl acetate adhesive or binder; a water-based glue which is quick drying and clear finishing, used for timber.

Rebate joint: A stepped joint for adding strength to any joint between two pieces of timber.

Render: A sand-lime cement mix applied to a masonry wall to give a sandy, smooth finish; may be further covered with a hard-set plaster.

Renovation: Update from the original.

Restoration: Process whereby the style of a piece is retained and its original finish restored.

Revamping: Process whereby the original form of an item is retained but its finish and character is altered.

Reveal: Timber extension of a window frame to the interior.

Riser: The height or vertical part of a step.

Rising damp: Movement of water into a wall from the ground by capillary action; associated mainly with old masonry houses that either have no damp-proof course (DPC) installed in the masonry, or where the existing DPC has failed due to deterioration or

physical damage.

River sand: Coarse rounded sand from rivers.

Sash: The frame and glass of a window, normally movable.

Screed: Levelling of materials using a straight edge; a thin layer, usually of mortar, used as a bed for tiles or a finishing application to rough concrete.

Scribed joint: A butt joint in which one surface matches the profile of the adjoining one.

Sealer: A coating to provide a suitable surface for final coatings.

Secret nailing: Method of nail-fixing panelling so that nails are not visible.

Shadecloth: Synthetic fibre netting either of split tape or filament used to screen out harsh sunlight and UV rays. Shadecloths are available in several grades – specified by their light transmittance – and can be woven or knitted.

Sill: The bottom horizontal member of a

window frame.

Soakaway: A pit filled with rubble into which rain or waste water drains.

Softwood: The open-grained wood of any coniferous trees such as pine and cedar.

Stencilling: Process of applying paint to a surface through a cut-out stencil design made of plastic, cardboard or metal.

Stopping compound: A filler or putty for filling blemishes in timber and other materials.

Straight edge: A ruler or perfectly straight piece of timber or metal used to give a clean and consistent edge when cutting or trimming.

Stretcher: A brick or stone laid horizontally with its length parallel to the length of a wall.

String line: Any type of string stretched between two points to mark the correct lines of a building project, e.g. a wall, path or paving project.

Strip floor: Strips of wood

cramped together forming a floor.

Stud: The vertical member of a timber frame.

Sub-base: The lowest part of a base or foundation.

Subfloor: A load-bearing wooden or concrete floor which is covered by a finish of timber floorboards or other flooring materials, e.g. ceramic tiles.

Timber studs (wall studs): Vertical wall framing member.

Toggle bolts: Type of bolts for use with hollow walls. Two types are available: spring toggles and gravity toggles. In both cases the toggles open behind the wall lining for fixing.

Trenching: See Housing.

Trompe l'oeil: A painted or decorated effect which gives an illusion of reality.

Underlay: A preparatory surface prior to fixing floor covering.

Vent: An outlet for air, including water vapour, through a ventilating duct.

INDEX

ACKNOWLEDGMENTS

In the course of putting this book together many people have helped. The publisher wishes to thank the following for their assistance:

Parts 1 & 2
Pel Fesq (Gemini Studio); Keith Atkins Bathrooms; Robyn Cosgrove Rugs; The Slate People; PGH Clay Products; Skydome Industries; NBL; Mitre 10 (Crows Nest); Ace Leadlight; Geoff Phillips; Stegbar Door and Windows; Sydney Window Installation; Tempo Interiors; Creative Wardrobe Company; Advance Parquetry; Porters Original Lime Wash

Part 3
Geoff Phillips; Graheme McIntosh; Gieffe Luxury Kitchens and Bathrooms; Laura Ashley; IKEA; FREEDOM; Country Form; Paul Frank; Judy Green Interiors; Clarke and Walker Pty Limited, Mitre 10; Hafele Australia; Sterling Mail Order; Australian Floral Designs; In Residence; Flossoms; Blue and White Drycleaners; Janet Niven's Antiques

Part 4
E.G. Lefever, Hardie & Coy Pty Ltd; Home & Garden, Skygarden store The Bay Tree, Woollahra; Cilla Campbell, Australian Floral Designs

Part 5
Classic Ceramics, Sydney; The Decorative Tile Company; Clarke and Walker Pty Limited, Mitre 10; E.G. Lefever, James Hardie & Coy Pty Ltd; IKEA; CSR Wood Panels; Australian Resilient Floor Covering Association; Wilson Fabrics and Wallcoverings; Armstrong Nylex Pty Ltd; Mistral RingGrip; Leader Bathrooms & Kitchens; Keith Atkins Bathrooms; Independent Living Centre; PROM

Part 6
E.G. Lefever, James Hardie & Coy Pty Ltd; A.D. Spring Pty Ltd; Clarke and Walker Pty Limited, Mitre 10; Amber Pty Ltd; Amdega Conservatories (Aust) Pty Ltd; Bruce Pollack Publicity; DUANE NORRIS

Note: Apologies to any individuals or companies not specifically mentioned.